D1223346

INTELLIGENCE: RECONCEPTUALIZATION AND MEASUREMENT

INTELLIGENCE: RECONCEPTUALIZATION AND MEASUREMENT

Edited by
HELGA A. H. ROWE
Australian Council for Educational Research

 LAWRENCE ERLBAUM ASSOCIATES, PUBLISHERS
1991   Hillsdale, New Jersey   Hove and London

 Australian Council for Educational Research

Lawrence Erlbaum Associates, Inc., Publishers
365 Broadway
Hillsdale, New Jersey 07642

Library of Congress Cataloging in Publication Data

Intelligence : reconceptualization and measurement / edited by Helga
   A.H. Rowe.
       p.   cm.
    "This book is the result of the Seminar on Intelligence . . . held
on August 26–28 in Melbourne, Australia"—pref.
   Includes bibliographical references and indexes.
   ISBN 0-8058-0942-2
   1. Intellect—Congresses.   2. Intelligence tests—Congresses.
   3. Human information processing—Congresses.   I. Rowe, Helga A.H.
   BF720.A85N48   1991
   153.9—dc20   91-7211
                                                                        CIP

Printed in the United States of America
10 9 8 7 6 5 4 3 2 1

Contents

Preface   xi

Notes on Contributors   xiii

1. Introduction: Paradigm and Context   1
Helga A. H. Rowe

  Intelligence and the Newtonian Paradigm   *3*
  Theoretical Reorientations   *5*
  The Emerging Holistic Paradigm   *7*
  References   *17*

2. Reconciling Views on Intelligence?   19
Marc N. Richelle

  A Brief Retrospective Look   *19*
  Sources of Discontent in Current
     Intelligence Research   *21*
  Towards Integration and Complementarity   *23*
  Conclusion   *31*
  References   *32*

3. Is the High IQ Person Really in Trouble? Why?   35
Kjell Raaheim

  Intelligence and Expectations   *37*
  Some Experimental Results   *39*
  Is Intelligence of no Further Use?   *40*
  Expectations Revisited   *41*
  Challenges Above the Upper Threshold   *43*
  Conclusion   *44*
  References   *45*

4. Intelligence as an Expression of Acquired Knowledge   **47**
Robert Glaser

Intelligence as a Cognitive Proficiency
in Domains of Knowledge   *49*
Properties of Intellectual Proficiency   *50*
Performance in Unfamiliar Domains   *51*
The Measurement of Domain Based
Intellectual Proficiency   *53*
References   *55*

5. Multimodal Learning and the Quality of Intelligent Behavior   **57**
John B. Biggs and Kevin F. Collis

Intelligent Behavior, Competence, and
Forms of Knowledge   *57*
Some Issues in Neo-Piagetian
Research   *60*
The Modes of Representation   *62*
Learning Cycles: The Solo Taxonomy   *64*
Some Qualities of Intelligent Behavior   *67*
Conclusions   *73*
References   *74*

6. Cognitive Developmental Perspectives on Intelligence   **77**
Susan R. Goldman and James W. Pellegrino

Perspectives on Cognitive Development   *79*
Empirical Observations   *80*
Practice and Addition Fact Performance   *81*
Collaborative Writing   *87*
Cognitive Development and Intelligence   *92*
References   *93*

7. The Effects of Training and Practice on Human Abilities   **97**
Lazar Stankov

The Effects of Training on Gf and Gc Abilities   *99*
The Effects of Practice on Gf and Gc Abilities   *103*
Practice and Changes in Correlations   *110*
Conclusion   *114*
References   *116*

8. **Intelligence, Task Complexity, and the Distinction Between Automatic and Effortful Mental Processing**   119
John D. Crawford

Defining Task Complexity   *119*
Task Complexity and Intelligence   *124*
Proposal of a New Model   *130*
Comparison with Other Accounts of Task
    Complexity and Intelligence   *137*
References   *141*

9. **On the Neurology of Intelligence and Intelligence Factors**   145
David L. Robinson

Arousability as the Determinant of
    Correlations Between EEG and IQ   *146*
A Systems Theory Approach to Analysis
    of EEG Responses   *148*
Arousability, Information Processing, and
    Intelligence Factors   *149*
Neurological Differences Determining Three
    Distinct High IQ Types   *155*
Conclusion   *159*
References   *160*

10. **Cognitive Integration: Alternative Model of Intelligence**   163
Jagannath P. Das and Ronald F. Jarman

Luria's Model   *164*
Model of Information Integration in 1975   *166*
Assessment of Cognitive Functions   *169*
Statistical Evidence for the Model   *169*
Luria's Model in Neuropsychology   *174*
Syndrome Analysis and Multivariate Analysis   *176*
Implications for Assessment   *177*
References   *179*

11. **Theory-Based Testing of Intellectual Abilities: Rationale for the Triarchic Abilities Test**   183
Robert J. Sternberg

The Differential Theories and Tests of Intelligence   *183*
The Triarchic Theory and Test of Intelligence   *186*
Uses of the Sternberg Triarchic Abilities Test   *199*
References   *200*

12. Cognitive Models for Understanding and Assessing Spatial Abilities   203
James W. Pellegrino and Earl B. Hunt

Psychometrics and Information Processing   *204*
Practice and Spatial Aptitude   *207*
Theory Based Assessment of Spatial Ability   *210*
Dynamic Spatial Reasoning Ability   *216*
Conclusions   *221*
References   *222*

13. The Control of Complex Systems and Performance in Intelligence Tests   227
Rainer H. Kluwe, Carlo Misiak, and Hilde Haider

Intelligence Tests Versus System
Control Tasks   *228*
Formal Aspects   *232*
Cognitive Aspects   *237*
Conclusion   *241*
References   *242*

14. New Intelligence with Information Technologies   245
Andrea A. diSessa

The Concept of a Computational Medium   *246*
Intelligence and Literacy   *247*
Examples   *250*
Where We Stand   *261*
Conclusion   *265*
References   *265*

15. Improving Intelligence by Fostering Creativity in Everyday Settings   267
Arthur J. Cropley

Some Relevant Studies   *276*
Promoting Creativity in Schools   *278*
References   *278*

16. Intelligence, Economics, and Schooling   **281**
   Kevin Harris

   Idealism and Materialism   *281*
   The Contemporary Context: Idealist
      Educational Theory   *284*
   Schooling, Education, and Intelligence:
      A Materialist Interpretation   *286*
   Conclusion   *294*
   References   *295*

Author Index   **297**
Subject Index   **305**

Preface

Most of us who are engaged in research agree that our work is more likely to be profitable when it results from the accumulation of knowledge acquired through projects undertaken within a coherent framework, rather than through single, isolated studies. To establish such a framework, researchers must be provided with the opportunity to exchange and refine their ideas and viewpoints. National and international conferences serve as examples of the role such meetings can play in providing a vehicle for increased communication, synthesis, summary and cross-area fertilisation among researchers working within specialised areas of psychological research and development. But conferences often serve more the sharing of specific information and keeping in touch. Conferences frequently fail to provide real opportunities for extensive reflection and debate.

The contributors to this book met together for two and one half days in just such reflection and debate in a *Seminar on Intelligence* from 26 to 28 August 1988 at the Southern Cross Hotel, Melbourne, Australia. They were asked not to present papers but to engage in a debate in front of an audience of nearly 300 academics and practitioners working in psychology and related disciplines. The aim was to offer a number of researchers who reflect current approaches to the investigation of 'intelligence' (conceived very broadly) and who have made significant contributions to existing knowledge, an opportunity to discuss their work in relatively broad perspective, and to consider explicitly how their findings and the knowledge they have gained could be brought to bear upon the development of more general theories, and upon approaches towards the solution of practical problems.

One year later chapters for this book were submitted. However, the purposes of the Seminar and the book were different. The aim of the Seminar had been to discuss unifying approaches to intelligence, and long term goals which might be shaping the course of research. The aim of the book was to give the authors of chapters the opportunity to write about their personal current research projects.

The Seminar was planned and arranged by the Australian Council For Educational Research (ACER) as its contribution to the Australian Bicentennial celebrations. Fourteen countries were represented at the Seminar. The Seminar was also regarded as a satellite conference preceeding the *24th International Congress of Psychology*, which took place in Sydney between 28 August and 2 September 1988.

I would like to express my thanks to everyone who contributed to the success of the ACER *Seminar on Intelligence*. I am especially indebted to the Council of the ACER for making the meeting possible. Without their support not only would there have been no Seminar, but this book would not have been written.

My largest debt is owed to the present and previous directors of the ACER, Dr. Barry McGaw and Dr. John P. Keeves for advice, financial assistance and, above all, moral support.

Helga A.H. Rowe
Principal Research Officer
Australian Council For Educational Research

Notes on Contributors

JOHN B. BIGGS is Professor and Chairman of the Department of Education, University of Hong Kong, a post he has held since 1987. Prior to that he was Professor of Education at the University of Newcastle, NSW, Australia for many years. His major research area, learning and motivation in institutional settings, has two interrelated strands: Students' approaches to learning, and assessing the quality of learning outcomes. The latter strand has largely been developed in cooperation with Kevin Collis. It uses the SOLO taxonomy for curriculum development, and for evaluating learning outcomes. John Biggs has written numerous articles and several monographs, including *Evaluating the Quality of Learning* (1987), and *The Process of Learning* (with R. Telfer, 1987). He is currently studying how students in Hong Kong schools and tertiary institutions approach academic learning and what kinds of learning outcome are obtained.

KEVIN F. COLLIS has been Professor of Education at the University of Tasmania since 1977. Before he began his academic research career at the University of Newcastle in 1968 he taught mathematics, science and logic in Queensland private and state secondary schools. His current research interests are in cognitive development, mathematics and science education, and evaluation. He is the author of many journal articles in both professional and adademic journals and has authored or coauthored several monographs.

JOHN D. CRAWFORD obtained his BSc in Physics and Master's degree in Electrical Engineering at the University of Sydney, and more recently a Ph.D. in Psychology at the University of New South Wales. He is now a Lecturer in Applied Psychology in the Faculty of Business at the University of Technology,

Sydney. His doctoral work was concerned with the relationship between common measures of intelligence and tests of sustained attention, and with the use of these tests to investigate different theoretical accounts of the nature of general intelligence. Present interests include the study of decision making skills and how they relate to current models of the structure of mental abilities, such as Gf/Gc theory, and to the concept of "practical" intelligence.

ARTHUR J. CROPLEY was born in South Australia in 1935 and graduated from Adelaide University in Arts and Education. After seven years as a school teacher in Australia, England and Canada, he attended the University of Alberta and obtained the Ph.D. in Educational Psychology in 1965. He is presently professor of psychology in the University of Hamburg, after a number of years as lecturer in psychology in the University of New England (NSW), and Assistant to Full Professor in the University of Regina (Canada). He is the author of 14 books on creativity, lifelong learning and adaptation of immigrants. In addition he has published about 100 papers and chapters on these topics, and has obtained a number of substantial research grants from various bodies.

JAGANNATH PRASAD DAS is Director of the Developmental Disabilities Centre, University of Alberta, Canada. He began teaching in India, subsequently taught at George Peabody College and the University of California at Los Angeles before his present position.

ANDREA A. DI SESSA is Professor, Division of Education in Mathematics, Science and Technology, and Associate Dean in the Graduate School of Education, University of California, Berkeley, USA. He was trained in physics with an A.B. at Princeton University and a Ph.D. at the Massachusetts Institute of Technology. He began his work in education with Seymour Papert's Logo Project, M.I.T. Artificial Intelligence Laboratory, and has continued to study and develop means of using advanced technology in education. In addition, Professor Di Sessa has extensively studied the development of intuitive knowledge of the physical world and its relation to learning science.

ROBERT GLASER's range of research takes in major problems in complex cognition and human abilities. He has studied the properties of subject matter competence and expertise, and the role of structures of knowledge in learning; the information processing requirements of performance on aptitude tests; and the differences between novices' and and experts' problem solving abilities in scientific problem solving. He has continuing interests in learning theory and the assessment of human performance. Robert Glaser is Professor of Psychology and Education, and Director of the Learning Research and Development Center at the University of Pittsburgh. He has served as president of major scientific and professional associations in his field and as editor of major journals. He has received numerous scientific awards and is recipient of honorary degrees from the Universities of Göteborg (Sweden), Louvain (Belgium), and Indiana (USA). Scientific reasoning, instructional theory and educational assessment are his current central interests.

SUSAN R. GOLDMAN is Professor of Psychology and Codirector of the Learning Technology Center, Vanderbilt University. Dr. Goldman's research focuses on cognitive and developmental characteristics of learning and thinking, especially for mathematical and language related skills. She is particularly interested in understanding sources of individual differences in performance in these areas.

HILDE HAIDER-HASEBRINK obtained a Diploma in Psychology (1985) from the University of Hamburg and is presently Assistant and Lecturer in Psychology at the Institute for Cognitive Research, University of The Federal Armed Forces, Hamburg.

KEVIN HARRIS is Professor of Education at Macquarie University, Sydney, Australia. One of his major interests is the role that formal educational institutions play in disseminating and legitimating of knowledge, and in fostering particular human abilities and qualities within societies. He is the author of *Education and Knowledge* and *Teachers and Classes*, both published by Routledge and Kegan Paul, and *Sex, Ideology and Religion*, published by Harvester Press. He has published numerous articles in academic journals.

RONALD F. JARMAN obtained a Bachelor of Science degree in mathematics from the University of British Columbia in 1970, a Master of Arts degree in educational measurement and evaluation and applied data analysis from the University of Toronto in 1972, and a Doctor of Philosophy in educational psychology from the University of Alberta in 1975. Since 1975, Dr. Jarman has been teaching and engaged in research at the University of British Columbia in the Department of Educational Psychology and Special Education, where he is a Professor. His Jarman's primary research interests are in the areas of models of human intelligence and the neuropsychological bases of cognitive processes.

RAINER H. KLUWE obtained a Diploma in Psychology (1971) and Ph.D. (1975) at the University of Trier, acquired a Dr. phil.habil. (1981) at the University of Munich, and became a Full Professor of Psychology (1980) at the Institute for Cognitive Research, University of The Federal Armed Forces, Hamburg.

CARLO MISIAK obtained a Diploma in Psychology (1983) at the University of Hamburg, and in 1988 became a Member of the AI-research group, Institute for Cognitive Research, University of the Federal Armed Forces, Hamburg.

JAMES W. PELLEGRINO is Professor of Psychology and holds the Frank Mayborn Chair in Cognitive Studies at Vanderbilt University. He is Codirector of the Learning Technology Center at Vanderbilt. His research focuses on individual differences in intellectual functioning, particularly as regards spatial and mathematical skills. He has applied this research to issues of testing and assessment.

KJELL RAAHEIM is Professor of Psychology at the University of Bergen, Norway. He graduated in psychology at the University of Oslo in 1955 and received his doctorate at the University of Bergen in 1963. He has been working towards making the Department of Cognitive Psychology in Bergen into one of the most influential institutions in Scandinavia in psychological research and the teaching of psychology at tertiary level. His list of published monographs, popular books and textbooks includes four books in English. With Dr. Wankowski at the University of Birmingham he was the author of *Helping Students to Learn at University*.

MARC N. RICHELLE was born in 1930 and has been Professor of Experimental Psychology and Head of the Psychology Laboratory, University of Liege, Belgium, since 1965. He received his university education at Liege, Geneva, and Harvard. His fields of research are in learning (animals and humans), cognitive development, experimental psychopharmacology, psychology of time, history and epistemology of psychology. He was President of the Belgian Psychology Society (1968–1970) and Société de Psychologie Scientifique de Langue Francaise (1989–1991). He is the author of more than 150 publications. Among the dozen books he has published are: *Les Conduites Créatives* (with C. Bodson, 1974), *Manuel de Psychologie* (with R. Droz, 1976), *L'acquisition du langage* (1972), *Skinner* (1978), *Time in Animal Behaviour* (with H. Lejeune, 1980, and *L'explicitation en Psychologie* (edited with X. Seron, 1980).

DAVID L. ROBINSON was born in Ireland where he spent his early adult years working in industry and developing a career in production management. At the age of 30 he left industry to study psychology at the University of Ulster. Later, after obtaining a Doctorate at the University of Oxford, he and his family moved to the United States. In the United States he was appointed Research Fellow at Brown University. This was followed by a research appointment with the United States National Institutes of Health. Dr. Robinson subsequently moved to Australia where he is now Senior Lecturer in Psychology at the University of Sydney. His abiding interest has been the relationship between brain-function and behavior and he takes the view that an integrated science of Psychology can only be achieved through better understanding of brain-behavior relationships.

HELGA A.H. ROWE is the Principal Research Fellow of The Australian Council For Educational Research. She was one of the first mature age students in the

Department of Psychology of the University of Queensland, where she enrolled for her degree in 1968, when her youngest child was 2-years-old. She and husband Harold have four sons and one daughter. In 1969 she was awarded a University of Queensland Teaching Fellowship. She graduated with first class honors in 1971 (BA, HONs) and was awarded the Gold medal of the University of Queensland. In 1980, she obtained a Ph.D. in the Department of Psychology, Melbourne University. Prior to her work with ACER whe was on the staff of the University of Queensland, first in the Department of Education, then in the Department of Psychology. She is the author of a number of psychological and educational tests and test batteries, including the *ACER Early School Series, Checklists for Schoolbeginners* and the *Non-verbal Abilities Tests* (*NAT*). She has published three books and contributed numerous chapters and articles covering a wide range of topics in educational psychology relating to individual differences and cognitive development. Her current research relates to the development of cognitive processes in real work and technological environments, and to implications of technology for learning and teaching.

LAZAR STANKOV was born in Belgrade in 1941. He completed a Masters degree at the University of Belgrade and a Ph.D. at Denver, where he worked with Professor John Horn, investigating auditory abilities in the context of a fluid and crystallized intelligence structure. In 1973 he took a post at the University of Sydney and is currently a Reader in Psychology. His major recent research makes use of competing tasks to investigate the relationship between attention and intelligence. He is living in the Blue Mountains west of Sydney with his wife Sondi (a manufacturing jeweller) and his two teenage daughters Naumi and Ise.

ROBERT J. STERNBERG is IBM Professor of Psychology and Education at Yale University. He received his BA summa cum laude, Phi Beta Kappa from Yale in 1972, and his Ph.D. from Stanford in 1975. He has been the winner of numerous awards, including the Early Career Award and Boyd R. McCandless Award of the American Psychological Association, the Outstanding Book and Research Review Awards of the Society for Multivariate Experimental Psychology, and the Distinguished Scholar Award of the National Association for Gifted Children (USA). He is a past winner of NSF and Guggenheim Foundation Fellowships. Sternberg's main research interests are in intelligence, creativity, and thought processes.

INTELLIGENCE: RECONCEPTUALIZATION AND MEASUREMENT

1 Introduction: Paradigm and Context

Helga A.H. Rowe
Australian Council for Educational Research

This book deals with theoretical issues relating to human "intelligence," its manifestation, development, and measurement. It focuses on intelligence because intelligence plays an important part in learning, involves higher-order thinking, problem solving, and creativity, and because of its importance to an individual's performance and personal success in everyday life. As reform in education continues, it is becoming particularly important that we develop a rich understanding of what intelligence is and how to foster it.

The authors call attention to some questions that have not been raised previously, and to many of the important and relevant issues that must be addressed in the study of cognition and in more general psychological research. One purpose of this book is to propose perspectives for future research, not so much with the intent of predicting it as with that of shaping it. However, perhaps to the dismay of some readers, the contributors to this book are not providing an agenda for future research. To suggest a single intellectual path or set of paradigms to guide research on intelligence is impossible, and if it were possible would probably be counterproductive. A forward move in intelligence research demands the reflection on its many facets and research from a variety of perspectives, which, hopefully, in the end might lead to certain syntheses.

Intelligence research in the 1980s might go down as a decade of publications that decried the quality of theories, and questioned the usefulness of the concept of intelligence and its measurement. This book is not about new theories. The term reconceptualization is used in the sense of "re-visiting" and "re-orientation" with the intention to come to know again and gain a new understanding of the processes underlying human intellectual functioning, i.e., the development and operation of human intelligence.

1

As suggested by Kuhn (1962, 1970a, 1970b) paradigmatic change in scientific communities announces itself through the discussion and questioning of the prevailing paradigm. Thus, the 1980s should have been an interesting time for intelligence research, but were they? Have research approaches developed? Have promising fields opened up (especially by the challenges resulting from computer use)? It is doubtful that many would answer these questions in the affirmative.

Paradigm and paradigm shifts have certainly become major topics of discussion among researchers in psychology and in other disciplines of science and social science (for an overview see e.g., Jacob, 1987, 1988). It is important to note, however, that different meanings are being attached to the term "paradigm" by different authors within the same and within different disciplines. For the purposes of this chapter I am using the term paradigm in a metaphorical sense as reflected in the literature of contemporary philosophy of science and new paradigm thinking, rather than equating it, as may be more typical within psychology and education, with a model of inquiry (e.g., Popkewitz, 1984) or with theory (e.g., Torgesen, 1986). I view paradigm as the *Weltanschauung* of the researcher, i.e., the central overall way of regarding and relating to phenomena and in the context in which he/she lives and works.

Such a conceptualization of paradigm allows for questioning at a more fundamental level than is the case at the level of theory or of model of inquiry. Paradigm directs attention to the basics of our thinking about what is reality and how it becomes known, not just within scientific investigation, but in all of life. It includes perceptions, beliefs, values and practices that collectively are part of the decisions that researchers make about what counts as real, and it also includes how researchers share and disseminate what they have found to be real.

Paradigms give rise not only to theories and research methodologies but also to criteria for the selection of research questions and for their evaluation (Capra, 1986; Lakoff & Johnson, 1980; Lincoln & Guba, 1985; Ogilvy, 1986; Prigogine & Stengers, 1984; Sadawa & Caley, 1985). The paradigm represents "the ultimate benchmarks against which *everything else* is tested" (Lincoln & Guba, 1985, p. 15). It does not frame the phenomena of interest as theory does, but rather presents a way of seeing (and not seeing) phenomena and thinking (and not thinking) about the world. It contains the perceptions, beliefs and values that ultimately determine our thinking, actions and reactions. When we articulate our paradigm we make explicit how we think about, know, and come to understand the phenomena that engage us in any area of our lives. Paradigms describe our personal epistemology. The need to become aware of and articulate (at least to oneself) the characteristics of one's ultimate benchmarks certainly arises when the paradigm one "unconsciously" lives by reaches its limitation (see also Capra, 1982, 1986; Lincoln & Guba, 1985; Prigogine & Stengers, 1984).

The prevailing paradigm in the natural and social sciences has arisen from the Newtonian, mechanistic, reductionist assumptions that have guided scientific and applied considerations since the rise of the natural sciences in the 17th century. However, evidence of a dawning awareness about the paradigmatic limitations within which we have worked are found in publications of an increasing number of scientists and philosophers of science during the 1980s (e.g., Berman, 1984; Bernstein, 1983; Capra, 1982; Hesse, 1980; Jantsch, 1980; Le-Shan & Margenau, 1982; Prigogine & Stengers, 1984; Wolf, 1981).

In the remainder of this chapter I (a) address the assumptions about the nature of reality and the nature of knowledge claims that underlie Newtonian mechanistic, reductionist thought in relation to intelligence and its measurement, (b) address the importance of theoretical re-orientation in the area of intelligence research, (c) outline some assumptions about what counts as real, and how we can know what is real within the emerging non-Newtonian, holistic paradigm and discuss the importance of these assumptions for research into intelligence and its application, and (d) introduce the chapters contained in this volume.

INTELLIGENCE AND THE NEWTONIAN PARADIGM

Mechanistic assumptions.   Current approaches to the conceptualization of intelligence and to its measurement have been shaped largely by the tenets of the Newtonian mechanistic paradigm. The Newtonian assumptions rely on the metaphor of the machine initially set out by Descartes. Newton established that the universe operates as a celestial clockwork following precise, mathematically statable natural laws. Mechanistic theory holds that the same natural laws that direct inanimate events direct the behavior of living organisms. This leads to the postulation of a uniformity and predictability analoguous of a machine-like (mechanical) process taking place throughout nature. A machine can be broken up into its smallest functional parts, and the causal relationships between the parts can be stated with precision. Once the mechanism is known, the future functioning of the machine can be predicted and controlled. Finally, in case of breakdown it is likely that the machine can be repaired.

Simplicity.   It is thus regarded as the foundation of the mechanistic paradigm. All complexity is broken down into components, which are to be operationalized as far as possible. The whole is to be understood by understanding the components, often arranged in so called logical and sequential order. In the Newtonian universe time and space are even and continuous, all movement is controlled by outside forces (assumptions that in psychology are reflected in stimulus control and systematic reinforcement theories), fact is separated from value, the observer is quite distinct from the observed, and knowledge is distinct from the person who has the knowledge. Personal meaning and context are irrelevant. Quantification, in terms of comparing what is being measured to an external standard, was the only means by which valid knowledge claims could be made. Certainty of knowledge is obtained by gathering sufficient data. Psychological phenomena came to be seen as observable or perceivable with one or more of the senses, measurable and quantifiable, and verifiable in that several observers should be able to agree on their existence and characteristics (Valle, 1981).

The machine metaphor has had and still has an enormous influence on psychologists' conceptions of learning, development and other human behavior, and on the criteria used in the selection of research questions, research methodology, and theory building. The assumptions of the mechanistic reductionist paradigm are at the core of practices such as task analysis, isolated skills training, programmed learning, the establishment of behavioral objectives, etc. They lead to the assumption that causality can be established and that prediction, and control become possible. One result is a glut of predictive tests and the practice of diagnostic/prescriptive assessment and instruction.

The mechanistic paradigm has had a particularly limiting effect on the conceptualization of "intelligence" and its identification. It led to the narrow and dogmatic view that educationists and industry evaluate performance potential and practice on the basis of what they regard as scientific and objective knowledge. We all have tended to rely too heavily on measurable outcomes, identified largely through the use of standardized tests. Only standardized procedures satisfy our *quest for certainty*. Theoretical approaches such as psychometric-, behavioristic-, psychological process-, or cognitive strategies models all share a mechanistic reductionist heritage that embraces assumptions of the following kinds:

- Intelligence (or the lack of it) resides within the individual; as do perceptual and learning problems.
- Knowledge, skills and learning can be segmented into pieces, and "intelligence" can be segmented into pieces of behavior and/or cognition.
- There are correct and incorrect strategies, facts, behaviors and processes that flow directly and indisputably from the assumptions of a particular theory.
- Cognitive skills can be taught in isolation through training that meets diagnosed "deficits".

One of the fundamental assumptions of the field is that certain limitations or deficiencies in basic psychological processes *cause* low levels of intelligence, as measured on traditional IQ-tests. Another assumption is that these cognitive limitations are caused by naturally occurring variation in the neurophysiological substrata that support all cognitive activity, or by damage to these areas caused by accident or disease. These two assumptions provide the rationale for intervention oriented research and practice in psychology and education.

Paradigm versus theory. As already noted, some major theoretical reorientations are occurring in an attempt to remedy the inadequacy of current approaches. In fact, there is considerable evidence in psychology and other social sciences of a shift from the mechanistic reductionist to an alternative, holistic paradigm. Within intelligence research a major obstacle to such a transition relates to a certain amount of confusion between theory and paradigm. Some authors refer to existing theories as paradigms. I believe that this is unfortunate because it gives the impression that a new level of inquiry has been reached, when in fact only variations in theory (however important they may be) are discussed within the assumptions of the mechanistic paradigm.

Paradigm and theory focus on different levels of inquiry. A paradigm delineates the assumptions held of reality and of knowledge per se. A theory is always more narrowly focused than a paradigm and delineates specific phenomena. When a group of researchers in a discipline come to share similar ideas about the basic assumptions they are making in their area, share criteria for the determination of the importance of questions that might be asked, the explanatory concepts that are preferred and the methodologies that are appropriate, they are seen as sharing a scientific paradigm (Kuhn, 1962, 1970a, 1970b). Paradigms can be distinguished from one another by their intellectual history, the research tools they employ and the language used by their adherents (Lachman, Lachman, & Butterfield, 1979). Theories are sets of propositions and hypothetical constructs that are developed to explain particular phenomena or a group of phenomena. Within a paradigm one can modify, expand or completely change a theory without changing the paradigm. It is possible to have several different theories about the same phenomenon within one paradigm. Whereas a paradigm sets a general orientation to inquiry, theories attempt to provide specific explanations for particular phenomena within a paradigm.

THEORETICAL REORIENTATIONS

The importance of interaction. The shift from a mechanistic to a holistic paradigm is a shift from the machine metaphor to a human metaphor. In a holistic paradigm, mechanistic assumptions are replaced by assumptions that emerge directly from the individual's perceptions and knowing. Knowledge and knowing result from processes of social interchange and interaction with the environment. The acquisition of knowledge is seen no longer as absorbing in one way or another the *truth,* as defined by some outside criteria, into one's mind, as it would be in mechanistic thought, but is seen as a direct outcome of processes of social interaction.

> We generally count as knowledge that which is represented in linguistic propositions - stored in books, journals, floppy disks, and the like. These renderings . . . are constituents of social practices. From this perspective knowledge is not something people possess somewhere in their heads, but rather something people do together (Gergen, 1985, p. 270).

This is not to say that all individual differences in learning and achievement can be explained on the basis of social interaction alone, or that cognitive processes are completely specific to the context and occasion in which they were originally acquired or applied. In order to function, people must be able to generalize some aspects of knowledge and skills to new situations. However, there is considerable support for the view that social interchange and interaction with the environment mediate knowing and intellectual development. What individuals perceive and experience is mediated by their own interpretation of the phenomena surrounding them. These interpretations are largely the result of interactions with other people and they are used by the individual to achieve specific goals (for review and further discussion see e.g., Manis & Meltzer, 1978; Meltzer, Petras & Reynolds, 1975; Rogoff & Lave, 1984).

> . . . individuals' experiences are mediated by their own interpretations of experience. These interpretations are created by individuals through interaction with others and used by individuals to achieve specific goals (Jacob, 1987, p. 27).

Social and cultural expectations and traditional patterns of social interaction make up a large part of the environmental context in which these idiosyncratic interpretations, which so strongly influence cognitive activity, are created (see also e.g., Cole & Scribner, 1975; Rogoff & Lave, 1984; Scribner, 1984; Scribner & Cole, 1981). Rogoff (1984) summarizes these influences as follows:

> Central to everyday contexts in which cognitive activity occurs is interaction with other people and use of socially provided tools and schemas for solving problems. Cognitive activity is socially defined, interpreted and supported. People, usually in conjunction with each other and always guided by social norms, set goals, negotiate appropriate means to reach the goals and assist each other in implementing the means and resetting the goals as activities evolve. . . The social context affects cognitive activity at two levels, according to Vygotsky (1978). First, sociocultural history provides tools for cognitive activity (e.g. writing and calculators) and practices to facilitate reaching appropriate solutions to problems (e.g., norms for the arrangement of grocery shelves to aid shoppers in locating what they need, common mnemonic devices, scripts and frames for interpreting events). Second, the immediate social interactional context structures individual cognitive activity (Rogoff, 1984, p. 4).

Erickson's (1984) overview of research from an anthropological view shows, for example, that mental abilities (including language and mathematical abilities) that were once thought to be relatively or even totally (as presumed by classical learning theory and Piagetian developmental theory) independent of context, are much more sensitive to context than traditionally thought. Cognitive processes such as reasoning and understanding develop in the context of personal use and purpose. The demand characteristics of a learning task can be changed by altering the context within which it is presented.

Change the physical form of the tools or symbols, or change the social forms of relations among the people with whom the individual is learning the practice (or is performing it once learned) and one has profoundly changed the nature of the interaction - the nature of the learning task. In doing so one has also changed what in ordinary parlance we call the *ability* of the individual.

From this point of view it is not surprising that a child can display arithmetic competence while dealing with change at the grocery store and yet seem to lack that performance when doing what seems to be the 'same' arithmetic problem on a worksheet or at the blackboard. . . a picture of a coin is not a coin, and relations with the teacher and fellow students are not the same as relations with a store clerk. . . The nature of the task in the store and in the classroom is very different and so is the nature of the abilities required to accomplish it (Erickson, 1984, p. 529–530).

As pointed out by Erickson (1984) differences in performance as described earlier can not be explained merely in relation to abstract versus concrete think-ing, as has been quite generally assumed. Rather, the differences in performance are very much related to differences in problem definition by self and others. When a person has made the problem his/her own, i.e., when he/she has formu-lated the task or question, he/she goes through a series of cognitive processes including decision making points, each involving personal abilities, knowledge and skills as well as processes of social interaction that do not come into play when, for example, he/she is engaged in completing a worksheet or doing an IQ test. It is not just that learning tasks are often "out of context" as Erickson (1984, p. 533) notes, but they are *in a context* in which the power relations and pro-cesses of social interaction are such that the student has no influence on problem formulation, and the tasks offer no context of personal use and purpose.

A full appreciation of the role of context, personal purpose and use, and of processes of social interaction would fundamentally reshape our conceptualiza-tions of and approaches to assessment as well as to teaching and learning. Our models for assessment and intervention have been explicitly based on the as-sumption that abilities and knowledge (and the lack of them) are lodged within the individual. The inability to perform certain tasks, low achievement on tests, learning problems, and the like, are variously explained in terms of deficits, disorders, delayed development, faulty learning, deficits in cognitive strategies, and so on.

THE EMERGING HOLISTIC PARADIGM

Adequacy of the mechanistic paradigm. Paradigms in themselves do not offer solutions, nor do they provide right and wrong ways to proceed. Rather, they offer sets of fundamental assumptions that might be adequate (or no longer adequate) for the identification and formulation of research questions and their evaluation. The mechanistic paradigm may have been adequate in relation to the assessment of certain general and specific abilities in restricted settings, i.e., by providing test scores reflecting certain outcomes. It is not adequate where the aim is to understand the *nature* of the processes, contexts and social interactions that have led to these test scores or might have resulted in different scores. It is not adequate when the focus is on how individuals actually construct the meaning of a task or situation. It does not take into consideration the impact of the relationship between the observer and the observed, tester and testee, learner and instructor, and so on, as persons. On the other hand, those working within the mechanistic paradigm have equipped investigators with a multitude of research tools, such as observational methods and measurement procedures, which help them to systematize observations that would otherwise not have been feasible in the more holistic and intuitive attempts to make, for instance, informal observations, or to conduct interviews.

The influence of quantum physics.   It is generally acknowledged that the demise of the Newtonian mechanistic assumptions in the physical sciences resulted from the revolutionary discoveries in quantum physics. Max Planck discovered that the energy of heat radiation is not emitted continuously, but appears in the form of energy "packets". Einstein labelled these packets "quanta" and recognized them as fundamental aspects of nature. Heisenberg theorized further and demonstrated in his "uncertainty principle" the inability of science to precisely predict atomic events.

> Quantum theory has thus demolished the classical concepts of solid objects and of strictly deterministic laws of nature. At the subatomic level, the solid material objects of classical physics dissolve into wavelike patterns of probabilities, and these patterns, ultimately, do not represent probabilities of things, but rather probabilities of interconnections. A careful analysis of the process of observation in atomic physics has shown that the subatomic particles have no meaning as isolated entities but can only be understood as interconnections between the preparation of an experiment and the subsequent measurement. Quantum theory thus reveals a basic oneness of the universe. It shows that we cannot decompose the world into independently existing smallest units. As we penetrate into matter, nature does not show us any isolated "building blocks", but rather appears as a complicated web of relations between the various parts of the whole. . . the properties of any atomic object can be understood only in terms of the object's interaction with the observer. This means that the classical ideal of an objective description of nature is no longer valid (Capra, 1975, pp. 56–57).

The implications for psychological research and measurement should be clear. Too long have we attempted to force wholeness into fragmentation, make the unpredictable predictable, the unmeasurable measurable, and regarded people as reactors rather than as creators of their own reality. Separations such as those made under the Newtonian mechanistic assumptions between self and the world, the knower and the known, ability and context are no longer tenable. They are, in fact, erroneous.

The contemporary paradigm shift thus represents the shift from a machine metaphor to a human metaphor. Prigogine and Stengers (1984, p. 23) refer to art forms as the new metaphor to characterize the fundamental importance of intuitive and idiosyncratic ways of knowing in present day science. Lincoln and Guba (1985, pp. 61–62) refer to the shift from "machine to human being" and from "reality as a machine toward reality as a conscious organism." Bernstein (1983) notes the shift from "rationality as method" to a "human rationality"; and Valle (1981, p. 428) speaks of a "person-world-view." This shift is occurring in virtually every major discipline. The basic principles of the emergent paradigm are reflected in "the analytic residue remaining after the particulars of physics, chemistry, brain theory, mathematics and so on have been boiled off" (Lincoln & Guba, 1985, p. 65).

Implications for intelligence research and measurement. The holistic paradigm views human beings (e.g., tester and testee, subject and researcher, student and teacher) as both active and reactive. Active, not as defined previously (i.e., actively engaged in responding to a direction, question or stimulus provided by someone else), but rather *immanently active* (i.e., a self-generating inner activity that gives meaning as it actively constructs and transforms reality), to use von Bertalanffy's terminology. Behavior is seen to result from active choices that are made by the individual on the basis of perceptions of purpose and meaning rather than because of the explanatory power gained from external "objective" knowledge and the collection of more data (see also LeShan & Margenau, 1982).

Central to a contemporary and future understanding and assessment of intelligence is that *purpose* is the driving force that is replacing traditional cause-and-effect relationships. The organism is viewed as a self-organizing and self-regulating open system, which always interacts with the environment and which transforms as a result of the individual's experience and perceived purpose of his/her actions (or the purpose of systems). The observer or tester and the observed are no longer independent.

Holistic assumptions reverse the mechanistic reductionist position. The dynamics of the whole can *not* be understood from the properties of its parts, rather the properties of the parts can only be understood from the dynamics of the whole. The whole is both different and more than the sum of its parts. Knowledge of parts can not lead to knowledge of the whole. There are no fixed and generalizable linkages between the parts.

Commitment to a holistic paradigm is not just a matter of a new set of prescriptive educational and/or research strategies. Because such a paradigm views human beings as immanently active, constructing meaning, self-organizing and self-regulating, there can not be a sequentially organized holistic "agenda."

Once one has accepted how holistic assumptions are fundamentally different from mechanistic reductionist ones, one begins to think differently about the nature of intelligence, learning, problem solving, assessment and measurement more generally.

Basic holistic assumptions include the following:

• Human learning involves understanding relationships, rather than the mere knowledge of pieces of information. It is the personal construction of meaning by the individual based on who he/she is and on what he/she knows (not based on what the test constructor understands or believes needs to be known). Whether they are aware of it or not, individuals bring their own personal, social, cultural histories, interpretations and purposes to any situation.

• Intellectual development and progress are transformative, rather than addictive. Development and progress occur when concepts are understood in new ways. As the individual is immanently active, what is learned is not necessarily directly and solely the result of how and what he/she has been taught. What is learned can not be captured by input-output or closed feedback models. New knowledge is not added on to previous knowledge but it transforms previous knowledge, just as previous knowledge shapes the nature of new knowledge.

• There is no best way to assess development, achievement or ability. Assessment involves monitoring what an individual does over time in purposeful (to the individual being assessed) engagements, in realistic and interactive settings. We no longer separate the question of what the individual is able to achieve from the question of how he/she constructs meaning in the assessment situation. In this context, *errors* are not instances that the individual is "wrong", but are ways of making sense that provide insights into how the testee thinks and reasons. Assessment also includes assessing the actual test and testee match, and an evaluation of the testee's opportunities and motivation for learning. The very criteria of assessment change from counting and ranking correct responses to controlled, often static tasks, to documenting and assessing real life processes and accomplishments (see also Messick, 1984).

A shift in paradigm leads to a transformation of the way research questions are identified, investigated and evaluated according to the different assumptions about what is regarded as "real" and how researchers can know. As noted earlier, various forms of inquiry have emerged from alternative paradigmatic assumptions such as the ones discussed here. They include phenomenological - and qualitative approaches, ethnography, naturalistic research, research as praxis (e.g., Lather, 1986) and research for empowerment (e.g., Heron, 1981). What these approaches have in common is the rejection of the mechanistic reductionist assumptions. They overlap to a considerable degree in their specific assumptions and research strategies. Differences between them relate to emphasis and purpose (for overviews of issues and approaches see e.g., Jacob, 1987; Lather, 1986; Morgan, 1983; Polkinghorne, (1983).

These forms of inquiry share the assumption that persons are immanently active, meaning constructing beings whose behavior is highly influenced by context and personal experience. This view leads to a fundamental change in the role of the *subject* as conceived in traditional research to that of participant in the research. The role of the researcher also changes from that of executor of the research design, i.e., controller and measurer of variables, to that of sensitive, empathic listener, observer, participator, and organizer of data. The traditional mathematical framework for data gathering, data preparation, judgment of significance and reporting of findings is supplemented and often replaced by more descriptive, qualitative information that is reported in natural language. Research method is no longer an unambiguous set of fixed rules but is defined as systematic inquiry and careful accounting of data gathering and analysis strategies, which are always designed to serve, rather than control, the research questions, the context, the interaction.

Method does not give truth; it corrects guesses (Polkinghorne, 1983, p. 249).

The necessity for human judgment is not only *not* an embarrassment, but is elevated to the level of precondition (Lincoln & Guba, 1985, p. 156).

There are no *best* general methodologies. Those who are searching for the *most efficient* modes of inquiry are in a way victims of the mechanistic approach that claimed to be able to arrive at generalizations applicable in just about every context. What is important is that cognitive functioning does not take place in a vacuum and that its development and the way it manifests itself is not independent of the physical, cultural, social, political and temporal context in which the individual operates.

The impact of the new holistic paradigm on the conceptualization and measurement of intelligence is not yet strong, but it does exist as is reflected in the chapters of this book. There is a need for much more debate and exploration of fundamental assumptions and strategies. It took the mechanistic paradigm over 300 years to refine its assumptions and work out its implications in order to serve and then outlive its promises. The machine metaphor provided scientists with an initial framework for gaining usable knowledge about nature. The human metaphor has different but equally profound implications for the way we view and conduct research. It acknowledges the understanding of complexity, rather than reduction to simplicity, as its major task and emphasizes that scientific inquiry is basically a process of personal *engagement*.

Scientists engage a subject of study by interacting with it through means of a particular frame of reference, and what is observed and discovered in the object (i.e., its objectivity) is as much a product of this interaction and the protocol and technique through which it is operationalized as it is of the object itself. . . we can see that the same object is capable of yielding many different kinds of knowledge. This leads us to see knowledge as a potentiality resting in an object of investigation and to see science as being concerned with the realization of potentials—of possible knowledges. This view emphasizes the importance of understanding the frameworks through which scientists engage their object of investigation and of understanding the possible modes of engagement (Morgan, 1983, p. 13).

Many readers are likely to feel that they have indeed embraced a holistic paradigm many years ago. I am sure this is so, but why then, do we continue to tolerate and, in fact, on many occasions actively support, mechanistic reductionist views, practices, and interpretations in particular in relation to intelligence and its measurement?

Contributions

My aim in producing this volume was to contribute to a reflective dimension in the investigation of intelligence and the cognitive phenomena it subsumes by providing diverse samples of the progress that is being achieved by highly engaged authors who advocate different approaches. Each one of the chapters broadens and deepens our understanding of intelligence and initiates new and constructive ideas concerning the nature of contemporary research, its possibilities and implications.

Drawing on different assumptions the contributors to this volume have generated different kinds of knowledge and quite distinctive kinds of insights and understanding. This diversity makes it clear to the reader that there are many different ways of studying the same phenomenon, and given that the insights gained on the basis of any one kind of investigation are at best partial and incomplete, the reader may gain much by reflecting on the nature and implications of different approaches before making a commitment to a particular mode of research.

The contributed chapters could be categorized in a number of different ways. They have been arranged into seven broad sections, in some cases somewhat arbitrarily. Some of the papers would have fitted into two or more of the sections. The only reason for using sections in this book is to provide the reader with a quick reference to the themes running through the book, and a certain amount of structure and overview. The major themes reflected in the sections following the introductory chapters relate to cognitive development and learning, responsiveness to instruction, neurological and neurophysiological explanations of cognitive process, theory based assessment of general and more specific abilities, intelligence and computer environments, creative aspects of intelligence, and intelligence viewed within an economic political framework.

The first section consists of two introductory chapters. Following Rowe's more general reflections on paradigm and research, Richelle, considers ways of integrating the fragments of knowledge gained to this point and, as reflected in the title of his chapter, reconciling theoretical views on intelligence. He is concerned about the ahistorical nature of psychological research. His view that "psychologists are prone to deny the value of what was done before" (p. 22) supports the observation made by Cattell more than 20 years ago when he wrote: "Today it has become a truism to say that major scientific theory triumphs not by converting its components, but by their deaths" (Cattell, 1966, p. vi).

Richelle is concerned about the consequences of this tendency for the progress of psychology. We clearly know more today than we have in the past about the processes underlying human intelligence and learning, but are we beginning to see the effects of this new knowledge in education? At the classroom level? In most cases the answer to these questions will be *no*. A likely reason for this negative answer is the impression created by psychologists that there is little agreement within the profession as to what the relevant new knowledge is. As noted by Richelle: "More often than not this knowledge has been conveyed together with and obscured by the turmoil of theoretical and ideological debates that are the rule in psychology" (pp. 22–23). He calls for a greater engagement in developmental studies by those who search for a better understanding of intelligence and points out that development has no explanatory status in a number of the information processing theories. As a unifying theoretical concept for intelligence Richelle proposes the concept of *dynamic variability* that he explains and discusses in relation to a number of theoretical approaches.

The methodological implications of the research on variability and change suggested in Richelle's chapter are certainly very different from those that would flow from the predictions made Detterman (1989) for the future of intelligence research. Detterman predicts that future research in human intelligence will use larger groups of subjects and that the concern with the *reliability* of measures will grow. Richelle's aims can only be fulfilled by a careful investigation of individuals, their history and general context. It is obvious that the 1990s will produce research within both the paradigms discussed earlier in this chapter.

The chapters contained in the second section of this book focus on the development of intelligence, on learning and on the role of knowledge. Raaheim reports a most interesting investigation of the generally perceived lack of correspondence between IQ-scores and success on various complex real life tasks. He finds that persons with high IQ appear to be *prevented* quite frequently from operating in keeping with their intelligence and from acting in more creative ways by their *sensitivity* to the needs and wishes of other people.

Glaser believes that "people think largely by using quite specific knowledge," (p. 53) and thus discusses intelligence as an expression of acquired knowledge. He stresses the importance of knowledge structures that are developed in specific domains to the development of cognitive processes that make possible the acquisition of further proficiency in the same and other domains. He discusses the properties of intellectual proficiency with respect to acquired domain knowledge and performance in unfamiliar domains for well defined and ill-structured tasks. His chapter also addresses the measurement of domain based intellectual proficiency through "indicators of the development of knowledge" such as principled performance, active knowledge, change in personal epistemology, problem representation, automaticity and attention, and self-regulatory skills.

Can the development of intelligence explain the different qualities of intelligent behavior is the question Biggs and Collis have addressed in their chapter. They review and discuss a number of current theoretical models of intelligence and issues relating to the development of intelligent behavior through learning in academic and everyday environments. Their Neo-Piagetian theory of learning cycles and resulting *SOLO Taxonomy* provides a model for the explanation of the relationship between learning and development, and makes a considerable contribution to the understanding of intelligence.

The third section of this volume contains two chapters concerned with individuals' responsiveness to training. The subject of Goldman and Pellegrino's chapter is cognitive development, defined as "the ability to learn" or "the ability to profit from practice" (p. 79) and the dynamic assessment of cognitive development. The chapter contains the discussion of two empirical studies, one relating to mathematics learning and the other to writing, which demonstrate how cognitive developmental perspectives on change in cognitive performance can highlight various attributes of intelligence. These studies show that static, general measures of intelligence and achievement do not predict who will benefit from repeated practice. Rather the changes that occurred as a result of practice were changes that had been predicted on the basis of information processing accounts of acquisition of skill in a specific domain. These findings relate very well to the findings of Biggs and Collis reported in the preceding chapter, and to the view expressed by Glaser in Chapter 4. Furthermore, Goldman and Pellegrino are finding that their work is permitting them not only to describe intellectual development, but to pursue conditions that foster change, and thus allow them to better understand some constraints on the malleability of intellectual functioning.

Stankov is concerned with the enhancement of performance on cognitive tasks and with individual differences in intellectual abilities. The work he presents in this chapter was motivated by a desire to achieve a better understanding of the nature of intelligence, in particular of fluid and crystallized intelligence. He explores how educational interventions can affect both Gf and Gc processes. Stankov distinguishes between *practice* and *training*. Practice refers to repeated performance on the same task. Its main aim is the acquisition and maintenance of a particular skill. Training differs from practice in that the activity on repeated trials involves processes that are theoretically distinct from those of the skill of interest. In other words, the essential feature of training is the presence of *transfer*. His results show that general intelligence can be influenced by educational processes that depend on transfer and that fluid and crystallized intelligence are affected to about the same degree. However, he describes differences in cognitive processes called forth by tests of fluid and crystallized intelligence respectively. His discussion of the results of practice re-addresses some of the traditional issues regarding the relationship of learning and human abilities. One of these issues relates to the effects of practice in doing test items on correlations with other measures of intelligence and on the formation of psychometric factors. He also discusses jointly practiced tasks.

The next three chapters are concerned with the neurophysiological basis of intelligence. Crawford discusses the notion of task complexity in relation to concepts from cognitive theories of attention. He defines task complexity in terms of a person's ability to perform effortful, nonautomatic mental processes. Finally, he proposes a model of task complexity and intelligence that is based on the distinction between diffuse and constricted neural pathways and compares his model with other theories of intelligence and task complexity. His work provides a most interesting and possibly more scientific acceptable account of Spearmans' early notion that higher g-loading (or more complex) tasks are those performance on which requires larger amounts of "mental energy."

Robinson discusses the neurological basis of intelligence and intelligence factors and reports on investigations of the relationship between cortical arousability and WAIS-IQ. Apart from the generally optimal effect of middling arousability, he reports indications that high and low arousability respectively relate to special aptitudes for the performance of some verbal and some manipulative visiospatial tasks with the individuals concerned also differing on the introversion-extraversion dimension of personality. He also found that individuals with high IQs might fall into three distinct neurological categories with corresponding differences on the major dimensions of personality and WAIS profiles. This chapter makes a novel contribution to the research relating EEG data to cognitive processing.

The fifth section of this book provides three excellent examples of theory-based approaches to assessment. Obviously, the chapter by Jarman and Das could have been included in the previous section equally well as it proposes a largely neurophysiological model of cognitive functions. However, it proposes more than this. "The model has its roots in both neuropsychology and cognitive psychology" (p. 163). Its structural basis is provided by the nervous system but its four major functions are constrained by the individual's knowledge base, i.e., his/her accumulated experiences. The scientific basis of this integration model are assessed carefully and its implications for assessment are discussed.

Sternberg takes a truly holistic approach to the conceptualization of intelligence in his *triarchic theory*. In this chapter he briefly discusses conventional differential theories of intelligence and the kinds of tests they have generated. He contrasts these with the triarchic theory and the kind of test it has generated. The main advantages of the triarchic theory and test, and uses of the test in educational and employment settings are discussed.

Pellegrino, as is evident from the title of his chapter, is concerned with *Cognitive Models for Understanding and Assessing Spatial Abilities*. He poses the question "Have we reached a point where the knowledge from research and development activities is sufficient to significantly impact contemporary approaches to measurement?" (p. 204) - which he answers in the affirmative "for various specific domains of cognition and aptitude" (p. 204), including the domain of visual spatial ability. In fact, Pellegrino believes that, in the domain of visual spatial cognition and aptitude, we are currently better off as regards validation problems with the construct, measurement and improvement of intellectual abilities. Major psychometric and information processing issues, including practice and transfer, related to computer-based and non computer-based testing and training are addressed in this chapter. Pellegrino shows that the assessment of dynamic spatial reasoning ability is possible in the context of computer technology. However, Pellegrino's most important message might well be that the application of current theory and technology can lead to the discovery of previously unspecified cognitive abilities.

The sixth section of this book contains three chapters that address intelligence somewhat differently from the other contributors. The first two, like Pellegrino and Goldman address issues within the environment of computer technology. Kluwe, Misiak and Haider investigate the relationship of intelligence, as assessed by traditional IQ-tests, and performance in the control of complex systems in a computer driven *microworld*. Their chapter addresses cognitive, information processing and measurement issues, including problems of assessing validity and reliability in both environments. Di Sessa provides an interesting illustration on how information technology might expand human intelligence. He and his research team are engaged in the development of *Boxer,* a prototype of a *computational medium*. The theoretical underpinnings of Boxer are described in this chapter and examples of its use in educational settings are provided.

Cropley's chapter is concerned with improving intelligence by fostering *creativity* in everyday settings. Currently we witness calls for more creative thinking in just about every country. But what exactly is creativity, and how, if at all, does it relate to intelligence? Are creativity and intelligence differentiable or are they different aspects of a single phenomenon? Cropley argues for a conceptualization of creativity as a *style* of applying one's intelligence. He illustrates his theory with examples from school and everyday life settings.

The last chapter in this book provides a philosophical and political view of *Intelligence, Economics and Schooling*. Harris argues that a major reason why many people will not be able to realize their cognitive and personal potential is political and economic, rather than educational. He discusses idealist and materialist values and their implications for educational theory and policy, curriculum and the development of intelligence.

As was noted at the beginning of this chapter, one expectation of the editor is that this book might in one way or another help shape future progress in intelligence research. This is an important purpose. Equally important is to reveal to readers the questions that those who concern themselves with the construct of intelligence in psychology are now willing to ask. The value of this book should thus be assessed as a whole, as well as on the basis of individual contributions. In other words, the importance of this volume lies as much in the questions posed as in the proposed solutions.

REFERENCES

Berman, M. (1984). *The reenchantment of the world.* New York: Bantam Books.
Bernstein, R. J. (1983). *Beyond objectivity and relativity: Science, hermeneutics, and praxis.* Philadelphia: University of Pennsylvania Press.
Capra, F. (1975). *The tao of physics.* New York: Bantam Books.
Capra, F. (1982). *The turning point: Science, society and the rising culture.* New York: Simon & Schuster.
Capra, F. (1986). The concept of paradigm and paradigm shift. Revision. *Journal of Consciousness and Change, 9,* 11–17.
Cattell, R. (1966). Preface. In R. Cattell (Ed.), *Handbook of multivariate experimental psychology.* Chicago: Rand McNally.
Cole, M, & Scribner, S. (1975). Theorizing about socialization of cognition. *Ethos, 3,* 249–268.
Detterman, D. K. (1989). The future of intelligence research. Editorial. *Intelligence, 13,* 199–203.
Erickson, F. (1984). School literacy, reasoning and civility: An anthropologist's perspective. *Review of Educational Research, 54,* 525–546.
Gergen, K. (1985). The social constructionist movement in psychology. *American Psychologist, 40,* 266–275.
Heron, J. (1981). Experimental research methods. In P. Reason & J. Rowan (Eds.), *Human inquiry.* New York: Wiley.
Hesse, M. (1980). *Revolutions and reconstructions in the philosophy of science.* Bloomington: Indiana University Press.
Jacob, E. (1987). Qualitative research traditions: A review. *Review of Educational Research, 57,* 1–50.
Jacob, E. (1988). Clarifying qualitative research: A focus on tradition. *Educational Researcher, 17,* 16–24.
Jantsch, E. (1980). *The self-organising universe: Scientific and human implications of the emerging paradigm of education.* Oxford: Pergamon Press.
Kuhn, T. S. (1962). *The structure of scientific revolutions.* Chicago: University of Chicago Press.
Kuhn, T. S. (1970a). *The structure of scientific revolutions.* Chicago: University of Chicago Press.
Kuhn, T. S. (1970b). Logic of discovery or psychology of research? In I. Lakatos & A. Musgrave (Eds.), *Criticism and the growth of knowledge.* Cambridge: Cambridge University Press.
Lachman, R., Lachman, J., & Butterfield, E. C. (1979). *Cognitive psychology and information processing: An introduction.* Hillsdale, NJ: Lawrence Erlbaum Associates.
Lakoff, G., & Johnson, M. (1980). *Metaphors we live by.* Chicago: University of Chicago Press.
Lather, P. (1986). Research as praxis. *Harvard Educational Review, 56,* 257–277.
LeShan, L., & Margenau, H. (1982). *Einstein's space and Van Gogh's sky. Physical reality and beyond.* New York: Macmillan.
Lincoln, Y. S., & Guba, E. G. (1985). *Naturalistic inquiry.* Beverly Hills, CA: Sage.
Manis, J., & Meltzer, B. (Eds.) (1978). *Symbolic interaction: A reader in social psychology.* 3rd edition. Boston: Allyn & Bacon.

Meltzer, B. N., Petras, J. W., & Reynolds, L. T. (1975). *Symbolic interactionism: Genesis, varieties and criticism*. London: Routledge & Kegan Paul.

Messick, S. (1984). Assessment in context: Appraising student performance in relation to instructional quality. *Educational Researcher, 13*, 3–8.

Morgan, G. M. (1983). *Beyond method. Strategies for social research*. Beverly Hills, CA: Sage.

Ogilvy, J. (1986). The current shift of paradigms. *Journal of Consciousness and Change, 9*, 11–17.

Polkinghorne, D. (1983). *Methodology for the human sciences*. Albany: State University of New York Press.

Popkewitz, T. S. (1984). *Paradigm and ideology in educational research. The social functions of the intellectual*. New York: Falmer Press.

Prigogine, I., & Stengers, I. (1984). *Order out of chaos. Man's new dialogue with nature*. New York: Bantam Books.

Rogoff, B. (1984). Introduction: Thinking and learning in social context. In B. Rogoff & J. Lave (Eds.), *Everyday cognition: Its development in social context*. Cambridge, MA: Harvard University Press.

Rogoff, B., & Lave, J. (Eds.). (1984). *Everyday cognition: Its development in social context*. Cambridge, MA: Harvard University Press.

Sadawa, D., & Caley, M. T. (1985). Dissipative structures: New metaphors for becoming in education. *Educational Researcher, 14*, 13–25.

Scribner, S. (1984). Studying working intelligence. In B. Rogoff & J. Lave (Eds.), *Everyday cognition: Its development in social context*. Cambridge, MA: Harvard University Press.

Scribner, S., & Cole, M. (1981). *The psychology of literacy*. Cambridge, MA: Harvard University Press.

Torgesen, J. K. (1986). Learning disabilities theory: Its current state and future prospects. *Journal of Learning Disabilities, 19*, 399–407.

Valle, R. S. (1981). Relativistic quantum psychology. In R. S. Valle & R. von Eckartsberg (Eds.), *The metaphors of consciousness*. New York: Plenum Press.

Vygotsky, L. S. (1978). *Mind in society*. Cambridge, MA: Harvard University Press.

Wolf, F. A. (1981). *Taking the quantum leap*. New York: Harper & Row.

2 Reconciling Views On Intelligence?

Marc N. Richelle
University of Liège, Belgium.

A BRIEF RETROSPECTIVE LOOK

Although scientific psychologists have been studying intelligence for a century, they do not seem to have come closer to a widely acceptable, consistent general theory of intelligence. On the contrary, they offer an array of limited, although usually sophisticated subtheories, addressing specific issues with little concern for integration with other views. The present state of the field contrasts with the picture prevalent around mid-century. Ambitious theories were then dominating. Some of them focussing on factor analysis of mental tests, some on the IQ concept, some on the ontogenetic approach. The latter theories are most typically examplified by Piaget's contributions. The explosion of the field into a variety of fragmented, and often unrelated subfields provides evidence for the fact that those earlier monolithic theories could not withstand their critics.

This is the common fate of scientific theories. But it also reflects a general trend in contemporary psychology, where highly productive research is conducted in a climate of neglect of integrative views. Awareness of this state of affairs is reflected in the title of the present volume, that calls for reconceptualization thus implying that traditional concepts have, to some extent been shown to be inadequate. A symposium that took place at the 24th International Congress of Psychology in Sydney in 1988, was devoted to *Intelligence: Contrasting Views:* the title correctly described the current situation in the field. The contributions were only a sample of the variety of approaches that are developing today. *Contrast* here, means more than variety: to some extent the domains of research on intelligence are not only unrelated, but conflicting with each other.

I will not enumerate all the views about the elusive concept of intelligence that are flourishing currently. The following chapters provide some typical illustrations. More complete pictures can be found in sources like Sternberg (1982a, 1982b), and dissenting views are expressed in their diversity in open peer commentaries to Sternberg (1982a). I shall focus on a few typical examples to illustrate my point.

Theories of intelligence derived from mental measurement tests and IQ have been attacked from several sides. They have been blamed for being culture-bound; the cross-cultural approach is being offered as an alternative. They have been blamed for restricting intelligence to those skills related to school achievement; it has been suggested that so called social skills are not less important than cognitive ones and that an ecological approach might provide a solution for those who wish to escape the circularity of Binet's famous words "Intelligence is what is measured by my tests". (Olerón, 1982). In as far as IQ has been used in most studies of the hereditary components of intelligence, these theories have been attacked by those who believe in environmental, and especially educational factors in intellectual performances. This has given rise to the most passionate debate that has taken place in modern psychology in the last 25 years (for a serene review, see Scarr & Carter-Saltzman, 1982).

Developmental theories such as Piaget's have also been criticised from various, and indeed sometimes quite opposite, points of view. To some critics, interactive constructivism left too large a part to the environment and to the progressive and active acquisition of intellectual competence by the individual. The study of competences in infancy aimed to demonstrate innate, latent abilities, something along the lines of Chomsky's internal *Language Acquisition Device (LAD)* for the development of language skills. Development was no longer seen as a phase of construction, but as the mere actualization of built-in capacities. An extreme case of this "developmental" approach has been Mehler's concept of "learning by loss" (Mehler, 1974). To other critics, the main flaw in Piaget's theory was its neglect of learning processes. However, critics rarely supplemented the genuine ontogenetic approach by bringing learning mechanisms into the picture. The explanatory value of a developmental analysis has usually been lost in the debate.

In another vein, learning theories grown in the context of the behaviorist era and based to a large extent on animal studies have fallen into disrepute, and their relevance to our understanding of intelligent, higher order processes has been denied repeatedly. Cognitivist approaches have taken over the stage, with an emphasis on information processing as a level of functioning distinct from and presumably more important than learning, or as an alternative to learning as it was thought of previously. In educational circles, concern for creativity has contributed to the view that the relevance of learning theories is limited to automatized, stereotyped simple motor behaviors. A general concern for species specific levels of functioning and behavior in learning has led many psychologists, interested in intelligence, to ignore phylogenetic continuities that have nonetheless been widely documented by students of animal behavior, field ethologists and laboratory researchers.

The major influence on the conceptualization of intelligence in the last decades has undoubtedly been the development of artificial intelligence (AI). This fascinating new field of modern technology has given an unprecedented impetus to psychological research on intellectual processes. It has provided researchers, including psychologists with a variety of models, which—though not necessarily intended by their authors to be models of natural intelligence and its applications—are a rich source of inspiration. AI also raises a number of challenging questions as to the limits (or the absence of limits) to the possibility of building machines that would be endowed with all the capacities of the best human minds, including their power to solve complex problems and to create novelty. AI is a crucial resource for cognitive psychology. The fact that engineers engaged in building automata sometimes turn to the natural functioning of living organisms in their search for solutions to their own problems has given psychology a somewhat unexpected source of recognition and status in a multidisciplinary framework, together with new insights. However, stimulating as it may be, the interaction with various structures and constraints of AI might result in the channelling psychological research along the narrow path of those issues that are important to researchers and practitioners of AI.

SOURCES OF DISCONTENT IN CURRENT INTELLIGENCE RESEARCH

The current state of affairs might be summarised as follows:

1. The psychology of intelligence is in very good shape if judged by the number and variety of subfields of basic as well as applied research.
2. In the present ninth decade of the 20th century, psychologists working in the area of intelligence have turned away from great synthetic theories that were dominant by mid-century.
3. The proliferation of unrelated research is leading to the proliferation of local theories.

The question I would like to address here is: Should we be satisfied with this state of affairs? And if the answer is "No" (the obvious answer suggested by the very fact that the question is being asked), what corrections should be brought in so that improvement results that would be profitable both for the progress of our understanding of intelligence and for developments in applied fields, most importantly in education?

Why not be satisfied with the present state of affairs? Fragmentation of a field of knowledge, although an inevitable situation at some stages in the history of any science, counteracts the development of global views and unified theories that seem to be the quest of all sciences. What is at stake here is not the aesthetic-rational argument that unified theories are more elegant, and therefore more satisfactory than dispersed knowledge (though this argument has been used by many prominent scholars throughout history). The main point is that compartmentalization and fragmentation are usually the consequence of the extreme complexity of the subject matter that is being studied. On the other hand, they also reveal the scientists' incapacity to account for complexity.

Another reason for the discontent with the current situation has to do with the way psychologists feel, and indeed behave, about the history of their own science. History has shown that all sciences undergo permanent evolution, the rate of which can vary from apparent stagnation for a given period to drastic changes comparable to revolutions. Kuhn's classical analysis has thrown light on the way such changes of paradigm occur and are prepared, and on the reasons why paradigmatic science at a given time resists changes. However, it is rarely the case in natural sciences such as physics, chemistry or biology that even those scientists taking part in some important "revolutionary" change think of their own work as being totally correct and of what has been done before as being all wrong. Even the most radical changes in paradigm seem to preserve a sense of continuity in the scientific endeavour. Curiously enough, psychologists are prone to deny the value of what was done before. Kuhn's concept of paradigm, often taken in oversimplified manner, has been peculiarly popular among them. Watson may have been an example of this already. He found it necessary to use the style of a manifesto to advocate behaviorism. Unfortunately, more recent schools of thought have hurried much further along the same path, claiming the death of previous schools or blaming great psychologists of previous generations for what they have failed to do or to say. Are we really prepared to ignore what those before us have contributed towards the accumulated knowledge that forms the basis of our current knowledge?

Again, it is not the ethical aspect of that historical neglect that is important, it is its consequences for the progress of psychology. The deliberate or naive ignorance of former theories, schools of thought or scientists (*ad hominem* attitudes are not rare in this context) leads to rediscovering things that we should know have been with us for a long time, even though possibly under different names.

Another reason for not being content with the current compartmentalization and fragmentation relates to the consequences such an attitude would have on the application of knowledge gained from research on intelligence. Education would, of course, be most affected and modern societies will suffer if the insights gained over the past decades are not made available to educators.

The training of people in education has for many years included basic knowledge gained from the psychological sciences, but more often than not this knowledge has been conveyed together with and obscured by the turmoil of theoretical and ideological debates that are the rule in psychology.

TOWARDS INTEGRATION AND COMPLEMENTARITY

I shall not engage here in elaborating a new general theory of intelligence, nor shall I attempt to bring together in a syncretic manner all the various views and specific approaches to intelligence. I shall only make a plea in favour of the integration of concepts proposed by theorists of the past (often the recent past) in the current thinking about intelligence. To that end, I shall use examples from fields I happen to be most familiar with. Other illustrations could be proposed in different, even more relevant domains. I believe that this effort towards integration is the essential task for psychology today. We have had our share of great monolithic theories for the first three quarters of this century, and we are left with the admittedly difficult task of looking for convergences where they have gone unnoticed, for complementarities beyond contradictions, and for novel concepts emerging from cross-fertilization.

Development as explanation.   The developmental approach and its place in cognitive research is an appropriate starting point for an European author, because a large number of major European contributions to psychological theory have been essentially developmental. From Freud to Piaget, from the Buehlers to Wallon, from Vygotsky to Lorenz, European psychology has had a typical developmental or ontogenetic (a term preferred from the old ambiguous work genetic) outlook. Four of the names just mentioned have exerted a direct and strong influence on the field of intelligence. The other two have certainly contributed indirectly to shape current views on intellectual functioning, be it from the very different perspectives of psychoanalysis or of ethology. The common denominator of these theories—whatever their important differences in other respects—is that the ontogenetic dimension is given not a simple descriptive status but an explanatory value. In the field of intelligence, this has been most impressively exemplified by Piaget's work and in his constructivist view. But it is no less central in Vygotsky's insightful account of mental growth as an interactive process in which social factors play a determinant role, or in the theory elaborated by the French psychologist H. Wallon (whose work, curiously enough, is known very little outside French speaking countries) in which the influence of biological and sociocultural factors are given balanced weightings.

There are, fortunately, still developmental psychologists studying intelligence, and as is reflected in a number of chapters of this book, there are also cognitive psychologists who study the development of intellectual functioning. However for a very large part, cognitive psychology has ignored the ontogenetic dimension. When cognitive psychologists deal with the early stages of development, they do not aim to explain a psychological function by its development, rather, they focus on its precocious effectiveness. Cognitive psychology in general can be said to be ahistoric, i.e., it does not assume that present functioning of cognitive systems is to be understood by the systems' past history, be it phylogenetic, ontogenetic or cultural. The efforts of cognitive psychology are turned mainly towards accounting for universal rules in information processing devices.

Robert Sternberg's influential contribution to the field of intelligence has been noted already. It must be stressed, however, that development has no place, and *a fortiori* not explanatory status, in the theoretical model eschewed under the label "triarchic theory of human intelligence" (see his chapter in this book). The *Handbook of Human Intelligence* published under his editorship (1982) devotes only one chapter, and typically the last of 14 (before the concluding "metatheoretical" chapter) to the development of intelligence. Basic explanatory concepts are, as a rule, not relegated to final parts of a carefully built editorial architecture. Reading this last chapter, coauthored by Sternberg and Powell, confirms this interpretation. *Age* is given some attention, not *development;* only to observe that "all existing theories of intelligence are age restricted to some extent" and to conclude:

> None of the experimentally based theories of intelligence has yet been widely tested on children's performance, and hence their validity for children is still, to some extent unknown (Sternberg & Powell, 1982, p. 995).

It is assumed that a theory based on empirical studies of adults could eventually be validated on children of any age. This is, of course, quite different from *looking at development in order to* understand intelligence in its final stage. Piaget is acknowledged in the same short section for having attempted "to account in some detail for intelligent behavior from infancy to adulthood" (p. 995; cited in Sternberg & Powell, 1982). This is misphrasing his endeavor, which had been to account for adult intelligence by following its development from infancy. It was not Piaget's intention to simply describe intelligence as a function of age.

The developmental dimension seems no less essential to contemporary neurobiological thinking than it has been to the great psychologists of the past. Discontent with the current information processing approach has been expressed recently by Edelman (1987) who emphasizes the dynamic aspects of neuronal group selection through somatic time in his account of neural organization underlying perceptual processes and learning.

Learning and development.   Another alley of integration is between the psychology of learning and the developmental approach. For those who are, as I am, equally interested in intelligence and in learning processes, it has been for long a source of astonishment that these major fields of twentieth century psychology have been growing along parallel tracks with very little, if any, interactions. The reciprocal ignorance that Piaget and Skinner kept each other throughout their careers is typical in this respect. The former argued obstinately against the behaviorist learning theories by referring to Hull's work, with almost no mention of Skinner's personal views. The latter could hardly see anything more than a description of behavior as a function of another independent variable in Piaget's developmental analysis, with no special status in explanation, apart from age.

Followers of Skinner who worked with young children have usually missed the developmental dimension as such, and limited their inquiry to demonstrating the effectiveness of reinforcement or stimulus control from earliest age. Such a position is indeed quite similar to that taken by cognitivists. Experimental psychologists have been very little concerned with the study of long behavioral histories (although modern laboratory technologies would make longitudinal studies much easier than before, we must go back to pioneers in research on experimental neurosis, like Liddell or Gantt, to find experimental subjects followed-up for periods of ten years or more). There have also been surprisingly few studies on young developing or on aging animal subjects in the learning laboratories.

A closer look at real life, however, indicates the obvious complementarity of learning and development. Research based on the recognition of that complementarity has been carried out over the past 15 or 20 years most successfully, showing not only that the methodological tools from both fields could crossfertilize, but that theoretical concepts could be fruitfully integrated. If the tendency of great theorists to develop their views as a closed system is overlooked, unexpected convergences might be unveiled on essential points, as I have shown to be the case for Piaget and Skinner (Richelle, 1976).

Current interest in the concept of *zone of proximal development,* a concept borrowed from Vygotsky, or in the concept of *dynamic assessment* clearly brings development and learning in close relation. Anyone who has undertaken to shape some new behavior in an animal or to teach a human being something new has come across the problem of the distance between the current state of the repertoire and the new state to be attained, with the resulting difficulty of identifying the ideal number of steps to be taken to cover the distance. Similarly, anyone who has been teaching a developing organism has come across the developmental constraints that dictate the direction and length of possible steps towards a given acquisition.

This integration is of course all the more necessary in the applied field of education, where it has often been left to the imagination of teachers to solve the contradictions between various psychological theories on important issues that common sense would recommend to look at in a global way.

The primacy of action.   The cognitivist approach appears to many as a major breakthrough in contemporary psychology, and a number of psychologists have felt so enthusiastic about it that they have proclaimed the end of the obscurantist era that preceded, referring particularly to behaviorism. They have identified their own position as nothing less than a new paradigm, as described earlier. I have been critical of cognitivism on several grounds with respect to its approach to development and to learning processes. I would like to intensify this criticism further, as far as intelligence is concerned. However, a word of caution might be advisable to introduce the following remarks.

Cognitivism is obviously not a unified doctrine. It has many different versions, with various implication; sometimes simply of a methodological nature, sometimes epistemological, sometimes ethical, and sometimes merely practical (see Richelle, 1987). This makes it likely that there will be someone somewhere who refers to him/herself as a cognitivist, whose work is an exception to the aspect under criticism. Thus, exceptions to the following statement can, most probably—and most fortunately—be found.

Besides its neglect of the, already mentioned, developmental explanation, cognitivism, by making information processing its central subject matter, has turned away from the primacy of action that had been recognized, and indeed given a central role, by influential students of intelligence—Piaget holding, in this respect also, a prominent place. Although perception had been by mid-century, quite generally viewed more and more as subordinated to action by several theories (some strictly psychological and some psychophysiological), it has regained so to speak an independent and dominant status. The reasons for this might have to do with the fascination of the computer metaphor, the computer—at least as psychologists experience it—performing highly complex functions, but with little direct action on the world around it. Whatever the reason, the present dismissal of action as the basis for knowledge can be taken as a theoretical regression, that will hopefully be corrected as soon as researchers rediscover its real place (in a similar way as psycholinguists have rediscovered the pragmatic aspects of verbal behavior after having claimed for a few years that language is all in the competence of the speaking subject). In the meantime, there could be a danger that those in charge of schooling and education more generally, under the influence of the popular cognitivist fashion, might be tempted to stop looking at observable manifestations of the intellectual activities of their pupils and to satisfy themselves with putting again "inside their students' heads" all that is deemed to be important, as well as the full responsibility for their own imperfections and learning difficulties.

Looking for unifying concepts.   When, contrary to expectation, various approaches to the same subject appear to diverge rather than converge, a good strategy towards theoretical breakthrough is to look for some unifying concept(s) in existing theories that might have been overlooked, or encapsulated at a covert level. I would like to argue that, in the field of intelligence, a good candidate is the concept of *variability*.

Rather than opposing laws of learning (as they have been drawn from the animal laboratories) to higher problem solving processes (as studied on verbal and symbolic materials in humans) and rather than opposing more or less automatized algorithmic strategies for problem solving and genuine production of creative solutions or products, we should look at all adaptive behavior emerging throughout the history of individuals resulting from dynamic variability. During an individual's lifetime *dynamic variability* plays a role similar to that of biological variability, be it by mutations or recombinations, at the scale of the evolution of a species. The concept of dynamic variability suggests the link between elementary learning from the simplest conditioning of a motor response to higher creative acts. It might also provide the unifying principle between psychological analysis, neurobiological descriptions and explanations, and abstract models taken from computer science.

The concept of dynamic variability implies, of course, a typically historical and developmental view of intelligence. This means that no behavior can be labelled as being more or less intelligent without reference to its place on a time sequence, and that the status of any intelligent behavior can be expected to change, as we all know, from one of genuine novelty (when it occurs for the first time, maybe in the history of the species) to one of routine action when a given set of conditions requires it, to one of fully automatized chain of movements or operations.

Traditionally, psychologists have been looking at variability as an undesirable property of their scientific data, resulting from the imperfections of their methods and from the peculiar characteristics of their subject matter. The aim is to neutralize variability where it cannot be avoided. This view reflects the psychologists' obsession of giving their field as much scientific dignity as possible. Physics (classical physics) was the model to imitate, both in its elegant measurements and formulae, and in its clarifying analysis of causal relationships. This results in a world view, in which nothing is left to chance and where reversibility is the rule, including phenomena such as movements and changes that only to our human eyes appear to be time-oriented. Within such a framework, variability appeared as noise, which every good experimenter should work to "get rid of".

The epistemological reference to the hard science par excellence converged with the legitimate methodological preoccupation for clean experiments. Variability, obviously, often reflects poor experimental control, and psychologists of the past and of the present are certainly not to be blamed for their efforts towards more rigorous experimental designs and treatments. But these efforts generally imply that variations are noisy interferences masking lawful relationships. If general laws are to be drawn from experiments, variation is to be eliminated or neutralized. This has been one of the major reasons for studying groups, rather than individuals, and for adopting statistical definitions of the events measured (as in sensory thresholds or reaction time experiments).

The concern for constancy and invariance has indeed been pervasive in most areas of psychology. Much energy has been spent to demonstrate the reliability of mental tests, i.e., the stability over time of the measurement provided by the instruments being implicitly transferred to whatever is being measured, be it intelligence or one of its components. In another area, many efforts have been devoted to identify stable personality characteristics, as in the various "brands" of typologies.

By taking this stand, psychologists have simply shared with many scientists and philosophers a particular view of the place of *chance* in the universe. Chance is only "the measure of our ignorance", to cite Poincaré. However, in another view, which goes back to Aristotle, chance is given its place, *in its own right,* in explaining reality. Probabilistic accounts or randomness proper are not necessarily the disguise of our ignorances. They eventually reflect the nature of things proper.

The conflict between these two opposite views has dominated, as is well known, the history of modern physics. Prigogine and Stengers (1988) have shown how Boltzmann, confronted with the problem of irreversibility in thermodynamic systems,

> forced to choose between opening physics to temporality and remaining faithful to the principles of dynamics, the constraints of which he was experiencing, made the choice of fidelity. For the dynamic [i.e., integrating the concept of irreversibility] interpretation of the second principle [of thermodynamics] he substituted a *probabilistic interpretation.* (p. 28).

"Probabilistic interpretation" is to be understood as an interpretation that accounts for the irreversibility observed in terms of the crude, "macroscopic" character of certain observations. If the observer were equipped with better tools, he would be in a position to follow each individual molecule, rather than populations, and would describe a reversible system, in conformity with traditional principles. Boltzmann was forced to this interpretation against his own intuitions.

No wonder that psychologists, fascinated as they were by the model of traditional physics, have been slow in facing the problem of variability. And yet, they have been repeatedly confronted with phenomena that could not be accounted for in the traditional manner.

Cases in point are changes of behavior as the result of learning, problem solving, and creativity. Variability has also been recognized in the field of developmental psychology, where the idea of a mere unfolding of prebuilt potentialities has been abandoned long ago; and in the field of ethology, where instinctive behavior has been shown to exhibit a much wider range of adaptability than had been recognized before. The study of exploratory behavior and of play in (satiated) animals and humans raised similar questions in another context.

The reluctance of psychologists to concern themselves with dynamic variability is all the more surprising because the key explanatory concepts had been offered, for some time, by biology within the framework of evolutionary theory. A number of psychologists have, of course, been aware of the possibility of approaching their own problems using those conceptual tools. Needless to say, researchers such as Thurstone and Tolman, influential scientists who contributed to the shaping of modern psychology in the recent past did appeal to the evolutionary analogy and the variability concept in their theories, whatever their divergences in other respects.

Skinner has explicitly and repeatedly exposed his view of the learning process as involving essentially the same sorts of mechanisms as biological evolution, namely a combination of variation and selective pressure. (Skinner, 1966, 1985) This should have suggested (at least from the mid 1950s on) to experimenters in that particular field, the importance of paying systematic attention to the nature and the sources of variations. Curiously enough, with very few exceptions that went largely unnoticed, practically none of Skinner's followers engaged in that sort of inquiry until the publication of Staddon and Simmelhag's (1971) seminal paper. Even then, much more attention continued to be devoted to the selective action of the environment (under the familiar concept of *contingencies of reinforcement*) than to the *sources of variation*.

The state of affairs has consolidated the idea, that has eventually been adopted by many psychologists in other fields as well as by laymen, that conditioning is a process of stereotyped repetition of simple motor behaviors that has little to do with more complex adaptive behavior, and certainly no link whatsoever to problem solving or creativity. This has resulted in a most curious disassociation between the current picture of a basic behavioral mechanism (and indeed the bunch of empirical data accumulated in the laboratory) and the main theoretical tenets, which in Skinner's mind, offered the unified treatment of individually adapted behaviors from the apparently simple forms observed in animals up to the most elaborate actions of creative humans.

Lorenz played a central role in putting the study of animal behavior into an evolutionary perspective, and he has given, in his later works, extensive attention to the concept of variation in relation to mechanisms of individual learning. The notion of *open versus closed programmes for learning* contrast species exhibiting high behavioral variability, and consequently high capacity for learning, as a consequence of having evolved in a changing environment and species that, because they have evolved in a homogeneous environment, are equipped with very limited although very efficient behavior patterns with little place for flexible adjustment to unusual conditions.

Piaget has, throughout his monumental work, continuously resorted to evolutionary thinking. His search for continuity from elementary forms of biological processes and the most complex achievements of the human mind in logic and science is likely to make him the most biologically orientated psychologist in our century. I have argued elsewhere that, in spite of important differences, Piaget and Skinner share basic views with respect to the evolutionary analogy and with respect to the role of variations in the dynamics of behavior (Richelle, 1976).

To these three major contributions, one could add a number of possibly less ambitious or less prestigious, although no less significant works, which I shall not undertake to enumerate here. Suffice it to point out to those who study intelligence, the evolution observed in the field of differential psychology. Differential psychology deals with *interindividual variations*. Interindividual variations are of no less interest in biological thinking than *intraindividual variations*. Variability within a population, that is between individuals, is an essential factor in the dynamics of evolution.

In psychology, interindividual variations have been looked at in exactly the same way as intraindividual variations. They have been treated as unfortunate and uninteresting deviations from the norm or central tendency of a population, i.e., as divergences that go counter to the strict lawfulness of nature. Differential psychologists have been keeping themselves busy with identifying the factors accounting for these deviations mainly because for practical purposes they cannot be ignored. If people are different, you have to take these differences into account when individuals enter school or apply for a job. However, individual differences essentially remain minor violations to basic similarity. Thus differential psychology has been regarded as a minor field, imposed, so to speak, by daily life's practical constraints and with little bearing on a general and deep understanding of behavior and mind. Significantly enough, differential psychology had no place of its own in the well known *Handbook of Experimental Psychology* (Fraisse & Piaget, 1963) which has been regarded as the major reference work by French speaking psychologists for the last 25 years. A full section was devoted to it, however in the comparable reference book in applied psychology (Pieron, 1949).

No doubt this peculiar status of differential psychology resulted to some extent from the popular ideology of the equality of men. Many psychologists failed to make the important distinction between the ethical concept of *equality* and the empirical fact of *diversity*. Psychological differences were regarded as blemishes, with the consequence that the productive and constructive aspects of variation were lost in the process.

However, a change of perspective has emerged in the last few years. Some differential psychologists have adopted a radically different view of their own field. Interindividual variations are being analyzed as reflections of the richness of adaptive potential at the level of a population. This approach has been applied to cognitive development and problem solving. Various strategies observed in different individuals confronted with a problem situation are seen as offering a range of alternatives, each having its heuristic value, especially in the context of *change*. The obsession with rank ordering various strategies hierarchically has been abandoned. (For an example of this new approach to differential psychology, see Lautrey, 1988).

CONCLUSION

We witness converging from very different alleys ideas and facts that confirm the hypothesis that behaving organisms are to some extent *generators of variability*. The selection on variations is the general unifying mechanism at work in the production of novelty in the living world, be it at the level of phylogeny, at the level of individual learning (not to be conceived of outside the species anyhow) or, as has been suggested by several schools of thought in cultural anthropology, at the level of cultural history.

The concept of variability, if it is to be applied to intelligent behavior, clearly requires a diachronic perspective, be it at the level of ontogency (as discussed earlier) or, more generally, of knowledge gaining in an individual's history. It provides for dynamic links between automatized action and original problem solving and creative work; with continuity of time making for the progressive transformation of the latter into the former. The diachronic dimension has been overlooked by some of the most influential trends of thought in present cognitive psychology. For example, in Johnson-Laird's account of mental models, or Fodor's modularity theory it had typically been overlooked, as it also has been by structuralist views that were popular in the 1960's.

Though lack of space does not allow an elaboration of this point here, a brief allusion should be made to congenial views such as "variability looked at in its own right" in other fields of science that are no less important than psychology to our understanding of human intelligence, i.e., epistemology and the history of science, neurobiology and AI.

An evolutionary approach to the problem of science development had already been adopted years ago by Popper's (1972) *Objective Knowledge: An Evolutionary Approach.*

Especially relevant to our argument is Popper's characterization of the growth of knowledge as a special case of learning:

> The growth of knowledge—or *the learning process* [italics by the author]—is not a repetitive or a cumulative process but one of error elimination. It is Darwinian selection, rather than Lamarckian instruction. (Popper, 1972, p. 144).

> All this may be expressed by saying that the growth of our knowledge is the result of a process closely resembling what Darwin called *natural selection;* that is *the natural selection of hypotheses:* our knowledge consists, at every moment of those hypotheses which have shown their (comparative) fitness by surviving so far in their struggle for existence; a comparative struggle which eliminates those hypotheses which are unfit. (Popper, 1972, p. 261).

Popper continues by framing this view of the evolution of scientific knowledge in the general view of the development of knowledge or learning in living systems:

This interpretation may be applied to animal knowledge, pre-scientific knowledge, and to scientific knowledge. [He further emphasises the status of the analogy:] This statement of the situation is meant to describe how knowledge really grows. It is not meant metaphorically, though of course it makes use of metaphors. . . From the amoeba to Einstein, the growth of knowledge is always the same. . .' (Popper, 1971, p. 261).

In neurobiology, a field quite close to psychology, major recent theoretical advances have centered on similar concepts. After Changeux's theory of '*selective stabilisation*', that unfortunately missed a real encounter with current relevant research in psychology, the recent book by Edelman (1987) *Neural Darwinism: The theory of neuronal group selection,* will certainly appear as a decisive breakthrough, as well as a unique source of inspiration for psychologists involved in research on variability.

Finally, in the field of A.I., the main challenge for the near future is to build, if this eventually becomes possible at all, machines endowed with a capacity for learning from their previous "experience" not only in terms of increased memory storage, but with the improved adaptation to unexpected problems; in other words, creative machines. There are some indications that adequate models for the production of such "automata" (maybe this is an inappropriate label for a novelty producing device) will imply some variability generating systems. They might well be designed on the basis of the evolutionary analogy that will have succeeded in accounting for changes and the emergence of new forms at all levels of the living world.

REFERENCES

Edelman, G. M. (1987). *Neural Darwinism*. New York: Basic Books.

Fraisse, P., & Piaget, J. (Eds.). (1963). *Traité de psychologie expérimentale* [Treatise on experimental psychology.] Paris: Presses Universitaires de France.

Lautrey, J. (1988). *Inter and intra-individual variability: What can it teach us about cognitive development?* Paper presented at the Symposium on Behavioral Variability in Learning and Cognitive processes, 24th International Congress on Psychology. Sydney. (Unpublished).

Mehler, J. (1974). Connaître par désapprentissage. In E. Morin & M. Piatelli-Palmarin, (Eds.), *Unité de l'homme*. Paris: Le Seuil.

Oléron, P. (1982). *Savoirs et savoirs-faire psychologiques chez l'enfant*. Bruxelles: Mardaga.

Pieron, H. (1949). *Traité de psychologie appliquée*. Livre I: La Psychologie Différentielle. Paris: Presses Universitaires de France.

Popper, K. R. (1972). *Objective knowledge: An evolutionary approach*. Oxford: Oxford University Press.

Prigogine, I., & Stengers, I. (1988). *Entre le temps et l'éternité*. Paris: Gallimard.

Richelle, M. N. (1976). Constructivisme et behaviourisme, *Revue Européenne de Sciences Sociales et Cahiers Vilfredo Pareto,* Numéro Spécial, Hommage à J. Piaget, *14,* 291–303.

Richelle, M. N. (1987). Les cognitivismes: progrés, régression ou suicide de la psychologie? In M. Siguan (Ed.), *Comportement, cognition, conscience: la psychologie à la recherche de son objet*. Paris: Universitaires de France.

Scarr, S. & Carter-Saltzman, L. (1982). Genetics and intelligence. In R. J. Sternberg (Ed.) *Handbook of human intelligence*. Cambridge: Cambridge University Press.

Skinner, B. F. (1966). The phylogeny and ontogeny of behaviour. *Science, 153,* 1205–1215.

Skinner, B. F. (1970). Creating the creative artist. In R. Soloman *On the future of art.* New York: Guggengheim Museum.

Skinner, B. F. (1981). Selection by consequences. *Science, 213,* 501–504.

Skinner, B. F. (1985). The evolution of behavior. In C. F. Lowe, M. Richelle, D. E. Blackman & C. M. Bradshaw (Eds.), *Behavioural analysis and contemporary psychology.* London: Lawrence Erlbaum Associates.

Staddon, J. E., & Simmelhag, V. L. (1971). The "superstition" experiment: A re-examination of its implications for the principles of adaptive behaviour. *Psychological Review, 78,* 3–43.

Sternberg, R. J. (1982a). Toward a triarchic theory of human intelligence. *The Behavioural and Brain Sciences, 7,* 269–315.

Sternberg, R. J. (Ed.) (1982b). *Handbook of human intelligence.* Cambridge: Cambridge University Press.

Sternberg, R. J., & Powell, J. S. (1982). Theories of intelligence. In R. J. Sternberg (Ed.), *Handbook of human intelligence.* Cambridge: Cambridge University Press.

3 Is the High IQ Person Really in Trouble? Why?

Kjell Raaheim
University of Bergen, Norway

Again voices are heard among front-line psychologists, expressing the view that present day society asks of its citizens, for their successful problem solving in actual life, abilities or skills, above or beyond what is assessed by traditional IQ-tests. Sternberg (1988) for one, illustrated how the top performer on IQ-tests, with school marks to match her test performance, sooner or later reaches a point, along the line of university training, where she cannot cope any longer anywhere nearly as effectively as before with the challenges of scientific enterprise.

We are also being told that it is now high time to leave the notion of general intelligence behind, and to concentrate on those more specific factors that are found to correlate with various other measures of intellectual performance. One cannot escape the feeling of being a witness to a "crusade," to knock off the IQ-pedestal the very person being put there by no one but the psychologists themselves.

Clearly it is of importance to demonstrate, as do Kluwe and his colleagues (this volume), that persons with high IQ-scores will not necessarily perform better, where problem solving in complex environments and tasks of everyday life are concerned. What we ought not to do, however, is to suddenly stop wondering why a faithful servant does not deliver, on occasions where one, initially at least, had reason to expect him or her to be successful.

In the present author's opinion, it seems more than a little strange that the high-IQ person, who has been with you all the way in solving the fanciful tasks of the various intelligence tests, should inevitably be left behind when some less structured or "creativity"—demanding tasks pop up.

In actual fact, being "left behind" is not the correct description of the phenomenon in question. So far, we have rarely, if ever, observed negative correlations between IQ and problem solving success. What has been found in a number of cases is simply that the person with a higher IQ is no better off than those with lower IQs.

This, of course, adds nothing to what was observed already in the laboratory studies of the pioneers in the field of experimental studies in cognition. With the so called Hatrack Problem, which asks for a way of turning two poles and a C-clamp into a sturdy construction for hanging up a heavy coat, Burke and Maier (1965) undertook an extensive study with hundreds of students and using 18 different tests and instruments of assessments to find out what could possibly explain the success of some people and the limited success of others in this situation. Burke and Maier did not find the answer despite extensive testing of the subjects. The IQ scores of the solvers and the non-solvers were not found to differ significantly.

With many of the so called "mental puzzles" similar findings are obtained. (See Sternberg & Davidson, 1982, for a discussion of this.) Also with longer series of situations of the same type, where a pitfall occurs sooner or later (e.g., the water-jar problems of Luchins, 1942) it has been observed that people with high IQ scores are no better off than subjects who are found to be less intelligent as measured by traditional psychometric tests.

Why is the ability to discover that a trap has been laid, or that a change of system of solution procedure is needed, not part of being intelligent? The answer is: this is, in fact, something that is achieved by intelligence. But because a more general and frequent exposure to puzzles and parlor games is experienced by a limited number of people, only some subjects have a sufficient background for intelligence to come into play in a useful way. Undoubtedly, a person who has been through the whole literature of puzzles and parlor games would profit immensely from that experience when challenged by yet another intriguing task of a similar kind. If this were not so, a negative correlation would, in fact, be found between mental abilities and problem-solving performance.

It is possible that the intelligent person will only prove his/her intelligence on the *recurrence* of a more or less familiar type of challenge. The present author has repeatedly argued (see, e.g., Raaheim, 1988a) that human intelligence is likely to be at its best when the task confronting the individual is a novel one, but, at the same time, one that is not totally outside the person's past experience. Figure 3.1 is an attempt to illustrate the author's view, and is intended to show how the importance of the intelligent use of past experience may vary with the degree of novelty of the present situation.

Figure 3.1 indicates that as soon as a situation that a person is confronted with *deviates* in some respects from what has been seen in the past, intelligence is called on. The *lower threshold* of the problem area has now been passed.

With increasing novelty of the situation, heavier demands are made on intelligence. However, when a certain (large) degree of novelty has been reached, the

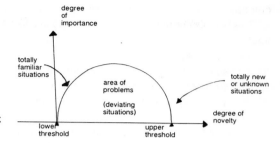

FIG. 3.1.   Intelligence and task novelty.

importance of intelligently using one's past experience starts *decreasing* as far as adaptive problem solving behavior is concerned. Instead one is faced with an increasing challenge of discovering important details of the present situation, which may be crucial for a successful handling of the task.

The *upper threshold* is passed when a familiar pattern is no longer recognizable. The tasks encountered here are, *initially,* outside the individual's range of comprehension (Sternberg, 1984). However, it is not necessary to assume that the situations above the upper threshold *remain* outside this range for any considerable time. After a short period of exploration the individual may well be able to treat the situation in an intelligent way once again.

It does not follow from the aforementioned argument (that there *is* an upper threshold above which intelligence is of little help) that the individual will always recognize this state of affairs and hence stop his or her attempts at exploiting past experience, now to explore the present more fully. Nor does one need to take it for granted that a person will more or less automatically come to discover that a particular way of classifying a problem, which within our framework is a situation found *between the thresholds,* is not particularly well suited to fill the need for an appropriate solution to the problem. For one thing a person may sometimes, out of a sheer lack of awareness, try to treat the present challenge as a familiar sort of problem, totally ignoring the radically new conditions that may be of vital importance. But there is, also, the possibility that something (or someone) is *preventing* the intelligent person from delivering the goods asked for, here and now.

INTELLIGENCE AND EXPECTATIONS

Sternberg tells the story about two boys who are threatened by a grizzly bear, rapidly closing in on them in the forest. The very intelligent boy seems to be the loser in this case. He has quickly calculated the number of seconds the bear needs to overtake him, and hence feels very frightened by the thought of the final outcome. The less intelligent, but more creative boy looks more composed, smilingly explaining to his friend: "All I have to worry about, is to run faster than you!"

It is highly inappropriate, of course, to dismantle a good joke such as this one. At the same time it is all the more tempting, in particular because it provides, or at least so it seems, an excellent example of what we tend to overlook at times when we feel disappointed in the problem-solving efforts of the intelligent person.

At the outset the story is, of course, less funny if the very intelligent boy is not seen as rather clumsy at the same time, but conceived instead (in line with the normal findings of the test psychologist) as a well fit and coordinated person, fully capable of running as fast as the next man.

And what then, if the intelligent boy is not only able to figure out precisely how quickly the bear will be at his own side, but to find out, also how much *sooner* his friend will be captured? As a former Boy Scout he himself might be able to "pull a few tricks," to make things a bit more difficult for the grizzly bear. But then, as a former Sunday School student, at an even earlier age, does he feel free to even *think* of deserting his friend?

One may well ask questions like these. The human being—as far as the present author can judge—has not only the ability to see the past reflected in the present (which is what we consider to be the trademark of intelligence), but has also a sensitivity to other people's needs, or wishes, so as to automatically adjust his or her problem solving behavior according to these needs, and, generally, to what seems to be expected in the situation.

Thus, before we accuse high-IQ persons of not being able to free themselves from the old routine of copying the solution patterns of yesterday, we ought, perhaps, to make it a bit clearer that now we want them to use their wits in a different way.

There may be a number of reasons why the intelligent person has to be told, in so many words, that under the present circumstances he or she must feel free to come up with creative suggestions. For one thing, in school one has been trained in intelligent problem solving, and not in "creative thinking." Even at tertiary level a student is seldom encouraged to engage in enterprises the outcome of which are highly uncertain, or to take on questions, the answers to which are not known by one's teachers beforehand. And, secondly, on a more fundamental level, human intelligence as a means of survival in challenging situations is built on the ability to discern the familiar features. In many instances of daily life, we come to discover that the real novelty of a situation is much less than it might have appeared initially, or that some change that has occurred is less pronounced or of a more superficial nature than initially thought. Also, throughout our lives we are regularly rewarded for making use of the knowledge we have been presented with.

In a given instance, then, we must perhaps—when we take on the role of a teacher or a psychologist—emphasize rather strongly that now there is another claim on the individual than the usual "Remember what you have been told." But then, also, if we want students e.g., at a university to be more creative on a general basis, or at some particular stage during their studies, we ought to consider giving much more encouragement towards creative production in primary and secondary schools.

SOME EXPERIMENTAL RESULTS

Without further speculation about possible grounds for a particular line of reasoning by named or unnamed subjects of psychological investigations, the author wishes to draw the reader's attention to some recent findings from a series of experiments set up to clarify further to what extent the familiarity of a task will account for the degree of correspondence between "intelligence" and problem solving success.

The immediate point of departure for the experiments was a study by Sternberg and Davidson (1982), where a closer look was taken at the so called "mental puzzles," and where the "mysterious" lack of correspondence between IQ and success on many such tasks was also discussed.

The main body of the present author's research findings has been reported elsewhere (Raaheim, 1988a). Generally, in line with the author's model of the relationship between intelligence and task novelty, it was found that when a series of five equivalent puzzles was presented to subjects (such as university students), a correspondence between intellectual ability (as indicated by IQ-scores) and problem solving ability was *built up* during the first few tasks of the same type.

Figure 3.2 shows the typical results obtained with a series of five problem tasks requiring the same general principle of solution. Curves with almost identical shapes have in fact been found in a number of different experiments.

It should be emphasized that the different series of problems are made up of tasks that are, initially, unfamiliar to the subjects. In some cases a number of more or less artificial tasks had been constructed for the purpose of the experiment. At other times, a puzzle found in the literature among those famous for causing headache in most people, was taken as the model for making up a set of five equivalent problems.

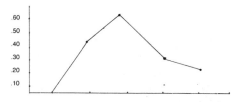

FIG. 3.2. Correlation between IQ and success in solving the separate problems.

The highly interesting thing is, of course, that we do find, in either case, that the more intelligent subjects, although being no better off than the less gifted ones when confronted with Task 1, will prove more successful with Task 2 and/or Task 3 of the same general type.

IS INTELLIGENCE OF NO FURTHER USE?

By now, in the author's opinion, a reasonable amount of evidence has been produced to establish the fact that only when a task has a basis in previously experienced circumstances, will human intelligence come to bear on its solution in a straightforward way. What is, however, far from clear, is the reason why the curve of correlations between intelligence and task solution shows *decreasing* levels after the first two or three problems of a series such as the one described earlier. Surely the initial increase must mean that at least some of the "brighter" subjects have discovered the *principle* on which the series of problems is based? And is it not strange, then, that problems later in the series are solved almost equally well by students with high and not so high IQs?

An alteration of the sequence of problems—such as has been attempted with the tasks of a series leading initially to results like those presented in Figure 3.2—does not result in a different shape of the curve of correlations (Raaheim, 1989). There is, thus, no reason to believe that some of the problems are of a different nature or much more difficult to solve than the rest.

A possible interpretation of the results in terms of a problem turning into an all too easy task when preceded by a number of equivalent challenges, proves to be incorrect on a closer inspection of the data. The percentage of solution does not increase towards the end of the problem series. (See Raaheim, 1988a, for details of solution percentages.)

What we do know is that some 40% of the subjects come up with the correct answer to a problem within three minutes, and that with the problems towards the end of the five-task series, subjects on various IQ-levels perform about equally well, as indeed they seemed to do with the very first task of the series. What will happen, then, if a series of tasks is presented, and the built-in principle for solution is that of a puzzle previously found to be a good predictor of intelligence?

Figure 3.3 gives the results with a series of five problems based on the principle at work in the so called "water lilies problem," found by Sternberg and Davidson (1982) to be the best predictor of intelligence among a number of puzzles studied.

In the original version of this task, one is told that water lilies on a particular lake double in area every 24 hours. The subject is further informed about the number of days it takes to cover the lake completely, from a start of only one lily at the beginning of the summer. The task is to determine on what day the lake is half covered.

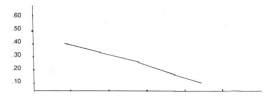

FIG. 3.3. Correlation between IQ and success in solving the separate problems.

Five problems of a similar nature were given to a group of 65 female students at a Nursing Training College. There were questions of increasing temperature in a room, of the increase in the weights of fish in a sea farm, and the length of jogging trips (with increasing fitness), to mention some of the main topics covered by the puzzles. The subjects were presented with the problems after having been administered an intelligence test of the traditional type. The latter had six sub-tests: Sentence completion, arithmetic, verbal classification (similarities), digit series, verbal analogies, and comprehension.

The results depicted in Figure 3.3 must be taken as yet another indication of the fact that even when the solution of a certain type of task has been shown to be influenced by intelligence, further task solution along the same general lines appears to be losing contact with this human talent.

In the present series of tasks the correlation between IQ and success on the first problem was found to be .46. For each successive problem the correlation drops, to .39, .35, and .28, respectively, and finally reaches .18 for the fifth and final problem in the series. To this author this development seems more than a bit strange.

EXPECTATIONS REVISITED

There is, as already suggested earlier, ample evidence that human beings tend to behave in a manner that they think is in accordance with what is expected of them. This will, of course, also hold true for subjects of psychological experiments. The *Einstellungseffekt,* described by Luchins (1942), may result in a phenomenon that even the brightest of subjects fail to treat a particular task in a different way from what has been the procedure for solving a preceding series of (seemingly) equivalent problems. In our own experiments the failure may be said to be that of subjects no longer taking into account what had been seen before. How, then, can we explain why intelligent subjects are unable to produce the correct solution throughout the whole series of "equivalent tasks"?

"Equivalent tasks" are, of course, similar only to the extent that one is willing, or feels obliged, to overlook the more or less marked differences among the tasks. And, by the same token, a common feature may well be disregarded, once one is given to understand that the discrepancies are what really count, today. So, with respect to our experimental set-up, this leads to the following question: What is it that might influence the problem solver to "think in this way" rather than in another? Would some condition lead him or her to believe, e.g., that tasks towards the end of the problem series are "meant to be" different from the initial ones?

Examining the details of our research procedure, one may find that the experimenter, in an endeavour to make sure that all subjects spend the "correct" amount of time on each problem, has placed a sheet of red paper between the individual tasks that are presented, one at the time, on sheets of ordinary white paper. Is it possible that this "red signal" has somehow made the subjects believe that sooner or later a "new" type of task would appear?

To look into this possibility, the author changed the experimental procedure in the following way: Instead of having the problems presented on separate sheets of paper, the subjects received all five problems on one sheet, the total time allowed for solution being the same as before. The sequence of the tasks was the one that had previously produced the results shown in Figure 3.2.

The details of the results of this experiment have been presented elsewhere (Raaheim, 1988b). Here only the main finding will be focused on. With the change of procedure, which made, in fact, the whole problem solving session *look like* a subtest or other of an ordinary intelligence test, a significant positive correlation was found, between test results and problem solution, including the final task of the series of five problems. It seems likely, then, that the altered form of presentation of the problems resulted in the subjects feeling free to concentrate on the common features of the tasks.

As has been suggested earlier, as far as problem definition is concerned the human problem solver is regularly faced with a twofold task: (a) There is a need to have more than one interpretation of the way the things before you appear to be arranged—by nature or by the fellow human being, e.g., the experimental psychologist or another examiner; (b) (and this is perhaps a demand that is attended to without too much hesitation) There is a need to choose the interpretation that fits with the expectations of other people.

It might be safe to assume that a human being, whether he or she is very bright or not, has *overlearned,* as a result of numerous reinforcements, what other people's expectations are. And so, during the normal course of problem solving behavior, one "knows instantly" what to do, once the alternatives have been recognized.

But then, when someone has decided to take the problem solver by surprise, the latter is all the more vulnerable to unexpected maneuvers. With little or no warning that "today is another day" ("Now be creative!"), there is, as far as the author can see, the inevitable outcome of the problem solver needing some time to recover, so to speak.

In the laboratory of the experimental psychologist the subject naturally enough often needs to look again, in order to make a sound judgment of what is really going on. But when you don't know what to expect, you don't know what is expected of you, either. Some research efforts within the Test Anxiety tradition (Hagtvet & Raaheim, 1987) have indicated that when subjects are confronted with a series of equivalent puzzles, they are only influenced by conditions of worry when, after a few initial tasks, the whole problem solving affair has become familiar enough for intelligence to come into play.

The sensitivity to one's surroundings, in the form of an immediate awareness of the expectations or wishes of other people, may, as suggested earlier, be at its highest when the task in front of you is a novel one. As far as the present author can judge, there is, however, a lack of recognition among researchers of the extent that this sensitivity may come to influence intelligent action.

A final and quite recent observation (Johnsen & Hagtvet, in preparation) is worth mentioning here. When students were asked to suggest solutions to a series of five different, but equivalent problem tasks presented by computer, the level of anxiety was found to be lower than with the paper and pencil version, administered by the experimental psychologist. The computer program was written, in this case, in such a way as to ask the subjects to assess their state of anxiety after having been confronted with two of the five tasks. This interruption of problem solving seemed to have led the subjects to believe that here were two different sets of problems. In any case, the correlation between intelligence test results and problem solving, instead of reaching its highest figure with Task three, came close to zero with this problem (with an increase for the subsequent tasks).

CHALLENGES ABOVE THE UPPER THRESHOLD

In situations where the degree of novelty is such as to make each and every effort of intelligently exploiting one's past experience turn into a fruitless enterprise, the more intelligent person, on reflection, might feel particularly helpless. At least this may be so in the early phase of the solution process. To the extent that this is true, the following might serve as an explanation:

We have suggested earlier that situations above the upper threshold of intelligent problem solving may, by some quickly performed search for information, be transformed into a situation where intelligence again has a role to play. It is conceivable, then, that the very bright person, or someone who is highly experienced in some particular field or other, may be partly *unaware* of the trips he or she takes into uncertainty because they are of such short duration. It may be that a very brief inspection of the particulars of a situation so frequently turns out to be more than enough to set the intelligent problem solver on the right track, that under normal circumstances the individual comes to underestimate, or even ignore, the importance of seeking new information to be fed into the knowledge store.

The helplessness felt by the very intelligent problem solver when he or she is placed in a situation distinctly outside a familiar field, may at times have important consequences. Where the less intelligent person, out of sheer habit, asks questions and makes lengthy and systematic observations, the person who has come to rely more strongly on his or her intelligence in the past, expects to understand the matter without too much information seeking.

This seems to be at least part of the story behind a lot of initial failures, or poor academic results among tertiary students who have had a brilliant career in school. Some subjects at tertiary level (but not all) place demands on new students with which they are quite unfamiliar, irrespective of marks received during secondary schooling. And because some of the students have had a greater chance of forgetting what it is like not to know the answers, and what one has to do if this turns out to be the case, their despair in the new situation and their awkwardness is all the greater.

So far, only a very tentative study has been performed to look into this question (Raaheim & Raaheim, 1987). As far as psychology students and their struggle with academic problems are concerned, it seems that students who had "an easy task" getting good marks at school are no better off initially in coping with the demands of tertiary courses than students who report that they had to work hard at school in order to obtain decent marks. Our results so far seem also to be indicating that initial difficulties have more longlasting effects on those students to whom good school marks came easy.

When we looked into the career of the students in their third year of university study, the following picture emerged: Whereas students who had stated that they worked hard at secondary school had done equally well at university irrespective of their initial difficulties, students who were unfamiliar with having to work hard to obtain good results, seemed to have had their university career determined by their initial experience at university. In this subgroup students meeting difficulties during their first term had a greater number of failures later on. A considerable number of these students, on our inspection of results two years later, were found to have simply given up their courses. It ought to be added, perhaps, that the results of a verbal intelligence test administered to the students in the initial phase of this study, revealed that students who reported having had an easy time at school actually obtained higher scores on the intelligence test than their hard working peers.

CONCLUSION

Our argument concerning the relationship between IQ (as measured by traditional intelligence tests) and actual problem solving behavior can be summarized in three points as follows:

1. When persons who have performed very well on IQ tests are found to be unsuccessful when challenged by new tasks in the psychologist's laboratory or in

real life, one ought to consider the possibility that something is preventing the person from doing his or her best, before drawing the conclusion that "other abilities"—that the person is thought to be lacking—are needed in the situation in question.

2. If intelligence is regarded as the ability to see the past reflected in the present, as *pattern recognition* in its widest sense, a talent to look on a changing world in such a way that it seems to be unchanging (Edwards, Lindman, & Phillips, 1965), then one ought to make sure that more than one instance of a given type of task is used in assessing "intelligence at work."

3. Furthermore, one ought to take into consideration that the human being is able to perceive a given situation in many different ways and to sort it accordingly into different and multiple categories. With a rich variety of ways that an individual may come to classify his or her experience, he or she might, at a given time, place great importance on certain similarities between tasks, while ignoring some of the perceived differences, only, in the next moment, to turn to the "opposite" strategy of concentrating on the differences. As a researcher, one must be sensitive to this type of flexibility in human cognitive processing when making judgments about problem solving capacities.

The computerized administration of psychological tests and tasks of problem solving may have some definite advantages (see Goldman & Pellegrino, Pellegrino, Stankov, Di Sessa, & Kluwe et al., in this volume and also again Johnsen & Hagtvet, in preparation). As already indicated, subjects may feel less threatened because in the computer environment neither the father figure, nor the mother are represented. Yet, human sensitivity to possible situational demands may operate also in such cases, in particular, perhaps, among more intelligent subjects. Thus, if as educators, psychologists or administrators we feel we have to pass judgment on the intellectual skills of our fellow human beings, we must never stop taking precautions to ensure that the subjects we talk about are not using their "wits" primarily to please someone else, instead of thinking for themselves.

REFERENCES

Burke, R. J., & Maier, N. R. F. (1965). Attempts to predict success on an insight problem. *Psychological Reports, 17,* 303–310.

Edwards, W., Lindman, H., & Phillips, L. D. (1965). Emerging technologies for making decisions. In *New directions in psychology II.* New York: Holt, Rinehart & Winston.

Hagtvet, K. A., & Raaheim, K. (1987, September). *A process oriented study of intelligence and anxiety.* Paper prepared for the Invitational Workshop and Symposium on Applied Psychometrics, Plymouth, England.

Johnsen, T. B., & Hagtvet, K. A. (in preparation). Assessing anxiety or destroying performance.

Luchins, A. S. (1942). Mechanization in problem solving: The effect of Einstellung. *Psychological Monographs, 54,* No. 248.

Raaheim, K. (1988a). Intelligence and task novelty. In. R. J. Sternberg (Ed.), *Advances in the psychology of human intelligence,* Vol. 4. Hillsdale, NJ: Lawrence Erlbaum Associates.

Raaheim, K. (1988b, September). *Intelligence and its limitation in problem-solving tasks.* Paper presented to the XXIV International Conference in Psychology, Sydney, Australia.

Raaheim, K. (1989). The dilemma of the intelligent problem solver. In I. Bjorgen (Ed.). *Basic issues in psychology.* Bergen: Sigma.

Raaheim, K., & Raaheim, A. (1987). *Hvem far vansker i studiestarten?* Report to The Faculty of Psychology, University of Bergen.

Sternberg, R. J. (1988). *Beyond IQ.* Invited Keynote Address delivered at the opening of the ACER Seminar on Intelligence, held in Melbourne, 24–26 August, 1988.

Sternberg, R. J. (1984). Mechanisms of cognitive development: a componential approach. In R. J. Sternberg (Ed.), *Mechanisms of cognitive development.* New York: W. H. Freeman.

Sternberg, R. J., & Davidson, J. E. (1982). The mind of the puzzler. *Psychology Today,* June 16, pp. 37–44.

4 Intelligence as an Expression of Acquired Knowledge

Robert Glaser
University of Pittsburgh

The attitude with which I approach the study of intelligence can best be conveyed by noting the similarities between intellectual and athletic proficiency. Certainly, the comparison is not new. In his book on thinking, Bartlett (1958) introduced his studies by discussing the nature of "bodily skill" and the properties of skilled performance. He suggested that:

> It seems reasonable to try to begin by treating thinking provisionally as a complex and high level kind of skill. Thinking has its acknowledged experts, like every other known form of skill, and in both cases much of the expertness, though never, perhaps, all of it, has to be acquired by well-informed practice. (pp. 11–12)

It should not be surprising that the phenomena apparent in one domain of human performance resemble those of other domains, and it seems to me that certain characteristics are salient in intellectual performance as well as athletic prowess (Glaser, 1986). A number of the characteristics that are important in both domains are listed here:

- An available knowledge structure of the domain of competence (the game or skill) that is elaborated with experience.

---

[1]This article is a revision of the author's address at the Australian Council for Educational Research Seminar on Intelligence, Melbourne, August 1988. It relies upon "Intelligence as Acquired Proficiency" (Glaser, 1986). Its preparation was sponsored in part by the Cognitive Science Program of the Office of Naval Research. Additional support was provided by the Center for the Study of Learning (CSL) at the Learning Research and Development Center of the University of Pittsburgh. CSL is funded by the Office of Educational Research and Improvement of the US Department of Education.

- Automated performance components that allow precise timing and fast perceptual reactions to information.
- Chunking of discrete events into groupings and classifications that enable pattern recognition and planful sequences of actions. This is revealed, for example, in the play of the badminton champion or baseball professional, who think in terms of sequences of actions that go beyond a particular stroke or throw.
- Inherited physiological systems, for example, musculature and cardiovascular system, that are further developed with appropriate exercise.
- A constancy of performance that is maintained over a long period of time, declines with disuse and with aging of the physiological system, and recovers with use. Sometimes this performance is maintained over longer periods because of the well-organized knowledge structures of experienced performers.
- A tacit understanding in experts that often makes them unable to describe the full particulars of their performances. Coaches who observe skill and its development are much better at analyzing skilled competence for the purposes of training.
- Parameters of individual differences and individual styles are very apparent.
- Proficiency that is specific to particular domains of performance. Although some performance components and a good physiological system contribute to all around ability, expertise of one kind is not necessarily transferable to other types of performance.
- Competence that can be assisted and extended by artificial aids and specially designed inventions and equipment (such as high jump poles, track shoes, and track surfaces) that are derived from study and increased understanding of performance. Over time, with good motivational conditions, such aids improve records of performance and foster new forms and levels of proficiency.
- At the limits of expert performance, flexibility, adaptiveness, and inventiveness allow further elaboration of knowledge and skill, especially when novel, nonstandard situations are encountered.

These resemblances are a useful guide for considering the nature and nurture of intelligence. By conceiving of intelligence as a form of proficiency, we can remove it from the realm of mysterious capacities and render it trainable, amenable to external support, and open to discovery of its limits. The parallel between intellectual and athletic proficiency has its limits, but it can serve to redirect our thinking about the nature of intellectual competence. In this chapter, I propose a conception of intellectual proficiency in the context of domains of knowledge, the characteristics of expertise, and performance in unfamiliar domains. In addition, I discuss dimensions of domain competence as a basis for assessing the growth of intellectual proficiency.

INTELLIGENCE AS A COGNITIVE PROFICIENCY IN DOMAINS OF KNOWLEDGE

The notion of the cultivation of intellect, through targeted experience, that is implied by the resemblance between athletic proficiency and intellectual proficiency is illuminated when we consider the role of knowledge in intelligence. By this view, of intelligent performance as largely manifested in and derived from experiences that build structures of knowledge, knowledge of two interactive kinds: artifactually constrained and naturally constrained. Intelligence in *artifactual domains* refers to cognitive proficiency in such invented knowledge domains as the sciences, vocational-technical proficiencies, and the social and personal skills typical of a culture and its subcultures. These competencies are usually acquired under relatively formal instructional conditions in school, through intentional self-instruction, or through social learning and modeling in a family and community.

Intelligence in *natural domains* refers to pervasive competences that occur early in human development, for example, first language proficiency, general spatial knowledge and related perceptual abilities, knowledge of the regularities in elementary concepts of numbers, causal thinking, and classification skills (such as observed by Gelman & Gallistel, 1978; Keil, 1981; and others). Intelligence in natural domains, like intelligence in artifactual domains, evolves from the constraints of available cognitive structures, but it is learned more informally and spontaneously than artifactual domain intelligence. Proficiency in natural domains is broadly applicable in acquiring artifactual proficiencies.

Through interaction of stage of development and situational or task requirements, both artifactually derived and natural knowledge and skill comprise forms of intellectual performance and attained cognitive proficiencies that can be called intelligence. Thus, adults who become highly proficient and expert in performances required in their jobs and in dealing with problems of daily life display intelligence, as do children who become highly skilled in the representation of quantity and in numerical reasoning through early categorization and counting skills. Such performances represent intelligence, as encouraged and valued by a culture and as defined by the structure of a domain.

The domains of artifactually and naturally constrained intelligence overlap and interact as a function of the tasks and environmental situations encountered by a child or an adult. For example, number concepts and principles start out as primarily natural knowledge domains and become integrated into the artifactual domains of mathematics. Other intelligent capacities like musical talent and spatial ability seem to develop similarly. The quality and degree of these attainments, as with athletic proficiency, are determined by the interactive knowledge-process requirements of a domain, the opportunities for experience, the assistance available from invented aids, as well as the cultural demands and social motivation that inhere in performance.

In large measure, knowledge structures associated with domain-specific proficiency enable the cognitive processes that are critical to the acquisition of further proficiency. These processes foster the rapid access to organized memory, chunking, forms of representation, and self-regulatory skills that are required for coping with tasks and problem situations and that lead to new organizations and integrations of information. Learning occurs through the utilization of such proficiencies and results in the intelligences that exist in the context of natural and artifactual domains.

The generalized cognitive processes identified by psychometric analyses, as well as the general methods of heuristic processes uncovered in cognitive studies of human problem solving on knowledge lean–tasks, appear to have particular importance when an individual is confronted with unfamiliar domains, that is, domains in which specific proficiency may not have been attained. However, these general processes may be less differentiating of individual variation in cognitive proficiency than the domain specific intelligences that are nurtured over the course of life span development. It is also conceivable that generally applicable processes are acquired and elaborated as an individual operates in a wide variety of domains, so that the common structures and processes employed become available for mapping and analogical reasoning in new domains.

PROPERTIES OF INTELLECTUAL PROFICIENCY

When intelligence is considered as cognitive proficiency manifested in a domain, the performances that index the quality and level of intelligence are displayed in the context of acquired knowledge. Recent investigations of expertise in various domains (Chi, Glaser, & Farr, 1988; Glaser, 1987) suggest the following general properties that describe such intellectual proficiency:

Intelligence in a domain of knowledge is manifested by the ability to perceive large, meaningful patterns of information rapidly. Pattern recognition occurs so rapidly that it takes on the character of the "intuitions". Individuals with less proficiency recognize patterns that are smaller, less articulated, more literal and surface-structure oriented, and less related to abstract principles.

Intelligence is characterized by dynamic proceduralized knowledge. Concepts and declarative knowledge are not rote and inert items in memory, but are bound to procedures for their application and to the conditions under which these procedures are useful.

Intellectual proficiency facilitates the perception and representation of situations in ways that greatly reduce the role of memory search. Individuals who are less proficient in a domain display a good deal of general search and processing.

Intellectual proficiency depends on the development of automaticity in basic performance processes. Automaticity frees working memory for higher level processing, and high levels of competence may emerge after extended practice, leading to the development of performance automaticity.

Intellectual proficiency is accompanied by the development of skilled self–regulatory (metacognitive) processes, such as performance monitoring, allocation of attention, sensitivity to informational feedback, and so on. Such cognitive skills enable the use of information in new situations and facilitate transfer.

Proficiency in one domain is no guarantee of proficiency in others, and forms of intellectual proficiency differ as a function of the domains in which they develop. However, competence in certain domains may be more generalizable and lead to possibilities for a wide span of intellectual proficiency. Also, individuals competent in a number of different domains may develop generalizable proficiencies (mapping and analogical strategies) that enable them to transfer abilities across domains.

Intelligence is limited and shaped by the task structures and environment in which it is exercised. Hence, in efficiency-oriented environments, where there is repeated application with little variation, routine forms of intelligence develop. In contrast, analytical tasks and environments or cultures where understanding and innovation are valued along with efficient performance encourage variation and nonroutine adaptations.

Intelligence in both artifactual and natural domains, and their interactions, show these various properties. They are constrained by organized structures of knowledge and depend on automated basic performance processes. They also engender metacognitive, self-regulatory processes and are influenced by environmental and cultural requirements and limits. The structures involved in the development of natural proficiencies are available early in life, before extensive experience with artifactual domains. As the structures of formally instructed domains are introduced, they interact with natural proficiencies, and, increasingly, knowledge specific manifestations of intelligence are developed.

PERFORMANCE IN UNFAMILIAR DOMAINS

So far, I have described findings about levels of competence as they are determined by acquired domain knowledge. In this respect, I have pictured intelligence primarily in a sense that does not account for the competence that is demonstrated when people work at the frontiers of their knowledge. When the problems they confront are novel, or in relatively unfamiliar domains, or not well structured, the pattern recognition that drives expert performance cannot readily be accomplished. Working such problems requires the resolution of open constraints that are not given or defined when the problem is presented or conceived, and a search for analogies and for equivalents to the principles that underlie solutions for more familiar problems. Problem solution in situations where acquired domain knowledge is inadequate requires the definition of subproblems for which patterns can be seen that entail particular approaches. The solver must impose an organization that synthesizes various partial understandings. He/she must come up with some potentially useful representation or model as a basis for proceeding. The global problem must be decomposed into a set of well structured subproblems that can be handled (Simon, 1973; Voss & Post, 1988).

With an ill-structured problem, for example in the social sciences, the community of experts little agree on how to achieve a solution, or on which attributes of the problem situation have referents in analogous instances or established principles. Nor is there agreement about evaluating the adequacy of correctness of a solution, for example, what solution operations are permissible, and what are their consequences? Under these circumstances, the solver must impose organization, as well as explore alternative solutions (or explanations) and assess their power. Several may be acceptable, so that individual differences and personal creativity are more exposed in such performances than in well structured problem situations.

With novel problems in their domains and with problems in unfamiliar domains of knowledge, experts, somewhat like novices, bring *general* problem solving processes to bear. They decompose the problem into a structured set of sub-problems, but with greater facility than a novice would. They also are better able to select values for open constraints that lead to a possible meaningful solution by supplying testable candidate problem representations. They often resort, for example, to analogies with systems that they understand well and search for matches and mismatches. They may attempt to impose some model of the workings of a phenomenon they know as they try to understand how it would behave in the context of the unfamiliar situation. They may pose extreme case arguments or construct simplified problems of a similar sort to deal with the original problem. In general, wherever problems do not yield to straightforward approaches based on experts' attempts to see the deep structure or principle underlying a problem, they employ these general strategies.

The use of general heuristics may become apparent when experts address atypical problems, but they do not take on significance as substitutes for domain knowledge. On the contrary, general heuristics serve mostly in the attempt to gain access to and apply whatever domain knowledge might prove relevant to problem solution. In a sense, experts' uses of general heuristics are attempts to move ill-structured problems into familiar domains where extant knowledge can be brought into play. Rather than using general heuristics in a decontextualized way, as free-floating interrogators of a situation, the expert uses them as links to available knowledge and the solution processes it might afford. The abstract use of general heuristics, as might be taught in courses on thinking skills or reasoning, may not be successful because it is decontextualized.

Finally, it is important to say that in no way do I dismiss the analysis of processes of general intelligence that scientific study has pursued over the years through factor analytic theory and more recent cognitive information processing approaches and theory. People use these processes in the course of acquiring domain knowledge and skill, and then the influence of growing knowledge structures on intellectual processes is displayed in new levels of performance. Thus, as well as working on general theories of intelligence, we should concentrate on examining the details of knowledge use in all forms of intelligent performance. When we know what people know, we can offer more realistic theories about determinants of performance because people think largely by using quite specific knowledge.

THE MEASUREMENT OF DOMAIN BASED INTELLECTUAL PROFICIENCY

On the basis of the foregoing description of the properties of acquired intellectual proficiency, it seems useful to suggest a framework for assessing levels of intelligent performance that are attained in the course of education and experience. Much as the details of athletic performance as evaluated by a coach are integral in efforts to improve performance, the dimensions of cognitive assessment suggested here could yield diagnostic information for the further development of intellectual proficiency.

At various stages of the acquisition of intellectual proficiency, there exist different integrations of knowledge, different degrees of procedural skill, and differences in access to memory and in forms of task representation. These variations in developing competence can be a basis for test construction that is coordinate with or prior to psychometric considerations. The underlying assumption is that measurement of intellectual proficiency in a domain can be grounded by theory that describes the acquisition of knowledge and its accompanying competence (Glaser, Lesgold, & Lajoie, 1987). Measurement theory that accommodates theories of knowledge acquisition is at an early stage. Many of the essential ideas are yet to be worked out, but enough research has been done to indicate the shape of a guiding framework. Consider as a tentative representative sample the following closely linked six dimensions of cognitive proficiency: principled performance, active knowledge, theory change, problem representation, automaticity to reduce attentional demands, and self-regulatory skills.

Principled performance.   As competence is attained, elements of knowledge and components of skill become increasingly interconnected and based on abstracted principles and generalizations, so that individuals access principles and rules for their performances rather than fragmentary pieces of information. This is apparent in various domains of subject matter. A beginner's knowledge consists of incomplete definitions, too widely or narrowly applicable rules, and superficial understandings. As learning occurs, the pattern of a student's test responses can show systematic patterns of performance that determine progress or blockages to further achievement. The diagnosis of effective and ineffective principles of performance becomes a candidate dimension for the assessment of developing knowledge.

Active knowledge. The course of acquisition of knowledge proceeds from an initial accumulation of information in declarative form to a form that is more active and useful. In essence, we can know a principle, or a rule, or an item of specialized vocabulary without knowing initially the conditions under which it is to be used effectively. Studies of the difference between experts and novices indicate that beginners may have requisite knowledge, but this knowledge is not bound to the conditions of applicability. When knowledge is accessed by experts, it is associated with indications of how and when it is to be appropriately used. Assessments of the development of achievement in an area of knowledge through this progression from declarative to active information can be a useful measure of competence.

Theory change. Learning takes place on the basis of the novices' existing theories and mental models that either enhance or retard learning. With appropriate instruction, learners test, evaluate, and modify their current theories on the basis of new information, and, as a result, develop new schemata that facilitate more advanced thinking. However, the naive theories relied on at the beginning of a course may make learning difficult. And, even after extended instruction, these naive theories may persist. Although students have learned to solve problems in some mechanical fashion, they may have little understanding. Thus, theories of knowledge become targets for assessment. Assessments that capture the characteristics of naive theories might indicate which are amenable to change under certain instructional conditions, or whether a theory is more intractable and will result in learning difficulties. Such assessments might also monitor future shifts in theory over a course of learning.

Problem representation. As indicated, novices process information on the basis of the surface features of a problem or task situation, and more proficient individuals go beyond surface features to identify inferences or principles that subsume the surface structure. This growing ability to quickly recognize the underlying principles indicates developing achievement and could be assessed by appropriate pattern recognition tasks in verbal and graphic situations. Because certain forms of representation appear to be highly correlated with the ability to carry out the steps of a problem solution, test items might concentrate on assessing the initial understanding that is displayed by problem representation, as well as the details of solution procedures.

Automaticity to reduce attentional demands. When the subtasks of a complex activity simultaneously require attention, the efficiency of the overall task is affected. This fact has particular implications for diagnostic assessment of the interaction between components of performance. Although component processes may work well when tested separately, they may not be efficient enough to work together. If a task demands an orchestration of skills, then measurement procedures should be able to diagnose inefficiencies. Criteria for assessment should include the levels of automaticity required for subprocesses to have minimal interference effects and the levels required to facilitate efficient, integrated performance and new learning.

Self-regulatory skills. The experience of experts enables them to develop executive skills for approaching problems and monitoring performance. Experts rapidly check their progress toward problem solutions. They are more accurate at judging problem difficulty, apportioning their time, asking questions, assessing their knowledge, and predicting the outcome of their performance. These self-regulatory skills vary in individuals and appear to be less developed in those with performance difficulties. Superior monitoring skills reflect the domain knowledge and representational capabilities of experts, and these skills contribute to the utility of knowledge. Knowledge of a rule or procedure is enhanced by overseeing its applicability and monitoring its use. Thus, self-regulatory skills are important candidates for learning and instruction. Assessments that monitor their development can be significant predictors of problem solving abilities that result in new learning.

The measurement of intellectual proficiency, as defined here, is a method of assessing competence through indicators of the development of knowledge, skill, and cognitive process. These indicators reveal stages of performance that have been attained and that provide a basis for further learning or for specific instructional attention. The measurement of performance, thus conceived, must be informed by theories of the acquisition of subject matter profiency. A focus on various dimensions of proficiency invites us to consider the ways that the use of knowledge is an index to the growth and development of intellectual competence.

REFERENCES

Bartlett, F. (1958). *Thinking: An experimental and social study.* New York: Basic Books.
Chi, M. T. H., Glaser, R., & Farr, M. (Eds.). (1988). *The nature of expertise.* Hillsdale, NJ: Lawrence Erlbaum Associates.

Gelman, R., & Gallistel, C. R. (1978). *The child's understanding of numbers*. Cambridge: Harvard University Press.

Glaser, R. (1987). Thoughts on expertise. In C. Schooler & W. Schaie (Eds.), *Cognitive functioning and social structure over the life course*. Norwood, NJ: Ablex.

Glaser, R., Lesgold, A. M., & Lajoie, S. (1987). Toward a cognitive theory for the measurement of achievement. In R. R. Ronning, J. Glover, J. C. Conoley, & J. C. Witt (Eds.), *The influence of cognitive psychology on testing and measurement*. Hillsdale: NJ: Lawrence Erlbaum Associates.

Glaser, R. (1986). Intelligence as acquired proficiency. In R. J. Sternberg & D. K. Detterman (Eds.), *What is intelligence? Contemporary viewpoints on its nature and definition*. Norwood, NJ: Ablex.

Keil, F. C. (1981). Constraints on knowledge and cognitive development. *Psychological Review, 88*(3), 204–205.

Simon, H. A. (1973). The structure of ill-structured problems. *Artificial Intelligence, 4*, 181–201.

Voss, J., & Post, T. (1988). On the solving of ill-structured problems. In M. T. H. Chi, R. Glaser, & M. Farr (Eds.), *The nature of expertise*. Hillsdale, NJ: Lawrence Erlbaum Associates.

5 Multimodal Learning and the Quality of Intelligent Behavior

John B. Biggs
University of Hong Kong

Kevin F. Collis
University of Tasmania

INTELLIGENT BEHAVIOR, COMPETENCE, AND FORMS OF KNOWLEDGE

Academic and everyday intelligence.   Two assumptions about intelligent behavior have dominated psychology for the greater part of this century. The first is that a construct of general intelligence underlies much competent behavior, and the second, that academic achievement is determined by that one construct more than by any other single factor. As is well known, the original brief of Binet and Simon (1908) was to construct a battery of tests that would help identify the educability of children attending Paris schools. This they did, and with remarkable efficiency, for the kinds of test items they used, and their concept of an intelligence quotient, have endured at least in generic form until the present day.

As Sternberg has pointed out in his chapter in this book and on other occasions (e.g., Sternberg & Wagner, 1986), this history determined until recently that the focus of intelligence research was on measurement, not on theoretical issues. "Intelligence" was accepted as whatever it was that intelligence tests were measuring. Intelligent behavior in extracurricular or everyday domains scarcely received any attention, either by theorists or by those who designed the tests.

Currently however, researchers are studying the display of competence in nonacademic contexts, and such competence, commonly referred to as everyday intelligence, has quite different characteristics from that associated with performance on intelligence tests. In contrast to academic intelligence, everyday intelligence appears to have the following characteristics:

- It is context specific. Seemingly general skills, such as tallying sales, are demonstrated only in the context in which they are learned and practiced, and do not generalize across contexts (Scribner, 1986). Schooled intelligence, on the other hand, focuses on pure mental processes and operations of wide generality (Resnick, 1987).

- It makes much use of concrete aids and relatively little use of the abstract algorithms, or even the symbol and notational systems themselves, that are taught in school.

- It is frequently socially mediated, whereas academic intelligence and problem solving functions within contexts that stipulate the solitary involvement of the learner and that exclude shared problem solving.

- It functions on directly experienced problems that are of existential moment to the individual. Schooling, on the other hand, deals with a codified abstraction and formalization of what others have already discovered. This disembodied and depersonalized character of school learning creates motivational problems. Codified knowledge does not often provide its own motivation for learning, except in that special case we call intrinsic motivation.

A multiplicity of intelligences?   It is a moot point how far we can subdivide intelligence. Sternberg and Wagner (1986) simply distinguish between academic and everyday intelligence, with the latter displaying high context specificity. Is there one basic form of intelligence, "g" in the Spearman model and its derivatives, or several forms of intelligence that are basically unrelated to each other?

Gardner (1985) has identified seven autonomous intelligences, or "frames of mind", within which some people manifest prodigious performance, often from an early age, and across which prodigies within one frame perform little better than anybody else. These frames are content based and include: Bodily-kinaesthetic (e.g., gymnasts and dancers), musical, linguistic, logico-mathematical, spatial, interpersonal (e.g., skilled negotiators), and intrapersonal (e.g., mystics). These particular frames were identified on the basis of studies of brain localization, particularly where particular lesions have resulted in specific behavioral impairments, and of exceptional attainment in specific areas, such as child prodigies in music, mathematics, and language.

Demetriou and Efklides (1987) postulate six "autonomous capacity spheres," in which cognitive development takes place. Some of these appear directly to overlap the Gardner intelligences (e.g., imaginal with spatial, verbal with linguistic), whereas others share characteristics of several.

The precise list of autonomous intelligences may well become larger, or reorganized. Both Gardner and Demetriou and Efklides agree that a generalized intelligence construct cannot account for the facts of exceptional performance even within the confines of academe, let alone beyond.

Task specific competencies.   Another recent view of exceptional performance is that the notion of general, or even specific abilities should be replaced by that of individual competencies (e.g., Tyler, 1978), a view currently most evident in Glaser's chapter and the novice-expert research of the Pittsburgh school (Chi, Glaser, & Rees, 1982; Chipman, Segal, & Glaser, 1984). High level competence, or expertise, is seen as largely accountable for by the acquisition of a well structured knowledge base that bears directly on the task in hand. Thus, the difference between novices and experts in such diverse tasks as chess, physics, radiography, and so on, is simply that the expert has, over much familiarity with this kind of task and its associated database, developed strategies that make use of this ordered knowledge and can generalize it to new contexts.

Forms of knowledge. One outcome of competent behavior is the attainment of a particular form of knowledge. For present purposes we may note the following:

Tacit knowledge is manifested by doing and is usually not verbally accessible. Some forms of tacit knowledge may be verbalized, others may not (Wagner & Sternberg, 1986). A gymnast, for example, may be quite unable to express how she performs a particular act; the important thing is that she can do it perfectly at will, and that is the evidence for her knowledge.

Intuitive knowledge is directly perceived or felt, and may include aesthetic knowledge and the kind of knowledge displayed when mathematicians or scientists apprehend an idea or solution before they are able to elucidate it symbolicaly.

Declarative knowledge is expressed through the medium of a symbol system in a way that is publicly understandable. Declarative knowledge for present purposes is not at a level of abstraction beyond first order descriptions within the given system.

Theoretical knowledge is at a higher level of abstraction than that declared within the given system, and can be mapped onto, and often subsumed under, a more abstract statement of knowledge.

Anderson (1980) distinguishes between declarative knowledge as "comprising the facts we know," and procedural knowledge as "the skills we know how to perform" (p.222). His description of procedural knowledge appropriately emphasizes the performance aspects. In this respect it would be suitable for our use of "tacit." Subsequent usage of the term however implies a more abstract meaning than is allowable for current purposes.

Any theory of intelligence should have something to say about expressions of competence in both academic and everyday contexts, and about the attainment of knowledge in its various forms. Differences between academic intelligence and everyday intelligence, and forms of knowing, involve essentially the concreteness or abstractness of what is known, which is also at issue in descriptions of cognitive development. We are led, then, to a question that was of vital concern to Piaget (1950) himself, which Richelle (in this volume) sees as essential, and which is addressed by other contributors to this book in different ways: Does the development of intelligence throw light on the nature of intelligence?

In the present chapter, we outline a theory of development that we believe addresses this question.

SOME ISSUES IN NEO-PIAGETIAN RESEARCH

In traditional Piagetian theory, cognitive development proceeded in discrete stages, each state being defined in terms of a logical structure (*structure d'en-semble*) that governed all performances within that stage. Examples of uneven performance, referred to as *décalages,* were regarded as aberrant and rare.

In the last decade, several neo-Piagetian theories of cognitive development have been put forward, including those of Biggs and Collis (1982), Case (1985), Demetriou and Ecfklides (1987), Fischer (1980), Halford (1982), and Mounoud (1986). It is possible to discover consensus on some key issues of development and disagreement on others.

On the question of the relative frequency of *décalage,* there seems to be a major difference between neo-Piagetians. Case (1985), Halford (1985), and Mounoud (1986) reported strong evidence for evenness across tasks, Fischer and Silvern (1985), and Demetriou and Efklides (1987) finding little. Part of the problem is task selection. Halford bases most of his theorizing on a board game, Mounoud on reaching and lifting objects, and although Case himself uses tasks over different content areas, these tasks drew consistently on covariation or analogical reasoning (Demetriou & Efklides, 1987). Fischer, on the other hand, used several tasks, including traditional Piagetian type problems (the weight and spring) but also social role play. A rough summary of the position would be that evenness is found within a domain of performance, but not across domains. However, what constitutes a domain is not clear.

An important attack on the problem of "décalage" was the demonstration that context played a major role in correct responding to several of the standard Piagetian tasks (Borke, 1978; Donaldson, 1978). In the context of school "dé-calage" is extremely common (Biggs & Collis, 1982). A student can be "early formal" in mathematics while "early concrete" in history, or even formal in mathematics one day and concrete the next. Such observations cannot indicate shifts in cognitive development, but rather shifts in more proximal constructs, such as learning, performance, or motivation.

The nature of a stage.   If "décalage" is in fact so frequent, then stages ought not be defined structurally (Fischer & Bullock, 1984; Meadows, 1983). On the other hand, all neo-Piagetians agree on the existence of stages in some form. The following considerations are fairly clear evidence of stage like phenomena:

• It is possible to describe age periods when all but exceptional children at least in Western society learn key tasks. In infancy, all children learn to coordinate their actions with the environment. In early childhood they learn to speak. From around 6 years to adolescence they learn to use second order symbol systems. From adolescence they learn to form theories about their world and how it might be ordered otherwise.

• During such key periods of optimally complex learning, the performances of different children on particular tasks resemble each other more than the performances of the same child at earlier or later periods.

• The activities from earlier to late key periods are increasingly abstract.

• There are clear qualitative differences, or discontinuities, between the way the same task is handled at various periods.

What is varying across such periods of optimal learning is clearly not the structure of all tasks handled within a stage, as suggested by the *structure-d'ensemble* model, but the mode of representation on the contents learned. These modes range from the most concrete, physical acts in infancy, through mental images in early childhood, to symbolic representations in later childhood, and to formal theories by late adolescence. These modes accrue from birth to maturity. The more abstract ones, which develop at later ages, do not replace those operating earlier, in the sense that later developing structured wholes were said to subsume immature ones, but to coexist with them. In other words, the latest developing stages represent a current ceiling to abstraction, not the level that all performances must conform to.

As to the number of stages, there is less agreement. Case (1985) and Halford (1982) postulate four, corresponding in timing but not in name to the sensorimotor, preoperational, concrete, and formal stages of Piaget. Mounoud (1986) and Fischer (1980) postulate three, effectively merging pre- and concrete operations, but Fischer preserves an open mind: "The number of levels beyond formal operations is not yet clear, but theory and research suggest at least one additional level emerging at approximately 14 to 16 years" (Fischer & Silvern, 1985, p. 635).

Substages or levels.   Several theorists postulate substages that recycle during successively higher stages (Biggs & Collis, 1982; Case, 1985; Fischer, 1980; Mounoud, 1986). Fischer and Pipp (1984), for instance, distinguish between *optimal level* and *skill acquisition,* the former referring to the highest level of abstraction available for representing a problem, which is indexed by developmental stage, and the latter to the way skills or competencies grow until they reach that optimal level, which is a matter of learning. To maintain the distinction, we might refer to the first as stage, and to the second substage, within a stage, as level.

Shifts in the structural complexity of performance in different school subjects (Biggs & Collis, 1982) thus refer to level, not stage; and as outlined more fully later, we postulate four hierarchical levels, which recur across stages. Other theorists also refer to a number of levels, usually four, each subsuming the preceding one, the topmost becoming the lowest unit at the next stage (Case, 1985; Fischer, 1980; Mounoud, 1986). Disagreement exists, however, on the nature of the organization of the levels, their content specificity, and the level and mechanism of generalization to the next stage.

We thus see a notable shift in the nature of stages and levels. Structural complexity is no longer the discriminating characteristic of stage, but as one important way of characterizing the growth of skill across levels within a developmental stage, the discriminandum of stage now becoming the level of abstraction of the mode that the contents of experience are represented.

THE MODES OF REPRESENTATION

Modes, then, are levels of abstraction, progressing from concrete actions to abstract concepts and principles, which form the basis of the developmental stages. There is general consensus amongst contemporary theorists that four stages can be distinguished up to late adolescence, but for our purposes, it is convenient also to distinguish a fifth, postformal, stage in adulthood. Further, each of these modes as it emerges is postulated not to replace its predecessor, as is suggested in Piagetian theory, but to coexist with it, thus enhancing considerably the modal repertoire of the mature adult as compared to that of the young child. The modes, and the age that each typically emerges, are described in the following discussion:

1. *Sensorimotor* (from birth). The infant can only interact with the world in the most concrete way: by giving a motor response to a sensory stimulus. Sensorimotor learning becomes quite complex during the first year or so of life, but its nature remains that of coordinating actions with each other and with the environment. During infancy, the sensorimotor mode is the only one available for learning. Sensorimotor learning leads to tacit knowledge, exemplified by skilled gymnasts or sportspeople, who know by the "feel" during the execution of an act when and how to adjust their performance. The distinction between this form of knowledge and declarative knowledge is well illustrated with Gardner's (1985) quotation of Isadora Duncan (a bodily-kinaesthetic prodigy) who, when asked to explain the meaning of a particular dance, replied: "If I could tell you what it is, I would not have danced it." (op. cit.; p. 225).

2. *Ikonic* (from around 18 months). If an action is to become more abstract it must be represented in some way. Piaget (1950) defined thought as the internalization of action. The simplest way of internalizing an action is to imagine it, by forming what Bruner (1964a, 1964b) referred to as an internal picture or "ikon". This generalizes with the help of language (for which it is a necessary prerequisite) after 18 months. Ikonic thought draws heavily on imagery and is frequently affect laden. With such a mode as this for their most powerful tool for

encoding reality, young children explain the mysteries of human interaction in terms of stories with clear stereotypical characters and obvious plots, in what Egan (1984) calls the "mythic" stage; a tendency also displayed by adults with manipulative intent, for example using images of an evil empire in order to bolster national loyalties. Adult versions of ikonic thought can however rise beyond myth-making, as is evident in the intuitive knowledge displayed in aesthetics, and by mathematicians (Hadamard, 1954) and scientists. As Gardner (1985) relates, Kekule's realization of the structure of the organic ring compounds was preceded by a hypnogogic dream of six snakes chasing each others' tails, and only later was his "truth" established to the satisfaction of the scientific community by evidence and argument. The ikonic mode is thus not merely a presymbolic mode of information processing restricted to early childhood. It continues to grow in power and complexity well beyond childhood. Whether that increase occurs solely within the ikonic mode, or in interaction with other modes, is an important question to which we return later.

3. *Concrete-symbolic* (from around 6 years). The next mode involves a significant shift in abstraction, from direct symbolization of the world through oral language, to written, second order, symbol systems that apply to the experienced world. There is logic and order both between the symbols themselves, and between the symbol system and the world. The symbol systems of written language and signs give us one of the most powerful tools for acting on the environment, and they include writing itself, mathematical symbol systems, maps, musical notation, and other symbolic devices. Mastery of these systems, and of their application to real world problems, is the major task in primary and secondary schooling according to any curriculum theory. Learning in the concrete-symbolic mode leads to declarative knowledge, demonstrated by symbolic descriptions of the experienced world.

4. *Formal* (from around 14 years). The concrete symbolic mode is that in which the higher cognitive aspects of everyday living are conducted. For example, an everyday understanding of evaporation involves the specific case of the three states of solid, liquid, and gas, and the relationship between these states and the application of heat. A theory about that relationship, however, involves more abstract constructs, and that of latent heat is one critical part of that new, more abstract, system (see Table 5.2). Formal thinking thus refers to a superordinate abstract system, in which any given topic is embedded, and which can be used to generate hypotheses about alternative ways of ordering the world. This superordinate system becomes identifiable with the body of knowledge that currently prevails in a discipline. Professional (as opposed to technical) competence requires an understanding of the first principles underlying the discipline so that the practitioner can generate viable alternatives when rule of thumb prescriptions prove inadequate. Thinking in the formal mode thus both incorporates and transcends particular circumstances. This mode begins to appear, in some individuals with respect to their particular specializations, from around 14 years of

age, but does not generalize to all thinking, and in some individuals may not develop at all. The formal mode is the level of abstraction usually required in undergraduate study, and some evidence of formal thought in the proposed area of study should be essential for admission to a university (Collis & Biggs, 1983).

5. *Postformal* (from about 20 years). As noted earlier, there is some debate about the existence of a postformal stage. Certainly, lifespan psychologists describe qualitative improvements in cognition well into adulthood, in the affective and social domains (e.g., Erikson, 1959; Jung, 1956; Levinson et al., 1978), in purely cognitive processes (Knox, 1977; Schaie, 1979), and in the metacognitive aspects of thinking (Biggs, 1987; Demetriou & Efklides, 1985; Lawrence, Dodds, & Volet, 1983). Thus if formal thought is usually the maximum level of abstraction required at undergraduate level and in professional practice, questioning the conventional bounds of theory and practice, and establishing new ones, is presumably what constitutes postformal thinking. Postformal thought may be seen in high level innovations in many fields. Many of the prodigious performances in music, mathematics, literature and the arts noted by Gardner (1985) seem to be of this kind. Educationally, it is institutionalized in postgraduate study, and in basic research. Demetriou and Efklides (1985) operationally define postformal thought with tests requiring the respondent to operate in novel systems, and, in a metacognition test, to report on their processing while solving novel problems. They found, as did Commons, Richards, and Kuhn (1982), that postformal thought defined in this way was rare even amongst university students. Nevertheless, some kind of postformal thinking is required in original research, and its absence may explain the difficulty some hitherto high achieving undergraduates have in coming to terms with the requirements of research higher degrees (Collis & Biggs, 1983).

LEARNING CYCLES: THE SOLO TAXONOMY

These five modes of representation thus open out progressively abstract possibilities by means of which people may conduct their learning. The next question is that of growth within stages, the ordering of *levels* of response within a mode.

In the progression from incompetence to expertise, learners display a consistent sequence, or learning cycle, that is generalizable to a large variety of tasks and particularly school-based tasks (Biggs & Collis, 1982). This sequence refers to a saccadic and hierarchical increase in the structural complexity of their responses, whatever the mode that the learning is expressed in. This hierarchy can tell us how far learning has progressed towards expertise, with reference to any particular mode, and may therefore be used to classify the outcomes of learning within any given mode. We call this hierarchical system the SOLO Taxonomy, SOLO being an acronym for "structure of the observed learning

TABLE 5.1
Modes and Levels in the SOLO Taxonomy

Mode		Structural Level (SOLO)
Next	5	*Extended abstract.* The learner now generalizes the structure to take in new and more abstract features, representing a new and higher mode of operation.
Target	4	*Relational.* The learner now integrates the parts with each other, so that the whole has a coherent structure and meaning.
	3	*Multistructural.* The learner picks up more and more relevant or correct features, but does not integrate them.
	2	*Unistructural.* The learner focuses on the relevant domain, and picks up one aspect to work with.
Previous	1	*Prestructural.* The task is engagaed, but the learner is distracted or misled by an irrelevant aspect belonging to a previous stage or mode.

outcome," and it may be used to evaluate learning quality, or to set curriculum objectives (Biggs & Collis, 1989). Our interest here, however, is to bring change across levels, via the learning cycle, into the broad framework of cognitive theory.

Five basic levels in the learning cycle can be distinguished: Prestructural, unistructural, multistructural, relational, and extended abstract. The middle three fall within the mode in question, the first and last fall outside it. Prestructural responses belong in the previous mode, indicating that learning is at too low a level of abstraction for the task in question. Extended abstract responses are, as the name suggests, at a level of abstraction that is extended into the next mode, and which become the first, or unistructural level of that next mode. Table 5.1 describes these levels in relation to a given mode, here called the "target" mode.

The focus of learning is the target mode, in which levels 2, 3, and 4 may be used *descriptively,* to refer to the point in the learning cycle that the learner has already reached, or *prescriptively,* to refer, for example for instructional purposes, to a desirable or logical end-point for a learning episode for a particular task. Examples of responses at the various SOLO levels within different modes are given for the topic of evaporation in Table 5.2.

Putting the concepts of mode and learning cycle together, we postulate that:

- Modes appear additively at particular ages.
- The unistructural, multistructural, and relational levels of the learning cycle repeat within all modes; extended abstract responses indicate a transition to the next higher mode.
- Increasing competence within any given mode leads to a particular kind of knowledge.
- Particular tasks may require the integration of several modes. The general model is given in Fig. 5.1

TABLE 5.2
The Concept of Evaporation Through Modes and Levels

Postformal	(EA)U	Developing and testing a new theory.
Formal	R	Working understanding of the discipline of physics.
	M	Other physical concepts involving principles of energy, matter.
	U(EA)	The heat energy supplied speeds praticles so that water changes state into steam. The latent heat is the amount of energy supplied.
Concrete-Symbolic	R	The heat turns the water into steam and it evaporates off, remaining invisible but in the atmosphere (15 years).
	M	The flame makes the steam come and the water goes (9 years).
	(EA)U	It soaks into the pan (7 years).
Ikonic	R	The steam causes the water to disappear (7 years old). This does not happen at our house. There's still water in the pan because my mum makes the tea with it (8 years).
	M	You put he pan on top of the flame and the water goes.
	U	The flame does it (5 years).

EA = Extended Abstract
R = Relational
M = Multistructural
U = Unistructural

Sources: Beveridge (1985)
         Collis and Biggs (1983)
         Shayer and Adey (1981)

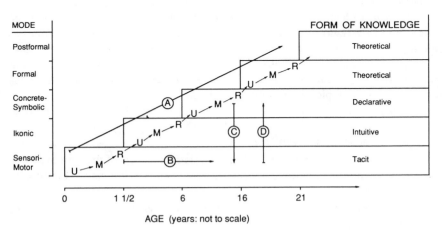

FIG. 5.1.   Modes, learning cycles and forms of knowledge (see text for explanation).

Modes typically appear at the ages indicated on the abscissa. The modes themselves accumulate as indicated on the ordinate, remaining as potential media for learning throughout life. The learning cycle progresses from unistructural (U), through multistructural (M), to relational (R) within each mode, the extension from relational to extended abstract becoming unistructural in the next mode. At the right, are the nature of the contents learned within each mode, and the form of knowledge most associated with a particular mode. The four lines, (a), (b), (c) and (d), each represents an important aspect of intelligent behavior:

(a) The course of optimal development,

(b) The course of learning within a mode (unimodal)

(c) "Top-down" facilitation of lower order learning (multimodal)

(d) "Bottom-up" facilitation of higher order learning (multimodal).

SOME QUALITIES OF INTELLIGENT BEHAVIOR

The course of optimal development.   The diagonal line (a) represents the course of development as it is usually studied by developmental psychologists. Part of the course runs within a stage, and hence indicates levels of substages, but the interest is on what happens across stages, and specifically on the maximum degree of abstraction that can be successfully handled by a group or individual at any given age, both within and across tasks. This optimal growth is slow and spontaneous, and quite probably physiologically linked.

The key here is the extended abstract transition from relational in one mode to unistructural in the next. The following factors appear to be involved:

(a) *Physical maturation.* A necessary but not sufficient condition for the development of higher order thinking is almost certainly physiological (Fischer & Bullock, 1984; Mounoud, 1985); Case (1985) in fact suggests that the mechanism may be the progressive mylenisation of the nervous system.

(b) *Relational level responding in the previous mode.* In all his work on concept development, Piaget never once reported the emergence of a new stage from the middle of the previous one. Indeed his frequent reporting of vacillatory transitional responses emphasizes how crucial immediately prior competence is. Likewise, from quite a different background, the novice-expert studies strongly imply high competence with the given before generalizing to new domains. Thus, both evidence and logic would suggest that a prerequisite to the shift into a new mode, via the extended abstract response, would be relational level responding in that same topic in the previous mode. Like the question of physiological maturation, however, this would have to be a necessary rather than a sufficient condition for a change in mode.

(c) *Availability of working memory*. Several writers have emphasized the role of working memory in development (e.g., Case, 1985, Halford, 1982). If working memory is of fixed capacity, the information to noise ratio improves with use from level to level up to multistructural, information becoming better organized from multistructural to relational. Any increase after relational, however, requires a change in the basis of organization, in other words a modal shift. This description, however, simply provides a background for (b) mentioned earlier: working memory itself does not explain why this change of base occurs, only that it occurs.

(d) *Social support*. Several writers refer to social support as a factor in hastening development (Fischer & Bullock, 1984; Vygotsky, 1978/1934). It was the latter who observed that children may at first only accomplish some tasks in collaboration with supportive adults, or with older children, but are later able to pursue those tasks unaided. The "zone of proximal development" refers to that area bridging the socially and the psychologically possible. When a child is within that zone, appropriate social support from parent or teacher may enable the child to operate at a higher level than without such support. Interaction with other people seems to hasten developmental growth, in particular in the form of "scaffolded" mental states (Fischer & Bullock, 1984).

(e) *Confrontation with a problem*. When an individual is presented with a problem that creates an "optimal" mismatch between what is known and what is needed to be known, that person becomes involved in a cognitively complex way that is motivated intrinsically (Hunt, 1961). White (1959) argues that such motivated mismatches occur at times that are significant developmentally. This is perhaps another way of saying that sufficient prior knowledge, and confrontation with a problem that requires us to use and reorganize that knowledge, are both necessary for a modal shift that permits extended abstract responding.

Change in mode thus cannot easily be ascribed to any one particular factor. After the stage has been set physiologically, further development seems to depend on the confluence of several factors, including social support, prior knowledge base and associated expertise, and confrontation with particular problems that are cognitively involving.

The course of learning within a mode.   Line (b) represents the simplest case of learning, the learning cycle that occurs from U to M to R within a mode. The original work with the SOLO Taxonomy (Biggs & Collis, 1982) described the course of such learning in particular topics within the secondary school curriculum, with reference to the concrete-symbolic mode.

The first and purest case of unimodal learning is sensorimotor learning in infancy. We have argued that ultimately this leads to tacit knowledge of sensorimotor skills, sometimes of an extremely high order of complexity, obviously beyond that of which infants responding at the relational level are capable of performing. The questions is: What lies beyond relational if we remain within the same mode? Is the response of an adult gymnast just a "better" relational response than an infant's or is it qualitatively different? We suggest later that the latter is the case: That such qualitative differences in performance, apparently homogeneous modally speaking, are not in fact unimodal, in that adults draw on higher order modes in order to augment their performance in lower order modes.

Figure 5.1 highlights an important educational issue raised here. Schooling centers on the concrete-symbolic mode, and as discussed in the introduction to this chapter, much of the content taught in school is decontextualized, abstract, impersonal, and almost by definition, not within the student's direct experience. Nevertheless, it may be seen from Fig. 5.1 that concrete-symbolic mode evolves from sensorimotor and ikonic foundations, so that any topic raised at the concrete-symbolic stage has an "ancestry" in the earlier modes. The problem with direct instruction is that it may short circuit this existing experiential hierarchy, substituting a network of concepts and propositions that are self-referential, and that coexist within the concrete-symbolic mode itself. There is a depressing amount of evidence showing that students compartmentalize their schooled knowledge from their experience. Marton and Ramsden (1988) cite examples of students who correctly describe, with detailed diagrams, what photosynthesis is, but who are unable to see the difference between how plants and animals obtain food. Gunstone and White (1981) describe several experimental demonstrations with first year physics students, showing that although they pass examinations in a post-Newtonian world, they are still living existentially in an Aristotelean one.

School learning is likely to become even more remote from real life when the language used for teaching is not the mother tongue, as in the case in many South East Asian and African countries. This is understandable in polyglot societies. Hong Kong, however, presents an interesting case of an essentially monoglot society. The mother tongue for over 95% of the population is Cantonese, where, after having been taught in Chinese throughout primary school, English becomes the official language of instruction and of examination in most subjects throughout secondary school. The great majority of students therefore use one language for encoding and expressing classroom knowledge, and the mother tongue for all forms of knowing and of experience.

When students perceive school learning as unrelated to their personal goals, for whatever reason, they tend to adopt a "surface approach" to learning (Biggs, 1987; Marton & Saljo, 1976). Learning then becomes focused on the concrete and literal aspects of the task, which are seen as discrete and unrelated to each other, and rote memorization tends to become a major strategy for learning them. The outcome of such an approach is a response that may be rich in detail, but is structurally impoverished, being in SOLO terms usually no more than multistructural (Biggs, 1979, Van Rossum & Schenk, 1984; Watkins, 1983).

Unimodal learning thus seems to provide another way of looking at such "pathologies" as surface learning, and to help understand what happens when, for linguistic or other reasons, competence in the concrete symbolic and formal modes may not be linked with their sensorimotor and ikonic precursors.

"Top-down" facilitation of lower order learning.   It is obvious that adolescents and adults do not learn sensorimotor acts in the same way as do babies. Not only are the brains and nervous systems of adults more highly developed than those of infants, adults are higher order modes to facilitate lower order learning. For example, motor skills can be considerably enhanced by mental rehearsal alone (Paivio, 1986) or by explaining the mechanics of an act at a concrete-symbolic level (Fitts, 1962). Such a mechanism is meant to be depicted by line (c) (Fig. 5.1).

Fitts, for example, postulates three stages in motor skill learning: *Cognitive* analysis of the task and verbalization of what is involved so that the learner understands what to do; *fixative,* to practice to the point of minimal error; and *autonomous,* to reach the point where the skill may be run off without error and without conscious deliberation. The first stage does not even primarily involve the target mode. The kind of knowledge aimed at here is declarative although sensorimotor, ikonic, and possibly formal, modes are also engaged. The fixative stage focuses primarily on the sensori-motor mode, and the final goal of autonomous skill involves tacit knowledge.

Activation within several modes is thus likely to enhance performance of the skill in the sensorimotor mode. There are, however, likely to be considerable differences in the extent that different individuals, with different purposes, utilize different modes in the service of skill learning. Performing artists will naturally focus on the skill itself, almost to the point of unimodality. This is perhaps most evident in Olympic gymnasts, who at their peak are somewhat younger than other athletes, and whose training is focused on performance. Other prodigious performers are more multimodal. Isadora Duncan's dancing, for example, although requiring immense sensorimotor skill also had strong ikonic aspects, and in fact it is the latter that defines her performance as a dance, rather than as callisthenics. Coaches would be more oriented towards the higher order modes, involving declarative and theoretical knowledge of physiology, nutrition, and mechanics, in order to derive better strategies for training and for performance.

It was suggested earlier that the notion of professionalism lay in the formal mode, but professional practice more accurately implies multimodality. A professional person is one whose role in the community requires informed action, i.e., skill in carrying out the role and a theory guiding its deployment. One of the most difficult features of professional training is the integration of the practicum with theory. Historically, the two roles were kept apart. The tyro lawyer was articled or apprenticed to a firm, and he (it usually was a "he") read for a law degree. In teacher education, practice teaching was one thing, the psychology of learning very much another, with the inevitable result that student teachers saw the latter as a time wasting irrelevance in their education.

Such a multistructural conception of professional training is now disappearing; problem-based learning in the professions is one increasingly popular alternative. The content learned, of a medical, paramedical, agricultural, or other degree (see Boud, 1985), is presented in context; anatomy is taught in so far as it is required for the treatment of (very carefully selected) patients, so that the content itself has a relation both to the body of knowledge of which it is part, and to a palpable problem, in which particular skills need to be developed.

Bottom-up facilitation of higher order learning. The second form of multimodal learning is where the target is a high level mode, and lower levels are invoked to achieve learning, as indicated by line (d) (Fig. 5.1). Bruner (1964a) has given this version of multimodal learning its most straightforward formulation. In tracing the developmental sequence he described as enactive-ikonic-symbolic, Bruner concluded that the most effective way of learning at the symbolic level was to retrace through enactive (or sensorimotor) and ikonic levels; to come straight in at the symbolic level was to produce a form of learning that was shallow and narrow in its range of application, in much the same way as we argued earlier concerning unimodal learning. His theory of development thus gave rise to a technique of instruction, in which enactive and ikonic involvement preceded symbolic representation. He has illustrated this with an experiment in teaching mathematics using Dienes Blocks (Bruner, 1964b) and to the concept of the "spiral curriculum" (Bruner, 1960/1977).

This form of learning has had considerable mileage in progressive education, where it is variously realized in inductive, experiential, workshop, constructivist, or discovery classroom methods, but it has been comparatively neglected in psychological theory.

Children's alternative frameworks. An interesting and important issue refers to the case when the appropriate level of development to handle the task at hand is not yet attained. This occurs when children attempt to explain phenomena with as yet inadequately developed constructs by using alternative frameworks to those used by scientists (Driver, 1983; Driver & Easley, 1978; Gilbert, Osborne, & Fensham, 1982), so that the nature and level of explanation is at odds with the official accepted frameworks taught in the science curriculum.

Alternative frameworks span several developmental stages. They comprise a rational means of constructing an explanation consistent with the child's stage of cognitive development. They should not be seen as a blind alley or as an aberration. To show how they fit the general model, let us take as an example a study by Beveridge (1985) who examined how 5-, 7-, and 9-year old children spontaneously explained the phenomenon of evaporation. A metal pan of water was heated on a gas ring until all the water had evaporated; the children were asked to explain "what had happened to the water." Our concern is with the nature of the explanations, which show shifts across mode, from ikonic to concrete symbolic, and various SOLO levels within each mode. To Beveridge's own data, we have added abbreviated examples obtained from secondary school students and constructed general statements that illustrate the higher concrete symbolic and formal levels (see Table 5.2).

The responses in the ikonic mode refer to what was perceptually evident. The unistructural response simply takes one dominant perceptual feature "the flame" and makes that the explanation, whereas the corresponding unistructural response in the concrete symbolic mode refers to a process (the wrong one, as it happens). The multistructural response at the ikonic stage describes what was done; it too omits reference to a process. The first relational response in the ikonic mode weaves the event into a nicely observed personal anecdote, but that is beside the paradigmatic point; the second seizes on the appropriate change of state, steam, but transductively ascribes causality to the result, not the cause.

Concrete symbolic responses imply a process. The unistructural one is incorrect in this context; the multistructural one actually has the essential ingredients, suggesting that steam has a part to play in the process, but falls short of specifying that part. The relational explicitly refers to a change in state.

The formal responses are of an entirely different kind. The first was given by a Year 12 student, and the content transcends the tangible; we are here dealing with theoretical constructs, physical laws, and unobservables. The multistructural example illustrates at a macro level what a multistructural conception of physics would be: this would be held by Year 12 and undergraduate students in the process of acquiring a range of knowledge in theoretical physics, before they have formed a comprehensive idea of the structure of the discipline, and thence before they are "thinking like physicists" (Bruner, 1960/77). The postformal response is again at the macro level; postformal thought questions current conventional wisdom, sees an inadequacy, develops an alternative hypothesis, and designs a study to test the new hypothesis.

Adults everyday learning. Another example of a different quality of intelligent or competent behavior is in everyday performance by adults in their jobs or avocations. Scribner (1986) studied how workers in a dairy carry out their everyday tasks. The striking thing was the irrelevance of the paradigms and declarative knowledge taught in schools. In taking inventories of stacked milk crates, the workers had memorized short cut methods of enumeration, and when a stack was not amenable to these directly, they mentally transformed array configurations so that they were: "when a large array was not a solid rectangle, but had gaps, the men mentally squared off the array by visualizing phantom stacks and counting them" (op. cit. p. 20). Numerous other examples are given of pricing delivery tickets, and other aspects of production. She found that whereas novices used school taught procedures with varying accuracy, experts used highly specific, ikonically based, techniques with near perfect accuracy.

Even more startling is the study by Ceci and Liker (1986) of compulsive racetrack gamblers. Sixteen "experts," who predicted the winning horse in 93% of races, were compared with "nonexperts," who only predicted 53% (which is still much greater than chance would predict). There were no differences between experts and nonexperts, or between the gamblers and the normal population, on IQ.

In arriving at their predictions, gamblers took account of 14 independent variables, derived from the horses' past performances, including jockey ability, racetrack conditions, lifetimes earnings of horse, and so on. The major difference between the experts and nonexperts, to cast the problem in a multiple regression algorithm, was that the latter took into account important interactions between these variables, whereas the nonexperts took account only of additive effects (but still 14 of them!). The calculations frequently took 8 hours of intensive study, but without the aid of calculating devices. In fact, it is quite unclear how these enormous "regression equations" were in fact calculated; certainly those carrying them out could not explain how they did it. Equally, none used, or knew, the appropriate statistical paradigms; paradigmatically parallel problems, with different data from those actually in their experience or knowledge, could not be solved. One can only conclude that their knowledge was derived intuitively, from the ikonic mode.

CONCLUSIONS

We return to our original question: Does the development of intelligence throw light on the different qualities of intelligent behavior? The answer undoubtedly is that it does. Traditionally, intelligent behavior has been related to school performance, in which the concrete-symbolic and formal modes are involved, but here we see that that area is only one of many manifestations of high competence. The study of development itself has been "along the diagonal" of fig. 5.1, i.e., "optimal" performance.

There are, however, many performances that are suboptimal, or involve different modes than the target mode in a given performance:

Top-down facilitation of lower order learning. The prime example is motor skill learning, but the same principles apply at all levels: in fine arts (ikonic, augmented by concrete-symbolic and formal), even declarative knowledge (concrete-symbolic, augmented by formal and postformal).

Bottom-up facilitation of higher order learning, as in constructive play, and the progressive movement generally in education, which has often produced the results, but has not had adequate back-up (formal and postformal) from psychological theory.

Children's alternative frameworks for interpreting natural phenomena. Here the quality of thinking is captured by looking at SOLO levels within modes, below the mode that the paradigms of science demand as that which provides a satisfactory explanation. The problem here is that the explanation arising out of the child's own experience is sufficiently compelling to preempt higher order explanations, even when the individual is developmentally able to handle such explanations.

Everyday displays of competence by adults. There is now an impressive amount of evidence that adults perform in highly competent ways that do not necessarily invoke the traditional concrete-symbolic, formal and postformal modes of institutionalized learning. Two examples mentioned here involved the performance of workers in a dairy and compulsive gamblers predicting horse race results. Although the mechanisms of such performance are far from clear, it is clear that such performance is irrelevant to performance in the higher modes, as are Gardner's frames of mind, which represent prodigious performance manifested in particular content areas, not in levels of abstraction.

In conclusion, then, the discussion of the quality of intelligent behavior needs to take into account the ontogenesis of behavior. Prodigious performance can be placed within a complex context, involving: (a) the structure of the behavior, (b) the levels of abstraction (or modes) in which it can be located, (c) whether these modes are one or several, and if several, which modes, (d) the content areas in which such performance is manifested. Four forms of knowledge emerge from each of the five modes: tacit, intuitive, declarative, and theoretical (formal and postformal). Within each, the learner can arrive at a level of competence that may be based in unimodal or multimodal learning.

For as long as traditional stage theory held sway, the notion that successive stages added to the repertoire of adults was not considered, although progressive educators have tacitly acknowledged the fact of multiple modality. The present model has important educational implications in the areas of curriculum, instructional method, and assessment; these are explored in Collis and Biggs (in press).

REFERENCES

Anderson, J. R. (1980). *Cognitive psychology and its implications.* San Francisco: Freeman.

Beveridge, E. (1985). The development of young children's understanding of the process of evaporation. *British Journal of Educational Psychology, 55,* 84–90.

Biggs, J. B. (1979). Individual differences in study processes and the quality of learning outcomes. *Higher Education, 8,* 381–394.

Biggs, J. B. (1987). *Student approaches to learning and studying.* Australian Council for Educational Research, Hawthorn, Vic.

Biggs, J. B., & Collis, K. F. (1982). *Evaluating the quality of learning: The SOLO Taxonomy.* New York: Academic Press.

Biggs, J. B., & Collis, K. F. (1989). Towards a model of school-based curriculum development and assessment: Using the SOLO Taxonomy. *Australian Journal of Education, 33,* 151–163.

Binet, A., & Simon, T. (1908). Le développement de l'intelligence chez les enfants. *Année Psychologique, 14,* 1–94.

Borke, H. (1978). Piaget's view of social interaction and the theoretical construct of empathy. In L. S. Siegel & C. J. Brainerd, (Eds.), *Alternatives to Piaget*. New York: Academic Press.

Boud, D. (Ed.) (1985). *Problem-based learning in education for the professions*. Sydney: Higher Education Research and Development Society of Australasia.

Bruner, J. S. (1960/77). *The process of education*. Cambridge, MA: Harvard University Press.

Bruner, J. S. (1964a). The course of cognitive growth. *American Psychologist, 19*, 1–15.

Bruner, J. S. (1964b). Some theorems on instruction illustrated with reference to mathematics. In E. R. Hilgard (Ed.), *Theories of learning and instruction*. Sixty-third Yearbook of the National Society for the Study of Education. Chicago: University of Chicago Press.

Case, R. (1985). *Cognitive development*. New York: Academic Press.

Ceci, S. J., & Liker, J. (1986). Academic and nonacademic intelligence: An experimental separation. In R. J. Sternberg & R. K. Wagner (Eds.), *Practical intelligence*. Cambridge: Cambridge University Press.

Chi, M. T. H., Glaser, R., & Rees, E. (1982). Expertise in problem solving. In R. Sternberg (Ed.), *Advances in the psychology of human intelligence*, Vol. 1). Hillsdale, NJ: Lawrence Erlbaum Associates.

Chipman, S., Segal, J., & Glaser, R. (Eds.). (1984). *Thinking and learning skills*. Hillsdale, NJ: Lawrence Erlbaum Associates.

Collis, K. F., & Biggs, J. B. (1983). Matriculation, degree requirements, and cognitive demands in universities and CAEs. *Australian Journal of Education, 27*, 41–51.

Collis, K. F., & Biggs, J. B. (in press). Developmental determinants of qualitative aspects of school learning. In G. Evans (Ed.), *Learning and teaching cognitive skills*. Hawthorn, viz.: Australian Council for Educational Research.

Commons, M. C., Richards, F. A., & Kuhn, D. (1982). Systematic and metasystematic reasoning: A case for levels of reasoning beyond Piaget's stage of formal operations. *Child Development, 53*, 1058–1069.

Demetriou, A., & Efklides, A. (1985). Structure and sequence of formal and postformal thought: General patterns and individual differences. *Child Development, 56*, 1062–1091.

Demetriou, A., & Efklides, A. (1987). Experiential structuralism and neo-Piagetian theories: Towards an integrated model. *International Journal of Psychology, 22*, 679–728.

Donaldson, M. (1978). *Children's minds*. Glasgow: Fontana.

Driver, R. (1983). *The pupil as scientist*. The Open University Press, Milton Keynes.

Driver, R., & Easley, J. (1978). Pupils and paradigms: A review of literature related to concept development in advanced science studies. *Studies in Science Education, 5*, 61–84.

Egan, K. (1984). *Educational development*. Oxford: Oxford University Press.

Erikson, E. (1959). *Identity and the life cycle*. New York: International Universities Press.

Fischer, K. (1980). A theory of cognitive development: The control and construction of hierarchies of skills. *Psychological Review, 57*, 477–531.

Fischer, K., & Bullock, D. (1984). Cognitive development in school-age children: Conclusion and new directions. In W. Collius (Ed.), *Development during middle childhood: The year from six to twelve*. Washington DC: National Academy of Sciences Press.

Fischer, K., & Pipp, S. (1984). Process of cognitive development: Optimal level and skill acquisition. In R. Sternberg (Ed.), *Mechanism of cognitive development*. New York: W. H. Freeman.

Fischer, K., & Silvern, L. (1985). Stages and individual differences in cognitive development. *Annual Review of Psychology, 36*, 613–648.

Fitts, P. (1962). Factors in complex skill training. In R. Glaser (Ed.), *Training research and education*. Pennsylvania: University of Pittsburgh Press.

Gardner, H. (1985). *Frames of mind*. London: Paladin.

Gilbert, J., Osborne, R., & Fensham, P. (1982). Children's science and its consequences for teaching. *Science Education, 68*, 623–633.

Gunstone, R., & White, R. T. (1981). Understanding of gravity. *Science Education, 65*, 291–299.

Hadamard, J. (1954). *The psychology of invention in the mathematical field*. New Jersey: Princeton University Press.

Halford, G. S. (1982). *The development of thought*. Hillsdale, NJ: Lawrence Erlbaum Associates.

Hunt, J. McV. (1961). *Intelligence and experience*. New York: Ronald.

Jung, C. G. (1956). *The integration of the personality*. London: Routledge & Kegan Paul.

Knox, A. B. (1977). *Adult development and learning*. San Francisco: Jossey Bass.

Lawrence, J., Dodds, A., & Volet, S. (1983). *An afternoon off: A comparative study of adults' and adolescents' planning activities*. Paper presented to Annual Conference, Australian Association for Research in Education, Canberra.

Levinson, D., Darrow, C., Klein, E., Levinson, H., & McKee, B. (1978). *The seasons of a man's life*. New York: Knopf.

Marton, F., & Ramsden, P. (1988). What does it take to improve learning? In P. Ramsden (Ed.), *Improving learning: New perspectives*. London: Kogan Page.

Marton, F., & Saljo, R. (1976). On qualitative differences in learning—I: outcome and process. *British Journal of Educational Psychology, 46,* 4–11.

Meadows, S. (1983). Piaget's theory of cognitive development. In S. Meadows (Ed.), *Developing thinking*. London: Methuen.

Mounoud, P. (1986). Similarities between developmental sequences at different age periods. In I. Levin (Ed.), *Stage and structure*. Norwood, NJ: Ablex.

Paivio, A. (1986). *Mental representations: A dual coding approach*. New York: Oxford University Press.

Piaget, J. (1950). *The psychology of intelligence*. London: Routledge & Kegan Paul.

Resnick, L. B. (1987). Learning in school and out. *Educational Researcher, 16,* 13–20.

Schaie, K. W. (1979). The primary mental abilities in adulthood: An exploration in the development of psychometric intelligence. In P. Baltes & O. Brim (Eds.), *Life span development and behavior*. New York: Academic Press.

Scribner, S. (1986). Thinking in action: Some characteristics of practical thought. In R. J. Sternberg & R. K. Wagner (Eds.), *Practical intelligence*. Cambridge: Cambridge University Press.

Shayer, M., & Adey, P. (1981). *Toward a science of science teaching*. London: Heinemann Educational.

Sternberg, R. J., & R. K. Wagner (Eds.). (1986). *Practical intelligence,* Cambridge: Cambridge University Press.

Tyler, L. E. (1978). *Individuality*. San Francisco: Jossey Bass.

Van Rossum, E. J., & Schenk, S. M. (1984). The relationship between learning conception, study strategy and learning outcome. *British Journal of Educational Psychology, 54,* 73–83.

Vygotsky, L. (1978/1934). *Mind and society*. Cambridge, MA: Harvard University Press.

Wagner, R. K., & Sternberg, R. J. (1986). Tacit knowledge and intelligence in the world. In R. J. Sternberg and R. K. Wagner (Eds.), *Practical intelligence*. Cambridge: Cambridge University Press.

Watkins, D. A. (1983). Depth of processing and the quality of learning outcomes. *Instructional Science, 12,* 49–58.

White, R. W. (1959). Motivation reconsidered: The concept of competence. *Psychological Review, 66,* 297–333.

6 Cognitive Developmental Perspectives on Intelligence[1]

Susan R. Goldman
James W. Pellegrino
Vanderbilt University

The construct intelligence has occupied a key position in psychology and in education from the very beginning of those fields. For almost as long, there has been disagreement and sometimes controversy over the definition of intelligence. With the exception of E. G. Boring's (1923) operational definition of intelligence, namely that intelligence is what the tests test, no other single definition has emerged in the field, despite the existence of at least two major symposia designed to yield consensual definition. What emerged from those symposia, held 65 years apart in 1921 and 1986, were lists of attributes of intelligence (Sternberg & Detterman, 1986). Table 6.1 is a synthesis of the attributes generated at both points in time (Sternberg & Berg, 1986). In general, theorists in 1986 preferred a multidimensional, non-factorial view emphasizing general and specific knowledge and cognitive processes that are used within practical as well as academic venues (see Pellegrino & Goldman, 1990). Further examination of the two lists shows precious little in the way of consensual agreement about even the top ranked attribute, higher level processes: At the 1986 symposium, only 50% of the participants mentioned this attribute, down from 57% in 1921. The 1986 list included several attributes not included in the 1921 list, including *what is valued by culture, process knowledge interaction,* and *automated performance.* Executive processes and metacognition were included more frequently in 1986 than in 1921; ability to learn and adaptation to the environment were listed somewhat less frequently in 1986 than in 1921.

[1]The research reported in this chapter was supported by grant #G0083-002860 from the Office of Special Education and Rehabilitation Services, US Department of Education, to Project TEECh, Special Education Research Laboratory, University of California, Santa Barbara.

77

TABLE 6.1
Attributes of Intelligence Mentioned in 1921 and 1986 Symposia[a]

	% Mentioned	
	---	---
	1986	1921
Higher level processes	50	57
What is valued by culture	29	0
Executive processes	25	7
Elementary processes	21	21
Knowledge	21	7
Effective/successful responses	21	21
Metacognition	17	7
Process - knowledge interaction	17	0
Ability to learn	17	29
Discrete abilities	17	7
g	17	14
Not easily defined, not one construct	17	14
Adaptation to environment	13	29
Speed of processing	13	14
Automated performance	13	0
Capacities prewired at birth	13	7
Physiological mechanisms	8	29
Real world manifestations	8	0
Restricted to academic/cognitive abilities	8	14

[a] Reprinted from Pellegrino and Goldman (1990).

The changes in theorists' conceptions of the attributes of intelligence clearly show the impact of several theoretical trends including contemporary cognitive developmental perspectives on intellectual functioning. In the late 20th century we are most strongly experiencing the impact of two cognitive developmental perspectives. The first perspective reflects the confluence of (a) Piagetian notions regarding the organization of knowledge and operative structures for thinking and (b) information processing theories of human cognition. We refer to this perspective as a *cognitive information processing perspective* on development. The second perspective reflects the influence of Soviet psychology and stresses the notion that intellectual functioning and its development are mediated through social interactions (Vygotsky, 1978). We adopt Cole's terminology in referring to this perspective as a *sociocultural framework* on development (Cole, 1985). Our goal in this paper is to illustrate how these cognitive developmental perspectives can enhance the understanding of intelligence by focusing on critical issues associated with the development of intellectual competence. A useful byproduct of such an emphasis is the related interest in the conditions that foster the acquisition of such competence, an emphasis that leads to a prescriptive rather than simply descriptive focus on intellectual assessment.

PERSPECTIVES ON COGNITIVE DEVELOPMENT

Both the cognitive information processing perspective and the sociocultural perspective reject the view that intelligence is relatively stable and inert, an assumption underlying traditional mental testing, particularly the use of intelligence tests for predictive purposes. Rather, the two cognitive developmental perspectives share the view that intelligence is malleable. As we have indicated previously (Pellegrino & Goldman, 1985) the assumption that intelligence can change shifts the focal issues away from the psychometric properties of intelligence tests and conditions that affect performance on those tests. Rather, issues associated with the ability to learn and the conditions that optimize learning take on central importance. Critical to efforts to examine the ability to learn are determinations of the entry level skills of the learner and the development of diagnostic rather than predictive tests. Thus, both the sociocultural and the cognitive information processing perspectives on development lead to the rejection of assessments of intellectual functioning that deal only with the products of learning but do not address issues of teachability and potentially effective intervention techniques.

In place of such "static" assessment, there has been renewed interest in dynamic assessment of intellectual skills and intervention efforts that might provide information regarding individuals' learning potential and responsiveness to instruction (e.g., Brown & Ferrara, 1985; Campione & Brown, 1988, 1990; Feuerstein, Rand, Jensen, Kaniel, & Tzuriel, 1988; Ferrara, 1987a,b; Vye, Burns, Delclos, & Bransford, 1988). As Lidz (1988) has cogently pointed out, measuring intelligence as the *ability to learn* or as *the ability to benefit from practice* is not a novel interpretation of intelligence, having been popular in the 1920s.

With respect to understanding development and mechanisms of developmental change in intellectual functioning, the cognitive information processing and sociocultural perspectives generate somewhat different empirical emphases. The cognitive information processing perspective emphasizes detailed analyses of the macro and microstructure of cognition as manifest in specific tasks and content. The tasks and content include those found on tests of intelligence and academic achievement as well as in the classroom. The specific concerns are how knowledge is represented and processed and the changes in knowledge and processing associated with the acquisition of competence. This can be traced out longitudinally within individuals or cross sectionally across individuals varying in age and/or expertise.

According to the sociocultural perspective, interactions between people are the principal mechanism by which learning and development occur. The intellectual skills that children acquire are considered to be directly related to how they interact with adults and peers in specific problem solving environments. Children internalize the kind of help they receive from others more capable and eventually come to use the means of guidance initially provided by another to direct their own subsequent problem solving behaviors. There is thus an explicit and direct connection between interpersonal and intrapersonal psychological processes (e.g., Bruner, 1985; Vygotsky, 1981). Because the *process* of learning and the child's participation in that process are focal, emphasis is placed on assessment methods that estimate the child's ability to benefit from instruction. Individual differences in intellectual levels may be described in terms of task-specific variation in this ability. Assessment simultaneously provides an indication of the child's current level of functioning and a prescription for intervention activities that are likely to bring about change in that level of functioning.

Despite the somewhat different empirical emphases of the cognitive information processing and the sociocultural perspectives, both view peer interactions as important to intellectual development. From the cognitive information processing perspective, peer interactions are a primary way that individuals encounter information that challenges their views of the world. The resulting cognitive conflict leads to modification of their knowledge system (Piaget, 1970). Vygotsky (1978) viewed interaction with others as important not only because of the scaffolding provided by a more competent peer. He proposed that when individuals verbally express developing concepts, they must be broken down into more clearly conceptualized units; thus, the process of verbalizing becomes a stimulus for development. The mere presence of someone as an observer or listener could be educationally valuable.

EMPIRICAL OBSERVATIONS

In the remainder of this chapter, we discuss two research projects on the assessment and development of intellectual competence. Both focus on learning disabled students who, according to standard assessment tests, don't function very well intellectually. In the first research project, derived from a cognitive information processing perspective, we examine two issues. The first is the strategies used by learning handicapped students in solving basic addition facts. The second is how practice affects strategy acquisition and use. Individual differences in strategy use and strategy acquisition are shown to be independent of conventional measures of intelligence and achievement. In contrast, such individual differences are readily accommodated by developmental theories and data on the normal acquisition of competence in the domain of basic mathematics.

In a second project, we have examined cognitive and social characteristics of collaborative writing by learning handicapped students (Goldman, Cosden, & Hine, 1988). This work demonstrates the importance of group composition to learning processes and outcomes in two ways. First, changes in intellectual functioning resulting from peer interactions are more closely tied to the task-specific competence levels of the participants than to more general and conventional measures of intellectual ability or academic intelligence. Second, the interaction situation requires social and practical intelligence that adds an additional dimension of complexity to the learning process. Adequate social skills for collaborating may themselves need to be modeled for peer interactions to have the intended beneficial effects on intellectual development.

PRACTICE AND ADDITION FACT PERFORMANCE

The theoretical perspective of our work investigating handicapped students' strategies for solving basic addition facts involves several assumptions common to cognitive information processing accounts of learning and to theories of mathematics skill development. Critical to successful mathematical problem solving and computation is a readily accessible knowledge base of the basic number facts (e.g., Pressley, 1986; Suydam & Dessart, 1980). Practice is a primary way that basic facts become readily accessible (e.g., Ashlock & Washbon, 1978; Davis, 1978). Information processing explanations of why a readily accessible knowledge base is important and of why practice is important to its development are related to general theories of cognitive skill acquisition (e.g., Anderson, 1982; van Parreren, 1978). Cognitive skill acquisition theories explain the importance of a readily accessible knowledge base in terms of attentional resource constraints on the human's limited capacity processing system. In such a system, specific skills need to reach a level of proficiency where skill execution is rapid and accurate and requires little conscious attention. This state comes about through extended practice. As fewer demands are made on the limited attentional resource pool, attentional resources can be allocated away from the specific skill to other tasks and/or processes such as those required in advanced mathematics (for further discussion see Goldman & Pellegrino, 1987).

From cognitive information processing accounts of the development of addition fact skill in normally achieving children (Ashcraft, 1987; Siegler, 1987) and in learning disabled children (e.g., Goldman, Pellegrino, & Mertz, 1988), it has become clear that children use a variety of strategies to solve these problems. The different strategies are differentially efficient. Siegler (1987; Siegler & Shrager, 1984) has related strategy choice to the contents and patterns of associations among problem addends and their solutions. The stronger the association between the addends and the correct response, the more likely it is that the child will directly retrieve the answer to the problem. If no response exceeds the child's criterion for responding, an alternative strategy, usually counting, will be tried. The strength of the association is determined by frequency of exposure to and production of the various candidate answers.

The model assumes that over time, the strongest association will be that between the problem and the correct answer. Thus, the frequency of occurrence of an item in a student's personal history becomes an important factor in the strategy choice model. As we have argued elsewhere, if practice does nothing else, it increases the frequency of occurrence for the practiced items. Thus, the strategy choice model assigns an important role to practicing the basic facts. However, the strategy choice model also implies that incorrect responding has a distinctly negative impact on learning because the associative strength between that incorrect answer and the problem is increased (Goldman et al., 1988).

Given that there exist developmental theory and data on the normal acquisition of competence for basic mathematical facts, it is essential to show its applicability to individuals of varying intellectual abilities, as conventionally defined. In the present context we are concerned with demonstrating three things with respect to issues of individual differences among learning disabled children with similar demographic profiles. First, theories of knowledge and performance derived for "normal" children are applicable to children who are psychometrically characterized as "abnormal". Second, conventional measures of intellectual skill bear no relationship to the individual differences observed among such children. Third, significant learning occurs for such children as a result of practice and, furthermore, the learning is consistent with models of the normal development of competence.

Table 6.2 shows the general characteristics of nine learning disabled children whom we studied at a particular school site. The site was one of several different sites where we studied the effects of practice on the performance of both normal and learning handicapped children. The nine students represented in Table 6.2 were enrolled in an elementary level (Years 1–4) special day class in one school in Southern California. The students had a mean age of 8 years 3 months with a range from 6 years 7 months to 10 years 6 months. The aptitude data reflected the generally lower level of students placed in special day classes in comparison with those who are mainstreamed. The average WISC-R Verbal IQ was 79 with a range of 70–87. The average WISC-R Performance IQ was 91 with a range of 78–108. The average mathematics percentile level on the Peabody Individual

TABLE 6.2
Characteristics of the Students Participating in the Addition Practice

Student	Age	WISCR Verbal	WISCR Performance	PIAT Math Achievement	Number of Sessions
1	6,11	77	88	58	28
2	8,0	81	97	70	31
3	7,8	76	97	58	23
4	8,11	87	95	57	26
5	9,9	83	78	41	31
6	8,4	83	108	69	29
7	7,6	73	92	61	32
8	6,7	80	90	22	30
9	10,6	70	78	43	33

Achievement Test (PIAT) was 53 with a range of 22–70. These students worked each day in a mobile van and were supervised by a member of the research team. The microcomputer practice was, in effect, a pull-out program for these special day class students. The program operated five days per week for eight weeks and students participated in anywhere from 23 to 33 individual sessions of practice (Mean = 29).

We administered a pretest that consisted of the presentation of 44 basic addition facts, to which the students responded orally and another 44 that they responded to by typing their responses at a keyboard. Problems were presented on a microcomputer screen. At the conclusion of the eight week duration of the practice intervention, these tests were readministered. Accuracy on the oral pretest ranged from 42% to 97%, Mean = 86%, although eight of the nine students were correct on 86% or more of the problems. There was a general effect of practice in that each student's accuracy score improved: at posttest, six students were 100% accurate, and the remaining three scored between 89 and 95% correct. What was quite variable, however, were the response latencies and the strategies that the students were using to answer the problems.

Figure 6.1 is a plot of the median response latencies for each of the students on the oral pretest. Two groups of students can be reliably differentiated from one another. One group has a mean accuracy level of 90% and a median latency of 3.77 seconds. In previous work, we identified a group of mainstreamed learning disabled students who performed at this level (Group C in Goldman et al., 1988). In contrast, the other group consisted of four students whose accuracy level was 9 percent lower and whose response times are extremely slow—11.42 seconds.

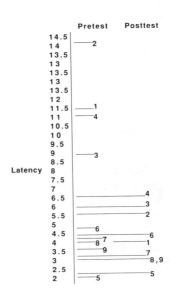

FIG. 6.1. Distribution of individual student's oral pretest and posttest median response latencies (correctly answered problems only) for basic addition facts.

Referring back to Table 6.2, the students in the "Fast" group, students 5, 6, 7, 8, and 9, have IQ and achievement test scores (and ages) that are indistinguishable from those in the "Slow" group.

In addition to differences in the median latency, we used the distributions of individual items across 1 second latency classes to determine the strategies that students were using to answer the problems. (A full explanation of how item distributions are used to determine strategy use is provided in Goldman et al., 1988; and in Goldman, Mertz, & Pellegrino, 1989). Strategies that are typically used to solve basic addition facts are of two types: direct retrieval and counting. Direct retrieval involves "answering from memory." There are several types of counting strategies that differ in terms of which addends the child actually enumerates. The Sum strategy involves the child counting out each of the addends and the answer is the total number (or sum) that results. Another counting strategy involves fewer enumerations than the Sum strategy and is thus thought to be more efficient: the child starts with the larger addend and counts on the number indicated by the smaller addend. This strategy is called the Minimum Addend (Min) strategy.

The strategy analyses of the individual item distributions revealed that the fast and the slow groups were using different mixtures of strategies to answer the basic addition facts. In fact, within the "Fast" group, one of the students (Student 5) proved to be different from the other four. This student had a median response latency that was 1.5 seconds faster than the latencies of the other four students, a time comparable to the more advanced mainstreamed learning disabled students that we have tested (Goldman et al., 1988). Student 5's item distribution is shown in Fig. 6.2 and indicates use of the Min strategy, with 40% of the problems responded to in under 2 seconds. These were problems with minimum addends of 1, 2, and 3. In the 2 to 3 seconds latency class were problems with minimum addends of 3, 4, and 5. Problems with minimum addends of 4 and 5 were answered in 3 to 4 seconds and those with mins of 6, 7, and 8 in the 4 to 6 seconds range. The tie problems with larger addends (e.g., 6+6 and 8+8) also had latencies in the 4 to 6 seconds range, a fact that provides further support for Student 5's consistent use of the Min strategy. The effects of practice for this student were negligible: the item distribution continued to reflect Min counting, although there was a somewhat greater concentration of problems in the 2 to 3 second range than had been the case at pretest (Fig. 6.2b).

The other four students in the "Fast" group had performance characteristics that were more similar to one another, with the median latency ranging from 3.74 to 4.68, Mean 4.16 seconds. The shape of the item latency distribution at pretest (Fig. 6.3a) is relatively normal and the mode is in the 4 to 5 seconds interval, indicative of Sum counting. In addition to the prevalent use of Sum counting for most of the problems, the ordering of the problems having minimum addends of 1 and of a number of the ties (e.g., 4+4, 3+3, 2+2, 6+6 and 9+9) indicates some use of Minimum counting and, perhaps, direct retrieval of the tie problems.

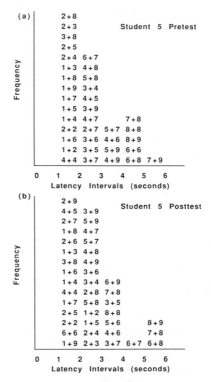

FIG. 6.2. Distribution of correctly answered items over response latency classes for student 5 on the (a) pretest, and (b) posttest. On the pretest items 2+6, 5+6, 6+9, and 2+9 are missing values.

The posttest distribution, shown in panel b of Fig. 6.3, indicates a decided downward shift, reflected by a mode in the 2 to 3 second interval and a median of 3.53 seconds. The posttest distribution clearly reflects a more prevalent use of Minimum counting, particularly for problems with minimum addends of 1, 2, and 3. Over the course of the practice, these students appear to have shifted to a greater use of a more efficient strategy.

The greatest benefit of practice was on the performance of the four students in the Slow group. The oral pretest item distribution for the students in this group (Fig. 6.4a) indicates highly variable and relatively idiosyncratic response strategies. The distribution is relatively flat and has a range in excess of 20 seconds. Practice substantially improved the performance of students in this group, as the posttest median latency of 5.54 seconds indicates. Their individual median response latencies at posttest were much closer to those of the "Fast" group (refer to Fig. 6.1). The change is evident as well in the more systematic item distribution (panel b of Fig. 6.4). These students now appear to be using Minimum counting for problems with minimum addends of 1, 2, and 3 if the sum is 10 or less; and Sum counting for the remaining problems.

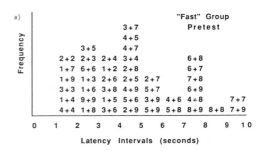

```
a)                                              "Fast" Group
                                  3+7             Pretest
     >                            4+5
     u                  3+5       4+7
     c      2+2 2+3 2+4 3+4             6+8
     e      1+7 6+6 1+2 2+8             6+7
     q      1+9 1+3 2+6 2+5 2+7        7+8
     e      3+3 1+6 3+8 4+9 5+7        6+9
     r      1+4 9+9 1+5 5+6 3+9 4+6 4+8        7+7
     F      4+4 1+8 3+6 2+9 5+9 5+8 8+9 8+8 7+9

            0   1   2   3   4   5   6   7   8   9   10

                    Latency Intervals (seconds)
```

```
b)                      2+8
                        5+5               "Fast" Group
                        2+7 4+8            Posttest
                        2+6 2+9
     >          1+5 1+9 4+9
     c          1+3 3+6 3+7       9+9
     e          1+8 3+4 3+9       5+9
     q          1+6 3+3 5+7       4+7
     e          1+4 3+8 7+7 7+9 5+6
     r          2+3 1+7 4+5 5+8 8+8
     F          1+2 4+4 2+4 3+5 6+7       8+9
                2+2 6+6 2+5 4+6 6+9 6+8 7+8

            0   1   2   3   4   5   6   7   8

                    Latency Intervals (seconds)
```

FIG. 6.3. Distribution of correctly answered items over response latency classes for the "Fast" group on the (a) pretest, and (b) posttest. On the pretest, 5+5 is a missing value.

Our data on strategy use and strategy change following practice are not unique to this sample of children. Rather, similar patterns of performance have been observed with various subgroups of normal and learning handicapped children at various school sites. Of greater significance is the fact that cognitive developmental theories of the acquisition of competence in this domain subsume almost all of the various patterns we have observed. The demographic characteristics provided in Table 6.2 are in no way helpful in predicting the differences that we have observed among these nine children: differences in response latency at the pretest, in the strategies used to solve the problems and in the effects of practice. In short, differences in the specific knowledge of basic math facts were not related to static measures of intelligence or mathematics achievement. Furthermore, and consistent with the results of practice studies done some 30 years ago (as reviewed by Lidz, 1988), the benefits of practice were greatest for those students whose initial performance was the poorest. Moreover, learning disabled children demonstrated substantial learning consistent with normal developmental progress. We can only speculate at this point about the causes of their developmental delay.

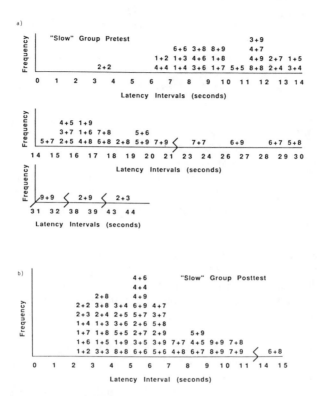

FIG. 6.4. Distribution of correctly answered items over response latency classes for the "Slow" group on the (a) pretest, and (b) posttest. On the pretest, 2+6, 3+3, and 3+5 are missing values.

COLLABORATIVE WRITING

The sociocultural perspective on cognitive development (Vygotsky, 1978) has given rise to a functional interactive approach to writing. Stress is placed on the interpersonal aspects of writing and the importance of writing for a specific purpose and audience. Writing is an example of a specific task context, in which what children learn about writing may be directly related to how they interact with adults and peers. This perspective thus emphasizes the nature of the intellectual environment created by the teacher and/or the student's peers (e.g., Goldman & Rueda, 1988). The purpose of considering our work on collaborative writing in the context of this chapter is to examine how the cognitive outcomes of peer interactions are related to the social intelligence of the children involved as well as to their cognitive skill levels.

Collaborative writing groups have been shown to be a mechanism for improving the writing skills of students. For example, Dickinson (1986) conducted an ethnographic study of a combined first and second grade classroom's writing program into which a computer was introduced. He found that the computer increased the amount of peer collaboration in the classroom. The nature of the peer collaborations led to children becoming more aware of what they knew implicitly about writing. Furthermore, peers provided instruction and feedback as soon as problems arose and there was more focus on meaning and style than when children worked individually (handwritten compositions). Dickinson attributed the facilitated emphasis on meaning and style to the fact that the two children could share responsibilities, one doing the generation and one doing the editing.

In the case of learning handicapped students, we were interested in examining whether collaborative interactions on a writing task would indeed lead to improvements in the writing performance of the individual students. What we illustrate in the present context is a rather simple point, yet one that is often ignored: Whether there were benefits of working together depended on the skill levels of the individuals involved in the interaction, specifically on their individual verbal fluency levels, and on the nature of the social interactions that took place between the children. We illustrate this for various measures of the quality of the written products and discuss the nature of the social interactions that gave rise to the written products. (Complete descriptions of this research can be found in Cosden, Goldman, and Hine (in press), Goldman et al., (1988), and Hine, Goldman, and Cosden (1990).

Briefly, the procedure we used was to have students write a series of stories, entering their text directly into the computer, either working by themselves or in pairs. The students WISC-R scores were similar to those of the students who participated in the mathematics study but in the writing study, students were about two years older, on average, and were in grades Three, Four and Five. The written products were described in terms of five measures of verbal fluency and story quality.

Table 6.3 shows the results for five measures of verbal fluency. First versus final draft refers to the written product after an initial writing attempt (first) and after the student or the dyad had had a chance to revise and edit the story (final). The results across the five measures were relatively consistent: Final versions of the stories contained more words, more unique words, more propositions, more predicate propositions and were more structurally complex than the first drafts. There were no differences between single and dyad conditions in these analyses. Only on the story structure measure was there an interaction of grouping and draft ($F(1,10) = 14.33, p < .01$). There was a greater degree of improvement in the quality of the story structure from first to final version in the dyad condition (3.20 compared to 3.96) than in the single condition (3.27 compared to 3.55).

Although the statistical analyses indicated few significant differences in these

TABLE 6.3
Means and Analysis of Variance Results for the Five Measures of Fluency of the Written Products

	First Draft	Final Draft	$F(1, 10)$	p
Word tokens	34.07	51.68	36.19	<.001
Word types	22.70	32.05	29.48	< .001
Propositions	13.91	21.63	49.59	< .001
Predicates	6.21	9.54	53.45	< .001
Story structure	3.24	3.76	24.75	< .01

fluency measures as a function of whether students worked together or alone, our observations during the work sessions suggested that there were substantial differences between dyads and between students within dyads in terms of group interactions and productivity. To examine this, we classified the 11 students into high, low and medium fluency based on their writing when they worked by themselves. The distribution of students across dyads produced three dyads, in which high fluency students worked with low fluency students, three dyads in which high fluency students worked with medium fluency students and one dyad in which a medium fluency student worked with a low fluency student. There were two dyads where low fluency students worked together and one where medium fluency students were paired. We then examined the written products of each of the dyads and compared these to the written products produced by the members of the dyad when they worked alone.

Figure 6.5 shows the percent change in performance on the number of propositions in the stories. The change is plotted against the performance level of the low fluency member of the dyad. Figure 6.6 shows the percent change in this measure plotted against the performance level of the high fluency member of the dyad. The difference in these two figures tells the story: Relative to the performance of the lower fluency students the written product was better when they worked with a more competent peer than when they worked alone. The performance of the more competent peers, was, however, negatively affected by working with a less fluent partner. Note that for the homogeneous dyads, there was little change from performance in the single condition.

The social interactions of the dyads provided insight into these outcomes. In the dyads where the less fluent student benefitted but the more fluent did not, there were several interaction patterns. In one instance, the more fluent student took major responsibility for the group effort and produced less here than when alone because he solicited input from the less fluent student. The less fluent student, however, was relatively unresponsive and appeared to have little to contribute. In two other instances, both members of the dyad were concerned about the written production; even though performance skills were disparate, the needs of both students to be an active part of the joint project were accommo-

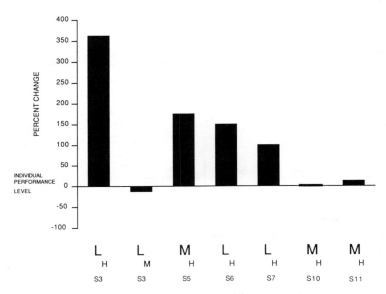

FIG. 6.5. Percent change in performance on the number of propositions included in the stories, relative to the individual performance of the low fluency students.

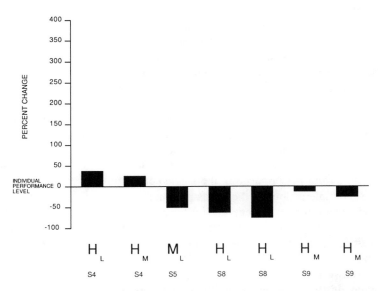

FIG. 6.6. Percent change in performance on the number of propositions included in the stories, relative to the individual performance of the high fluency students.

dated by discussions about what to include and how to say it. This resulted in less actual written text being generated by the dyads. Finally, in two dyads, the interactions were marked with extensive conflicts. In one case both students wanted to participate in the project, but were antagonistic toward each other and spent considerable time fighting and not working. In the other instance, the less fluent child was willing to do little, but the more fluent child wanted him to participate. However, when the less fluent student did offer his help and ideas, the more fluent belittled his imperfect performance.

There was one high fluency student who had more elaborate dyad than individual products in both dyads that he participated in. The interaction patterns differed in the two cases. In one case, the less fluent partner did not want to participate, and this was acceptable to the more fluent student. The more fluent student merely used the less fluent student as an audience for his work. It is interesting to note that the less fluent student still felt that the writing sample was a group product. In the second instance, the two students took turns working, much like parallel play. Although this also resulted in a more elaborate group product than was created by either of the students alone, the *collaborative* process left much to be desired; that is, the students paid little attention to each other and made independent but cumulative contributions to the product.

To summarize the interactions that occurred in the dyads, from the perspective of the individuals and the dyads that they worked in, the effects of collaborating on the writing task were mixed. Whether the final written product was superior to that produced when an individual student worked alone depended on the student's individual fluency level and on the nature of the interaction that occurred in the particular dyad. In general, students whose individual fluency levels were low, relative to the group, benefitted from writing with a higher fluency partner; and at the same time, the fluency levels of the stories produced in these dyads were below the level of the higher fluency students' individual stories.

Our analysis of the interactions in these dyads indicated two major patterns associated with this product relationship: Either the members of the dyad, particularly the more fluent, sought the input of the less fluent students, or the pair engaged in antagonistic behavior, arguing about who would compose the text and whose ideas to include in the story (see for examples Goldman & Rueda, 1988). The interaction process, whether collaborative or argumentative, actually took time away from the actual composing task. As Heap (1987) noted, children engaged in collaborative writing have to worry about a variety of social interpersonal issues over and above the best way to write: They have to worry about whether their rights are being respected and whether the other person's rights are being respected.

From a cognitive processing perspective, it is clear that the demands of the interaction situation may create enough overload on an already taxed system that the collaboration does not yield apparent benefits. However, it must be borne in mind that the less fluent students in the dyads could claim ownership of a written product that was superior to any they produced on their own. In fact, one student who contributed absolutely nothing to one of the stories sat back in his chair at the end of the session and said, "That's the best story I ever wrote."

The learning outcomes and the interactions in the dyads are telling with respect to the value of peer collaboration in bringing about changes in levels of intellectual functioning. Not only must attention be paid to the cognitive skill levels of the participants in the group, but the social dynamics are critical to the outcomes of the interactions. Children who possess high degrees of social intelligence—a construct perhaps as elusive as academic intelligence—will readily exploit the interaction context. Sometimes, as in the cases of the dyads where the more fluent students attempted to solicit input and involve the less fluent in the writing task, the social dynamics may lead to increased participation and competence for the "lower" member of the dyad. However, we also observed a high number of socially intelligent behaviors that derailed the writing process per se by changing the dyad agenda from the "academic" writing task to a social agenda, the goal of which seemed to be to avoid the writing task and engage in "play" behaviors. In still other cases, we observed some highly competent social intelligence at work: Some students knew exactly what to do to get their partner to do all the work.

COGNITIVE DEVELOPMENT AND INTELLIGENCE

We have presented two examples of ways that cognitive developmental perspectives on intellectual change highlight various attributes of intelligence and suggest useful instructional interventions. In particular, we have illustrated that static, general measures of intelligence and achievement do not predict who will benefit from repeated practice. Rather, the changes that occurred as a result of the practice were changes that are predicted by cognitive information processing accounts of the acquisition of skill in the specific domain of addition. Brown and Ferrara (1985) have suggested that one benefit of dynamic as opposed to static assessments of intellect is that dynamic measures permit one to distinguish between those individuals who are handicapped in their learning and those who are more severely retarded. The students in our addition fact practice study were indeed able to benefit from the repeated presentations of the basic facts. At the same time, the practice did not make them comparable to same aged nonhandicapped peers. Thus, the results of the practice study suggest that their intellectual functioning in this area of mathematics is malleable but the etiology of their need for instruction that differs from nonhandicapped students is unclear. It remains to be determined whether these individuals reach some plateau beyond which no amount of practice would increase the efficiency with which they access their knowledge or whether with additional interventions of the sort we have presented here these learning handicapped students would continue to close the gap and approach the access speeds of nonhandicapped peers.

Our work on collaborative writing groups illustrates a second important dimension of cognitive developmental perspectives on intelligence. The impact of interacting with others on an individual's intellectual functioning is very much a function of the skill levels of the interactants. These skill levels relate to social skills as well as to academic skills. Benefits derived from interactions need to be conceptualized in terms of increased knowledge of how to negotiate the learning process and the social interaction process. Cognitive-academic competence and social competence were not vested to the same degree in the various students we observed. For some, an inability to negotiate the social, interpersonal dynamics of an interaction will disrupt the learning process.

The addition practice and the collaborative writing study both illustrate an important change in focus that cognitive developmental perspectives bring to considerations of intelligence. In both instances we have examined instructional interventions that are theoretically predicted to foster intellectual change. Our work permits us to not only describe intellectual change but to pursue conditions that foster change and better understand some constraints on the malleability of intellectual functioning.

REFERENCES

Anderson, J. R. (1982). Acquisition of cognitive skill. *Psychological Review, 89,* 369–406.

Ashcraft, M. H. (1987). Children's knowledge of simple arithmetic: A developmental model and simulation. In J. Bisanz, C. Brainerd, & R. Kail (Eds.), *Formal methods in developmental psychology* (pp. 302–338). New York: Springer Verlag.

Ashlock, R. B., & Washbon, C. A. (1978). Games: Practice activities for basic facts. In M. N. Suydam & R. E. Reys (Eds.), *Developing computational skills* (pp. 39–50). Reston, VA: National Council of Teachers of Mathematics.

Boring, E. G. (1923). Intelligence as the tests test it. *New Republic,* June, pp. 35–37.

Brown, A. L., & Ferrara, R. A., (1985). Diagnosing zones of proximal development. In J. V. Wertsch (Ed.), *Culture, communication, and cognition: Vygotskian perspectives* (pp. 273–305). New York: Cambridge University Press.

Bruner, J. (1985). Vygotsky: A historical and conceptual perspective. In J. V. Wertsch (Ed.), *Culture, communication, and cognition: Vygotskian perspectives* (pp. 21–34). New York: Cambridge University Press.

Campione, J. C., & Brown, A. L. (1990). Guided learning and transfer: Implications for approaches to assessment. In N. Frederiksen, R. Glaser, A. Lesgold, & M. Shatto (Eds.), *Diagnostic monitoring of skill acquisition* (pp. 141–172). Hillsdale, NJ: Lawrence Erlbaum Associates.

Campione, J. C., & Brown, A. L. (1988). Linking dynamic assessment with school achievement. In C. S. Lidz (Ed.), *Dynamic assessment: An international approach to evaluating learning potential* (pp. 82–115). New York: Guilford Press.

Cole, M. (1985). The zone of proximal development: Where culture and cognition create each other. In J. V. Wertsch (Ed.), *Culture, communication, and cognition: Vygotskian perspectives* (pp. 146–161). New York: Cambridge University Press.

Cosden, M. A., Goldman, S. R., & Hine, M. S. (in press). Learning handicapped students' interactions during a microcomputer-based group writing activity. *Journal of Special Education Technology.*

Davis, E. J. (1978). Suggestions for teaching the basic facts of arithmetic. In M. N. Suydam & R. E. Reys (Eds.), *Developing computational skills* (pp. 51–60). Reston, VA: National Council of Teachers of Mathematics.

Dickinson, D. K. (1986). Cooperation, collaboration, and a computer: Integrating a computer into a first-second grade writing program. *Research in the Teaching of English, 20,* 357–379.

Ferrara, R. A. (1987a, April). *Dynamic assessment of responsiveness to beginning mathematics instruction: Determinants of the zone of proximal development.* Poster presented at the American Educational Research Association meeting. Washington, D.C.

Ferrara, R. A. (1987b). *Learning mathematics in the zone of proximal development: The importance of flexible use of knowledge.* Doctoral dissertation. Department of Psychology, University of Illinois at Urbana-Champaign.

Feuerstein, R., Rand, Y., Jensen, M. R., Kaniel, S., & Tzuriel, D. (1988). Prerequisites for assessment of learning potential: The LPAD model. In C. S. Lidz (Ed.), *Dynamic Assessment: An interactional approach to evaluating learning potential* (pp. 35–51). New York: Guilford Press.

Goldman, S. R., Cosden, M. A., & Hine, M. S. (1988, April). *Microcomputer-based collaborative writing by learning handicapped students: Cognitive characteristics* (Technical Report #55). University of California, Santa Barbara: Project TEECh.

Goldman, S. R., Mertz, D. L., & Pellegrino, J. W. (1989). Individual differences in extended practice functions and solution strategies for basic addition facts. *Journal of Educational Psychology, 81,* 481–496.

Goldman, S. R., & Pellegrino, J. W. (1987). Information processing and educational microcomputer technology: Where do we go from here? *Journal of Learning Disabilities, 20,* 144–154.

Goldman, S. R., Pellegrino, J. W., & Mertz, D. L. (1988). Extended practice of basic addition facts: Strategy changes in learning-disabled students. *Cognition and Instruction, 5,* 223–265.

Goldman, S. R., & Rueda, R. (1988). Developing writing skills in bilingual exceptional children. *Exceptional Children, 54,* 543–551.

Heap, J. L. (1987). *Organizational features of collaborative editing activities at a computer.* Paper presented at the annual meeting of the American Educational Research Association, Washington, D.C.

Hine, M. S., Goldman, S. R., & Cosden, M. A. (1990). Error monitoring by learning handicapped students engaged in microcomputer-based writing. *The Journal of Special Education, 23,* 407–422.

Lidz, C. S. (1988). Historical perspectives. In C. S. Lidz (Ed.), *Dynamic Assessment: An interactional approach to evaluating learning potential* (pp. 3–32). New York: Guilford Press.

Piaget, J. (1970). Piaget's theory. In P. H. Mussen (Ed.), *Carmichael's manual of child psychology* (Third Edition, Vol. 1). 703–732.

Pellegrino, J. W., & Goldman, S. R. (1990). Cognitive science perspectives on intelligence and learning disabilities. In H. L. Swanson & B. Keogh (Eds.), *Learning disabilities: Theoretical research issues* (pp. 41–58). Hillsdale, NJ: Lawrence Erlbaum Associates.

Pellegrino, J. W., & Goldman, S. R. (1985, July). *Intelligence and intellectual development: An information processing perspective.* Invited address presented to the XX InterAmerican Congress of Psychology, Caracas, Venezuela.

Pressley, M. (1986). The relevance of the good strategy user model to the teaching of mathematics. *Educational Psychologist, 21,* 139–161.

Siegler, R. S. (1987). The perils of averaging data over strategies: An example from children's addition. *Journal of Experimental Psychology: General, 116,* 250–264.

Siegler, R. S., & Shrager, J. (1984). Strategy choices in addition and subtraction: How do children know what to do? In C. Sophian (Ed.), *Origins of cognitive skills* (pp. 229–293). Hillsdale, NJ: Lawrence Erlbaum Associates.

Sternberg, R. J., & Berg, C. A. (1986). Quantitative integration: Definitions of intelligence: A comparison of the 1921 and 1986 symposia. In R. J. Sternberg & D. K. Detterman (Eds.), *What is intelligence?* (pp. 155–162). Norwood, NJ: Ablex.

Sternberg, R. J., & Detterman, D. K. (Eds.). (1986). *What is intelligence?* Norwood, NJ: Ablex.

Suydam, M. N., & Dessart, D. J. (1980). Skill learning. In R. J. Shumway (Ed.), *Research in mathematics education* (pp. 207–234). Reston, VA: National Council of Teachers of Mathematics.

van Parreren, C. (1978). A building block model of cognitive learning. In A. M. Lesgold, J. W. Pellegrino, S. D. Fokkema, & R. Glaser (Eds.), *Cognitive psychology and instruction.* New York: Plenum Press.

Vye, N. J., Burns, M. S., Delclos, V. R., & Bransford, J. D. (1988). A comprehensive approach to assessing intellectually handicapped children. In C. S. Lidz (Ed.), *Dynamic assessment: An interactional approach to evaluating learning potential* (pp. 327–359). New York: Guilford Press.

Vygotsky, L. S. (1978). In M. Cole, J. Scribner, V. John-Steiner, & E. Souberman (Eds.), *Mind in society: The development of higher psychological processes.* Cambridge, MA: Harvard University Press.

Vygotsky, L. S. (1981). The genesis of higher mental function. In J. V. Wertsch (Ed.), *The concept of activity in Soviet psychology.* Armonk, NY: Sharpe.

7 The Effects of Training and Practice on Human Abilities

Lazar Stankov
University of Sydney, Australia

The ability of educational intervention to enhance performance on cognitive tasks is of major importance to human societies. Our work has been concerned with two types of interventions, practice and training. *Practice* refers to repeated performance of the same cognitive task. Its role lies in the acquisition and maintenance of cognitive skill. *Training* also involves repeated performance but differs from practice in that the repeated activity consists of processes that are theoretically distinct from those of the skill of interest, i.e., its efficacy rests on the presence of transfer.

Discussion of the relationship between human cognitive abilities and the learning process is probably as old as our attempts to understand psychological functioning. Definitions of intelligence as "the ability to learn" are still very much with us today. Thus, Humphreys (1979) states that, "[General] intelligence is the resultant of the processes of acquiring, storing in memory, retrieving, combining, comparing, and using in new contexts information and conceptual skills" (p. 115).

A similarly important role is ascribed to learning in theories proposed by many other contemporary writers on intelligence. For example, Sternberg (1985) considers learning within the experiential subtheory of his triarchic theory, which he discusses in this volume, suggesting that novel and nonentrenched concepts as well as various aspects of performance that are related to the achievement of automaticity, are important components of intelligence. Similarly, Jensen's (1969) distinction between Level I and Level II ability rests on the differentiation of cognitive processes that call for mental manipulation and transformations of input material from simple rote learning.

The role of learning is also critical in the theory of fluid and crystallized intelligence (Gf/Gc theory). From the early stages of the development of this theory, its two main proponents differed in their views of the role of learning. Much of the original distinction between Gf and Gc depended on R. Cattell's (see his 1971 book) review of the literature on the role of environment and heredity in the shaping of human cognitive abilities. In particular, Cattell claimed that about 80% of Gf phenotypic variance can be attributed to heredity, and that heredity is responsible for about 40% of Gc. Although more recent studies show that heritability of the two major organizations of abilities is about the same (and rather high), contemporary textbook accounts and common understanding of the Gf/Gc theory have not changed. The genetic argument for the Gf/Gc distinction rests nowadays on the evidence that these two groups of abilities derive from distinct gene pools. Because high heritability of a trait is often taken to imply the absence of susceptibility to educationally induced change, it is usually claimed that Gc, but not Gf, is affected by training and practice. This feature is often seen as the most salient distinction between Gf and Gc.

Perhaps under the influence of views expressed by Humphreys, Horn believed that learning is at the core of the development of all abilities and that the distinction between Gf and Gc derives largely from the nature of learning; Gc being the outgrowth of formal education and acculturation, and Gf deriving by and large from incidental and casual learning situations. Thus, both Gf and Gc should be affected by training and practice, perhaps differently depending on the nature of the exercises, but significantly nevertheless. There has been a relative scarcity of studies of the effects of practice and training on the well defined Gf and Gc abilities. A few that have been published clearly show that Gf can be improved (Stankov, 1986; Willis, Bliezner, & Baltes, 1981) supporting Horn's interpretation.

Both Cattell and Horn have written extensively on the mechanisms that are responsible for the differentiation of human abilities. In Cattell's structured learning model, there is an interrelationship between personality and ability traits; learning is driven by interests and motivational traits that act as potent sources shaping the structure of abilities during development. To this Horn adds a number of other psychological and sociological influences. Horn also accepts the early Ferguson (1956) model, which presents ability factors as overlearned skills and views intellectual development as cumulative learning. Ferguson's transfer model postulates that performance on task y is some unspecified function of performance on task x and the amount of practice on the two tasks. It is the learning of specific acquisitions that transfers and thus generates a relatively broad ability factor. This transfer provides for the growth of ability factors and is responsible for the correlations among the ability measures during development.

Whereas orthodox experimental studies of learning have been concerned largely with overall levels of performance (i.e., changes in arithmetic means), studies that link learning with human abilities have traditionally investigated changes in measures of dispersion (i.e., variances and covariances) in addition to arithmetic means. A recent attempt to relate the study of individual differences to skill learning was made by Ackerman (1986, 1987, 1988). Because much of the work in this area deals with the acquisition of simple perceptual and psychomotor skills, it is not entirely clear what findings should translate directly to training and practice studies of the complex cognitive processes of intellectual abilities. Nevertheless, we see that there is a considerable similarity among the issues of theoretical interest (e.g., the concepts of limited capacity and controlled and automatic processing) and also in the methodology employed.

Our work on practice and training was motivated by a desire to achieve a better understanding of the nature of intelligence and, in particular, fluid and crystallized intelligence. The aim was to:

1. Establish whether educational interventions can affect both Gf and Gc processes and, if so, explore the relative magnitudes of these effects.
2. Employ theories and methods that have emerged within cognitive experimental psychology, particularly recent developments in studies of skill acquisition, for the purpose of distinguishing between Gf and Gc.
3. Explore changes in correlation, and the relative roles of fluid and crystallized intelligence, at different stages of practice.

The studies of training were guided by the first of the three goals. The practice studies have been concerned largely with the second and the third goal. My aim here is to provide a brief overview of this work.

THE EFFECTS OF TRAINING ON Gf AND Gc ABILITIES

Because training denotes transfer across tasks that are not identical, evidence of its effectiveness provides an important justification for educational enterprise: Skills that are taught in schools are likely to be transferred to real life situations. Traditionally of course, the educational system makes this assumption. The problem lies in finding effective means for achieving the maximum transfer.

A series of experiments designed and carried out in Yugoslavia by R. Kvashchev during the early 1970s was based on training exercises in what he called "creative problem solving." These exercises were designed after extensive searches of the psychological literature on thinking by both experimental psychologists (e.g., Gestaltists, Bartlett, Piaget, Vygotsky) and differential psychologists (e.g., Spearman, Thurstone, Cattell). Studies of creativity carried out by Guilford, Torrance, and others were particularly influential in all stages of this work.

Stankov (1986) and Stankov and Chen (1988a, 1988b) provide more detailed information about Kvashchev's experiments. Briefly, Kvashchev took syllabuses for virtually all school subjects that are taught in secondary schools in Yugoslavia and engaged teachers to design lectures to cover various topics in a way that would elicit use of principles of creative problem solving. Thus, he encouraged teachers to ask students to design critical experiments in order to arrive at answers to particular problems in science subjects, to develop creative writing exercises in language subjects, to look for hidden meanings in texts dealing with history and other social science subjects. Over the years, he spent a lot of time with individual teachers helping them to change their teaching methods and developing teaching modules for individual topics within school subjects. In addition, he spent many hours working with the students on his own. This was made possible on a regular weekly basis through arrangements with the school authorities and also through his willingness to act as a replacement teacher whenever the need arose. He taught strategies for creative thinking such as the need to consider different meanings of the elements of a problem, the need to seek unusual and novel relationships among the elements of a problem and so on. In his encounters with the students, these principles were illustrated using examples which, by themselves, had little in common with the actual school subjects; they were general problem solving exercises described in the psychological and educational literature.

It is particularly important to note, however, that no exercise—neither those presented by teachers nor the ones presented by Kvashchev—contained any problems that were part of the intelligence test battery that was used to assess the effects of the experiment. The new learning involved crystallized abilities to the extent that the exercises were still based on school material. However, because general skills, strategies, and ways of looking at problems that are not taught in the typical school system were emphasized, the involvement of fluid abilities was implicated as well.

These exercises were given to an experimental group consisting of some 150 secondary school students over a period of 3 school years—an effort of major proportions given the limited resources at his disposal. A control group of equal size was taught in the traditional middle-European manner which means that, for the most part, students used rote learning to master the material that was presented to them within a typical ex-cathedra lecturing framework.

Both the experimental and control groups were tested with a battery of 36 psychological tests, including 28 paper and pencil tests of intelligence, at the beginning of the experiment—i.e., at an average age of 15 years and again at average ages of 18, 18.2, and 19 years. These tests were selected to measure both fluid and crystallized intelligence.

Using Kvashchev's data Stankov (1986) presented the results of analyses involving single tests (i.e., univariate analyses), and Stankov and Chen (1988a, 1988b) employed multivariate procedures of covariance structure analysis. These two latter studies were based on different and nonoverlapping subsamples of tests from the set of 28. Stankov and Chen fitted a model developed by McDonald (1984) that postulates an invariant factor pattern over occasions of testing and allows for observing changes in the means of factor scores. In other words, the model assumes that a given test has precisely the same loading on a factor on each occasion of testing and that changes occur in the factor scores of individuals. This model allows for a test of the hypothesis that Gf and Gc are indeed the two factors measured by the battery. The hypothesis was supported. The substantive interpretation of the model is that transfer produces no change in task structure (i.e., in factor loadings) but it does lead to changes in intra-individual cognitive structure (i.e., in factor scores).

The results of both univariate and multivariate analyses can be summarized quite simply. First, both Gf and Gc performance significantly improves as a result of training in creative problem solving. We have to conclude that training in creative problem solving is effective, that transfer occurs and, above all, that performance on tests of general intelligence can be improved. Second, in the Stankov (1986) and Stankov and Chen (1988a, 1988b) studies, improvement was slightly greater for the Gf than for the Gc abilities.

The comparisons between training effects on Gf and Gc in both multivariate and univariate analyses, are open to criticism because of the differences in scale. The various tests used in Kvashchev's work, and indeed in research of all psychologists, have different ranges of scores, and different means and standard deviations. Under many conditions this is not a problem. Thus, even though measures of dispersion may vary from condition to condition and from one group to the next, if the same test is used under different treatment conditions (testing occasions, or with different groups of subjects) the existing statistical machinery can cope with the problem through the use of pooled estimates of population dispersions.

A serious problem arises, however, when one wishes to compare different classes of abilities. How can one say confidently that improvement in Gf is greater than improvement in Gc, if the tests used to measure Gf have different scale properties than the measures of Gc? Even if the scale properties were the same, one may question this comparison because of qualitative differences between Gf and Gc. The answer to this question may never be solved to everybody's satisfaction but the first step in the right direction is to ensure scale equivalence. I wish to describe now the result of our reanalysis of Kvashchev's data, in which an attempt was made to provide the same scale for Gf and Gc abilities.

In this work, estimates of Gf and Gc were obtained by simple summation of the scaled scores on four measures of Gf and four measures of Gc from Kvashchev's battery. Prior to summation, scaling was carried out in the following way. For each variable maximum and minimum scores were found over all four occasions of testing and values of 100 and 0 respectively were attached to these extremes. Scores in between the extremes were expressed in terms of their distances on the 100 points scale. The same scaling was also carried out on the composite sum of Gf and Gc scores. The obtained scores are in fact similar to

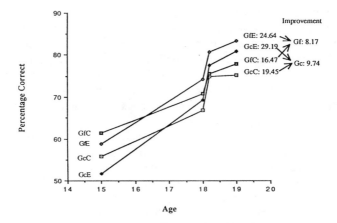

FIG. 7.1.   Changes in fluid (Gf) and crystallized (Gc) intelligence as a result of training in creative problem solving. E = Experimental group; C = Control group.

percentage scores often used in school practice; they are easily understood by teachers and parents alike. In this way both fluid and crystallized intelligence composites are expressed on the same scale, and the resulting means for each group over all occasions of testing can be easily compared. These scores were analyzed using the procedures developed by Jack McArdle for his *Reticular Analysis Model (RAM)* (McArdle, 1988).[1]

The major outcome of this work is summarized in Figure 7.1, which displays the means for Experimental (E) and Control (C) groups at different average ages of testing. We may note that at the beginning of the experiment, the control group was superior to the experimental group on both Gf and Gc but at the end of the experiment the reverse was true. The superiority of the experimental group remained at the second retesting, i.e., a year after all training in creative problem solving had ceased. The numbers on the right hand side of Fig. 7.1, which appear following the labels for various curves indicate the amount of gain between the ages of 15 and 19.

The gain over the 4-year period is somewhat greater for crystallized ability (about 24.32% point on the average for both experimental and control groups) than for fluid ability (about 22.04%) but the difference is rather small. Both gains are statistically significant.

The improvement due to training per se can be assessed through a comparison of the experimental and control groups on Gf and Gc abilities separately. This improvement is shown following the arrows at the right hand side in Fig. 7.1. The improvements of the experimental group in both crystallized intelligence (9.74%) and in fluid intelligence (8.17%) are statistically significant. In order to

[1] I am grateful to Kuei Chen and Jack McArdle for their help with these analyses.

evaluate the psychological significance of these results, it is useful to note that the initial standard deviations for both fluid and for crystallized intelligence and for both experimental and control groups were around 11%. The improvement is, therefore, close to one standard deviation. However, the change in crystallized intelligence is only 1.57% points higher than the change in fluid intelligence. Because this difference in improvement is rather small, I believe that Kvashchev's data should be interpreted to mean the Gf and Gc were affected to about the same degree by training in creative problem solving.[2]

Kvashchev's work produced a finding that was not anticipated but may have important educational implications. In all our analyses of these data, it was observed that the variance on measures of fluid intelligence reduces significantly between ages 15 and 19. For the data in Fig. 7.1, the standard deviation for fluid intelligence is halved during this period (from about 11.70% at 15 to about 6.20% at 19 years of age). Although the present analysis shows that both the experimental and control groups had reduced variance, in analyses of Stankov (1986) and Stankov and Chen (1988a, 1988b), the reduction was much more pronounced in the experimental group than in the control group. It is as if education has an equalizing effect on Gf abilities, in the sense of reducing individual differences. Similar effects on crystallized abilities have not been observed in Kvashchev's data.

We may conclude that the exercises developed by Kvashchev seem to have qualities that are affecting, through transfer, both the formal learning reflected in Gc and also the casual learning processes of Gf that are typically not specifically taught in school but, obviously, could and perhaps should be taught.

It is perhaps pertinent to observe that although much of Kvashchev's work was designed to elicit creativity, this was never interpreted as the "complete freedom and lack of discipline within the school settings" that appears to be causing a negative reaction in our society nowadays and has precipitated the "back to the basics" movement in our schools. Exercises in creative thinking are obviously effective, and their use in our school systems should be encouraged.

THE EFFECTS OF PRACTICE ON Gf AND Gc ABILITIES

Practice in doing a test itself, of course, leads to a much more dramatic improvement in performance, especially if it takes place within a short period of time, say twice a day for a week. However, the main aim of our practice studies was

---

[2]It is useful to note that at the end of experimental trials the gain in Gf was greater than the gain in Gc and also that another selection of markers for Gf and Gc may produce the opposite outcome to what is found here—i.e., somewhat greater improvement in Gf abilities. Perhaps the most convincing argument, of course, is in terms of statistical findings: Interaction between intelligence (Two levels: Gf and Gc) and group membership (Two levels: Experimental vs Control) was not significant. For these reasons, too, we should not attach particular significance to the observed differences in improvement.

different from that of the training studies. We did not wish to demonstrate the effect of increasing the level of performance but rather we wished to use the information available in the practice curves to distinguish between different kinds of abilities. Of particular interest to us was, of course, the distinction between fluid and crystallized intelligence.

Arguments in favor of the Gf/Gc theory as opposed to the single factor (Spearman/Jensen) or multiple factors (Thurstone/Guilford) theories of the organization of human abilities derive from structural findings (hierarchical factor analysis) involving large batteries of psychometric tests (see Carroll, 1987) from life span developmental evidence and genetic studies (see Horn, 1986) and from theories of contemporary experimental cognitive psychology (see Horn, 1986, Stankov, 1988). Practice studies belong to this last mentioned category. In order to place the outcomes of these studies in a proper perspective it is necessary to introduce briefly two constructs that emerged within experimental psychology and became relevant for the study of individual differences. These are the ideas of *limited capacity* and of *controlled versus automatic* processing.

Much of our recent investigation has been informed by the idea that the human cognitive apparatus has a limited capacity. This limited capacity can be thought of either as a unitary construct or as a pool of elementary and atomistic processing resources. An example of the former is the construct of working memory—a dynamic, centrally located system often divided into "active" and "passive" parts corresponding to what is happening within immediate awareness as we try to solve a problem. An example of the latter is the construct of attentional resources that subsumes all elementary operations including input related processes that are needed for the solution of a problem. Various paradigms can be used to demonstrate limited capacity, but the most common illustration derives from changes in performance that are observed when two cognitive task are presented simultaneously, i.e., dual or competing tasks.

As differential psychologists, our interest in competing tasks was aroused by the finding that they are better measures of the general factor than single tests. It seemed reasonable to hypothesize that individual differences in cognitive capacity are responsible for the individual differences we observe with measures of intelligence; a simple and rather satisfying explanation. However, we should note that competing tasks are a convenient methodological tool and have no special relationship to limited capacity. The concept of limited capacity is useful as a means of assessing *all* cognitive tasks, not only competing tasks, with respect to the demand or effort that they place on the person.

Because intelligence tests belong to the class of cognitive tasks, they too can be ordered in this way. Conceptual analyses of the demands of various measures of intelligence suggest that typical tests of fluid ability tend to be demanding of processing resources, but crystallized intelligence tests, like Synonyms and Vocabulary for example, appear to be less so; if available, the meanings of the words are retrieved quickly and rather easily. Similarly light in processing capacity are some other tests of abilities, such as those that measure perceptual or motor processes. On this analysis, decrement in performance with competing Gf tasks should be more pronounced than decrement with competing Gc or perceptual abilities tasks.

The other idea that emerged from experimental cognitive psychology, and suggested the use of practice studies to support the distinction between fluid and crystallized intelligence, is that of controlled and automatic processing. Controlled processes are characterized (see Schneider & Shiffrin's, 1977) as requiring a large allocation of cognitive processing resources, as relatively slow, and as readily alterable to meet changing requirements. Automatic processes require little allocation of processing resources, are fast, and are not easily altered by conscious control. The importance of this distinction for our purposes here derives from the use of practice data (particularly the so called consistent and varied mapping conditions) to distinguish between the automatic and controlled processes. Whereas practice represents the process of automatization, it has been found that over a large number of practice trials controlled processes fail to reach automaticity in performance. Schneider and his associates used both single and competing tasks and produced data from which we can deduce general principles in order to determine if the processes called for by a particular task are predominantly automatic or controlled.

It is necessary to keep in mind that the tasks that will be presented in the remaining sections of this paper differ from those of the initial work on controlled and automatic processing. In our studies, practice consists of doing a set of several hundred different single and competing items from a given psychometric test over a period of five days. In terms of Ferguson's (1956) transfer model, all psychometric tests measure abilities that are the result of a prolonged period of learning and therefore have reached their asymptote; thus rendering any further practice ineffective. Competing tasks may escape this effect to some degree because simultaneous presentation typically results in lower performance on the component tasks than is achieved for their single versions. Therefore, we might expect competing tasks undergoing automatization to reach asymptotic performance over rather more practice trials than their single counterparts, as more automatic processes will need to be developed, and as resources will be released more slowly by developing automaticity. We might also expect a rapprochement of single and competing tasks within the limits of the resources available. However, tasks requiring controlled processing while showing a similar or, as argued earlier, greater drop in performance initially, should fail to achieve a rapprochement of practice curves for single and competing versions, as the demands on resources will not be reduced, with practice, to much the same level for both.

On past experience, the single test provides an indicant of the maximum score to be expected from the competing task. Attainment of the single test level of performance in a competing task may serve as an alternative criterion of automaticity, for comparison with practice curve results.

The design of tasks for our practice studies was relatively simple: subjects worked on three tests—two single tests and on a competing task. The competing task was always composed of items from the single tests, presented simultaneously. Under competing conditions subjects were instructed to work on both items, and at the end of item presentation one of the two tasks was designated to be answered first (primary), and the other second (secondary). On every occasion of testing, the numbers of items for each of the three conditions of a given test (single versions and primary and secondary conditions of competing version) was 20.

We consider the outcomes of three practice studies here. Comparisons among the practice curves from these studies allow us to substantiate our argument that measures of intelligence can be divided into those using automatic processing, and those that are controlled and resource limited (dependent on the available pool of processing resources).

Study 1: Perceptual Abilities.   The top part of Fig. 7.2 displays examples of the items used in this study. In the Tonal Memory test, a sequence consisting of three, four or five tones is presented. The sequence is then repeated with one of the tones changed. The subject must identify the position of the tone that changed. In the Hidden Figures test, two drawings are presented at the top left and the top right

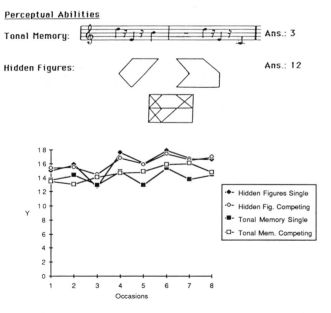

FIG. 7.2.   Performance on single and competing versions of the perceptual abilities tests on eight occasions of practice. Y = total test scores.

respectively. A more complex figure appears in the middle lower half of the screen. The subjects were required to state which figure was present (both, none, left figure, or right figure). These two tests are measures of broad auditory function and of broad visualization respectively. The practice curves at the bottom part of Fig. 7.2 are based on the performance of 40 subjects. In order to avoid clutter, I present an appropriately scaled composite for the competing task rather than separate primary and secondary curves.

Figure 7.2 clearly shows that single and competing versions of the two perceptual tests were performed at the same level of competence from the very beginning of the practice sessions. Some improvement due to practice was present in the data but this trend was not particularly impressive. Differences between single and competing versions of the tests were not significant.

The results of this study suggest that these two marker tests of different perceptual factors can be performed in parallel (i.e., without loss in the level of performance under the competing condition) and that they reach asymptote quickly. This finding is consistent with the theory of multiple pools of processing resources of C. Wickens (1980).

Study 2: Crystallized Intelligence.   The top section of Fig. 7.3 illustrates the two tests of crystallized intelligence used in this study. In the Similarities test subjects are asked to choose, from among four words, two that have similar meanings. Elements of the items for this test were presented sequentially on the computer screen. In the Scrambled Words test, subjects have to rearrange four letters to form a word. This test was presented through earphones. Due to the sequential nature of the item presentation, these two tests are not identical with typical tests of crystallized intelligence (e.g., Vocabulary tests), and bear some similarity to fluid intelligence tasks. These two tests were presented to 50 students from the University of Sydney. The overall level of performance on different occasions of practice is displayed at the bottom part of Fig. 7.3.

The results of this study differ from those of Study 1. First, at the beginning of practice, competing task performance was inferior to the single task performance for both tests. This indicates that in contrast to the perceptual measures of Study 1, the competing tasks of Study 2 draw on more processing resources. After two occasions of practice, both versions of the Scrambled Words test and the single Similarities test reached the same asymptote. The competing version of the Similarities reached the single level of performance after eight occasions of practice. This means that although crystallized ability tests draw on more resources than perceptual tests at the beginning of practice trials, but practice results in rapid automatization, so that overall, the present measures of crystallized ability appear more akin to automatic than to controlled processes.

Study 3: Fluid Intelligence.   The top parts of Figs. 7.4 and 7.5 illustrate the two fluid intelligence marker tests that were used in order to trace practice effects in this study. A larger number of subjects (N = 100) were used than in the

Crystallized Intelligence tasks

Similarities:	TRY	GET	ATTEMPT	PLAY	Ans.: 13
Scrambled Words:	E	T	R	E	Ans.: Tree.

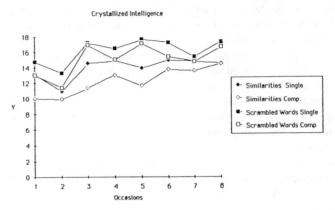

Crystallized Intelligence

◆- Similarities Single
◇- Similarities Comp.
■- Scrambled Words Single
◻- Scrambled Words Comp

FIG. 7.3. Performance on single and competing versions of the crystallized intelligence tests on eight occasions of practice. Y = total test scores.

Letter Reordering test:

R S T   T R S   Answer: 312

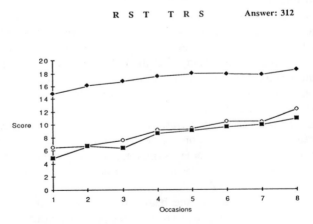

FIG. 7.4. Performance on single and competing versions of the Letter Reordering test (a marker for fluid intelligence) on eight occasions of practice. Y = total test scores; black diamonds = single test; open diamonds = competing task, primary scores; black squares = competing task, secondary scores.

108

Number Series test:

1   2   4   7   11   16   Answer: 22

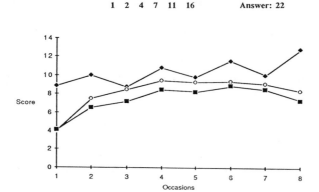

FIG. 7.5. Performance on single and competing versions of the Number Series test (a marker for fluid intelligence) on eight occasions of practice. Y = total test scores; black diamonds = single test; open diamonds = competing task, primary scores; black squares = competing task, secondary scores.

previous two studies, and because this provides for a more reliable outcome, we consider some issues that were omitted from our earlier discussion. Of the two marker tests, the Number Series is a well known marker of inductive reasoning at the first order of analysis and of fluid intelligence at the second order. The other test, Letter Reordering, involves listening to a set of three letters, attaching numbers to the letters in accordance with the order of their presentation, listening to the same three letters that are now presented in a different order, and writing the answer to indicate that second order. This test is a good measure of the Temporal Tracking factor at the first order of analysis and of fluid intelligence at the second order.

It is apparent from both Figs. 7.4 and 7.5 that performance in the competing presentation is inferior (much more so than in the previous two studies) to single presentation, especially at the beginning of practice. This means that the Gf makers are more demanding of resources than perceptual tests or measures of Gc. Also, for both tasks, secondary scores are lower than primary scores. This is typical of all our studies because secondary scores reflect the capacity remaining after processing of the primary task is accomplished.

Figure 7.4 presents the single, primary and secondary scores for the Letter Reordering test. The curve for the single test scores is clearly separated from the curves for competing task scores and, even though it appears that the top curve might have asymptoted, we should keep in mind the fact that during the last three occasions of practice, single test performance was close to ceiling level. The competing task curves approach the single task curve at a much slower rate and, given the ceiling effect of the single curve, it is doubtful that the two would ever coincide even after much longer periods of practice than we employed. This pattern of results is typical for measures of controlled processing and measures that are sensitive to limited capacity.

Figure 7.5 presents the results for the Number Series test, which are obviously different from those for the Letter Reordering test. First, the single Number Series test is clearly more difficult than the Letter Reordering test. This greater difficulty might have influenced the subjects to adopt a particular strategy during the competing presentation (e.g., invest more effort working on the Number Series test). Second, even though there is a considerable difference between the single and competing scores on the very first and the very last occasions of practice, indicating that indeed we are dealing here with controlled processing, these differences are noticeably smaller in-between these two extreme occasions. In a separate study we found that the three different sets of items that were used in the present study differed somewhat among themselves with respect to difficulty thus explaining the saw-tooth quality of the single test curve in Fig. 7.5. Third, there is an appearance of asymptotic performance level for the competing tasks after the fourth occasion of practice. As this occurred without the secondary performance reaching the level of the primary, it suggests that this task will not be fully automatized, but will remain controlled.

The results of Study 3, warn us that determination of the type of processing called for by a particular task may not be a simple matter and that careful attention should be given to the design of the study (i.e., issues of test difficulty and strategy use). Viewed in isolation from the Letter Reordering results, Number Series presents a rather unclear picture—it could be seen either as controlled or as an automatic task. Nevertheless, when viewed jointly the measures of Gf clearly behave differently from either tests of perceptual abilities or measures of crystallized intelligence when tested for capacity limitations via the use of competing tasks and for automatization using practice.

PRACTICE AND CHANGES IN CORRELATIONS

Studies of the link between learning and human abilities have sought understanding of the changing interrelationships among practiced tasks and different outside measures of abilities or among the same measures at different stages of practice.

The first of these interests calls for the use of an experimental design that will have a task that is being practiced and an independent assessment of abilities. In our practice Studies 1 and 2 of the preceding section, subjects were given *Wechsler's Adult Intelligence Scale–Revised (WAIS-R)* in addition to the single and competing tasks that were used for practice. Following the work of Fleishman and Hempel (1954, 1955) with perceptual/motor tasks, it was widely accepted that

TABLE 7.1
Correlations Between a Measure of Intelligence (WAIS-R Total Score) and Single and Competing
Versions of Tonal Memory and Hidden Figure Tests

Occasions	Single Competing	Tonal Memory	Hidden Figures	Single Competing
WAIS-R				
1	.15	.31	.54	.52
2	.19	.11	.44	.52
3	.13	.18	.46	.45
4	.14	.05	.29	.20
5	.07	.15	.25	.27
6	.22	.23	.49	.47
7	.07	.04	.60	.41
8	.34	.29	.40	.46

although intellectual abilities might correlate with initial task performance, correlations dropped over trials. Ackerman (1987) reanalysed Fleishman's data, and collected data of his own to challenge this conclusion. In non-motor learning such as concept attainment, Cronbach and Snow (1977) show that intellectual abilities correlate with performance at early *and* late stages of practice.

Our results are in general agreement with the conclusion of Cronbach and Snow (1977). Table 7.1 presents correlations for Study 1, i.e., correlations between single and competing versions of the Tonal Memory and Hidden Figures tests and total WAIS-R scores.[3] We can see that the correlations of the Hidden Figures test are higher than those of the Tonal Memory test, but no clear trend in correlations can be observed over practice trials. As initial correlations are not noticeably higher than final correlations, there is no justification for a claim that Gf abilities take over as practice continues. Observations along these lines have been reported by some students of perceptual and motor skills (see Ackerman, 1988).

The second correlational issue addressed in our studies has to do with changes in correlations among the practiced tasks. Most published studies in this area have only one practiced task and the question is, basically, what pattern of correlations among the trials appears. The usual answer is: *simplex*. Generally, correlations among trials that are close together are higher than correlations among the trials that are further apart. If trials are ordered from first to last, the correlational matrix will contain higher values close to the main diagonal and gradually lowered values as one moves to the top-right or bottom-left hand corners. Interpretations of the processes underlying an empirically observed simplex vary. They include the "simplification" process proposed by Jones (1962) and the "accretion" process proposed by Anderson (1939) but, as pointed

---

[3]Study 2 leads to the same conclusion.

out by Corballis (1965) the presence of a simplex pattern is not sufficient to confirm either one of these or, indeed, simultaneous presence of both processes.

Situations in which practice on each trial involves more than one test, like our practice of single and competing tasks, are not common in the literature. This situation, however, is important in practice studies because it allows for the examination of the changes in latent dimensions, rather than in simple observed variables. After all, we usually assume that our interventions have deeper effects than those detected by our tests. Perhaps the notion of transfer can be understood in terms of changes in factor loadings and factor scores. A statistical model for examining data such as ours was proposed by Swaminathan (see McDonald, 1978, 1984) who described a way to test this model with *COSAN*. Basically the model assumes a particular common structure among the different measures (in the present case one factor on each occasion of testing), simplex structure on factor scores, and correlations among the "unique" parts of each variable across the trials. It is important to observe that in this model the simplex on factor scores was constructed with Anderson's (1939) accretion interpretation in mind, i.e., it is assumed that something new is added on each occasion of practice and the simplex reflects the amount of overlap between the trials.

This model was fitted to the data obtained in what was described earlier as Study 3. The correlational matrix that provided input data for this analysis consisted of 30 variables. These were 6 tests (Single-, Primary-, Secondary-Number Series scores, and Single-, Primary-, Secondary-Letter Reordering scores) on 5 occasions of practice. In order to have manageable matrices for the *COSAN* analysis only occasions 1,2,4,6, and 8 were included.[4] The resulting common factor structure and factor intercorrelations are presented in Table 7.2. (Unique factor variances, and covariances among the unique part of the variables are not presented in Table 7.2 in order to save space.) This solution had a Chi-square = 733.15 with df = 341. Because this Chi-square is about twice as large as the number of degree-of-freedom, the obtained fit is satisfactory according to the standards accepted today.

Considering factor loadings first, it is immediately noticeable that the Number Series test tends to have higher loadings on each occasion of testing than the Letter Reordering test. This difference is not of importance to us here, because it may be due to psychometric features of our tests rather than to profound characteristics of the psychological processes involved in performance.

Much more important is the change in the size of the factor loadings over the occasions of practice. It is obvious the factor loadings increase as practice continues, implying that the correlations among the jointly practiced tests are higher at the end of practice than they are at the beginning. We may also note that the

---

[4]The same kind of analysis was carried out on the data of Study 2—i.e., with crystallized intelligence tests. The results of this analysis are essentially the same as those obtained with Study 3 data. I do not report this second set of data here in order to save space.

TABLE 7.2
Factor Matrix: COSAN Solution for Study 3 (Gf Practice Data)

	Occasions of Practice				
	1	2	4	6	8
Number Series Single 1	.64	0	0	0	0
Number Series Primary 1	.69	0	0	0	0
Number Series Secondary 1	.63	0	0	0	0
Letter Reordering Single 1	.46	0	0	0	0
Letter Reordering Primary 1	.35	0	0	0	0
Letter Reordering Secondary 1	.34	0	0	0	0
Number Series Single 2	0	.62	0	0	0
Number Series Primry 2	0	.83	0	0	0
Number Series Secondary 2	0	.79	0	0	0
Letter Reordering Single 2	0	.45	0	0	0
Letter Reordering Primary 2	0	.34	0	0	0
Letter Reordering Secondary 2	0	.41	0	0	0
Number Series Single 4	0	0	.70	0	0
Number Series Primary 4	0	0	.72	0	0
Number Series Secondary 4	0	0	.78	0	0
Letter Reordering Single 4	0	0	.48	0	0
Letter Reordering Primary 4	0	0	.47	0	0
Letter Reordering Secondary 4	0	0	.48	0	0
Number Series Single 6	0	0	0	.80	0
Number Series Primary 6	0	0	0	.81	0
Number Series Secondary 6	0	0	0	.91	0
Letter Reordering Single 6	0	0	0	.41	0
Letter Reordering Primary 6	0	0	0	.49	0
Letter Reordering Secondary 6	0	0	0	.51	0
Number Series Single 8	0	0	0	0	.82
Number Series Primary 8	0	0	0	0	.79
Number Series Secondary 8	0	0	0	0	.82
Letter Reordering Single 8	0	0	0	0	.44
Letter Reordering Primary 8	0	0	0	0	.41
Letter Reordering Secondary 8	0	0	0	0	.52
Factor Intercorrelations					
Occasion 1	1.0				
Occasion 2	.79	1.0			
Occasion 4	.76	.96	1.0		
Occasion 6	.71	.89	.93	1.0	
Occasion 8	.68	.86	.89	.96	1.0

largest increases in the size of factor loadings are for the single Number Series test and for its two secondary competing task scores. I believe that the observed increase in loadings over the occasions of practice is of importance. It shows that practiced tasks tend to develop more characteristics in common. This is an interpretation of transfer that captures Ferguson's ideas about the development of abilities quite well.

Turning now to factor intercorrelations, we may note that apart from the correlations of the first factor, the size of the coefficients is rather high and the difference between the highest and the lowest values is rather small. A simplex structure on the factor scores is clearly visible. In fact, our analyses of a subset of these data and of the results of Study 2, show that a satisfactory fit may be obtained by restricting all factor intercorrelations to a value of 1.00. This indicates that the changes in factor scores are fairly equal across occasions and that individual differences in these changes are not very pronounced. This outcome is in striking contrast to our attempts to constrain factor loadings across the occasions of practice; such attempts lead inevitably to poor fit.

CONCLUSION

The results of our training and practice studies have shed light on some issues of interest to students of individual differences in intellectual abilities. These are:

1. The use of training to improve performance on tests of general intelligence.
2. Differences in the cognitive processes called forth by tests of fluid and crystallized intelligence.
3. Effects of practice in doing intelligence test items on correlations with other measures of intelligence and on the formation of psychometric factors.

Kvashchev's attempts to use training in what he called creative problem solving were obviously successful. Several reanalyses of his data have shown that both fluid and crystallized intelligence are affected to about the same degree. We must conclude that general intelligence can be influenced through educational processes that depend on transfer. There is also some evidence that this kind of training leads to performance that is less variable between individuals, i.e., it seems to have an equalizing effect. Horn's interpretation of Gf and Gc as the outgrowths of learning (casual and formal, respectively) have been supported.

Stankov (1986) observed that analyses on raw scores and univariate ANOVA procedures lead to improvements in performance on all tests that is, on the average, equal to or less than half of one standard deviation of the variable of interest. This led him to question whether the enormous effort exerted by Kvashchev was truly justified; the gain may be too small. Analyses of the present report employed a convenient "percentage" scores rescaling of the Gf and Gc composites in order to compare improvements in these two intelligence estimates. The overall gain through training is close to one standard deviation (i.e., about as large as the Black-White difference) and there can be little doubt about its usefulness, especially because the effects last at least one year beyond the end of the active training.

Our studies of practice show that cognitive processes of fluid intelligence differ from those of crystallized and broad perceptual factors. Basically, perceptual abilities and crystallized intelligence depend on automatic processing whereas fluid intelligence (and probably short-term memory abilities) depend on controlled, resource limited processing. This distinction is revealed through the examination of various features of practice curves for single and competing tasks. The distinction is not always easy to make because the nature of the competing task presentation may affect the relative importance of the processes involved. For example, sequential presentation of crystallized intelligence items may change these items to appear more akin to fluid intelligence tasks. Likewise, the adoption of strategies in competing tasks (for example, focussing on a more difficult test within a pair) may make this component of the competing task appear easier than when attention is equally divided between the two tasks.

It is not entirely clear at present whether the aforementioned analysis provides a basic distinguishing feature between Gf and Gc or whether this is an epiphenomenon due to our choice of tasks for practice studies. For, if we agree with Horn that the main distinction between Gf and Gc resides in the nature of learning (formal versus casual) which caused the formation of these broad factors, we may have to say that everything else is secondary or, in fact, has nothing to do with the essence of these broad factors. After all, we can use analogies items to measure both Gf and Gc; the critical aspect is the choice of elements for the analogies. This means that all that we have uncovered through our linking of fluid intelligence with the limited capacity controlled processing is a tendency among psychologists to use a particular type of task, i.e., a controlled processing task for its measurement.

Cattell's (1971) interpretation of fluid and crystallized abilities, on the other hand, allows for a stronger statement about the importance of our findings although a slight modification of his views seems necessary. He distinguishes between two basic kinds of contributors to the development of *agencies* which, in his triadic theory, correspond to primary abilities and crystallized intelligence. The first class of contributors are organismic contributors or powers that further subdivide into *provincial powers* of sensory inputs, and *capacities* that include Fluid power, Speed, (Short-term) Memory, and Fluency. The second class of contributors are motivational systems and rewarded experiences in particular areas of endeavor. Within this framework, the inability of competing and single Gf tasks curves to approach each other after long periods of practice (and other signs of controlled processing that could be discerned in practice curves) indicate that central fluid power is indeed being tapped by these tasks. Capacity of provincial powers, however, is of a different nature and it does reveal itself through the same experimental manipulation (see practice Study 1). Our work supports a distinction between the two kinds of organismic contributors and suggests that cognitive processes of provincial powers and capacities are different.

Our practice studies have also allowed us to address some old issues regarding the relationship between learning and human abilities. One of these issues was change in correlation with external measures of intelligence. We find that in accordance with other reports involving intellectual abilities (as opposed to perceptual/psychomotor abilities), no systematic change in correlation can be detected.

Finally, because our work involved practicing two tasks on each occasion and these tasks produced three scores each, it was possible to look at the changes in the interrelationship among the jointly practiced tasks. This situation has not been studied often in the past.[5] Our findings with the data of Study 3 indicate that fitting a model that assumes one factor on each occasion and simplex on factor scores, produces a solution that displays an important change in factor loadings in the course of practice. The tendency is to have higher loadings of most variables at the latter stages of practice indicating that a factor has become stronger and better defined. It appears that Ferguson's (1954, 1956) ideas about the role of learning and transfer in the formation of human abilities can be tested in this way.

REFERENCES

Ackerman, P. L. (1986). Individual differences in information processing: An investigation of intellectual abilities and task performance during practice. *Intelligence, 10,* 101–139.

Ackerman, P. L. (1987). Individual differences in skill learning: An integration of psychometric and information processing perspectives. *Psychological Bulletin, 102,* 3–27.

Ackerman, P. L. (1988). Determinants of individual differences during skill acquisition: Cognitive abilities and information processing. *Journal of Experimental Psychology: General, 117,* 288–318.

Anderson, J. E. (1939). The limitations of infant and school tests in the measurement of intelligence. *Journal of Psychology, 10,* 203–212.

Carroll, J. B. (1987). Psychometric approaches to cognitive abilities and processes. In S. H. Irvine & S. E. Newstead. *Intelligence and Cognition: Contemporary Frames of Reference* Derdrecht: Martinus Nijhoff Publishers.

Cattell, R. B. (1971). *Abilities, Their Structure, Growth, and Action.* Boston: Houghton-Mifflin.

Corballis, M. C. (1965). Practice and the simplex. *Psychological Review, 70,* 68–80.

Cronbach, L. J., & Snow, R. E. (1977). *Aptitudes and instructional methods.* New York: Irvington.

Ferguson, G. A. (1954). On learning and human ability. *Canadian Journal of Psychology, 8,* 95–112.

Ferguson, G. A. (1956). On transfer and the abilities of man. *Canadian Journal of Psychology, 10,* 121–131.

Fleishman, E. A., & Hempel, E. E. Jr. (1954). Changes in factor structure of a complex psychomotor test as a function of practice. *Psychometrika, 19,* 239–252.

Fleishman, E. A., & Hempel, E. E., Jr. (1955). The relation between abilities and improvement with practice in a visual discrimination task. *Journal of Experimental Psychology, 49,* 301–316.

Horn, J. L. (1972). State, trait and change dimensions of intelligence. *The British Journal of Educational Psychology, 42,* 159–185.

---

[5]Horn (1972) reported an important study that falls into this category—i.e., practicing several different intelligence measures on each occasion. His concern, however, was to distinguish between trait and state factors using methods of analysis that predate currently popular structural modeling approaches. He was not concerned with a model involving simplex on factor scores. In view of our findings, it would be interesting to reanalyse Horn's dateausing Swaminathan's or some related model.

Horn, J. L. (1986). Intellectual ability concepts. In R. J. Sternberg (Ed.), *Advances in the psychology of human intelligence*. Hillsdale, NJ: Lawrence Erlbaum Associates.

Humphreys, L. G. (1979). The construct of general intelligence. *Intelligence, 3,* 105–120.

Jensen, A. R. (1969). How much can we boost IQ and academic achievement? *Harvard Educational Review, 39,* 1–123.

Jones, M. B. (1962). Practice as a process of simplification. *Psychological Review, 69,* 274–294.

McArdle, J. J. (1988). Dynamic but structural equation modeling of repeated measures data. In J. R. Nesselroade & R. B. Cattell (Eds.), *The handbook of multivariate experimental psychology. Volume II*. New York: Plenum Press.

McDonald, R. P. (1978). A simple comprehensive model for the analysis of covariance structures. *British Journal of Mathematical and Statistical Psychology, 31,* 161–183.

McDonald, R. P. (1984). The invariant factors model for multimode data. In H. G. Law, C. W. Snyder, Jr., J. A. Hattie, & R. P. McDonald (Eds.), *Research methods for multimode data analysis*. New York: Praeger Scientific.

Schneider, W., & Shiffrin, R. M. (1977). Controlled and automatic human information processing: I. Detection, search, and attention. *Psychological Review, 84,* 1–66.

Stankov, L. (1986). Kvashchev's experiment: Can we boost intelligence? *Intelligence, 10,* 209–230.

Stankov, L., & Chen, K. (1988a). Can we boost fluid and crystallised intelligence? A structural modeling approach. *Australian Journal of Psychology, 40,* 363–376.

Stankov, L., & Chen, K. (1988b). Training and changes in fluid and crystallised intelligence. *Contemporary Educational Psychology, 13,* 382–396.

Stankov, L. (1988). Aging, intelligence and attention. *Psychology and Aging, 3,* 59–74.

Sternberg, R. J. (1985). *Beyond IQ*. Cambridge: Cambridge University Press.

Wickens, C. D. (1980). The structure of attentional resources. In R. S. Nickerson (Ed.), *Attention and performance, VIII*. Hillsdale, NJ: Lawrence Erlbaum Associates.

Willis, S. L., Bliezner, R., & Baltes, P. B. (1981). Intellectual training research in aging: Modification of performance on the fluid ability and figural relations. *Journal of Educational Psychology, 73,* 41–50.

8

Intelligence, Task Complexity, and the Distinction Between Automatic and Effortful Mental Processing

John D. Crawford
University of Technology, Sydney, Australia

In recent years, increasing attention has been given to the concept of task complexity, firstly, as a way of describing the observed correlational structure of mental abilities, and secondly, as an explanatory concept by means of which certain aspects of this structure can be related to models and theories derived from the cognitive and other areas of psychology. In this chapter a model is proposed in which task complexity is interpreted in terms of a person's ability to perform effortful, or non-automatic, mental processing. Although similar to previous suggestions involving concepts such as mental energy, active mental processing or attentional resources, the proposed model attempts to provide an account of these terms in a way that avoids many of the limitations of earlier ones, and that relates in a natural manner to accepted views on certain elementary aspects of neurological functioning.

The chapter is divided into four parts. First, several definitional and conceptual issues related to the notion of task complexity are considered. Second, a number of previous views on intelligence or task complexity, which are relevant to the proposed model, are briefly evaluated. In the third part, a model of task complexity and intelligence based on the distinction between diffuse and constricted neural pathways is presented. Finally, a comparison is made between the proposed model and other theories of general intelligence and task complexity.

DEFINING TASK COMPLEXITY

Although Spearman (1927) identified general intelligence as the common factor "g," his theorizing on its psychological nature derived more directly from his observation that certain types of tests tended to exhibit relatively higher g-loadings than do others. Two important features that he suggested characterize tests with higher g-loadings are as follows. Firstly, performance on these tasks appeared to require higher levels of concentration, or "mental energy," than those tasks with lower g-loadings. Second, they seemed to involve the processes of reasoning and problem-solving, in contrast to the more mechanistic, or algorithmic, processes that appeared to underlie performances on the lower g-loading tasks. In Spearman's terms, the high g-loading tests exhibit the principle of "noegenesis," or involve the "eduction of relations and correlates."

Despite the wide influence of Spearman's single common factor theory towards the beginning of this century, data were becoming available that suggested that more than one factor was required to adequately account for the common variance between performances on mental tests. In response to such data, and assisted by advances in factor-analytic techniques, more pluralistic, or oligarchic models based on correlated group factors were gaining popularity. Within these models, the concept of general intelligence has little of the importance accorded to it by the earlier monistic model of Spearman. The most well known of these early pluralistic models was that of Thurstone (1938) in which performances on cognitive tasks are described in terms of a number of independent, although positively correlated "primary mental abilities." Despite being positively correlated these are regarded as independent, in the sense that they are held to reflect distinct psychological structures or processes.

The development of pluralistic models occurred in two directions, each of which can be seen as an attempt to cope with the ever increasing number of primary ability factors being discovered through the application of multiple-group factor analysis. The first of these, as typified by the work of Guilford (e.g., 1967), represents an acceptance of a large number of distinct ability factors, but attempts to bring order to such diversity by posing the existence of a much smaller number of dimensions by means of which these ability factors can be classified. The second direction that the pluralistic approach may be seen to have developed is in the formation of models based on truncated hierarchical factoring procedures. In such models (e.g., Horn & Cattell, 1966; Vernon, 1950) the correlations between the primary factors are described in terms of a smaller number of positively correlated higher-order factors. For example, in the Horn/Cattell theory of fluid and crystallized intelligence, attention focuses on a series of positively correlated second-order factors (e.g., Cattell, 1987; Horn, 1986). Thus an important similarity between this theory and Thurstone's is the assertion of the functional independence of a number of positively correlated ability dimensions, and the belief that a description in terms of higher order factors, (and in particular the general factor, "g"), would loose most of what is of psychological significance (Horn, 1985, 1986).

In recent years, there has been renewed interest by some authors in the concept of general intelligence (e.g., Snow, 1980, 1986; Marshalek, Lohman & Snow, 1983; Jensen, 1982b; Humphreys 1979, 1981). A number of possible reasons for this may be suggested. First, there is the availability of psychometric models, such as Guttman's (1954) radex model, or ones based on hierarchical factoring procedures, which do provide for an operational definition of "general intelligence" without the commitment to the single common factor model of Spearman. Within these more recent models allowance is made for the existence of independent ability domains (corresponding to the lower-order group factors in the hierarchical model, or the facets in the radex model) in ways that do not preclude a definition or general intelligence. For this reason, Sternberg (1981) suggests that such models can be regarded as a synthesis of earlier monistic and pluralistic ones. It should be noted, however, that the inability of Spearman's original single common factor model is quite often forwarded as evidence against the concept of general intelligence (e.g., Horn, 1985).

A second possible reason for this increased interest in the concept of general intelligence is that it has suggested, for some theorists, one way of relating ideas that have emerged from the more recent cognitive or information processing approach to the structure of mental abilities. It is in this context that the concept of task complexity has been suggested as an important construct. Spearman had noted that a fundamental difference can be observed in the nature of tasks that exhibit relatively high, and low, g-loadings in mental test batteries. The concept of task complexity has been used to describe this difference, with tasks that are found to correlate more highly with the general factor being seen as a consequence of their greater complexity. In turn, concepts derived from the cognitive or information processing theories have been used to define possible mental processes or capacities that are critically involved in the successful performance of more complex tasks.

A clear illustration of the way that the notion of task complexity has been used to describe the structure of abilities can be seen in Fig. 8.1, which has been taken from Marshalek, Lohman and Snow (1983). This is a multidimensional scaling, in two dimensions, of a large number of traditional ability tests, and is an illustration of the radex model of abilities suggested by Guttman (1954). Roughly, individual tests are represented here by points in two dimensional space in such a way as to attempt to place more highly correlated tests closer together in the plane. In this diagram, tests of higher complexity are those towards the centre, whereas those of lower complexity are distributed towards the periphery. The angular position around the diagram reflects the various different ability domains (content areas, special abilities, etc.), with figural, or spatial, tasks towards the right, perceptual/clerical speed tasks towards the upper left, a fluency test towards the top, and short-term memory tasks towards the lower left of the diagram. In terms of the Horn/Cattell theory of fluid and crystallized intelligence, the different angular regions can be seen to correspond to the broad, second-order abilities. Note that fluid intelligence, Gf, is distinguished from the remainder of the ability dimensions by being located at the center, rather than defining an ability content area or domain.

Task complexity and task difficulty are distinct concepts. Although there may be some intuitive appeal in the proposition that more difficult tasks are better

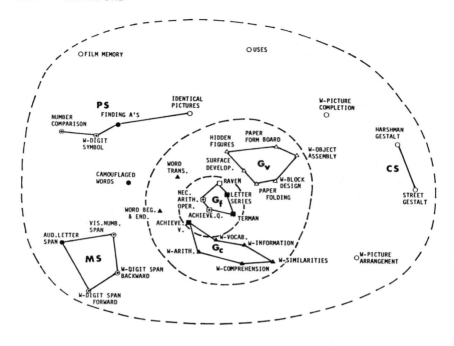

FIG. 8.1.   A multidimensional scaling of a number of traditional mental tests. Taken from Marshalek, Lohman and Snow (1983).

measures of intelligence, this is in general not correct. For example, Jensen (1977) found that paired associate learning correlates more highly with IQ when, in the learning phase, the stimuli are presented more slowly, even though the slower presentation makes the task easier. The explanation offered was that the slower presentation allows a greater involvement of higher order executive control processes, the functioning of which is assumed to be linked, in individual differences, with intelligence. A similar result was reported by Crawford and Stankov (1983). The immediate recall of digit and letter lists was found to correlate more highly with fluid intelligence than did a similar task that was made more difficult by the inclusion of an interpolated attention distracting filler task between the presentation and recall of the stimuli. These examples show that, for at least some pairs of similar tasks, task complexity and task difficulty can be negatively correlated. It is, however, easy to find such examples if pairs of dissimilar tasks are considered. A test comprising the easier items of, say, the Raven's Progressive Matrices tests, is likely to be more strongly associated with general intelligence than, say, a very difficult visual closure, incidental memory, or perceptual discrimination task.

This notion of complexity, defined in terms of a task's association with the general factor, is not the only (or even the most usual) one. In the description of concept learning, reaction time or memory tasks, for example, the term complexity is often used to denote some task parameter, usually associated with the number of stimulus features present, the number of hypothesized mental steps, or stages, required for task completion, or the depth of processing involved. The account of complexity proposed by Wood (1986) to describe work-related tasks would be of this type. In these contexts, task complexity and difficulty are probably more closely associated conceptually than for a definition of complexity based on a task's association with the general factor. However, when used in this way, it is not always the case that more complex tasks are more highly correlated with intelligence. (For example, see Jenkinson, 1983, for an investigation of the effect of apparent task complexity on correlations with intelligence).

Another point that should be noted is that when complexity is operationally defined in terms of relative size of its g-loading, it is assumed that its correlations with other tasks in the battery are not significantly affected by what may be regarded as artifacts of measurement. For example, varying a task's reliability by changing the number of items in the test would not be regarded as a valid means of affecting the test's complexity. In a similar but less obvious manner, the effects on correlations between tests of the skewness in the distributions of test scores and their coarseness of measurement (see Carroll, 1945, 1961), would need to be taken into account when evaluating a task's complexity. Such factors would tend to produce spuriously higher correlations between tests of greater difficulty, and in certain circumstances could tend to increase the g-loadings of the more difficult tasks in the battery. Such a spurious effect could also occur as a result of nonability factors such as carefulness or persistence (Horn & Bramble, 1967; Eysenck, 1953; White, 1982) which would be expected to have a greater influence on the scores of more difficult tests.

Finally, the relationship between a definition of complexity in terms of a test's correlation with the general factor, and the nature of the critical mental processes during the performance of the test should be considered. This issue arises because performances on tests such as Vocabulary and other crystallized intelligence measures do not appear to involve the same sorts of mental processes as characterize other typical high g-loading tests. Commonly suggested psychological bases for the complexity dimension such as those involving strategic processes, mental energy, and working memory are plausible explanations of why, say, the Raven's Progressive Matrices test is a good measure of "g," or why Backward Digit Span is more strongly related to "g" than is Forward Digit Span, but are not plausible descriptions of the more automatic memory retrieval processes involved in the performance of a Vocabulary test. There is a commonly stated view that this apparent anomaly can be explained by assuming that the prior acquisition of verbal knowledge, assessed by the Vocabulary tests, depends significantly on the types of mental processes that are more directly measured by tests such as the Raven's Progressive Matrices. Similar ideas can be found in the writing of Cattell (1987), Horn (1985), Hunt (1980) and others.

This issue is of particular significance as it is a likely source of confusion in the use of the term task complexity. If the term is defined strictly in terms of a task's association with "g" (as proposed by Jensen, 1977) then both the Raven's Progressive Matrices and Vocabulary tests would be described as tests of high complexity. If, however, the term complexity is used to indicate the extent that certain critical types of mental processes are required in the actual performance of the task then it would be more appropriate to regard Vocabulary as a task of relatively low complexity. Although such an approach to the definition of complexity was argued against by Wood (1986), it would allow the rather natural statement to be made, that more complex tasks are those that involve more complex sorts of mental processing. It would thus allow the construct of task complexity to function as a more direct link between the psychometric and cognitive areas.

TASK COMPLEXITY AND INTELLIGENCE

In this section a number of ideas that have been put forward as underlying the concept of general intelligence, or that of task complexity, is discussed. A comprehensive review will not be attempted. Rather, an evaluation of two broad approaches is given in a way that will serve as background to the presentation of a new model later in the chapter. The first of these involves ideas that relate most closely to the model that is proposed later, such as mental energy and attentional resources. Secondly, a currently more popular process oriented view of intelligence is discussed.

Complexity and "Mental Energy" or "Attentional Resources." Spearman (1927) suggested that "g" reflects the varying amounts of mental energy possessed by different individuals. Tasks were hypothesized to vary with respect to the extent that the availability of this mental energy determines level of performance, with performances on more complex tasks, (that is, those with higher g-loadings), being relatively more affected by the supply of such energy.

The influence of the concept of mental energy, and particularly Spearman's assumption of its primarily biological and genetic basis, can be seen in the later writings of authors such as Jensen, Eysenck and Cattell. However, its influence on more modern theories of intelligence has not been as strong as that of Spearman's other ideas on the nature of "g," associated with his "principal of noegenesis." A possible reason for this is the problem of circularity in the definition of the term "mental energy." An adequate account of the nature of this mental energy, independent of its relation to tasks with observed high and low g-loadings, is required to remove this circularity. Such an account was not seriously attempted by Spearman, possibly because of a belief that significant advances in the science of neurophysiology were required before this were possible.

One way that the notion of mental energy may be more adequately defined is via the more recent concept of attentional resources that is associated with the variable allocation models of Kahneman (1973) or Norman and Bobrow (1975). In such models, "central" limitations on the simultaneous processing of multiple sources of information is restricted by the limited availability of a general purpose source of attentional resources, which is capable of fuelling concurrent activity in different mental structures.

The fairly obvious and direct parallel between Kahneman's notion of attentional resources and Spearman's concept of mental energy was, in fact, noted by Hunt and Lansman (1982). Thus tasks more highly correlated with the common factor, "g," are those for which the levels of performances are more strongly dependent on the amount of available attentional resources. The uncorrelated specific factors (the s's in Spearman's model) are interpreted as reflecting the more automatic processes in those mental structures, postulated by Kahneman to underlie the non-central, or structural, sources of interference between concurrent mental processing. An obvious difficulty is the questionable assumption of the single common factor model of Spearman. However, this account can be easily modified by identifying the various specific mental structures postulated by Kahneman with the more peripheral tasks or factors rather than with the uncorrelated specific factors in Spearman's model. Such an account preserves the essential idea that task complexity is linked with the concept of attentional resources, but does not rely on Spearman's single common factor model.

In view of the widespread use of the distinction between automatic and effortful mental processes, and the fairly direct and obvious manner that this can be related to the structure of mental abilities, it is perhaps surprising that more attention has not been given to the possibility of such a theoretical link. A number of reasons may be suggested for the lack of serious consideration of attentional resources as an explanation of general intelligence, or of task complexity. First, in some quarters, where the trend is towards a more pluralistic view of human intelligence (or "intelligences"), the need for such explanations does not arise, and, indeed, would be inappropriate (e.g., Horn, 1986; Gardner, 1983).

A further reason for the relative neglect of attentional resources as an explanatory construct for intelligence is simply lack of direct empirical evidence in favor of such an explanation. One line of investigation that could be seen as being relevant to this issue is the study of individual differences in the performance of dual tasks. Such studies commonly focus on the question of the existence of a general time sharing factor or ability. Reviews of the results of these studies have generally concluded against the firm acceptance of time sharing ability. Hawkins, Church, and de Lemos (1978) suggested, instead, that different task combinations may call on different specific abilities. In a slightly more positive tone, Sverko (1977), and Ackerman, Schneider, and Wickens (1982) argued that evidence does exist to indicate the possibility of such an ability, but that its status is still uncertain. Similar conclusions could be drawn from results reported by Stankov (1985) and Fogarty and Stankov (1987) which showed that, in some but not all instances, correlations with "g" were greater when tasks were presented under competing conditions than when presented singly.

Studies such as those just described, were not intended, nor adequately designed, as direct tests of the validity of the concept of attentional resources, or of its manifestation in individual differences as general intelligence. However, a number of studies reported by Hunt (1980), Hunt and Lansman (1982) and Lansman and Hunt (1982), using a paradigm more suitable for the investigation of this issue, did, however, produce results generally (though not completely) consistent with a link between intelligence and the concept of attentional resources. Weighing against such an explanation of general intelligence, however, is the growing criticism by a number of authors of the validity of single attentional resource models of attention. Allport (1971, 1980a, 1980b), and Navon and Gopher (1979), for example, have argued, on the basis of the observed pattern of interference between different tasks, for a multi-processor, or multiple resources model. Such models do seem more suggestive of a multiple intelligences view (Horn, 1985; Gardner, 1983), rather than one based on the concept of general intelligence. An attack from a different direction on the notion of attentional resources came from Spelke, Hirst, and Neisser (1976), and Hirst, Spelke, Reaves, Caharack, and Neisser (1980) where it was shown that two tasks, after much practice, can be successfully performed simultaneously, and, according to the latter authors, without alternation of attention, and without the tasks becoming automatic.

Another source of evidence, generally supportive of an interpretation of general intelligence in terms of effortful, or nonautomatic, mental processing comes from Ackerman's (1988) review of studies on motor skills acquisition. Here Ackerman pointed to the decreasing correlations with general intelligence of a variety of psychomotor tasks as they became more automatic with increasing practice. Even more supportive of such an interpretation was the finding that, for a given amount of practice, this decrease in correlations with intelligence was greater for tasks containing "consistent mapping" (see Schneider and Shiffrin, 1977). Little or no change in correlations occurred for tasks containing so-called "varied mapping" and which therefore did not automate significantly with extended practice.

A different type of task that might be related, at least at an intuitive level, to Spearman's concept of mental energy, (although not necessarily to a single-source theory of attentional resources), is one investigated by Wittenborn (1943). He devised a number of tasks, the construction of which was guided by a number of design principles. The most important of these was that their performances should depend on a continuous, sustained application of mental effort, or concentration. It was also assumed by Wittenborn that individual differences in performances on these so-called "attention" tasks should not be strongly related to intellectual level nor should they depend to a significant extent on differences in subjects' previously acquired knowledge. Wittenborn's assumption that they should not be strongly related to intelligence can possibly be understood as resulting from the apparently repetitive, or algorithmic, mental processes involved in their performances. However, despite this assumption, there is good evidence that they are, in fact, closely related to traditional measures of intelligence. For example, in Wittenborn's (1943) study, these tasks were those with the highest loadings on the general factor formed by a battery of fairly diverse mental tests. A reanalysis of Wittenborn's data by Stankov (1983) using more modern factor analytic methods confirmed this result. Similar conclusions were drawn by Crawford (1988) who found that a number of tests based on Wittenborn's attention tasks were good measure of fluid intelligence. Such results are clearly consistent, at least at an intuitive level, with Spearman's account of intelligence in terms of the concept of mental energy as an explanation of general intelligence.

Complexity Involving Strategy Variation: Here we consider a particular view of intelligence whose conceptual framework can be traced to early theories of attention and memory, such as that by Atkinson and Shiffrin (1968). The key concept here is that mental processes are hierarchically organized into at least two levels of control. On the lower level are the more basic, elementary or mechanistic (Hunt, 1978) information processing functions, or the cognitive/performance components (Sternberg, 1983). These more basic processes are, in turn, organized and coordinated by the higher order executive control processes, or metacomponents. Within such a framework, general intelligence is seen as reflecting individual differences in the operation of the higher order executive control processes, which are held to manifest themselves primarily, at the level of task performance, in the selection of strategies used in the solution of the task. Strategy-intensive tasks are defined as those tasks that involve a greater variety of different strategies in their performance, as compared with strategy-free tasks. For example, in terms of this distinction, it was concluded by Campione, Brown, and Bryant (1985) that it is performances on the strategy-intensive tasks that are related to intelligence. A similar explanation of group differences in general intelligence was suggested by Borkowski and Krause (1983).

Sternberg (1981), as well as proposing a link between psychometric "g" and the functioning of executive control processes (metacomponents), also suggests that individual differences in the lower level processes (the components), are reflected by the more specific abilities, or group factors. A clear statement of a similar position was given by Hunt (1980) where he refers to the multidimensional scaling diagram shown in Fig. 8.1. Hunt suggests that the tests towards the periphery are those that present people with very restricted problem-solving situations, in which there is only one reasonable way to attack the task. Performance in such a situation will be more determined by mechanistic information-processing functions than by a choice of problem solving strategy simply because of the limited range of strategies possible. By contrast, performance on tests in the centre of the space may be much more dependent on a person's having available a store of strategies to deal with the varied problems presented by different items within each test. A similar idea is being expressed by Sternberg when describing the role of "task novelty" (e.g., Sternberg, 1985) in his triarchic theory of intelligence. Novel tasks (but not ones that are too novel) call for the greater involvement of strategic or metacomponential processes, and are therefore more closely related to measures of general intelligence.

One of the most frequent arguments given in favour of the strategies view is the failure, despite an enormous research effort, to find reliable and high correlations between intelligence and performances on relatively simple and strategy-free cognitive tasks. Empirical research on mental abilities, within the information processing framework, has followed two main approaches. These Pellegrino and Glaser (1979) have called the "cognitive correlates" and the "cognitive components" approaches. In the cognitive correlates approach, performances on relatively simple cognitive tasks, typically selected from the wide range of experimental paradigms, formally used in cognitive research, are correlated with traditional measures of intelligence, or specific mental abilities. A wide variety of so-called "elementary cognitive tasks" (ECT's) (Carroll, 1981), have been examined in this way. These include simple and complex reaction-time, memory scan, lexical access, inspection-time and many other paradigms. When reviewing data derived from this type of research, Hunt (1980) concluded that, for subjects in the normal range of ability, correlations between individual ECT's and traditional psychometric measures of general intelligence are only small, with values similar to those produced by common lower complexity tasks, such as perceptual/clerical speed or memory span tests. Keele (1979) described this generally weak result in terms of a "0.3 barrier" in the sizes of correlations between ECT's and intelligence. However, it should be emphasized that, as with other lower complexity measures such as memory span, correlations much higher than 0.3 can easily be obtained if subjects of sufficiently low levels of ability are included in the sample. It is also important to note that this is not simply a question of the restriction of range. Higher correlations between ECT's and intelligence are to be found with groups of lower ability than with groups of higher ability but with comparable ranges of ability. For example, the stronger relation between general intelligence and the digit span subtest of the WAIS for subjects of lower ability, was noted by Zimmerman and Woo-Sam (1973) and Matarazzo (1972). Nettlebeck and Kirby (1983) reported a similar pattern of results with reaction-time and inspection-time tasks.

Essentially the same negative conclusion was drawn from work using the cognitive components approach. Here subjects' performances on relatively complex tasks (such as analogies and series-completion tasks) are analyzed in terms of some stage, or "componential," model. Subjects' performances on the elementary, cognitive components are obtained indirectly as regression estimates of parameters within the relevant model. Such findings led Sternberg (1977) to conclude that intelligence is associated more with the functioning of the higher order strategic processes that coordinate the operation of the more elementary component processes.

Despite its strong intuitive appeal, and its current widespread popularity, a troubling aspect of such a view of general intelligence in terms of strategic functions is the lack of strong, direct positive evidence in its favour. There is, however, a substantial amount of evidence generally consistent with, but not directly supporting, such a view of intelligence in terms of strategic processes. A large number of studies have reported systematic differences between groups of varying ability in their use of problem solving strategies. Such studies have typically involved the comparison of retardates and normals, or children at different stages of development. (See studies quoted by Campione, Brown, and Bryant, 1985, in favor of their distinction between strategy-free and strategy-intensive tasks, and its relation to intelligence). The main limitation of such evidence in favour of a strategies view of intelligence, is that the observed differences in strategies could plausibly be the manifestation of more basic differences in mental capacity. This is emphasized by findings that suggest that lower ability groups have greater difficulty in learning and applying new strategies, as well as the generalizing of strategies to different, but similar tasks.

Such data operate most strongly against what might be termed a "software" position, where the difference in strategic functions between people of high and low intelligence is assumed to be primarily a result of the store of available problem solving strategies possessed by the person. These findings seem more compatible with a more structural view, that such strategic difference reflect a more fundamental limitation in the information processing capacity of the mental structures responsible for the learning and applying of cognitive strategies. For example, it could be the case, as Jensen (1979) suggests, that intelligence is linked to the ability to perform tasks requiring active, effortful mental processing, and that strategy selection is an important, but not the only manifestation of such processes.

Despite the large body of evidence generally consistent with the view that strategic functions underlie individual differences in intelligence, there do exist a few, but reliable, experimental results that weigh against such an interpretation. Cohen and Sandberg (1977) investigated the correlations with IQ of primacy and recency recall on a probed serial recall task. Multistore models of short-term memory, such as those proposed by Atkinson and Shiffrin (1968), or Waugh and Norman (1965), suggest that primacy recall and recency recall reflect different psychological processes. In particular, primacy recall depends on the transfer of items to a relatively long-term secondary memory system. This transfer was thought to be strongly influenced by executive control processes, such as those involved in the choice of efficient rehearsal strategies. Recency recall, on the other hand, was thought of as reflecting recall from a more sensory primary memory system, and was therefore assumed to be unaffected by such control processes. On the basis of these models, it was generally expected that primacy recall would be more strongly related to IQ than would recency recall. These expectations were initially confirmed, but largely with data comparing performances of normals and retardates (e.g., Ellis, 1970). However, Cohen and Sandberg (1977) in a series of separate studies, using normal children, showed that recency recall was consistently more highly correlated with intelligence, than was primacy recall. Their main conclusion was that it was non-strategic processes that were responsible for the higher correlations with intelligence.

Another set of data that does not seem consistent with an interpretation of general intelligence in terms of strategic processes involves the association between the rate of paired-associate learning and intelligence. In a study by Hughes (1983), subjects were divided into two groups. One group was given explicit instruction on strategies that would assist recall. The second group was given no such strategic instructions. As expected, it was found that the instruction group performed better on the learning task than the no-instruction group. However, correlations with intelligence (as measured by the Raven's Progressive Matrices) were much higher for the instruction group ($r = .59$) than for the no-instruction group ($r = .16$). This result would not be expected if correlations with intelligence were assumed to be mediated by subjects' ability to select, by themselves, the most appropriate strategies for the task.

A final set of data that does not seem compatible with a view of task complexity based on strategic variability comes from a series of studies by Crawford (1988). As mentioned earlier, it was found that a number of tasks based on Wittenborn's (1943) Attention Tests were good measures of fluid intelligence. Among these was a serial short-term memory task similar to those studied extensively by Monty and his associates (e.g., Monty, 1968; Monty, Taub, & Laughery, 1965). Consistent with Monty's interpretation of this task, examination of subjects' performances revealed no significant strategic variation, or any evidence that such variation mediated the close association between this task and fluid intelligence.

PROPOSAL OF A NEW MODEL

In this section a way of relating the psychometrically based notion of task complexity to concepts derived from cognitive attentional theories and models of neurological functioning is suggested. The proposed model relies on a number of existing theories, and can best be regarded as a demonstration of how these existing ideas can be combined in such a way as to give a plausible basis to the intuitive notion that more complex tasks are those that involve more effortful mental processing or mental energy.

The model is presented as follows. First, a number of well-known theories of attention are briefly reviewed and, where applicable, parallels with theories of intelligence are noted. Second, an attentional model is outlined, which is an extension of Kinsbourne's model of inter-task interference and which takes into account the observed pattern of functional localization in the brain's cortex. Third, an attempt is made to show how this attentional model can be related to the concept of task complexity, and to the structure of mental abilities as described by hierarchical factor or radex models of intelligence.

Attention and Intelligence.   Amongst the numerous meanings of the term attention (e.g., Moray, 1969) the one most often suggested as a possible explanation of individual differences in general mental ability, is that which has emerged from attempts to explain the pattern of performance deficits that occur in dual, or concurrent, task paradigms. One possible account of dual task performances is that interference between two concurrent tasks occurs when both tasks require the use of one or more specific information processing structures, which are assumed to be serial in operation, and are unable to simultaneously share the processing required by two tasks. In such structural theories, it is common that one of these structures (often termed the executive, or central processor) has a special and important place in the mental architecture. This derives from its position at the top of an assumed hierarchy of mental control, and its role in the execution of higher order mental processes, sometimes identified with consciousness or effortful mental processing (e.g., Kerr, 1973). Automatic processes refer to those not involving, or only minimally involving, the operation of the serial central processor. However, it is not always the case that such an executive structure is postulated. Allport (1980a, 1980b), for example, argues strongly against a strong hierarchical structure of control, and instead, for a system of "co-operating experts." Here, the concept of automaticity is suggested to be unnecessary, and even to be circular in its definition.

The most popular alternative to the structural theories are those such as proposed by Kahneman (1973), or Norman and Bobrow (1975), which postulate a limited supply of processing capacity, or attentional resources, capable of being shared between, or energizing a number of concurrent mental processes. Thus interference between performances on concurrent tasks can occur, not only as a result of competition for some specific mental structure, but can also occur between tasks not utilizing common structures. This can occur as a result of competition for a limited supply of general purpose attentional resources. Although, in theories such as Kahneman's, the existence of specific, serial processing, structures is allowed, no distinct structure with the functions of an executive, or central processor is assumed. However, it is generally regarded that executive, and higher order forms of processing are those that require relatively greater amounts of attentional resources. Processes needing less attentional resources are lower on the hierarchy of cognitive control. Although single resources theories tend to focus on resource limitations in producing inter task interference, the concept of structural interference is retained in order to account for what Wickens (1980) termed "structural alternation" effects. This is where the pattern of interference amongst pairs of tasks appears to be related to specific task content, or input/output modalities, and not only on the effortfulness, or resource require-ments, of the individual tasks.

The main way that structural and resource limited interference may be opera-tionally distinguished resides in the manner that performance on one task is affected by changes in the difficulty, or the priority given to, the other task. (This is provided that the level of performance on the second task does not alter as its difficulty or priority is varied. See Roediger, Knight, & Kantowitz, 1977). Pro-gressively decreasing levels of performance on one task as a result of increasing difficulty, say, of the other, would be taken as evidence of interference due to resource limitations. Structural interference, on the other hand, is characterized by a more discontinuous pattern of interference, with the presence of a concur-rent task producing performance deficits that are not sensitive to changes in the difficulty, or priority, of the concurrent task.

A third, and more recent, type of attentional theory is one that postulates a number of distinct pools of processing resource (e.g., Navon & Gopher, 1979). It is frequently suggested that each of these pools is associated with different neural sub-systems of the brain, such as hemisphere of processing, or those neural structures associated with different input/output modalities or modalities of more central processing. Experimental evidence for the existence of more than one form of resources derives from the resource-like characteristics of apparently content specific sources of interference between concurrent tasks (Wickens, 1980). However, much of the appeal of such a model derives from its apparent consistency with a view of the brain as containing a number of distinct, though interacting, functional subsystems, capable of operating in parallel without cost to performance. There does not appear to be, according to common interpreta-tions of brain functioning, a neural system or mechanism that could plausibly be identified with an executive, or central processor, or with a single, general-purpose pool of attentional resources.

There are two main ways that these attentional concepts have been related to theories of intelligence. First are the suggestions that individual differences in attentional resources, or in the operation of an executive system, might underlie differences in people's general intelligence. It is sometimes suggested that the operation of the specific mental structures, such as are assumed by Kahneman and others to produce structural interference between concurrent tasks, corre-spond to the lower g-loading group factors, or special abilities. The second way that these concepts have been related to the structure of mental abilities, is associated with the model of brain functioning consistent with the multiprocessor attentional theory of Allport (1980a), or the multiresource models of Navon and Gopher (1979) and Wickens (1980). Thus Gardner (1983) identifies separate neural subsystems, or functional cortical regions, with each of his various human intelligences. A certain degree of cortical localization was, in fact, one of Gardner's (1983) eight criteria for the identification of each of his multiple intelligences.

As emphasized by the advocates of pluralistic models of attention, or mental abilities, neurological studies have shown that certain types of mental processes, tend to be localized in different areas of the brain's cortex. Thus different broad regions of the cortex are primarily responsible for the perception and processing of visual, auditory, verbal, spatial, musical, and tactile material, and the coordination of the various motor outputs. However, superimposed on this organization of the cortex into different broad functional areas, there does exist another pattern of organization of a more hierarchical nature. A generally accepted aspect of the operation of the brain's cortex is that there is significant variation between the different cortical locations in the degree of specialization of function. The general model of cortical functioning described in this section is elaborated in books such as Lezak (1983), or Walsh (1987). Within each of the various broad regions of the cortex are found smaller areas of more highly specialized function. These are the so-called primary association, or projection, areas. Damage to these areas can produce a marked decline in the less complex, and more specific, forms of mental processing. Surrounding these centers of more specialized function are the secondary and the tertiary association areas. As one moves away from the primary association areas, functions become progressively less localized, and involve mental processes of higher apparent complexity. The tertiary association areas of each hemisphere of the brain merge to form a continuum in both form and function, and serve to coordinate the activities of the more specialized regions of the cortex. As well as being less content or modality specific, processing here appears to be more highly distributed. Damage to small local areas of the tertiary association areas produces minimal cognitive impairment, and the effects of damage to these areas seems to more closely follow the so-called "law of mass action" (Cattell, 1987, p. 221). That is, the degree of mental impairment is proportional to the mass, or volume, of damaged brain tissue.

It is important for later discussion to note that those mental functions that are more localized in the cortex, include not only the less complex, and largely innate, sensory and motor functions. Localization of functions also appears to occur for highly overlearned skills, such as in the understanding and production of language, the playing of musical instruments, or riding a bicycle. Localized cortical lesions in the appropriate locations can produce large deficits in the performances of such highly overlearned skills.

This distinction between the more, and less specialized neural processes forms the basis of the proposed model, which is outlined next.

The Concepts of Automatic and Effortful Mental Processes are defined in this model in a way similar to that above proposed by Kinsbourne (1981). Automatic processes are those corresponding to the more isolated, or channelled, and more functionally specific, neural pathways. Conversely, the less automatic, or more effortful processes, are those involving more diffuse, or distributed, neural pathways. These definitions make more explicit the similar ideas expressed by Kinsbourne (1981) on the differences between mental processes associated with a greater, and lesser, spread of neural activation.

Note that the concept of automaticity here is closely associated with, but does not correspond exactly to, that of the localization of brain functions. The key concept here is that of the *diffuseness* of neural pathways. A highly automatic task may involve critical neural pathways in numerous and widespread cortical locations, so long as these pathways are relatively constricted and functionally isolated from other neural processes. Also, it should be emphasized that the terms of "diffuse" and "constricted" represent a continuum in the nature of neural pathways, as do the corresponding notions of automatic and effortful mental processes. At the one end are the most highly automatic, and largely innate, processes of the primary sensory projection areas. Slightly more diffuse, and less automatic, processes would include those of the surrounding secondary association areas, and also the relatively localized neural pathways related to highly overlearned or automated skills. At the other end of the continuum are those neural pathways that may be postulated to involve the whole of the tertiary association areas of the cortex, of a hemisphere, or large portions of these association areas.

Interference Between Concurrent Tasks is assumed to be a function of the amount of overlap in the neural pathways involved in the performance of the tasks. Thus the model does not postulate one or more sources of attentional energy (resources, capacity, etc.). In this sense, (but not in the stricter sense used by Kahneman, 1973, or by Wickens, 1980) all interference between concurrent tasks can be regarded as structural interference. This is similar to the suggestion by Kinsbourne and Hicks (1978), and Kinsbourne (1981) that the amount of mutual interference between performances on dual tasks is determined by the proximity of the functional cortical space associated with the performances of each of the tasks.

The nature of the interference between concurrent tasks differs depending on whether this results from interference between relatively diffuse, or constricted, neural pathways. Competition for functional cerebral space (to use Kinsbourne and Hick's terms) by the overlapping of more diffuse neural pathways would tend to produce the type of interference between the tasks that Wickens (1980) suggests is indicative of resource limitations. That is, interference between the tasks is not "all or nothing," but exhibits a more or less continuous tradeoff between performances on the tasks as they compete for cortical space. This occurs in much the same way as in those models where tasks are held to compete for some hypothetical neuronal energy supply or attentional resources. In the present model, more attention being given to the performance of one of the tasks is interpreted as more cortical space being allocated to the processing of that task, at the expense of less cortical space being available for the other task. The notion that the efficiency of distributed neural processes can vary as a function of the amount of cortical space utilized is compatible with Pribram's (1971) "holographic" model, and other suggested distributed processing models (e.g., Anderson, 1983; Anderson & Hinton, 1981; Rumelhart & McClelland, 1986).

Interference between tasks due to highly constricted neural pathways, however, would tend to occur in a more "all or nothing" manner, which Wickens (1980) describes as being evidence of structural interferences. Because the constricted pathways are more isolated and functionally more specific, this would be more likely to occur when both tasks require the same, or very similar, forms of processing. Also, because the more highly automated neural processes tend to be those associated with specific sensory input and motor output, this is consistent with the types of structural interference suggested in the primarily capacity based models of Kahneman (1973) and others. However, the somewhat constricted neural pathways involved in the performance of overlearned sensorimotor, language and other skills, may also give rise to a more structural, rather than resource limited, form of interference between concurrent tasks.

The Process of Automatization and the Constriction of Neural Pathways.   It is common in neurological models of distributed processing, that the consolidation of neural pathways is hypothesized to occur through the increased conductances between neurones, which occurs as a result of repeated activation of these synaptic connections (Hebb, 1949; Anderson, 1983). The transmission of a signal along a given pathway becomes "easier" (more rapid, etc.), with greater use. A second assumption that will be made here, is that, accompanying such a process is a progressive constriction, or contraction, of the initially more diffuse neural pathways. Although such a notion is not usually found in mathematical models of distributed processing, it is consistent with the neurological evidence on the difference between the degree of cortical localization of new learning and highly practiced skills.

Comparison With Other Attentional Models.   Like Kahneman's (1973) theory, the present model does provide for both structural and resource limited patterns of interference between concurrent tasks. Resource-like effects, however, are assumed to occur through the competition for cortical area by overlapping diffuse neural pathways, rather than for a limited supply of some hypothesized attentional resources. The model is more similar to multiple resources ones insofar as it does allow minimal interference between apparently effortful or attention consuming tasks in some situations (see Allport, 1980a, for examples of these). This would occur when each task involves large, but well separated, areas on the cortex. This as would be the case, for example, if the tertiary association areas of separate hemispheres were involved in the simultaneous performance of, say, verbal and spatial tasks. Single attentional resource theories would not be able to account for such phenomena.

The main differences between the proposed model and the multiple resources ones are two-fold. First, the distinction between automatic and effortful processes is an important part of the present model, as is the distinction between resource-like versus structural interference effects. Multiple resources models are more likely to dispense with the notion of automaticity, as the latter concept is not needed to explain cases of minimal interference between pairs of tasks. It is assumed that different pools of resources are used by the two tasks. Also, the concept of structural interference is not needed in multiple resources models as this too can be explained in these models by assuming that different pools of resources are used by the two tasks. (However, Wickens, 1980, presents evidence for both a number of separate attentional resources, as well as sources of structural interference.)

The distinction between automatic and effortful processing was retained in the proposed model, mainly because of the easy way that these concepts could be related to neurological concepts (i.e., diffuse versus constricted neural pathways), and because of the natural way that the development and automation of skills can be interpreted within the model. In particular, it gives a ready explanation of the effect of more highly overlearned, or automatic, skills apparently consuming fewer attentional resources. This follows immediately from the assumption of the progressive contraction of neural pathways with increased automation, and the interpretation of resource like effects as resulting from the interference between more diffuse, or distributed, neural pathways.

It should be noted that, although this model does differ in important ways from single attentional resource models, it does share the following important property. More effortful tasks are, in general, more likely to be disrupted by other ongoing mental processes, and are more susceptible (compared with tasks that are performed more automatically) to various factors whose influence on mental performances has been interpreted as being due to a depletion in the amount of available attentional resources (e.g., M. Eysenck, 1979, 1982). The proposed model can thus be seen to predict effects similar to those expected from both single attentional resource and multiple resources models. Interference between concurrent tasks would tend to follow the arithmetic of a multiple resources models if remote cortical regions were involved in the performances of the tasks. However, results similar to those predicted by a single resource model would be expected if the two tasks compete for general purpose distributed processing space in the same region of the cortex. If adjacent, but still overlapping, cortical regions were involved in the processing of the two tasks, then the model would predict effects somewhere between those predicted by the single attentional resource and multiple resource models.

The Relationship Between the Attentional Model and Task Complexity. The central proposal here is that, in normal individuals, the efficiency of the more diffuse, or distributed, mental processes in the different regions of the cortex is reflected in individual differences by a single ability factor, which closely resembles the fluid intelligence factor, Gf. This proposal can be regarded as a restatement of Cattell's (1987) theory, that Gf reflects the efficiency of processing in the less specialized regions of the cortex, the tertiary association areas. In terms of the concept of task complexity, as discussed earlier in this chapter, complex tasks are those for which individual differences are largely a result of individual differences in the efficiency of more diffuse neural processes. Alternatively, both Gf and the notion of task complexity can simply be interpreted in terms of individual differences in more effortful mental processing. Tasks for which individual differences are more a result of differences in the more constricted, or localized, neural processes are associated with numerous other ability factors, with varying degrees of association with Gf. As a general rule, those highly localized and largely innate processes that are related to sensory and motor functions seem to be the ones least correlated with Gf. Somewhat more highly correlated with Gf are those relatively localized processes where it can be assumed that the localization is the result of prior learning, that is, where the degree of localization can be assumed to depend to some greater degree on the prior efficiency of more diffuse processes. In cases where individual differences in the efficiency of localized processes is primarily a function of the efficiency of prior more diffuse neural processes, (most plausibly in the case of tasks such as Vocabulary, and other Gc markers), relatively high correlations with Gf may occur. This may happen even though mental processing of relatively low complexity is involved at the time of their performance.

COMPARISON WITH OTHER ACCOUNTS OF TASK COMPLEXITY AND INTELLIGENCE

The suggested model is most obviously similar to those theories that interpret general intelligence in such terms as mental energy, attentional resources, and effortful mental processing. However, important differences between this model and similar ones should be noted. The main dissimilarity with Spearman's (1927) original single common factor model, apart from its attempting to give a more precise account of the notion of "mental energy," lies in the assumptions on the nature of the factors associated with the lower complexity tasks. In Spearman's model these factors (the s's) were assumed to be task-specific and uncorrelated. In the present model, these are allowed to be correlated, and are assumed to be much broader in content, with an importance comparable to that of the second-order factors. Another important difference is that in Spearman's and other similar statements individual differences in mental energy, or attentional resources, are assumed to be reflected in the "g" of batteries of diverse tests. In the present model it is suggested (as was also proposed by Hunt & Lansman, 1982) that certain types of high g-loading tasks, such as vocabulary and other common Gc markers, do not directly reflect individual differences in effortful, or complex, mental processing at the time of test performance. For this reason the present model identifies Gf, rather than "g," as reflecting more directly individual differences in effortful mental processing.

Hunt and Lansman (1982) suggested that Kahneman's notion of an undifferentiated pool of attentional resources might be a way of giving substance to Spearman's concept of mental energy as the source of individual differences in intelligence. Thus, in common with the present proposal, intelligence is seen as being associated with effortful mental processing. However, as emphasized earlier, in the present model the concept of effortful processing has a close, but not exact, link with that of a single, general purpose, pool of processing capacity. Here, effortful processing is defined in terms of the involvement of diffuse neural pathways, which may produce in certain circumstances, tradeoffs in the performances of concurrent tasks of the form that would be predicted from a single attentional resource model such as Kahneman's. However, effortful concurrent tasks which involve diffuse, but spatially well separated, neural pathways would give rise to lower mutual interference than would be expected from a single attentional resource model. This is an important difference between the model being proposed here and a theory of Gf (or of "g"), as suggested by Hunt and Lansman (1982), which is based on the concept of a single supply of attentional resources. The latter model would predict that two concurrently performed high Gf-loading (and therefore effortful) tasks would always show high levels of capacity-like mutual interference.

The proposed model, however, would allow, for certain combinations of Gf-loading tasks, that lower levels of intertask interference could occur in such dual task situations. Thus, for example, concurrently performed verbal reasoning and spatial visualization tasks (both relatively good markers of Gf) could be expected to show lower levels of mutual interference on the basis of the proposed model, than would be expected on the basis of the model suggested by Hunt and Lansman (1982). This would follow if the diffuse neural pathways associated with the performances on each of the tasks were well separated on the cortex, as might be expected if different hemispheres were primarily involved in the performances of the verbal and spatial tasks. The finding of a relatively low level of interference between such tasks might be taken as evidence for a multiprocessor, or multiple resources, attentional model (e.g., Allport, 1980a; Navon & Gopher, 1979). However, such multiprocessor, or multiple resources, models would not explain why both these tasks are good measures of Gf. It is the particular strength of the proposed model that it can accommodate the sorts of data commonly used to support multiprocessor or multiple resources, attentional models, but as well give an account of the concept of task complexity, which does seem to be more easily related to single attentional resource, or "central processor," types of attentional models.

In terms of the factorial description of the structure of mental abilities, the theory that most closely relates to the model being proposed in this chapter is the Gf/Gc theory of Horn and Cattell. The model suggested here could be regarded as an attempt to relate Gf/Gc theory to the notion of task complexity, and to those attentional theories that may give some basis to the notions of effortful processes or mental energy. The connection between the proposed model and Gf/Gc theory is particularly close for the presentation of Cattell's (1987) theory in which Gf is linked with the operation of the tertiary association areas of the cortex. The further development of these notions in terms of the concept of task complexity in this chapter however, does give Gf a special and central place in the architecture of mental abilities, an emphasis that is not always found in presentations of Gf/Gc theory. In this sense, the elaboration of Gf/Gc presented here does give greater acknowledgement to the radex-like structure of abilities, as displayed in Fig. 8.1 of this chapter, and to the notion of task complexity that is emphasized by others (usually those writers supportive of the concept of general intelligence) working outside of the conceptual framework of Gf/Gc theory.

More recent statements of Gf/Gc theory by Horn (1985, 1986), are, however, less consonant with the proposed interpretation of Gf/Gc theory. Here the equivalent status of the different human intelligences (corresponding to the various broad second-order factors of Gf/Gc theory) is emphasized. This would also apply to other more pluralistic types of theories, such as that of Gardner (1983), where the term "multiple intelligences" is often used as a means of emphasizing the equivalence, in importance or status, of a number of distinct ability domains. It should be pointed out, however, that from the perspective of structural organization of functioning in the brain's cortex, there is one sense in which the proposed model could be regarded as pluralistic. One of Gardner's (1983) eight criteria for the specification of a separate "intelligence" is its potential isolation by brain damage. It is consistent with the present model that damage to large areas of the tertiary association areas in one region of the cortex will result in significant deficits in the complex processing of material associated with nearby more localized processes, although complex forms of processing occurring in the other undamaged tertiary association areas may be relatively unaffected. Thus, for example damage to large areas of the tertiary association region of the right cortex would produce large deficits in the ability to perform spatial/visualisation tasks of high complexity, while leaving relatively intact the ability to perform a complex verbal task, whose critical processing is located in the association areas of the left hemisphere.

Thus, from a structural perspective, the model does have similarities to the multiprocessor one of Allport (1980a, 1980b), and the multiple intelligences approach of Gardner (1983). However, as a theory of intelligence it would be more appropriately regarded as monistic, as it is proposed that (at least for non brain-damaged people) various forms of more complex processing are related to a single dimension in individual differences. This follows from the assumption in the model that the efficiency of more highly diffuse or distributed neural processes is reflected in a single dimension in individual differences (namely Gf), irrespective of the cortical localization of the processing.

Except for the operational definition of task complexity in terms of "g," rather than in terms of Gf, the theoretical account of task complexity given by Jensen (1977, 1979) is largely consistent with the ideas being suggested in this model. Jensen describes complex tasks as being intentional and involving some kind of conscious mental effort, rather than being reflexive or automatic. He does not, however, attempt to define these notions in terms of any specific attentional theory. Similarly a close parallel between the present model and Jensen's (1969, 1973, 1974) earlier Level I/II theory can be drawn provided that some qualifications are made. It is clear from his theoretical descriptions of these abilities, and the tasks used to operationalize them in his empirical studies, that Level I and Level II abilities correspond to tasks of relatively low and high complexity, respectively. Apart from the issue discussed earlier, of whether it is "g" or Gf tasks that more appropriately represent complex mental processes, is the question of how Level I ability can be related to this model. How this may be done depends largely on whether Level I refers to a single low-complexity ability dimension, associated with the rote learning and memory, or whether it refers, collectively, to a number of different abilities (cf. Jensen, 1982a). Jensen's level I/II theory would more closely relate to the model presented earlier if Level I were regarded as a collective description of various distinct ability factors that represent mental processes of relatively low complexity.

Not so apparently consistent with the proposed model is the importance given by Jensen (e.g., 1980a, 1980b, 1982b) and H. Eysenck (1982) to the study of elementary reaction-time tasks and their relationship to intelligence. Correlations between such tasks and intelligence are typically of the same order of magnitude as are found for other more common low complexity tasks, such as perceptual/clerical speed or memory span. The main attraction, for these authors, towards the study of elementary reaction time tasks is that the finding of a significant relationship between these tasks and traditional measures of intelligence would be strong evidence against what they see as a popular, but erroneous, notion on the nature of intelligence. This notion is that "our current standard tests of intelligence measure nothing but a particular class of specific knowledge and acquired cognitive skills or strategies . . . ," and that "individual differences in intelligence are attributable to differences in opportunities afforded by the environment for acquiring the specific items of knowledge and skills that are called for by the standard tests of intelligence" (Jensen, 1982b, pp. 93–94). Although in basic agreement with Jensen and H. Eysenck on this point, the model proposed earlier would suggest that a type of task that is more suitable for their purposes is one similar to the serial short-term memory task discussed earlier, and others similar to Wittenborn's (1943) tests of sustained attention. As with reaction time tasks, performances on these tests of Attention could be regarded as relatively free from acquired knowledge or skills, but unlike reaction time tests, they have been found to be good direct markers of fluid intelligence.

Jensen's (1979) view on strategies, as a basis for the understanding of intelligence, is that they are a "red herring." To the extent that this implies that tasks whose performances are not strongly determined by a subject's choice of strategies can nevertheless be good measures of intelligence, the model presented earlier is in agreement with Jensen's statement. However, the model does imply a close and fundamental relationship between intelligence and what have been termed executive control and strategic processes. This follows from the generally accepted idea that a hierarchy of controls exists between the functions of the more specialized, and the less specialized, regions of the cortex. Psychoneurological accounts of the functions of the tertiary association areas emphasize their role in the coordination and control of the more specific and more localized neural functions. Such processes are also generally assumed to be more flexible (or less ballistic), and more directly associated with conscious or voluntary control, than are the more specific and localized processes. In other words, a major role of the tertiary association areas is the performance of what cognitive psychologists have termed executive control and strategic functions, and which have been postulated by numerous authors as underlying individual differences in general intelligence.

There is, therefore, a certain consistency between those more process-oriented, or strategies based, theories of intelligence and the model being suggested in this chapter. However, these theories do diverge from the one being presented here with respect to the question of whether the efficiency of processing in these association areas might be measured by tasks, performance on which does not depend significantly on individual differences in strategic processes. That this can be done is suggested by the supposed critical involvement of the tertiary association areas in functions other than strategic ones. Examples are tasks requiring the temporary holding in mind of information concurrent with other nonautomatic forms of processing and that have been described as reflecting the operation of an "active," or "working" short-term memory system. (The serial short-term memory task mentioned earlier is a good example). Because performances on such tasks reflect the efficiency of the less localized neural processes, they would be expected to be strongly related to intelligence, even though they do not directly reflect the role of the more distributed neural processes in being associated with the operation of strategic functions.

REFERENCES

Ackerman, P. L. (1988). Determinants of individual differences during skill acquisition: Cognitive abilities and information processing. *Journal of Experimental Psychology: General, 117*(3), 288–318.

Ackerman, P. L., Schneider, W., & Wickens, C. D. (1982). *Individual differences and time-sharing ability: A critical review and analysis.* Human Attention Research Laboratory, Psychology Dept., University of Illinois, Report HARL–ONR–8102.

Allport, D. A. (1971, March). *A new hypothesis on the nature of attention.* Paper presented at meeting of the Experimental Psychology Society, Reading.

Allport, D. A. (1980a). Patterns and actions: Cognitive mechanisms are content specific. In G. Claxton (Ed.), *Cognitive psychology: New directions.* London: Routledge and Kegan Paul.

Allport, D. A. (1980b). Attention and performance. In G. Claxton (Ed.), *Cognitive psychology: New directions.* London: Routledge and Kegan Paul.

Anderson, J. A. (1983). Cognitive and psychological computation with neural models. *IEEE Transactions on Systems, Man and Cybernetics, 13*(5), 799–815.

Anderson, J. A., & Hinton, G. E. (1981). Models of information processing in the brain. In G. E. Hinton & J. A. Anderson (Eds.), *Parallel models of associative memory*. Hillsdale, NJ: Lawrence Erlbaum Associates.

Atkinson, J. R., & Shiffrin, R. M. (1968). Human memory: A proposed system and its control processes. In K. W. Spence & J. T. Spence (Eds.), *The psychology of learning and motivation*. New York: Academic Press.

Borkowski, J. G., & Krause, A. (1983). Racial differences in intelligence: The importance of the executive system. *Intelligence, 7*, 379–395.

Campione, J. C., Brown, A. L., & Bryant, N. R. (1985). Individual differences in learning and memory. In R. J. Sternberg (Ed.), *Human abilities: An information processing approach*. New York: W. H. Freeman.

Carroll, J. B. (1945). The effect of difficulty and chance success on correlations between items or between tests. *Psychometrika, 10*, 1–19.

Carroll, J. B. (1961). The nature of the data, or how to choose a correlation coefficient. *Psychometrika, 26*, 347–372.

Carroll, J. B. (1981). Ability and task difficulty in cognitive psychology. *Educational Researcher, 10*, 11–21.

Cattell, R. B. (1987). *Intelligence: Its structure, growth and action*. Amsterdam: Elsevier Science Publishers.

Cohen, R. L., & Sandberg, T. (1977). Relation between intelligence and short-term memory. *Cognitive Psychology, 9*, 543–554.

Crawford, J. D. (1988). *Intelligence, task complexity and tests of sustained attention*. Unpublished doctoral thesis, University of N.S.W.

Crawford, J. D., & Stankov, L. (1983). Fluid and crystallised intelligence and primacy/recency components of short-term memory. *Intelligence, 7*, 227–252.

Ellis, N. R. (1970). Memory processes in retardates and normals. In N. R. Ellis (Ed.), *International review of research in mental retardation* (Vol. 4). New York: Academic Press.

Eysenck, H. J. (1953). *Uses and abuses of psychology*. Harmondsworth, England: Penguin.

Eysenck, M. W. (1979). Anxiety, learning and memory: A reconceptualisation. *Journal of Research in Personality, 13*, 363–385.

Eysenck, M. W. (1982). *Attention and arousal*. New York: Springer-Verlag.

Fogarty, G., & Stankov, L. (1987). Abilities involved in performance on competing tasks. *Personality and Individual Differences, 9*, 35–49.

Gardner, H. (1983). *Frames of mind: The theory of multiple intelligences*. New York: Basic Books.

Guilford, J. P. (1967). *The nature of human intelligence*. New York: McGraw Hill.

Guttman, L. (1954). A new approach to factor analysis: The radex. In P. F. Lazarfield (Ed.), *Mathematical thinking in the social sciences*. Glencoe, IL: Free Press.

Hawkins, H. L., Church, M., & de Lemos, S. (1978). *Time-sharing is not a unitary ability*. University of Oregon Technical Report No. 2, prepared for the office of Naval Research, Contract NOO14-77-C-0643.

Hebb, D. O. (1949). *The organisation of behaviour*. New York: Wiley.

Hirst, W., Spelke, E. S., Reaves, C. C., Caharack, G., & Neisser, U. (1980). Dividing attention without alteration or automaticity. *Journal of Experimental Psychology: General, 109*, 98–117.

Horn, J. L. (1985). Remodeling old models of intelligence. In B. B. Wollman (Ed.), *Handbook of intelligence*. New York: Wiley.

Horn, J. L. (1986). Models of Intelligence. In *Intelligence, measurement, theory and public policy*. Symposium, University of Illinois, Urbana: University of Illinois Press.

Horn, J. L., & Bramble, W. J. (1967). Second-order ability structure revealed in rights and wrongs scores. *Journal of Educational Psychology, 58*, 115–122.

Horn, J. L., & Cattell, R. B. (1966). Refinement and test of the theory of fluid and crystallised general intelligences. *Journal of Educational Psychology, 57*, 253–270.

Hughes, O. L. (1983). A comparison of error based and time based learning measures as predictors of general intelligence. *Intelligence, 7,* 9–26.

Humphreys, L. (1979). The construct of general intelligence. *Intelligence, 3,* 105–120.

Humphreys, L. (1981). The primary mental ability. In M. P. Friedman, J. P. Das, & N. O'Connor (Eds.), *Intelligence and learning.* New York: Plenum Press.

Hunt, E. (1978). Mechanics of verbal ability. *Psychological Review, 85,* 109–130.

Hunt, E. (1980). Intelligence as an information-processing concept. *British Journal of Psychology, 71,* 449–474.

Hunt, E. B., & Lansman, M. (1982). Individual differences in attention. In R. J. Sternberg (Ed.), *Advances in the psychology of human intelligence* (Vol. 1). Hillsdale, NJ: Lawrence Erlbaum Associates.

Jenkinson, J. C. (1983). Is speed of information processing related to fluid or crystallized intelligence? *Intelligence, 7,* 91–106.

Jensen, A. R. (1969). How much can we boost IQ and scholastic achievement? *Harvard Educational Review, 39,* 1–123.

Jensen, A. R. (1973). Level I and Level II abilities in three ethnic groups. *American Educational Research Journal, 10,* 263–276.

Jensen, A. R. (1974). Interaction of Level I and Level II abilities with race and socio-economic status. *Journal of Educational Psychology, 66,* 91–111.

Jensen, A. R. (1977). *The nature of intelligence and its relations to learning.* Paper delivered at the T. A. Fink Memorial Lecture at the University of Melbourne.

Jensen, A. R. (1979). g: Outmoded theory or unconquered frontier? *Creative Science and Technology, 2,* 16–29.

Jensen, A. R. (1980a). Reaction-time and intelligence. In M. P. Friedman, J. P. Das, & N. O'Connor (Eds.), *Intelligence and learning.* New York: Plenum.

Jensen, A. R. (1980b). Chronometric analysis of intelligence. *Journal of Social Biological Structures, 3,* 103–122.

Jensen, A. R. (1982a). Level I/Level II: Factors or categories? *Journal of Educational Psychology, 76,* 868–73.

Jensen, A. R. (1982b). Reaction time and psychometric g. In H. J. Eysenck (Ed.), *A model for intelligence.* Berlin: Springer Verlag.

Kahneman, D. (1973). *Attention and effort.* Englewood Cliffs, NJ: Prentice-Hall.

Keele, J. (1979). Presentation at the Office of Naval Research Contractor's Meeting on Information Processing Abilities, New Orleans.

Kerr, B. (1973). Processing demands during mental operations. *Memory and Cognition, 1,* 401–412.

Kinsbourne, M. (1981). Single-channel theory. In D. Holding (Ed.), *Human skills.* Plymouth, England: Wiley.

Kinsbourne, M., & Hicks, R. (1978). Functional cerebral space. In J. Requin (Ed.), *Attention and performance VII.* Hillsdale, NJ: Lawrence Erlbaum Associates.

Lansman, M., & Hunt, E. (1982). Individual differences in secondary task performance. *Memory and Cognition, 10,* 10–24.

Lezak, M. D. (1983). *Neuropsychological assessment.* New York: Oxford University Press.

Marshalek, B., Lohman, D. F., & Snow, R. E. (1983). The complexity continuum in the radex and hierarchical models of intelligence. *Intelligence, 7,* 107–127.

Matarazzo, J. D. (1972). *Wechsler's measurement and appraisal of adult intelligence* (5th ed.). Baltimore: Williams and Wilkins.

Monty, R. A. (1968). Spatial encoding strategies in sequential short-term memory. *Journal of Experimental Psychology, 77,* 506–508.

Monty, R. A., Taub, H. A., & Laughery, K. R. (1965). Keeping track of sequential events: effects of rate, categories and trial length. *Journal of Experimental Psychology, 69,* 224–229.

Moray, N. (1969). *Attention: Selective processes in vision and hearing.* London: Hutchinson Educational Ltd.

Navon, D., & Gopher, D. (1979). On the economy of the human processing system. *Psychological Review, 86,* 214–255.

Nettlebeck, T., & Kirby, N. H. (1983). Measures of timed performance and intelligence. *Intelligence, 7,* 39–52.

Norman, D. A., & Bobrow, D. G. (1975). On data-limited and resource-limited processes. *Cognitive Psychology, 7,* 44–64.

Pellegrino, J. W., & Glaser, R. (1979). Cognitive correlates and components in the analysis of individual differences. In R. J. Sternberg & D. K. Detterman (Eds.), *Human intelligence, perspectives on its theory and measurement.* Norwood, NJ: Ablex.

Pribram, K. H. (1971). *Languages of the brain.* Monterey, CA: Brooks/Cole.

Roediger, H. L., Knight, J. L., & Kantowitz, B. H. (1977). Infering decay in short-term memory: The issue of capacity. *Memory and cognition, 5,* 167–176.

Rumelhart, D. E., & McClelland, J. L. (1986). *Explorations in the microstructure of cognition* (Vol. 1). Cambridge, MA: Bradford Books, MIT Press.

Schneider, W., & Shiffrin, R. M. (1977). Controlled and automatic human information processing: I. Detection, search and attention. *Psychological Review, 84,* 1–16.

Snow, R. E. (1980). Aptitude processes. In R. E. Snow, P. A. Frederico, & W. E. Montague (Eds.), *Aptitude, learning and instruction* (Vol. 1). *Cognitive process analysis of aptitude.* Hillsdale, NJ: Lawrence Erlbaum Associates.

Snow, R. E. (1986). Toward a theory of cognitive aptitude for learning from instruction. In S. E. Newstead, S. H. Irvine & P. L. Dann (Eds.), *NATO Advanced Study Institute Study on Human Assessment: Cognition and Motivation.* Dordrecht: Martinus Nijhoff Publishers.

Spearman, C. (1927). *The abilities of man.* New York: MacMillan.

Spelke, E., Hirst, W., & Neisser, U. (1976). Skills of divided attention. *Cognition 4,* 215–230.

Stankov, L. (1983). Attention and intelligence. *Journal of Educational Psychology, 75,* 471–490.

Stankov, L. (1985). *Attentional resources and intelligence: A disappearing link.* Paper presented at the Australian Experimental Psychology Conference. Newcastle, N.S.W.

Sternberg, R. J. (1977). *Intelligence, information processing and analogical reasoning: The componential analysis of human abilities.* Hillsdale, NJ: Lawrence Erlbaum Associates.

Sternberg, R. J. (1981). The evolution of theories of intelligence. *Intelligence, 5,* 209–230.

Sternberg, R. J. (1983). Components of human intelligence. *Cognition, 15,* 1–48.

Sternberg, R. J. (1985). *Beyond I.Q.* Cambridge: Cambridge University Press.

Sverko, B. (1977). Individual differences in time-sharing ability. *Acta Instituti Psychologici Universitatis Zagrabiensis.* No. 80.

Thurstone, L. L. (1938). Primary mental abilities. *Psychometric Monographs.* No. 1. Chicago: University of Chicago Press.

Vernon, P. E. (1950). *The structure of human abilities.* London: Methuen.

Walsh, K. (1987). *Neuropsychological assessment: A clinical approach.* Edinborough: Churchill Livingstone.

Waugh, N. C., & Norman, D. A. (1965). Primary memory. *Psychological Review, 72,* 89–104.

White, P. O. (1982). Some major components in general intelligence. In H. J. Eysenck (Ed.), *A model for intelligence.* New York: Springer Verlag.

Wickens, C. D. (1980). The structure of attentional resources. In R. Nickerson (Ed.), *Attention and performance VIII.* Hillsdale, NJ: Lawrence Erlbaum Associates.

Wittenborn, T. R. (1943). Factorial equations for tests of attention. *Psychometrica, 8,* 19–35.

Wood, R. E. (1986). Task complexity: definition of the construct. *Organisational Behaviour and Human Decision Processes, 37,* 60–82.

Zimmerman, I. L., & Woo-Sam, J. M. (1973). *Clinical interpretations of the Wechsler Adult Intelligence Scale.* New York: Grune and Stratton.

9 On the Neurology of Intelligence and Intelligence Factors

David L. Robinson
University of Sydney, Australia

In general terms, it is useful and meaningful to think of intelligence as the total amount of "information" available to an individual. Since the merits of this conception are discussed in detail elsewhere (Robinson, 1989), it will suffice to state here that it has informed and directed the author's efforts to comprehend the nature of EEG-intelligence relations.

This research on EEG-intelligence relations has been carried on as an extension of earlier work which led to the discovery of theoretically meaningful relationships between personality dimensions such as introversion-extraversion and EEG measures of cortical arousability (Haier, Robinson, Braden, & Williams, 1984; Robinson, 1982, 1983, 1986a, 1986b, 1987; Robinson, Haier, Braden, & Krengel, 1984a). In the course of this earlier work the author was led to suppose that cortical arousability should also relate to intelligence.

The term cortical arousability refers to a characteristic or typical level of activation of thalamocortical neurons that is determined by the general availability and balance of excitatory and inhibitory neurotransmitter substances. In general terms, it was thought that differences in thalamocortical arousability might be a crucial neurological factor that can limit the amount of information available to an individual and thereby determine differences in general intelligence. In particular, it was hypothesized that intelligence test performance and arousability are related in a curvilinear fashion analogous to the Yerkes-Dodson law (Yerkes & Dodson, 1908; see also Broadhurst, 1959). Thus, across individuals, intelligence test performance would be optimal when there is an intermediate degree of arousability. For progressively higher or lower degrees of arousability there would be correspondingly lower intelligence scores.

Of course, the *general* notion of a link between intelligence and arousability is not new. To account for the effects of brain damage on intelligence test performance Hebb (1949) was forced to invent an arousal mechanism, the "cell assembly." According to Hebb, contemporary theories of behavior were inadequate since they did not account for some of the most fundamental psychological facts. Classical SR learning theory failed to allow for any autonomy of brain function and for related psychological facts such as selective attention. Field theory, on the other hand, tried to account for perception without reference to learning. Through the mechanism of the cell assembly, Hebb's theory was able to relate learning and perception while at the same time providing a basis for the autonomous brain activity or arousal that is necessary to account for behavior such as selective attention.

A decade later, Hebb (1959) refers to the gaps in neurological knowledge that existed when his theory was formulated and suggests that,

> the greatest omission of all is of course the brain-stem arousal system of Moruzzi and Magoun (1949) whose fundamental role in all higher processes is now clear. No account of intellectual processes and their relation to the brain can be taken seriously today when this is omitted from the reckoning. (pp. 266–267)

Hebb goes on to suggest that an intermediate degree of arousal would appear to be optimal for cognitive processing.

The psychological significance of brain arousal mechanisms has been considered in detail by Samuels (1959) and also by Magoun (1963). Both of these authors make the point that arousal mechanisms can modify cortical activity partially or globally and consequently they have the capacity to regulate the content of conscious experience with all that this entails.

AROUSABILITY AS THE DETERMINANT OF CORRELATIONS BETWEEN EEG AND IQ

In the publications referred to just now, both Samuels and Magoun review evidence which demonstrates conclusively that the activities of the arousal systems can be observed in EEG recordings. It follows directly that EEG measures relate to arousability and that there should be a relationship between such measures and intelligence test performance.

In fact, there is a considerable literature on the relationship of EEG and intelligence which shows many significant but apparently inconsistent correlations. However, the present author has found that this confused and confusing literature can be rendered comprehensible if reference is made to the "inverted-U" hypothesis of the relationship between arousability and intelligence. For the most part, studies of EEG and intelligence have not been guided by either theoretical expectations concerning the particular EEG variables which should relate to intelligence or by any expectation of the form such relationships should take. In practice, the results have often been evaluated in terms of rectilinear correlation coefficients which, by default, only test the validity of a simple rectilinear model. It follows that in a representative sample the proposed curvilinear inverted-U relationship would not be detected. However, significant positive or negative rectilinear correlation coefficients could be obtained in unrepresentative groups if the individuals concerned were either low on arousability or high on arousability, respectively.

In the earlier EEG studies, carried out prior to 1965, there are remarkably consistent reports of a positive relationship between the frequency of spontaneous EEG activity and intelligence in low arousability groups. That is to say, in groups of elderly people, children, or mentally retarded persons.

In recent times, technological advances have allowed the recording of EEG responses to specific stimuli, often a light flash or tone. From 1965, as many as 19 studies have investigated the possibility of a relationship between these evoked potentials and intelligence. Despite great variation of conditions and procedures, most studies did find some evidence of a relationship between intelligence and differences in evoked potential waveforms. Most of the correlations have been small but again there is some indication that the strongest evidence of a simple rectilinear relationship is to be found in low arousal groups.

The last point mentioned is well illustrated by Hendrickson's (1982) study of 219 London schoolchildren where a negative correlation coefficient of .83 was obtained between Full Scale WAIS IQ and a composite evoked potential measure. Two published studies and one as yet unpublished study carried out by the present author using similar, and in one case identical, evoked potential procedures, suggest that Hendrickson's findings do not generalize to adults in the middle years of the life span (Haier, Robinson, Braden & Williams 1983, Robinson, Haier, Braden, & Krengel, 1984b). However, significant correlations ranging up to 0.69 were found in three different samples composed of individuals in their late teens or early twenties. Evidence of a simple linear relationship was also found in a group of elderly subjects. Moreover, when behavioral criteria were employed to select out elderly individuals closest to the sleep threshold, there was an appreciable increase in the magnitude of the correlations.

These results led to the conviction that a simple linear model is inadequate and suggested that serious consideration be given to the arousability hypothesis. At the same time, it seemed clear that any advances in this area were unlikely to be achieved with conventional evoked potential procedures where the measurement of superficial features of the response waveform inevitably confounds the effects of different underlying variables and there is a general failure to take account of the dynamic nature of the relationship between stimulus inputs and EEG response outputs.

A SYSTEMS THEORY APPROACH TO ANALYSIS
OF EEG RESPONSES

To overcome the problems noted earlier, and to achieve a theoretically mean-ingful analysis of EEG responses, a new procedure was developed based on the concepts and techniques employed in systems analysis. Systems theory param-eters can summarize the dynamic character of a system and provide a compre-hensive description of arousability in terms that are precisely defined, well understood and generally accepted. Details of the systems analysis procedure are described by Robinson (1983). It will suffice here to state that by sinusoidal modulation of the luminance of a light stimulus, it is possible to obtain a si-nusoidal EEG response of the same frequency. As the frequency of the input stimulus is systematically altered there is variation of the peak-to-peak amplitude of the EEG response. If response amplitudes are plotted as a function of the stimulus frequency, then, for each subject, it is possible to obtain a characteristic frequency response curve with a peak at around 10 Hz. This kind of curve is produced by a system which effectively has two opposed elements that are capable of storing or integrating the inputs they receive. It is precisely the kind of curve that one would expect for opposed aggregates of inhibitory and excitatory thalamocortical neurons that are known to sum or integrate their inputs.

The shape of the curve reflects the fact that elements with the capacity to store or integrate their inputs will typically offer some impedance to the transmission of an input. For the kind of system producing these curves, the impedance due to one element increases as frequency increases. For the other element, impedance increases as frequency decreases. At one particular frequency of stimulation the impedances offered by the respective elements will be equal and they cancel out. At this frequency, the steady-state response amplitude is only limited by factors influencing the activity of the system that are not sensitive to changes in stimula-tion frequency. Thus, the particular shape of the curve obtained for any indi-vidual can be directly related to the transmission characteristics of thalamocor-tical processes of excitation and inhibition. Equally important, the shape of the curve also reflects any general effect on thalamocortical responsiveness due, for example, to external agencies such as the brainstem reticular activating system.

For specified conditions of stimulation, the frequency dependent effects of excitatory and inhibitory thalamocortical processes, and any general non fre-quency dependent effect, can all be represented in a model which yields an equation relating stimulus inputs to corresponding EEG outputs. Robinson (1983) has tested the empirical validity of this equation and found that it does account for variation of sinusoidal EEG responses, both within and across sub-jects, as a function of changes in stimulation frequency. The model is also valid in neurological terms since it represents the known organization and transmission characteristics of excitatory and inhibitory processes as well as accounting for a number of hitherto unexplained EEG phenomena, including the oscillatory character of the spontaneous EEG and the shape of the evoked potential waveform.

Robinson (1983) describes how the equation referred to in the preceding paragraph can be used to fit theoretical curves to the frequency response data obtained from different individuals. By fitting these curves, constants can be evaluated which provide *separate* estimates for the relative transmission characteristics of excitatory and inhibitory neurons and for any effect on responsiveness that is not frequency dependent.

The three constants have been designated L, C, and R because they represent effects that are analogous to the capacitance, inductance and resistance of electronics and because the functional significance of the constants can be understood more easily if reference is made to these familiar concepts. For any particular individual, the values of the constants can be used to calculate two systems theory parameters, natural frequency and damping ratio. These parameters are particularly meaningful and useful since they provide a summary description of the dynamic character or arousability of the whole system of excitatory and inhibitory neurons producing the sinusoidal EEG responses.

In general terms, higher natural frequencies indicate that a system will respond faster to any disturbance. In effect, there is faster transmission between the reciprocally interacting populations of neurons. A lower damping ratio, or less damping, indicates that the response to a transient input will continue or persist for a longer period. Thus, higher natural frequencies or lower damping ratios both indicate greater arousability although the two parameters relate to different aspects of arousability.

It is pertinent to note that the systems theory parameters describe the dynamic character of a closed thalamocortical loop or circuit that is analogous to the closed loop or cell assembly that Hebb postulated in order to account for autonomy of brain function. It is also noted that after Pavlov there are compelling theoretical reasons for evaluating arousability in terms of the relative balance of excitation and inhibition. This would provide no information about the intrinsic arousability of the thalamocortical system of neurons over and above that provided by the systems theory parameters, but it would be expected to influence the level of arousal of the brainstem reticular activating system and hence also influence the general level of arousal of the central nervous system.

AROUSABILITY, INFORMATION PROCESSING, AND INTELLIGENCE FACTORS

Robinson (1989) has described how the two arousability parameters, natural frequency and damping ratio, relate to WAIS IQ scores. In this analysis of data from 48 adult subjects it was found that the highest IQ scores do indeed coincide with middling *overall* arousability whether this is defined in terms of the relative contributions due to natural frequency and damping ratio or in terms of excitation-inhibition balance. That is to say, there is a strong relationship between IQ and arousability across individuals which is analogous to the inverted-U curve that has frequently been used to describe the relationship between performance and arousal within individuals.

This result has profound theoretical significance since the relationship between arousability and intelligence can be explained in terms of the way in which differences in thalamocortical arousability influence the acquisition, retention and utilization of information. At the same time, it is possible to discern the neurological bases for the general intelligence factor described by Spearman (1927) and for a bipolar ability factor that was frequently encountered in the early factor analytic studies reviewed by Burt (1949). In terms of arousability theory and related findings, it is also possible to account for a reported relationship between this bipolar factor and the introversion–extraversion dimension of personality.

An intermediate degree of thalamocortical arousability is conceived as optimal for information processing because of the way in which thalamocortical arousal influences:

1. The neurological system of information transmission.
2. The neurological system regulating attention and recall.
3. The neurological process of learning.

Arousability and Information Transmission.   An intermediate degree of cortical arousability should be optimal for information transmission because, as far as is known, all information received by the brain is transmitted centrally by variation of neural firing rates. This is also true for all information transmission within the brain. Since all physical systems including neurons have a limited operating range with upper and lower limits determined by physical constraints, it is clear that very high or very low levels of "background" activation or arousal will limit the variability of neural firing rates and hence limit the amount of information that can be transmitted. The brain receives much information by virtue of the contrasts provided by differential rates of firing of different neurons. These contrasts would be attenuated by high or low levels of arousal. Thus, while all aspects of information processing would be impaired by deviation from middling arousability, it can be suggested that a specific psychological effect would be a reduced capacity to make discriminations.

This accords with Spearman's (1904) interpretation of his early findings when he claimed that a single general function would suffice to account for practically all the correlations he observed between different ability measures. He identified this "fundamental general function" with the elementary process of "discrimination" and provided empirical support for the earlier ideas of Sully and Bain who both asserted that the discernment of difference is the most fundamental element in all intellectual activity (Burt, 1949). The fundamental importance of discriminative capacity is further suggested by recent findings reported by Lynn, Wilson, and Gault (1989) which show that the capacity to discriminate simple auditory tones is highly correlated with scores obtained on the WAIS. Similar findings have been obtained by this author in a study not yet published.

More generally, it is well known that at the extremes of very high or very low levels of arousal (whether due to traumatic experiences, sleep or drug effects) the psychological correlate of reduced information transmission is a total loss of discriminative power and unconsciousness.

Arousability, Attention, and Recall.   An intermediate degree of thalamocortical arousability should be optimal for information processing because it is optimal for the regulation of attention and recall and for the operation of "working memory." This follows from the premise that the content of conscious experience alters as a function of differences in the degree of thalamocortical arousability and resultant differences in the degree to which there is inhibition of the brainstem reticular activating system. The latter system provides background cortical activation that is necessary for perception to occur (Samuels, 1959). With higher intrinsic thalamocortical arousability there is a correspondingly higher level of thalamocortical activity or arousal and stronger inhibition of brainstem processes necessary for perception. While the overall effect of thalamocortical processes on the brainstem is known to be inhibitory, it is suggested that this inhibition is selective and graded in a manner which causes greater inhibition of familiar stimulus inputs when these do not signal positive or negative consequences.

In effect, learned and selective inhibition of brainstem processes is regarded as the mechanism which determines the psychological phenomenon of habituation and this is consistent with the fact that neurons of the brainstem reticular activating system are most easily activated by novel stimuli. If, as suggested, inhibition of the brainstem is selective and graded, it follows that a generally higher degree of thalamocortical arousability and correspondingly higher levels of cortical activation will increase the number of brainstem elements that are inactivated and thereby reduce the range of stimuli that can be perceived. This ensures that when there is high cortical arousability there can only be a very selective and serial mode of perceiving and representing the external environment.

At the same time, however, high intrinsic thalamocortical arousability must result in lower thresholds for the evocation of memories and ideation that is unrelated or less closely related to contemporary stimulus inputs than would otherwise be expected. The greater blocking of external inputs, which includes proprioception and other internal sources of stimulation, together with lower thresholds for memories and ideation, determines an introverted mental orientation that effectively limits the range of information that can be accessed, and determines a particular mode of information processing. The capacity of working memory is also reduced since the ability to "keep something in mind" will be impaired by irrelevant and distracting ideation.

With low intrinsic thalamocortical arousability the threshold for cortical activity associated with memories and ideation would be high, but weaker inhibition of the brainstem reticular activating system ensures that there are high levels of cortical activity mediated by this system and relating to a less selective and parallel mode of perceiving and representing the external environment in conscious experience. Again, it is emphasized that "external" means external to the CNS and does not exclude somatic inputs. In this case, the "broadband" and less selective perception of external inputs together with higher thresholds for the evocation of ideation determines an extraverted mental orientation. Again, the range of information that can be accessed is reduced and again the capacity of working memory is reduced since the ability to keep something in mind is impaired by irrelevant and distracting external stimuli.

Clearly, an intermediate degree of arousability is again optimal because transient shifts in arousal state will allow *both* internal and external sources of information to be accessed as necessary and this information can be better utilized in problem solving activities since the capacity of working memory is effectively increased when the distraction due to both irrelevant ideation and irrelevant external stimuli can be minimized.

Although attention has not always been defined in the same way, tests of the ability to concentrate attention have long been included in measures of general intelligence and some have had high loadings on general intelligence factors when these are extracted as the principal component in a battery of tests. So much so, that before the concept of general intelligence became less fashionable, various writers including Wundt suggested an identity with the "capacity for attention" (Burt, 1949).

When middling arousability is contrasted with both high and low arousability it is to be expected that those individuals with middling arousability will do better on tasks that involve keeping something in mind while executing related cognitive operations, as in oral arithmetic problems, and in tasks requiring a working memory of large capacity. It is only in this sense that the capacity to concentrate attention would be associated with a general intelligence factor.

If such a factor were extracted as the principal component in a set of tests and an orthogonal factor was subsequently extracted, one would expect this latter factor to contrast individuals high and low on arousability. In terms of cognitive abilities, one would expect a bipolar factor contrasting a very selective, idea-driven and serial mode of attention deployment with a relatively unselective, stimulus-driven and parallel mode of attention deployment. In fact, as Burt points out, when this method of factor analysis was more commonly employed such a bipolar factor was frequently encountered. Burt (1949, pp. 197–198) describes the contrast in terms of "fixating" as opposed to "diffusive" attention. He also points out that the same factor contrasts differences in perseveration, emotionality, objectivity and introversion-extraversion. This is precisely what would be predicted from arousability theory.

The effects of high and low arousability on the regulation of attention and recall has already been described in terms of introverted and extraverted mental orientations, but there is an actual and strong relationship between the arousability parameters described here and the introversion-extraversion dimension of personality (Robinson, 1982, 1987). Arousability theory explains this relationship and also accounts for the earlier findings described by Burt as well as accounting for the structural relationship between principal components or general intelligence factors and orthogonal bipolar factors.

Arousability and Learning. An intermediate degree of thalamocortical arousability should be optimal for information processing because it facilitates the development of a more valid world model through associative learning. In the first instance, this follows from the statements already made concerning information transmission and the regulation of attention and recall which specify optimal conditions for information processing *prior to* the occurrence of learning and the forming of associations.

The general advantage of enhanced information transmission and discriminative power is self evident but the way in which the regulation of attention would influence associative learning is not immediately obvious and must therefore be described in some detail. Clearly, the kinds of associations that are learned will depend on the manner in which attention is deployed. An introverted mental orientation will favour the learning of associations between discrete features of the external environment that are attended to selectively, in serial fashion, and in a way that is driven by ideation. This mode of learning favours the acquisition of cultural knowledge through language since language consists of circumscribed stimulus events that are arranged in serial fashion. Moreover, since learning is selective and driven by ideation, it is likely that any new learning will relate to the extension and development of existing ideas.

In contrast, an extraverted mental orientation, due to low thalamocortical arousability and weak inhibition of the brainstem reticular activating system will favour the learning of associations between many parallel stimulus inputs. In this case, the progression of learning in time is determined to a far greater extent by the nature of unfolding events and is much less influenced by ideation. Moreover, because there is an association of many parallel inputs through all sensory modalities this mode of learning favours the acquisition of knowledge concerning spatial and kinaesthetic relations which enhances all practical abilities involving physical interaction with the material environment. Other consequences of high and low thalamocortical arousability would be expected to influence the character of the associations that are formed. For example, high arousability can be associated with greater sensitivity to noxious stimuli and with feelings that are generally unpleasant. Low arousability can be related to greater sensitivity to appetitive stimuli and to feelings that are generally pleasant. Thus, there is a generally negative or positive quality of experience that is always present and therefore enters into all associations that are learned, as well as influencing expectations and determining differences in the situations that individuals will enter into and learn from.

Here it is sufficient to point to some of the more obvious consequences for associative learning that can be related to high and low arousability in order to demonstrate that there will be preferential learning of two very broad and distinct categories of associations. The world models that evolve as a consequence of either high or low arousability are inevitably distorted and unrealistic in that they derive from a biased sampling of all possible events and insofar as the quality of experience is subjectively biased in a positive or negative fashion.

In addition to these effects on learning, it can also be suggested that thalamocortical arousability has a direct influence on the development or selective facilitation of neural connections that is logically necessary to account for associative learning. This proposition is described in greater detail elsewhere (Robinson, 1989). Here it is sufficient to state that high chronic levels of cortical activation would be expected to have an effect on learning analogous to repetition or strong stimulation. Both high and low thalamocortical arousability will cause a high level of cortical activation. In the former case because intrinsic arousability is high. In the latter case, it is because low intrinsic arousability results in disinhibition of the brainstem reticular activating system and correspondingly high levels of externally mediated cortical arousal. Thus, as well as the preselection of two broad categories of inputs that can be associated, it may be argued that high and low arousability will ensure that, within these categories, associations are formed too easily and unselectively.

This would be advantageous in terms of "rote" learning and for the acquisition of special abilities of a reproductive character. However it would be disadvantageous insofar as associations within the introverted and extraverted domains would tend to have equal strength. A good world model should reflect the frequency with which events coincide so that, in conditions of uncertainty, there is a basis for discriminating associations that reflect chance coincidence from those that relate to frequently experienced coincidences and hence acquire the status of a relation.

If learning occurs too easily then all associations will tend to have equal weight or strength and there is no basis for discriminating valid relations from chance coincidence. On the other hand, if learning occurs with too much difficulty many relations will go unrecognized. A useful analogy here is the Type I and Type II errors of formal statistical inference. It should also be noted that, in the nature of things, elementary relations are experienced more frequently than complex ones. Thus, when learning occurs too readily there would be a reduced capacity to distinguish elementary relations within complex ones. In contrast, when learning occurs with too much difficulty, there should be a reduced capacity to perceive complex relations. In this way it can be argued that for associative learning, and especially for the development of a superior relational world model, middling arousability should be optimal. At this higher relational level, the effect of middling arousability would be manifest as the enhanced capacity to educe relations and correlates that eventually became a central feature of Spearman's (1927) conception of general intelligence.

Again, reference can be made to those earlier factor analytic studies reviewed by Burt (1949) where it was common to extract a principal component or general intelligence factor first and then subsequently to extract an orthogonal factor. Burt points out that in

> most researches in the cognitive field, the factor which accounts for the greater part of the individual variance, after the first or general factor has been removed, is a bipolar factor distinguishing verbal from non-verbal abilities. It appears with group tests and with individual tests, with psychological examinations and educational examinations, with Binet tests in the schoolroom and with tests of recruits for all the fighting services. It tends to divide both children and adults into verbal (or "intellectual") and nonverbal (or "practical") groups. (Burt, 1949, p. 184)

Once more it can be suggested that this factorial structure can be explained by arousability theory and that the bipolar factor again reflects a contrast between high and low arousability and the two different categories of associations that are preselected by the introverted and extraverted modes of attention deployment. Relevant studies carried out by this author do show that introverts and extraverts have different WAIS profiles such that introverts do better on the verbal subtests and extraverts do better on the performance subtests (Robinson, 1985, 1986c). Also, as noted earlier, there is a strong relationship between introversion-extraversion and thalamocortical arousability. Finally, from arousability theory it can be suggested that the bipolar factor relates to reproductive as distinct from eductive abilities.

NEUROLOGICAL DIFFERENCES DETERMINING THREE DISTINCT HIGH IQ TYPES

Without any contradiction of the finding that middling arousability determines high IQ, further analysis of the data described by Robinson (1989) reveals that high IQ scores are associated with three different and quite distinct combinations of the natural frequency, damping ratio and excitation-inhibition balance parameters. That is to say, middling arousability can be achieved by different combinations of the neurological parameters and all of these combinations are associated with high IQ scores. Data which illustrates this observation are shown in Table

9.1. To avoid any confusion it is noted that *high* natural frequencies indicate high arousability whereas *low* damping ratios indicate high arousability. Also it is noted that a zero value for the balance parameter, described here as "delta," indicates a balance between thalamocortical excitatory and inhibitory processes.

It is remarkable that in a sample of 48 individuals, described by Robinson (1989), all but one of the 17 subjects with IQ scores greater than 130 fall into the three quite distinct neurological categories shown in Table 9.1. The first two categories can be distinguished in terms of all three neurological parameters *with no overlap in the distributions*. In the first category, natural frequencies, damping ratios and delta values are all higher when compared with the corresponding values for the second group. In the third category, natural frequencies and delta values do not overlap with those of the second category and the damping ratios do not overlap with those of the first category.

Although high and low, respectively, on the three neurological parameters, the first two groups are similar in that there is a strong positive correlation between natural frequency and damping ratio. Indeed, the combined data for these two groups yield a highly significant product-moment correlation coefficient ($r = 0.81$). Thus, in these two categories, variation of arousability due to natural frequency is offset by corresponding but opposite changes in arousability due to

TABLE 9.1
The Means and Standard Deviations for Neurological Parameters, Personality Scores and Intelligence Test Scores in Three Different Neurological Categories

	Category 1	*Category 2*	*Category 3*
WAIS IQ	136.8(5.7)	137.1(3.2)	134.4(2.2)
Natural Freq.	64.9(0.88)	59.2(1.34)	64.8(1.23)
Damping Ratio	0.073(0.036)	0.027(0.022)	0.016(0.008)
E-I Balance	0.027(0.017)	-0.050(0.017)	0.004(0.007)
Extraversion	10.4(0.95)	13.9(5.81)	11.5(7.86)
Neuroticism	10.9(0.63)	8.2(2.46)	10.0(7.85)
Psychoticism	9.4(4.57)	3.3(1.70)	4.4(3.31)
Lie	1.3(0.96)	3.4(1.97)	4.2(3.17)
Information	0.49(0.66)	0.87(0.32)	0.85(0.41)
Comprehension	0.33(0.70)	0.40(0.81)	0.64(0.41)
Vocabulary	0.30(0.35)	0.93(0.21)	0.63(0.46)
Similarities	0.29(0.57)	0.40(0.35)	0.98(0.18)
P. Arrangement	0.72(0.74)	0.62(0.91)	-0.17(0.50)
B. Design	0.97(0.34)	0.57(0.66)	0.54(0.68)
Object Assy.	0.79(0.27)	0.32(0.90)	0.43(0.27)
Pict. Comp.	0.39(1.18)	0.20(0.74)	0.74(0.33)
Arithmetic	0.69(0.77)	1.13(0.40	0.09(0.70)
Digit Symbol	0.76(0.93)	0.95(0.57)	0.39(0.69)
Digit Span	0.60(1.02)	0.67(0.93)	0.89(0.54)

damping ratio. This constancy of thalamocortical arousability is reflected by remarkably similar personality profiles, especially in the first category.

In the third category, a near perfect negative correlation was found between natural frequency and damping ratio ($r = -0.99$). In this group, the negative correlation derives from the constraint that high IQ is primarily associated with excitation-inhibition balance and the covariation of the excitation-inhibition constants that is necessary to maintain balance results in a negative relationship between natural frequency and damping ratio. The result is that balance only guarantees high IQ within a limited range of covariation of the excitation-inhibition constants. Outside this limited range arousability due to natural frequency and damping ratio is either too high or too low and balance alone is no longer enough to sustain high IQ.

With respect to IQ scores, it appears that within a certain range, changes in arousability can be tolerated more than is usually the case provided there is an exact balance between excitation and inhibition. The same cannot be said for personality characteristics since there are large changes in extraversion (E) and neuroticism (N) as measured by the *Eysenck Personality Questionnaire* (Eysenck and Eysenck, 1975).

In Table 9.1 the patterns of mean WAIS subtest scores vary across the three categories in a way that suggests some relationship with the three main factors normally revealed by factor analysis of WAIS subtest scores. More generally, the patterns suggest that the three categories can be related meaningfully to the three major factors described by Cattell and Horn as "fluid" and "crystallized" intelligence and as "short-term memory and retrieval" (Cattell, 1971, 1987). The first four WAIS verbal subtests are considered markers for crystallized intelligence. The next group of performance tests are considered markers for fluid intelligence. Arithmetic and Digit Span, in the last group of three subtests, are markers for Cattell's "short-term memory and retrieval" factor. The differences in subtest means across the three categories suggest that the first category can be aligned with fluid intelligence, the second with "short-term memory and retrieval" and the third with crystallized intelligence.

One would not expect an exact correspondence between the ranking of category subtest means and loadings on intelligence factors. The profiles for categories two and three are similar in that higher scores were obtained on verbal as distinct from performance subtests. Factor analysis would almost certainly represent covariation of subtest scores related to these two categories in terms of a single "verbal" or "crystallized intelligence" factor with any residual variance assigned to a less important "attention-concentration," "freedom from distractibility," or "short-term memory and retrieval" factor.

When account is taken of this consideration the relationship between categories and factors is greatly clarified while at the same time a serious limitation of the factor analytic procedure is thrown into sharp relief. That is to say, factor analysis is blind to the influence of different agencies causing variation of test scores if these agencies are responsible for covariation of scores on the same set of tests. In the present case, different causal agencies are responsible for covariation of distinct but overlapping sets of tests. In this case, the operation of different causal agencies must influence the factor solution but there would be no one-to-one correspondence between the factors obtained and the causal agencies determining test variance. As already noted, the covariance of the overlapping subset of tests would tend to be represented by a single factor which would confound the influence of different causal agencies. The extent of any overlap would determine the degree of distortion but such distortion should be reduced if the factor analytic procedure allows correlated factors. Notably, Cattell has insisted that correlated factors have greater psychological relevance and, although this can now be disputed, it is clear that correlated factors do reveal structural features that would not be observed if only a principal component and orthogonal factors were extracted as described earlier. Taking account of the earlier discussion of principal components and orthogonal factors one is drawn to conclude that different factor analytic procedures reveal different aspects of structure and that these must all be accounted for in any comprehensive theory of intelligence.

In this account, a detailed analysis of subtest differences will not be presented but it is worth noting that even within a relatively small and highly selected data set, and with minimal variation of IQ, the three neurological parameters determine statistically significant differences in some WAIS subtest scores and this, of course, is why the three categories have different WAIS profiles. In particular, high scores on the Similarities subtest, which is the best marker for the third category, relate to low values of damping ratio (t = 2.20, df-15, $p<0.05$) and high values of natural frequency (t = 2.57, df-15, $p<0.05$). Block Design and Picture Arrangement are both good markers for the first category. High scores on Block Design relate to high damping ratios (t = 2.33, df = 15, $p<0.05$) and the same is true for Picture Arrangement (t = 2.29, df = 15, $p<0.05$). Finally, Arithmetic and Vocabulary are both good markers for the second category. High scores on Arithmetic relate to low values of natural frequency (t = 2.83, df = 15, $p<0.05$) as do high scores on Vocabulary (t = 2.94, df = 15, $p<0.05$). The difference between the Similarities and Picture Arrangement subtest scores proves to be particularly sensitive to variation of damping ratio. With a median split on damping ratio, there is no overlapping of the corresponding distributions of the difference variable. Thus, even when overall arousability is relatively invariant, high damping is associated with better performance on the Picture Arrangement subtest and relatively poor performance on Similarities. The converse is true for low damping. Notably, these particular subtests are considered the best WAIS markers for fluid and crystallized intelligence, respectively, which suggests that among high IQ subjects with middling overall arousability the fluid versus crystallized distinction relates mainly to variation of damping ratio.

High damping relates to fluid intelligence whereas low damping relates to crystallized intelligence. Insofar as there is a "verbal" versus "performance" distinction here the effect of variation in damping appears to mimic the effect of variation in overall arousability. This may be due to the fact that high damping would restrict the lateral spread of cortical activity and thereby restrict the development and accessing of ideation. Low damping would favour the development and accessing of ideation which would account for better verbal performance. In this case, however, owing to middling overall arousability, it is likely that verbal performance is eductive in character as distinct from the reproductive verbal abilities associated with low overall arousability. If this were indeed the case, then it is possible that the terms fluid and crystallized intelligence have misleading connotations. Also, if the fluid versus crystallized distinction depends on the relative involvement of ideation and better integrated neural activity, it is to be expected that as learning proceeds during the course of the lifespan, the progressive and experience-related integration of neural elements will ensure enhanced access to ideation and correspondingly improved verbal abilities but with a decline in performance on those tasks commonly associated with fluid intelligence.

The actual age related decline in performance of fluid ability tests has frequently been associated with degeneration of neural tissue. Here, it is suggested that such a decline is to be expected as a function of learning. That is to say, when the experience-related integration of neural elements proceeds beyond a certain point, individuals should become less able to perceive parts or elements and better able to perceive integrated Gestalt patterns. This accords with the data shown in Table 9.1 where the category associated with fluid intelligence is characterized by very high scores on the EPQ P scale and very low L scores. This particular combination indicates a psychopathic-like personality profile that can also be explained by an analytical as distinct from wholistic mode of perception, and by a restricted access to ideation.

It is emphasized that individuals in the three different neurological categories perform at an above average level on virtually all of the WAIS subtests and this is due to middling overall arousability. The different WAIS profiles in the three categories are clearly related to the particular way that middling arousability is achieved with some WAIS subtests relating more strongly to one or other of the three neurological parameters. Notably, these effects are distinct from the WAIS profile differences mentioned earlier, which do relate to differences in overall arousability.

CONCLUSION

In this chapter a new and more penetrating approach to the analysis of EEG activity and its implications for cognitive processing has been described. Apart from the generally optimal effect of middling arousability, and consistent with theoretical expectations, there are clear indications that high and low arousability relate, respectively, to special aptitudes for the performance of some verbal and some manipulative visuospatial tasks with the individuals concerned also differing on the introversion-extraversion dimension of personality. It is suggested that these arousability-related special aptitudes relate to the bipolar verbal/educational versus spatial/mechanical factor described in earlier factor analytic studies. The merit of this proposal is that the special aptitudes are aligned with a dimension of arousability that is effectively orthogonal to the contrast between middling arousability and both high and low arousability associated with general intelligence. Since the method of factor analysis employed in earlier studies was constrained to seek out precisely this kind of structure in any data set, there is good reason to assume that these early factor analytic solutions would reflect the two-fold influence of arousability differences described in the foregoing narrative.

Additional insights were obtained from an analysis of the data from high IQ subjects. It transpires that high IQ subjects fall into three distinct neurological categories with corresponding differences on the major dimensions of personality and WAIS profiles. These categories can be meaningfully related to the fluid intelligence, crystallized intelligence and "short-term memory and retrieval" factors described by Cattell and Horn although an exact correspondence would not be expected owing to limitations of the factor analytic techniques. It was suggested that the method of factor analysis favoured by Cattell and Horn, which involves rotation to simple structure and allows oblique or correlated factors, would be best able to discriminate psychological differences associated with the different neurological types. Thus it can be argued that different factor analytic procedures reveal different but complementary aspects of the structure of intelligence.

Finally, it is suggested that the data discussed in this chapter provide the first real insights concerning the biological basis of human intelligence and the causal agencies which give rise to intelligence factors. No less important, these findings extend the domain of arousability theory to include both intelligence and personality so that, for the first time, it is possible to present a truly comprehensive account of the biological bases of human individual differences.

REFERENCES

Broadhurst, P. L. (1959). The interaction of task difficulty and motivation. The Yerkes-Dodson law revived. *Acta Psychologica, 16,* 321–338.

Burt, C. (1949). The structure of the mind: A review of the results of factor analysis. *British Journal of Educational Psychology, 19,* 100–114, 176–219.

Cattell, R. B. (1971). *Abilities: Their structure growth and action.* Boston: Houghton Mifflin.

Cattell, R. B. (1987). *Intelligence: Its structure growth and action.* New York: North-Holland.

Eysenck, H. J., & Eysenck, S. B. G. (1975). *Manual of the Eysenck personality questionnaire.* London: Hodder and Stoughton.

Haier, R. J., Robinson, D. L., Braden, W., & Williams, D. (1983). Electrical potentials of the cerebral cortex and psychometric intelligence. *Personality and Individual Differences, 4*, 591–599.

Haier, R. J., Robinson, D. L., Braden, W., & Williams, D. (1984). Evoked potential augmenting—reducing and personality differences. *Personality and Individual Differences, 5*, 293–301.

Hebb, D. O. (1949). *The organization of behaviour.* New York: Wiley.

Hebb, D. O. (1959). Intelligence, brain function and the theory of mind. *Brain, 82*, 260–275.

Hendrickson, D. E. (1982). The biological basis of intelligence. Part II: Measurement. In H. J. Eysenck (Ed.), *A model for intelligence.* Berlin: Springer-Verlag.

Lynn, R., Wilson, G., & Gault, A. (1989). Simple musical tests as measures of Spearman's 'g'. *Personality and Individual Differences, 10*, 25–28.

Magoun, H. W. (1963). *The waking brain.* Springfield, IL: Thomas.

Moruzzi, G., & Magoun, H. W. (1949). Brain stem reticular formation and activation of the EEG. *Electroencephalography and Clinical Neurophysiology, 1*, 455–473.

Robinson, D. L. (1982). Properties of the diffuse thalamocortical system and human personality: A direct test of Pavlovian/Eysenckian theory. *Personality and Individual Differences, 3*, 1–16.

Robinson, D. L. (1983). An analysis of human EEG responses in the alpha range of frequencies. *International Journal of Neuroscience, 22*, 81–98.

Robinson, D. L. (1985). How personality relates to intelligence test performance: Implications for a theory of intelligence, ageing research and personality assessment. *Personality and Individual Differences, 6*, 203–216.

Robinson, D. L. (1986a). On the biological determination of personality structure. *Personality and Individual Differences, 7*, 435–438.

Robinson, D. L. (1986b). A commentary on Gray's critique of Eysenck's theory. *Personality and Individual Differences, 7*, 461–468.

Robinson, D. L. (1986c). The Wechsler Adult Intelligence Scale and personality assessment: Towards a biologically based theory of intelligence and cognition. *Personality and Individual Differences, 7*, 153–159.

Robinson, D. L. (1987). A neuropsychological model of personality and individual differences. In J. Strelau & H. J. Eysenck. (Eds.), *Personality dimensions and arousal.* London: Plenum Press.

Robinson, D. L. (1989). The neurophysiological basis of high IQ. *International Journal of Neuroscience, 46*, 209–234.

Robinson, D. L., Haier, R. J., Braden, W., & Krengel, M. (1984a). Evoked potential augmenting and reducing: The methodological and theoretical significance of new electrophysiological observations. *International Journal of Psychophysiology, 2*, 11–22.

Robinson, D. L., Haier, R. J., Braden, W., & Krengel, M. (1984b). Psychometric intelligence and visual evoked potentials: A replication. *Personality and Individual Differences, 5*, 487–489.

Samuels, I. (1959). Reticular mechanisms and behaviour. *Psychological Bulletin, 56*, 1–25.

Spearman, C. (1904). "General intelligence" objectively determined and measured. *American Journal of Psychology, 15*, 72–101.

Spearman, C. (1927). *The abilities of man.* London: Macmillan.

Yerkes, R. M., & Dodson, J. D. (1908). Relation of strength of stimulus to rapidity of habit formation. *Journal of Comparative Neurology and Psychology, 18*, 459–482.

10 Cognitive Integration: Alternative Model for Intelligence

J. P. Das[1]
University of Alberta

R. F. Jarman
University of British Columbia

The nature of intelligence is being debated today as vigorously as it was in 1927; Sternberg and Detterman (1986) demonstrate the various views on intelligence held by contemporary researchers. It is obvious to us, that if we abandon a one-dimensional view of intelligence, a legacy of Galton, we should have an alternative; a viable one is proposed in this chapter. A model for *cognitive functions* rather than intelligence is proposed. The model has its roots in both neuropsychology and cognitive psychology. Its structural basis is the brain; it comprises four major functions, and the functions are constrained by knowledge-base, the accumulated experiences of the individual.

First we present the model. Next, tests are considered; these tests operationalize the cognitive functions included in the model. Because current assessment techniques are heavily dependent on psychometric methods that seek justification by factor analyses, we present factor analytic work rather than empirical research that we have carried out (see Das & Varnhagen, 1986; Naglieri, 1989) for the assessment devices derived from the model. The model's neuropsychological roots are in Luria's work. Therefore, we have presented next a selective review in relation to its place in contemporary neuropsychology. This review is much needed to support the neoLurian perspective offered by the model. Finally, we discuss the implications of the neoLurian perspective for assessment.

[1]The first author was supported by a grant from S.S.H.R.C., Ottawa, Canada during the preparation of this paper.

LURIA'S MODEL

There are numerous cognitive functions, which Luria organized broadly to correspond to four different parts of the brain. Arousal-attention is organized in Block
1, in the brain-stem and the limbic system. It mainly involves the reticular
function. In the posterior region, which is Block 2, simultaneous and successive
information processes are located. Simultaneous processes are located in the
occipitoparietal region and successive in the fronto-temporal region. Planning
including decision making, judgment and evaluation is the function of Block 3,
the frontal region. Following Luria, (1966a, 1966b; 1973) the functions of these
three blocks of the brain can be described as follows:

Arousal-attention is concerned with cortical tone, i.e., cortical arousal. Ana-
tomically, this includes the brain stem, the diencephalon, and medial regions of
the hemispheres. The principal structure in this unit is the reticular formation
(RF). The integrity of the RF is crucial for the maintenance of cortical tone and
determination of levels of consciousness. The RF can be divided into ascending
and descending systems. The ascending RF activates and regulates cortical tone
(EEG desynchronization and behavioral arousal) whereas the descending RF
modulates control impulses from higher cortical centers to the periphery—such
as a limb movement or visceral activities. Lesions of the RF then can produce
decreases in cortical tone (such as production of sleep state EEG in waking
animals) and direction stimulation of the RF can produce lowering of the thresholds of peripheral sensory apparatus.

The RF can activate the central nervous system in three different ways: (a) by
influencing the control of metabolic processes (homeostasis) through its connections with the hypothalamus. These range from elementary processes such as
digestion to complex behavioural sequences such as sexual activities and food
gathering; (b) by influencing the orienting response through its connections with
the thalamic and hippocampal regions; (c) by influencing generally goal-directed
behaviour: Formulations of intentions and execution of programs. This is
achieved through the connection with the frontal cortex and (d) by modulating
the control functions of higher centers on the lower centers.

Luria considers the medial regions of the hemispheres as a part of the first
functional block. Lesions of these regions produce disturbances of consciousness
and symptoms that are quite different from other frontal lobe lesions. As well,
there are secondary memory deficits that are not modality specific. Clinically,
these patients show a marked lowering of cortical tone: There is marked slowing
of reaction times and a tendency to fatigue easily. The memory deficits seem to
be related to the increased distractibility of irrelevant, interfering stimuli on the
task at hand. These memory deficits become more severe if the hippocampus is
also damaged.

The orienting response—(Luria takes the concepts of excitation, inhibition
and orienting response from Pavlov, 1928)—is an elementary attentional process

that is cortically controlled by the arousal functions in Block 1, but at the same time, it is influenced by the programming and planning that goes on in the frontal lobes that are mainly associated with Block 3 functions. In fact, a close connection exists between Block 1 and Block 3 as evidenced from the following quotation from Luria:

> The systems of the first functional unit not only maintain cortical tone but also, themselves, experience the differentiating influence of the cortex, and the first functional unit of the brain works in close cooperation with the higher levels of the cortex. (Luria, 1973)

The coding functions are located in the posterior regions of the neocortex. They include the occipital, temporal, and parietal lobes. As in all other blocks of the brain, a hierarchical arrangement of cortical areas prevails. Luria developed tests for the assessment of two major coding functions that are either simultaneous or successive. *Simultaneous processing* refers to the synthesis of separate elements into groups. The essential nature of this sort of processing is that any portion is at once surveyable without depending on its position in the whole. *Successive processing* refers to processing of information in a serial order. The important distinction between this type of information processing and simultaneous processing is that in successive processing, the system is not totally surveyable at any point in time. Rather, a system of cues consecutively activates the components.

Returning to a former discussion of the neuropsychological aspects of Block 2, the interdependence between the three hierarchial areas with this is described next. The primary projection area receives external information and codes it in preparation for the secondary area. The secondary area in the system analyses this information and then passes it on to the tertiary area where the information supplies the building blocks for the formation of concepts. As mentioned earlier, the primary or projection area is modality specific in as much as an auditory neuron would not be sensitive to visual stimuli.

Examples of the functions of the tertiary zones in coding visual, auditory, or spatial information are the various activities that depend on simultaneous and successive processing such as map reading, copying a figure, monitoring a series of words, as in serial recall, or perception of syntax. All of these activities are examples of the function of the second block. Luria (1973) describes the difficulties that patients with lesions in the occipital, parietal or temporal lobes would have. Such patients would not be able to grasp information that has to be put together as a whole. They cannot convert consecutive presentations of words into different categories (for example, words that denote furniture or animals, but were presented randomly in a list) and they would experience great difficulty in temporal ordering of events. The relevance of Block 2 functions for solving standardized intelligence tests is apparent. Many of the items in these tests require coding.

Planning functions derive from the third block of the brain, i.e., the frontal lobes. This block is the most important, the last to develop, and occupies one third of the entire human brain. Luria singles out the prefrontal areas to be the most important ones for the formation of intentions, goals, and programs that regulate complex human behaviour. The tertiary zone in the prefrontal area has a massive system of neural connections to almost all parts of the brain. The prefrontal divisions not only receive information but send out information to various parts of the brain. They are most closely connected with RF. As mentioned earlier, the RF regulates arousal and attentional responses and interacts intensively with the frontal lobes in discriminating between relevant and irrelevant information for the purpose of allocating attention (Pribram & Luria, 1973).

Luria emphasizes over and over again (see Luria, Chapter 1 in Pribram & Luria, 1973) the connection between orienting response and the frontal lobes. Because attention and orienting responses are controlled by instructions, a subject with disturbances in the frontal lobe experiences an inability to regulate his/her behavior. Luria enthusiastically supports the research of Grey Walter on EEG changes, particularly, contingent negative variations, accompanying planful behavior. A person expects certain events because he has a pretty good idea of a scheme or a model for those events. The most important function of frontal lobes, therefore, is concerned with constructing a model and executing a program of activities that are controlled either through the instruction of an outside agent or through self-instruction. From this point of view, then, the close connection between attention and planful behaviour seems to be strongly entrenched in the neurophysiology of Block 1 and Block 3.

MODEL OF INFORMATION INTEGRATION IN 1975

A description of the model was first given in 1972 (Das, 1972) and later elaborated (Das, Kirby, & Jarman, 1975). A summary of the model as it was in 1975 follows.

Simultaneous integration refers to the synthesis of separate elements into groups, these groups often taking on spatial overtones. The essential nature of this sort of processing is that any portion of the results is at once surveyable without dependence on its position in the whole. It is hypothesized by Luria that simultaneous syntheses are of the following three varieties. (a) Direct perception: The process of perception is such that the organism is selectively attentive to the stimulus input in the brain. According to Luria, this type of formation is primarily spatial, even in the case of the acoustic analyser. (b) Mnestic processes: This refers to the organization of stimulus traces from earlier experience. Examples of this type of integration are the construction of the gestalt of a visual image by the subject when portions of the image are shown consecutively, and the organization of consecutively presented words into a group on the basis of a criterion. The stimulus traces, or, as we should refer to them, memory traces, can be either short-term or long-term, and the integration of the traces is performed on the basis of criteria that can be specified either by the organism or an external source. (c) The last variety of synthesis is found in complex intellectual processes. In order for the human organism to grasp systems of relationships, it is necessary that the components of the systems be represented simultaneously. In this fashion, the relationships among components can be explored and determined. Luria notes that the use of spatial presentation of the components is an aid in this process, for when a unitary representation of components is formed, the system is readily surveyable.

Successive information processing refers to processing of information in serial order. The important distinction between this type of information processing and simultaneous processing is that in successive processing, the system is not totally surveyable at any point in time. Rather, a system of cues consecutively activates the components. As in simultaneous processing, successive synthesis has three varieties: Perceptual, mnestic, and complex intellectual. According to Luria, the most obvious example of the last variety of successive processing is human speech. The structure of grammar is such that the processing of syntactical components is dependent upon their sequential relationships within sentence structure. Thus, grammatical structures that have to be understood in terms of their relationships are adversely affected by disturbance of simultaneous synthesis, whereas sequential structures are affected by successive synthesis.

The central processing unit has three major components: That which processes separate information into simultaneous groups, that which processes discrete information into temporally organized successive series, and the decision-making and planning components that use the information so integrated by the other components. The processing in these components is not affected by the form of sensory input—visual information can be processed successively and auditory information can be processed simultaneously.

The model assumes that both modes of processing information are available to the individual. The selection of either or both depends on two conditions: (a) the individual's habitual mode of processing information as determined by social-cultural and genetic factors, and (b) the demands of the task. The third component, which could be labeled thinking, uses coded information and determines the best possible plan for action. Perhaps it is also crucial for the emergence of causal thinking, which Hess (1967) describes as " an integrative activity which brings simultaneous and successive patterns of nervous excitation into a subjectively meaningful frame of reference" (p. 1283).

Both simultaneous and successive processing can be involved in all forms of responding. This is the case irrespective of the method of input presentation. Perhaps Lashley's (1951) work is relevant to the decoding or behavioral part in serial tasks. Serial ordering of behavior may be dependent on either the manner in which information was coded or on the motor aspects of the behavior itself.

The output unit, then, determines and organizes performance in accordance with the requirements of the task. For example, in memory tasks a subject may be required to recall serially or recall the items in categories supplied by the experimenter; appropriate output organization is necessary.

Arousal-Attention and Knowledge Base (Addition to the 1975 Model). Arousal is much more than the maintenance of wakefulness and the general energy level of mental activity. Neurophysiological relationships between the reticular formation and the frontal lobes are complex and intimate. Arousal may be the physiological label for a host of cognitive processes such as the orienting response, expectancy and intentions that blend with the processes of planning. Arousal as manifested in attention interacts with learning and memory, which are included in coding—the acquisition of information, its analyses, syntheses, storage and retrieval. Knowledge base was not explicitly mentioned in the original formulation of the model. Perhaps knowledge base should not be associated with the neuropsychological roots of the model.

Although Luria's writings on the three functional divisions of the brain (Luria, 1966a, 1966b, 1970) do not explicitly mention the role for knowledge base, nevertheless, in clinical practice he, like any other neuropsychologist, takes this into consideration.

Knowledge base is required for the operations performed by a human as well as a computer. But the human knowledge base is not quite the same as in a computer. The sum total of a person's experiences, habits and predispositions, conscious or unconscious, must make up the knowledge base. It is the accumulation of the person's learning and memories, attitudes and orientations, inborn capacities and energy level that interactively intervene in the interpretation of

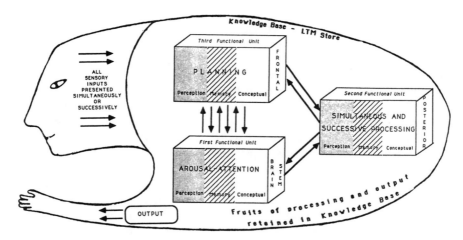

FIG. 10.1. A model for cognitive functions

reality as well as the structure and content of the thoughts of a person. The model is shown in Fig. 10.1.

ASSESSMENT OF COGNITIVE FUNCTIONS

A scheme for cognitive assessment is presented in Fig. 10.2. There are three major divisions following from the model within which cognitive functions need to be assessed. These are arousal-attention, simultaneous-successive processing and planning. Within each division the tasks can be further divided into those requiring perception, memory or higher symbolic processing such as conceptualization. As the scheme for simultaneous and successive processing tasks show, one could identify among these tasks perceptual, mnestic and conceptual groups. The tasks can be also divided into visual and auditory. The scheme can also be divided into verbal and nonverbal categories, and some which are mixed. In attention-arousal, for instance, vigilance would be a verbal test, whereas Posner's name and physical match in relation to pictorial stimuli could be a nonverbal test. Also in successive processing, serial recall and sentence repetition are verbal, whereas successive order for coloured chips presented in a sequence is nonverbal. In summary then, the tasks chosen for the assessment of the processes following form the model cut across such dichotomies in psychometric tests as verbal versus nonverbal, visual versus auditory or for that matter, memory versus reasoning, because examples from these dichotomous categories are found within the measures of the same cognitive function.

STATISTICAL EVIDENCE FOR THE MODEL

We provide evidence to the effect that the four functional units of Planning, Arousal-Attention, Simultaneous and Successive processing (PASS) can be confirmed by factor analytic procedures. Then, we make a distinction between the present model and two popular concepts associated with intelligence, namely, "g", and speed of processing.

The factor analytic evidence has been gathered over about 15 years in three stages of research on the model: First on simultaneous and successive processes, then on planning as well as the two preceding processes, and lastly on arousal-attention. Simultaneous and successive processes were consistently identified in factor analysis of data gathered on normal children; the samples of children varied in nationality, ethnic origin, socio-economic status, reading abilities, and intelligence. The performances of these various groups of children were consistent in that the same factors, simultaneous and successive emerged. In some analyses the tests were changed, but they fit the two constructs. These results are documented in a book on the two processes (Das, Kirby, & Jarman, 1979). An

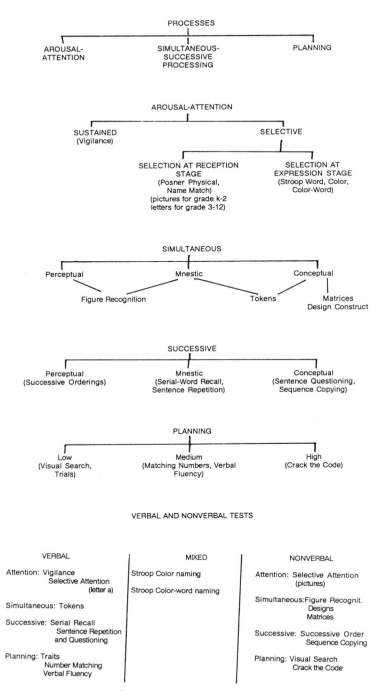

FIG. 10.2. A scheme for assessment of planning, attention, simultaneous and successive processing (PASS).

TABLE 10.1
Retated Factors for Grade 4[a]

| | Orthogonal Factors | | |
Test	Simultaneous	Successive	Speed
Raven's colored progressive matrices	.796	.132	-.201
Figure copying	.705	.182	.039
Memory-for designs	.786	.014	.098
Serial recall	.395	.624	-.240
Visual short-term memory	.164	.812	-.176
Digit span forward	-.108	.807	-.039
Word reading	-.053	-.273	.795
Color naming	-.140	-.039	.865
Percentage of total variance	23.89	22.84	19.01

[a]N = 202

example from the factor analyses is given in Table 10.1; the study was conducted on 202 Grade 4 children by Kirby (1976).The third factor was designated as speed of processing because the two Stroop cards that define the factor are scored for response time. More discussion on a speed factor is presented later.

There were many explorations before we discovered appropriate tests for planning. Examples of tests that had been shown to distinguish between frontal lobe damaged patients and others were included as planning tasks. In the two Tables, 10.2a and 10.2b, a planning factor orthogonal to simultaneous and successive processing has emerged. It will be noticed that the first group of subjects was mentally retarded (Das, 1980), and the second consisted of community

TABLE 10.2a
Orthogonal (Varimax) Rotations of Three Factors Following Principal Component Analysis

| | Orthogonal Factors | | | |
Variable	Planning	Successive	Simultaneous	h^2
Planned composition	697	126	376	641
Trail making	719	-341	260	699
Visual search	630	-419	105	582
Syllogistic reasoning error	-181	657	233	517
Syllogistic reasoning time (sec)	876	-011	-043	768
Auditory serial recall	060	831	080	699
Digit span	-150	724	-015	546
Memory for designs	-077	219	772	647
Figure copying	066	010	791	629
Variance	2.230	1.998	1.500	5.728
Percentage of total variance	24.77	22.20	16.66	63.63

Note. N = 55. Decimals are omitted.

TABLE 10.2b
Principal Components Analysis (Varimax Rotation) for the Trainable Mentally Retarded Group
(N = 64)

Variable	Simultaneous	Successive	Planning	h^2
Memory for design	924			872
Figure copying	938			891
Digit span		914		857
Auditory serial recall		901		835
Trail making			849	775
Visual search			666	646
% of total variance	32.94	28.49	19.84	81.27

Note. Decimal points and loadings below 400 have been omitted.

college students (Das & Heemsbergen, 1983). Naturally, some of the tests used for the college group were not suitable for the retarded. In spite of these variations in subjects and tests, a planning factor was obtained in each case.

By the time the last factor, arousal-attention, was added, we had begun to use confirmatory rather than exploratory factor analyses. Thus, in a study of 247 students from kindergarten to Grade 12, the confirmatory LISREL analysis (Joreskog & Sorbom, 1981) showed the four factors. The tests for Arousal-Attention were (a) selective attention-receptive, a variation of Posner & Boies (1971), physical and name-match tasks, and (b) stroop color-word interference card. The planning tasks were: visual search, matching numbers, and trail making. The simultaneous and successive tasks were: figure memory, matrices, sentence repetition, and word recall. Details of these PASS tasks are given in Naglieri and Das (1988).

The model was tested against three competing models that were a verbal/spatial/speed division of the aforementioned tests, a memory/reasoning division, and a one-factor "g" model. The comparative chi squares and p values are given in Table 10.3; it is evident that the PASS model appears to be superior to its competitor, verbal/spatial/speed for the Grades 5–12 sample, but not for kindergarten to Grade 2. The latter sample was administered different forms of the attention and planning tests in consideration of its ability. AGFI is the Adjusted Goodness of Fit Index and RSMR is the Root Mean Square Residual, whereas TLI is the Tucker Lewis Index. The chi square/df ratios should be 2 or less. In order to provide a more direct assessment of the relative fit of the alternative models, the difference in chi square values from one model to the next was computed, and a Bonferroni adjusted alpha level was used as a control for the use of multiple nonindependent comparisons: The PASS model showed significant improvements in goodness of fit as we proceeded from V/S/S model (in Grade 5–12 data). Earlier data analyses are described in detail by Naglieri, Das, Stevens, and Ledbetter (1990).

Speed is not to be regarded as a unitary factor at all, as (see Table 10.4) it

TABLE 10.3
Results of the Confirmatory Factory Analyses for Four Competing Models of Cognitive Functioning by Age Group

Model	Chi. Sq.	p	df	Chi Sq.	AGFI	RMSR	TLI[1]
Grades 5-12							
PASS	34.84	.210	29	1.20	.91	.05	.85
VSS	40.81	.090	30	1.36	.90	.05	.73
MR	88.19	.001	34	2.59	.81	.08	.20
VNV	117.20	.001	34	3.45	.71	.11	–
NULL	81.43	.001	35	2.33	.83	.08	–
Grades K-2							
PASS	26.50	.231	22	1.21	.85	.08	.81
VSS	34.94	.053	23	1.52	.81	.09	.51
MR	50.73	.003	26	1.95	.86	.10	.10
VNV	54.27	.001	26	2.09	.75	.11	–
NULL	55.56	.001	27	2.06	.75	.11	–

Note. PASS = Planning, Attention, Simultaneous, Successive
VSS = Verbal, Spatial, Speed
MR = Memory, Reasoning
NULL = One Factor
VNV = Verbal, Nonverbal

[1] = all TL1 values were computed in contrast to the Null Model. Values less than zero are not listed.

TABLE 10.4
Schmid-Leiman Hierarchical Orthogonalization of Simultaneous, Successive, and Planning Tasks for Grade 3 Children

	Factor					
	Second Order		First Order			
	$G1$	$G2$	Succ.	Simult.	Speed	Planning
Figure copying	.420	-.056	-.104	.675	.031	-.023
Memory for designs	.378	.135	.116	.638	-.065	.027
Serial recall	.433	-.029	.741	-.043	-.074	-.017
Digit span	.346	.068	.687	.046	-.024	.006
Word reading	.593	-.099	.067	-.031	.559	.023
Color naming	.395	-.172	-.014	.039	.345	-.022
Trail making	-.196	.537	.025	-.091	-.051	.175
Visual search	.026	.522	-.075	.075	.113	.187
	R_1[b]			R[a]		
	1.000	-.094 Succ.	1.000	.241	.305	.011
	-.094	1.000 Simult.	.241	1.000	3.66	-.013
		Speed	.305	.366	1.000	-.251
		Plan	.011	-.013	-.251	1.000

From Das and Dash (1983).
[a]R: Correlations among primary oblique factors
[b]R_1: Correlations among second-order factors

loads separately on two factors. The four-factor analysis demonstrates that speed scores in visual search and trails load on a planning factor as dictated by the model, whereas the two speed scores from Stroop load on a factor by themselves, as they did in Table 10.1. Speed, as seen in Table 10.4, is grouped together with simultaneous and successive processing, separate from Planning in the hierarchical factor analysis. These results reinforce the evidence in favor of the PASS model in contrast to the models that advocate a general factor of intelligence, or speed as a general index of intelligence.

LURIA'S MODEL IN NEUROPSYCHOLOGY

An issue that is implicit in all of the studies reported here and elsewhere (e.g., Das, Kirby, & Jarman, 1979), is the basis and stature of the model in neuropsychological terms. A second issue is the justification that may exist for utilizing a model that was formulated from clinical neuropsychological investigations for the development of a theory of cognitive processes. The theory is based on multivariate studies of individual differences. Lastly, a corollary consideration that flows from these issues is the implications of the Luria approach for the development of assessment techniques.

At present, attempts to explain human behavior by appealing to a model of brain functions is an extraordinarily active endeavour in the field of psychology. Within this area, as with many areas of psychology, distinct theoretical positions have gradually emerged, within which are those theorists that prefer to adopt simple global types of models, versus those theorists that prefer micro-analytic explanations of brain behavior. In the global category, for example, are the proponents of the well-known theory that the two hemispheres of the brain are to some varying degree dependent on the views of the particular theorist involved, specialized for certain types of processing, with the right hemisphere seen to be specialized for spatial types of processes, and the left hemisphere specialized for temporal types of processes (e.g., Gazzaniga, 1970; Sperry, 1968; [for less committed points of view see also Beaumont, 1988; Bloom, Lazerson, & Hofstadter, 1985; Dean (1986); and Hannay (1986)). In contrast, one example of the microanalytic category of theorists is Woodruff and Baisden (1986), who avoid a general model of complete brain functioning, and prefer instead, to make an attempt to taxonomize in very specific detail, the functions of each section and subsection of the brain.

Within the general stream of theoretical developments in neuropsychology, there appears to be a growing recognition of the value of Luria's (e.g., 1966a, 1966b, 1973) model; indeed, there is almost a parallel developing between the delayed recognition afforded Piaget after his many years of work in relative obscurity, and the recent recognition of Luria's research. One of the major reasons for this increased recognition of Luria's contribution is that his is the only theory in neuropsychology that deals with the brain as an integrated set of systems (Lewandowski, 1987), avoiding the global and somewhat trivialized models of the human brain such as the left-right hemispheric functioning model. At the same time, it is also avoiding the overly specific and the now theoretically untenable position of strict localization. Luria's view of the brain, as we have expressed elsewhere (e.g., Das, Kirby, & Jarman, 1979), incorporates the notion of functional systems that interlock with one another to govern behaviour, and which have varying levels of generality (Christensen, 1986; Russell, 1981). These systems have various anatomical bases, as established by Luria through many case study investigations of brain lesions, although the relationship of systems to specific brain locations is not fixed and immutable. Indeed, similar functional systems may be affected by different brain lesions, and conversely, the same functional system can be affected by disparate and distinctly different lesions (Bolter & Long, 1985). These apparently paradoxical conclusions by Luria are due to the relative plasticity of the brain and its compensatory capabilities following injury, in addition to the natural developmental effects of growth and experience.

A further, and very significant appeal of Luria's model to some neuropsychologists, is its ability to integrate and explain the results of research in some other areas of psychology. In this respect, there is no other model of brain functions that has comparable capability. For example, and once again as an interesting parallel to the delayed recognition of Piaget's work, Luria (1966a, 1966b) made substantial progress in the development of knowledge concerning the role of the frontal lobes in planning and decision making well before the advent of cognitive psychology with its attendant emphasis on metacognition and *knowing how to know.*

Since Luria's original work on the role of the frontal lobes, some researchers have extended his ideas to suggest, for example, that executive processes may take any of four different varieties: (a) the ability to formulate goals; (b) the ability to develop a plan to reach the goals; (c) the ability to execute plans; and (d) the ability to monitor the execution of plans and revise plans as required (Cicerone & Tupper, 1986). Other investigators have elaborated the psychological basis for Luria's theory of frontal lobe functions in terms of physiology, in order to supply a more differentiated and refined view of the various sectors of the frontal lobes. Damasio (1985), for instance, divides the frontal lobes into three major sectors, and suggests that the mesial sector is primarily responsible for affect and communication, the orbital sector is mainly responsible for the regulation of various personality traits, and it is the dorso-lateral section that is responsible for high level cognitive activity, including the extraction of meaning from ongoing experience, and the organization of mental contents in retroactive and proactive terms.

SYNDROME ANALYSIS AND
MULTIVARIATE ANALYSIS

Of fundamental concern here, is the question of the possible relationships between Luria's theory and data drawn from clinical investigations of brain-damaged subjects, and the various investigations as conducted by a variety of researchers using primarily multivariate statistical methods on data from normal and high incidence atypical populations (e.g., Das, Kirby, & Jarman, 1975, 1979). The relationship between these lines of research may be examined from several points of view, with a variety of interrelated questions asked about both lines of research, particularly the multivariate investigations. For example:

1. To what extent should these investigations accept Luria's model uncritically and merely apply it in the interpretation of the multivariate data?
2. To what extent does a logical and empirical relationship exist between the results of Luria's investigations, especially syndrome analysis and the results from multivariate studies?
3. To what extent can or should Luria's model itself be revised and affected by the outcome of various multivariate investigations?

With respect to the first question, although a general critique of Luria's theory is beyond the scope of this chapter, we noted increasing acceptance of his work among neuropsychologists, and the corresponding growing trend towards a *systems* perspective in neuropsychology (see Walsh, 1985, 1987). This trend is significant because it points to an opportunity for the integration of ideas from previously disparate areas, some that may ultimately contribute to revisions to Luria's model.

Our main focus here is on the third questions, particularly with respect to the relationship between the different varieties of research. Some of the basis for beginning to address the other questions raised here may be found in Luria's clinical technique, and the interlocking concepts of a functional system, and a behavioral syndrome. Luria's technique of clinical research was based on two principles:

1. That a qualitative analysis of behavior was necessary, utilizing virtually hundreds of tasks in some cases, to lead to the identification of a defect.
2. That a single lesion or defect may demonstrate itself in diverse behaviors (Cicerone & Tupper, 1986).

The concept of a syndrome, as an extension of these principles, was central to Luria's work (Walsh, 1985), whereby a syndrome was identified as a constellation of signs and symptoms, which, in turn, supplied what we would now term an operational definition for a functional system. Thus, Luria's clinical method entailed the accumulation of converging evidence from many tasks to define a syndrome. The syndrome, then, emerged as a common cognitive process that was disrupted in seemingly disparate tasks. This clinical method, in turn, allowed Luria to define various areas of regional specialization in the brain, and to map sets of functional systems that operate at various levels of generality within and between these areas.

The research process that Luria utilized, therefore, involved the definition of a variety of syndromes by identifying one or more cognitive processes that are common to tasks performed by brain-damaged subjects. A parallel approach is to operationally define constructs. This is achieved by identifying one or more cognitive processes that form the principal basis for individual differences within a set of tasks. Such differences among normal and various atypical subjects are to be supported using multivariate methods, particularly factor analysis.

What is the extent to which the processes that result in defective behavior in brain damaged subjects may be the same processes that form major dimensions of individual differences in normal subjects? The interpretation of factor analytic results in terms of Luria's clinical work depends on the answer to this question. The issue can be viewed as one of cross-validation. The approach adopted in the multivariate studies by the authors and their collaborators, has been to focus mainly on the use of tasks that were either employed extensively by Luria, or tasks that are very similar to them (although, as noted previously, the number of tasks used by Luria is very substantial and frequently too easy for a nonclinical population), combined with other tasks derived from the constructs of planning, arousal-attention, and so forth. Thus, in factor analytic terms, this research is confirmatory in both the selection of tasks and in the hypothesized outcomes of the analyses. By using a variety of tasks common to both Luria's investigations and a wide series of multivariate investigations, and by varying subject populations with known disorders (cf. Naglieri, Das, & Jarman, 1990), a set of multivariate research results have gradually emerged. We suggest that these may be interpreted in terms of, and in fact, may even extend our knowledge of, Luria's work on syndromes. With respect to the latter suggestion, there is increasing evidence that multivariate investigations of normal subjects can inform theory in neuropsychology. This is apparent in the recent discussions of problems in neuropsychological methods in which this need is emphasized (e.g., Clark, 1981; Dean, 1985).

IMPLICATIONS FOR ASSESSMENT

With respect to assessment, contemporary neuropsychology has found itself in a somewhat awkward position. The early work in localization led to the development of literally hundreds of narrow, highly homogeneous tests of brain function, nearly all of which lacked a comprehensive theoretical basis, and all of which were too narrow to explain and predict general behaviour. As the theoretical perspective in neuropsychology based on specific localization gradually fell into disfavor, these tests became interesting only as research tools. They had little relevance for the eventual development of, or integration into a comprehensive system of neurological assessment (cf. Walsh, 1985).

A second type of development in neuropsychologically based assessment that has taken place, in part as a reaction to the specific localization-based tests, is the development of several major batteries. These batteries were developed for the purpose of supplying a comprehensive view of brain functions, which was to be both theory-driven and psychometrically defensible. The two most obvious examples of these batteries are the *Halstead-Reitan Neuropsychological Test Battery* and the *Luria-Nebraska Neuropsychological Battery* (Bigler, 1987, 1988). Unfortunately, both batteries suffer to a degree from having been constructed by clinical neuropsychologists; for they have various scaling and measurement problems that despite several revisions, are still problematic.

A third, and rather ironic trend in neuropsychological assessment is evident in the use of major standardized intelligence tests and achievement tests, such as the *Wechsler Intelligence Scale for Children Revised (WISC-R)* and the *Wide Range Achievement Test (WRAT)*. Tests like the WISC-R have very good psychometric properties (Vernon, 1987), their use is ironic because many of them have little or no theoretical basis. Therefore they are regressive within the field of neuropsychology, which is attempting to move toward theory-based assessment. Despite the now well-documented importance of the frontal lobes in high-level cognitive functioning (e.g., Luria, 1973; Damasio, 1985), and despite the well-known finding that WAIS-R scores do not reflect this type of functioning due to their focus on coding processes (Bigler, 1987, 1988), these tests continue to be central to many reviews of neuropsychological assessment techniques (e.g., Chelune, Ferguson, & Moehle, 1986; Roberts, 1984).

Joint developments in cognitive psychology (such as metacognition research) and in neuropsychology (such as the recent recognition of the value of Luria's approach based on functional systems), therefore, have surpassed the development of assessment techniques. There have been several attempts in the assessment field to keep pace with these developments, most notably the development of the *Kaufman Assessment Battery for Children (K-ABC)*. However, these tests do not have many of the desirable features such as a theoretical basis, psychometric defensibility, and practical applicability. In the case of the K-ABC, for example, both problems with theory and psychometrics have led to critical reviews (e.g., Das, 1984; Bracken, 1985). These problems, combined with various administration problems in everyday utilization, have reduced the impact of the K-ABC in school psychological practice.

Looking ahead, it is evident that any new neuropsychologically-based assessment techniques that may be developed as an outgrowth of the type of work described here, should deal with a further problem that is inherent in Luria's approach to assessment. Luria's approach was highly dynamic. To elaborate the *dynamic* approach, many tests were chosen and used by Luria in the course of examining an individual patient, and the choice of tests was based on mainly qualitative data from the testing situation (Walsh, 1985). The *methode clinique,* a notable parallel with respect to Piaget's work, was adopted by Luria. Luria's clinical method is not easily convertible to a psychometric model in order to build an assessment battery, as is evident in Christensen's (1975) book.

The use of a theory based on qualitative clinical investigations for the creation of a quantitative assessment system is a problematic enterprise that has not been fully refined to date, but attempts are being made (see Naglieri, 1989, for a review of our effort). It appears that further progress in theory development, lies in both the clinical and multivariate investigations informing and influencing each other. Assessment methods to be developed in the future can then be the beneficiaries of both of these approaches, as well as of empirical research in cognitive processes.

REFERENCES

Beaumont, J. G. (1988). *Understanding neuropsychology.* New York: Basil Blackwell.

Bigler, E. D. (1987). Assessment of cortical functions. In L. C. Hartlage, M. J. Asken, & J. L. Hornsby (Eds.), *Essentials of neuropsychological assessment.* New York: Springer.

Bigler, E. D. (1988). *Diagnostic clinical neuropsychology.* Austin: University of Texas Press.

Bloom, F. E., Lazerson, A., & Hofstadter, L. (1985). *Brain, mind and behavior.* New York: W. H. Freeman.

Bolter, J. E., & Long, C. J. (1985). Methodological issues in research in developmental neuropsychology. In L. C. Hartlage & C. F. Telgrow (Eds.), *The neuropsychology of individual differences: A developmental perspective.* New York: Plenum.

Bracken, B. A. (1985). A critical review of the Kaufman assessment battery for children (K-ABC). *School Psychology Review, 14,* 21–36.

Chelune, G. J., Ferguson, W., & Moehle, K. (1986). The role of standard cognitive and personality tests in neuropsychological assessment. In T. Incagnoli, G. Goldstein, & C. J. Golden (Eds.), *Clinical application of neuropsychological test batteries.* New York: Plenum.

Christensen, A. L. (1975). *Luria's Neuropsychological Investigation.* Copenhagen: Munksgaard.

Christensen, A. L. (1986). Applying Luria's theory to the rehabilitation process of brain damage. In B. P. Uzzell & Y. Gross (Eds.), *Clinical neuropsychology of intervention.* Boston: Martinus Nijhoff.

Cicerone, K. D., & Tupper, D. E. (1986). Cognitive assessment in the neuropsychological rehabilitation of head-injured adults. In B. P. Uzzell & Y. Gross (Eds.), *Clinical neuropsychology of intervention.* Boston: Martinus Nijhoff.

Clark, C. M. (1981). Statistical models and their application in clinical neuropsychological research and practice. In S. B. Filskov & T. J. Boll (Eds.), *Handbook of clinical neuropsychology.* New York: Wiley.

Damasio, A. R. (1985). The frontal lobes. In K. M. Heilman & F. Valenstein (Eds.), *Clinical neuropsychology.* New York: Oxford University Press.

Das, J. P. (1972). Patterns of cognitive abilities in normal and retarded children. *American Journal of Mental Deficiency, 76,* 6–12.

Das, J. P. (1980). Planning: Theoretical considerations and empirical evidence. *Psychological Research, 41,* 141–151.

Das, J. P. (1984). Simultaneous and successive processes and K-ABC. *Journal of Special Education, 18,* 229–238.

Das, J. P., & Dash, U. N. (1983). Memory for spatial and temporal order in deaf children. *American Annals of the Deaf, 128,* 894–899.

Das, J. P., & Heemsbergen, D. B. (1983). Planning as a factor in the assessment of cognitive processes. *Journal of Psychoeducational Assessment, 1,* 1–15.

Das, J. P., Kirby, J., & Jarman, R. F. (1975). Simultaneous and successive syntheses: An alternative model for cognitive abilities. *Psychological Bulletin, 82,* 87–102.

Das, J. P., Kirby, J. R., & Jarman, R. (1979). *Simultaneous and successive cognitive processes.* New York: Academic Press.

Das, J. P., & Varnhagen, C. K. (1986). Neuropsychological functioning and cognitive processing. In J. E. Obzrut & G. W. Hynd (Eds.), *Child Neuropsychology, Vol. 1: Theory and Research.* New York: Academic Press.

Dean, R. S. (1985). Foundation and rationale for neuropsychological bases of individual differences. In L. C. Hartlage & C. F. Telgrow (Eds.), *The neuropsychology of individual differences: A developmental perspective.* New York: Plenum.

Dean, R. S. (1986). Lateralization of cerebral functions. In D. Wedding, A. M. Horton, & J. Webster (Eds.), *The neuropsychology handbook: Behavioral and clinical perspectives.* New York: Springer.

Gazzaniga, M. S. (1970). *The bisected brain.* New York: Appleton-Century-Crofts.

Hannay, H. J. (1986). Some issues and concerns in neuropsychological research: An introduction. In H. J. Hannay (Ed.), *Experimental techniques in human neuropsychology.* New York: Oxford University Press.

Hess, W. R. (1967). Causalty, consciousness and cerebral organization. *Science, 158,* 1279–1283.

Joreskog, K. G., & Sorbom, D. (1981). *LISREL V: Analysis of linear structural relationships by the method of maximum likelihood.* Chicago: International Education Services.

Kirby, J. R. (1976). *Information processing and human abilities.* Unpublished doctoral dissertation, University of Alberta, Edmonton.

Lashley, K. S. (1951). The problem of serial order in behavior. In J. A. Jeffreys (Ed.), *Cerebral mechanisms in behavior: The Hixon Symposium.* New York: Wiley.

Lewandowski, L. J. (1987). Brain-behavior relationships. In L. C. Hartlage, M. J. Asken & J. L. Hornsby (Eds.), *Essentials of neuropsychological assessment.* New York: Springer.

Luria, A. R. (1966a). *Higher cortical functions in man.* New York: Basic Books.

Luria, A. R. (1966b). *Human brain and psychological processes.* New York: Harper and Row.

Luria, A. R. (1970). The functional organization of the brain. *Scientific American, 222,* 66–78.

Luria, A. R. (1973). *The working brain.* Middlesex, England: Penguin Books.

Naglieri, J. A. (1989). A cognitive processing theory for the measurement of intelligence. *Educational Psychologist, 24,* 185–206.

Naglieri, J. A., & Das, J. P. (1988). Planning-Arousal-Simultaneous-Successive (PASS): A model for assessment. *Journal of School Psychology, 26,* 35–48.

Naglieri, J. A., Das, J. P., & Jarman, R. F. (1990). Planning, attention, simultaneous, and successive cognitive processes as a model for assessment. *School Psychology Review, 19,* 423–442.

Naglieri, J. A., Das, J. P., Stevens, J. J., & Ledbetter, M. F. (1990). Confirmatory factor analysis of planning, attention, simultaneous, and successive cognitive processing tasks. *Journal of School Psychology.*

Pavlov, I. P. (1928). *Lectures on Conditioned Reflexes* (Trans., W. H. Gantt). New York: International Publishers.

Posner, M. I., & Boies, S. J. (1971). Components of attention. *Psychological Review, 78,* 391–408.

Pribram, K. H., & Luria, A. R. (Eds.) (1973). The frontal lobes and the regulation of behavior. In K. H. Pribram & A. R. Luria (Eds.) *Psychology and the frontal lobes.* New York: Academic Press.

Roberts, J. K. A. (1984). *Differential diagnosis in neuropsychiatry*. New York: Wiley.

Russell, E. W. (1981). The psychometric foundation of clinical neuropsychology. In S. B. Filskov & T. J. Boll (Eds.), *Handbook of clinical neuropsychology*. New York: Wiley.

Sperry, R. W. (1968). Hemispheric deconnection and unity in conscious awareness. *American Psychologist, 23*, 723–733.

Sternberg, R. J., & Detterman, D. (Eds.). (1986). *What is intelligence?* Norwood, NJ: Ablex.

Vernon, P. A. (1987). Wechsler Intelligence Scale for Children-Revised. In D. J. Keyser, & R. C. Sweetland (Eds.), *Tet critiques compendium*. Kansas City: Test Corporation of America.

Walsh, K. W. (1985). *Understanding brain damage*. London: Churchill Livingstone.

Walsh, K. W. (1987). *Neuropsychology: A clinical approach*. London: Churchill Livingstone.

Woodruff, M. L., & Baisden, R. H. (1986). Theories of brain functioning: A brief introduction to the study of the brain and behavior. In D. Wedding, A. M. Horton, & J. Webster (Eds.), *The neuropsychology handbook: Behavioral and clinical perspectives*. New York: Springer.

11

Theory-Based Testing of Intellectual Abilities: Rationale for the Triarchic Abilities Test

Robert J. Sternberg
Yale University

Conventional psychometric tests of intelligence have been based on theories of intelligence that have their roots in differential psychology—the psychology of individual differences. Although the theories generating these tests have been somewhat different, the scope of the tests has been surprisingly similar, in large part because for whatever their differences, the various theories of intelligence have encompassed roughly the same range of mental abilities.

In this chapter, I discuss a new approach to intelligence testing, based on a theory of human intelligence—the triarchic theory (Sternberg, 1985, 1988)—that is broader than conventional differential theories. The chapter is divided into three main parts. In the first, I briefly review differential theories, and the kinds of tests they have generated. In the second, main part of the chapter, I describe the triarchic theory, and the kind of test it has generated. The test is compared and contrasted with conventional tests. In the third part, I describe what I believe to be the main advantages of the triarchic theory and test, and how I see it being used in educational and employments settings.

THE DIFFERENTIAL THEORIES AND TESTS OF INTELLIGENCE

There have been innumerable tests of intelligence, based on a number of differential theories of intelligence. Fairly comprehensive reviews of these theories can be found in Carroll (1982) and Sternberg (1990), and hence the present review will be brief. I discuss three main differential approaches: the approach of Alfred Binet, which started the intelligence testing movement and its emphasis on the measurement of judgment and higher order reasoning skills; the approach of Charles Spearman, on which tests of the general factor of intelligence are based; and the approach of Louis Thurstone and other multifactor theorists, on which tests of multiple factors of intelligence are based.

The Approach of Alfred Binet.   In 1904, the Minister of Public Instruction in Paris named a commission charged with studying or creating tests that would insure that mentally defective children received an adequate education. The commission decided that no child suspected of retardation should be placed in a special class for the retarded without first being examined. Thus, the first major intelligence test grew out of practical educational concerns, and particularly, out of a concern to protect children from being placed in classes for the retarded without adequate justification.

According to Binet and Simon (1916a), the core of intelligence is "judgment, otherwise called good sense, practical sense, initiative, the faculty of adapting one's self to circumstances" (p. 42). Binet and Simon (1916b) believed that intelligent thought comprises three distinct elements: direction, adaptation, and criticism.

Direction consists in knowing what has to be done and how it is to be accomplished. When we are required to add two numbers, for example, we give ourselves a series of instructions on how to proceed. Adaptation refers to one's selection and monitoring of one's strategy during the course of task performance. For example, one may discover that a problem solving strategy is not working by monitoring this strategy as it is being used. Criticism is the ability to critique one's thoughts and actions, for example, to realize that a decision one has made has not represented one's best in terms of the use of available information.

In its most recent form, the Stanford Binet Intelligence Scale (4th edition: Thorndike, Hagen, & Sattler, 1986) provides four area scores and a composite score. The areas are verbal reasoning, abstract/visual reasoning, quantitative reasoning, and short-term memory. This particular partitioning of areas is not based on a psychological theory—either Binet's or anyone else's. Rather, the partitioning is loosely based on factor analysis of the subtests. There are 15 subtests relevant per level, with the exact identities of the subtests depending on the age level. Examples of subtests include vocabulary, comprehension, absurdities, verbal relations, pattern analysis, matrices, paper folding and cutting, number series, memory for sentences, and memory for objects. The subtests are generally true to Binet's conception of intelligence, with perhaps somewhat more emphasis on short-term memory than was found in Binet's theory.

The Approach of Charles Spearman.   Charles Spearman (1904, 1927) based his theorizing about intelligence on factor analysis, a psychometric technique that he invented. The idea of factor analysis is to identify the latent abilities that underlie scores on a set of mental ability tests. Spearman believed that two basic kinds of factors underlay these tests. The most important kind of factor, a general factor, is common to all of the tests. Less important are specific factors, each of which applies to a single test and represents variation in performance that derives solely from the single test.

As already discussed by Crawford, Spearman (1927) hypothesized that the general factor might represent individual differences in mental energy, although he never clearly defined what mental energy might be. Earlier, Spearman (1923) had proposed that three mental processes seem to be common to many kinds of reasoning of the kind found in tasks requiring intelligence. The first, apprehension of experience, refers to the perceptual encoding of stimuli. The second, eduction of relations, refers to inferring relations between stimuli. And the third, eduction of correlates, refers to application of the inferred relation to a new domain.

The Spearmanesque view of intelligence is represented in tests providing a single IQ score based on the three processes he identified. Tests such as matrix problems, series completions, classifications, and analogies seem to provide particularly good measurement of the general factor, especially if they use figural stimuli or other stimuli that do not require a large amount of prior knowledge when they are thought about in the context of taking a test. Verbal items requiring a high level of vocabulary for their completion are generally not good measures of Spearmanian general ability. For a more detailed discussion of Spearman's work see Crawford's chapter in this volume.

The Multifactor Approach of Louis Thurstone and His Successors.   Louis Thurstone (1938) believed that the general factor is a statistical artifact that only poorly describes the structure of intelligence. He suggested that intelligence is better understood as comprising a set of primary mental abilities, including verbal comprehension, verbal fluency, number, spatial visualization, inductive reasoning, perceptual speed, and memory abilities. He and his wife constructed a test measuring the primary mental abilities, which is still published in revised form to this day by Science Research Associates.

Other multifactor theorists proposed somewhat different theories based on the idea that intelligence cannot be well understood in terms of just a single factor of intelligence. For example, Guilford (1967) suggested that intelligence comprises 120 factors, obtained by crossing five different kinds of mental operations with six different kinds of products and four different kinds of contents. Horn and Cattell (1966) stayed closer to the original Spearmanian conception of intelligence, subdividing the general factor into a fluid subfactor that was similar to Spearman's general factor, and a crystallized subfactor that encompassed the knowledge based use of abilities. Most contemporary psychometric tests are loosely based on multifactor theories, although they do not usually follow the theories closely in terms of the scores they generate.

THE TRIARCHIC THEORY AND
TEST OF INTELLIGENCE

The triarchic theory of human intelligence seeks to explain in an integrative way the relationship between intelligence and:

1. The internal world of the individual, or the mental mechanisms that underlie intelligent behavior.
2. Experience, or the degree of relative novelty or lack of novelty involved in the application of the mental mechanisms of intelligence.
3. The external world of the individual, or the use of mental mechanisms in everyday life in order to attain an intelligent fit to the environment.

I discuss each of these three parts of the theory in turn, and how abilities are assessed by means of the Sternberg Triarchic Abilities Test. This test is an eight-level, two-form pencil and paper test of intelligence appropriate for administration to students from kindergarten through college. The college form may also be used with adults.

The test is equally divided into three contents, each representing a different form of mental representation of information: Verbal, quantitative, and figural. Crossed with these three content domains are four areas of mental processing. The general abilities domain is most similar to what is found on conventional intelligence tests, and measures the relation of intelligence to the internal world of the individual. The coping with novelty domain measures the relation of intelligence to novel experience. The automatization domain measures the relation of intelligence to highly familiar experience. And the practical domain measures the relation of intelligence to the external world of the individual. The experiential domain is measured through two separate sections because of the differences in processing to be found in novel versus familiar realms of experience.

At the time this chapter is being written, the test is being tried out in various cities in the United States. When published, the test will yield three content and four process scores, as well as an overall score. Various norm referenced scales will be provided, and current plans call for linking the test to achievement tests. Through such linking, it will be possible to relate more closely ability to achievement.

Intelligence and the Internal World of the Individual. In the triarchic theory, understanding of the relation between intelligence and the internal world of the individual is sought through an understanding of three basic kinds of information processing components: metacomponents, performance components, and knowledge acquisition components, each of which will be considered in turn.

Metacomponents are higher order, executive processes used to plan what one is going to do, to monitor it while one is doing it, and to evaluate it after it is done. These metacomponents include (a) recognizing the existence of a problem, (b) deciding on the nature of the problem confronting one, (c), selecting a set of lower order processes to solve the problem, (d) selecting a strategy into which to combine these components, (e) selecting a mental representation on which the components and strategy can act, (f) allocating one's mental resources, (g) monitoring one's problem solving as it is happening, and (h) evaluating one's problem solving after it is done. Consider some examples of these higher order processes.

Deciding on the nature of a problem plays a prominent role in intelligence. For example, with young children as well as older adults, their difficulty in problem solving often lies not in actually solving the given problem, but in figuring out just what the problem is that needs to be solved (see e.g., Flavell, 1977; Sternberg & Rifkin, 1979). A major feature distinguishing retarded persons from normal ones is the retardates' need to be instructed explicitly and completely as to the nature of the particular task they are solving and how it should be performed (Butterfield, Wambold & Belmont, 1973; Campione & Brown, 1979). The importance of figuring out the nature of the problem is not limited to retarded persons. Resnick and Glaser (1976) have argued that intelligence is the ability to learn from incomplete instruction.

Selection of a strategy for combining lower order components is also a critical aspect of intelligence. In early information processing research on intelligence, including my own (e.g., Sternberg, 1977), the primary emphasis was simply on figuring out what individuals do when confronted with a problem. What components do subjects use, and into what straegies do they combine these components? Soon, however, information processing researchers began to ask the question of why subjects use the strategies they choose. Consider some examples.

Cooper (1982) has reported that in solving spatial problems, and especially mental rotation problems, some subjects seem to use a holistic strategy of comparison whereas others use an analytic strategy. She has sought to figure out what leads subjects to the choice of one strategy or another. Siegler (1986) has actually proposed a model of strategy selection in arithmetic computation problems that links strategy choice to both the rules and mental associations one has stored in long-term memory. MacLeod, Hunt, and Mathews (1978) found that high spatial subjects tend to use a spatial strategy in solving sentence-picture comparison problems, whereas high verbal subjects are more likely to use a linguistic strategy. In my own work, I have found that subjects tend to prefer certain strategies for analogical reasoning over others because they place fewer demands on working memory (Sternberg & Ketron, 1982). Similarly subjects choose different strategies in linear-syllogistic reasoning (spatial, linguistic, mixed spatial-linguistic), but in this task, they do not always capitalize on their ability patterns so as to choose the strategy most suitable to their respective levels of spatial and verbal abilities (Sternberg & Weil, 1980). In sum, the selection of a strategy seems to be at least as important for understanding intelligent task performance as is the efficacy with which the chosen strategy is implemented.

Performance components are lower order processes that execute the instructions of the metacomponents. These lower order components solve the problems according to the plans laid out by the metacomponents. Whereas the number of metacomponents used in the performance of various tasks is relatively limited, the number of performance components is probably quite large. Many of these performance components are relatively specific to narrow ranges of tasks (Sternberg, 1979, 1983, 1985).

One of the most interesting classes of performance components is that found in inductive reasoning of the kind measured by tests such as matrices, analogies, series completions, and classifications. These components are important because of the importance of the tasks into which they enter: Induction problems of these kinds show the highest loadings on the general intelligence factor (Jensen, 1980; Snow & Lohman, 1984; Sternberg & Gardner, 1982). Thus, identifying these performance components can give us some insight into the nature of the general factor. In saying this, I am not arguing for any one factorial model of intelligence over others: To the contrary, I believe that most factor models are mutually compatible, differing only in the form of rotation that has been applied to a given factor space (Sternberg, 1977). The rotation one uses is a matter of theoretical or practical convenience, not of truth or falsity.

The main performance components of inductive reasoning are encoding, inference, mapping, application, comparison, justification, and response. They can be illustrated with reference to the analogy problem, LAWYER : CLIENT :: DOCTOR : (A) PATIENT, (B) MEDICINE. In encoding, the subject retrieves from semantic memory semantic attributes that are potentially relevant for analogy solution. In inference, the subject discovers the relation between the first two terms of the analogy, here, LAWYER and CLIENT. In mapping, the subjects discover the higher order relation that links the first half of the analogy, headed by LAWYER, to the second half of the analogy, headed by DOCTOR. In application, the subject carries over the relation inferred in the first half of the analogy to the second half of the analogy, generating a possible completion for the analogy. In comparison, the subject compares each of the answer options to the mentally generated completion, deciding which, if any, is correct. In justification, used optionally if none of the answer options matches the mentally generated solution, the subject decides which, if any, of the options is close enough to constitute an acceptable solution to the examiners, whether by means of pressing a button, making a mark on a piece of paper, or whatever.

Knowledge acquisition components are used to learn how to do what the metacomponents and performance components eventually do. Three knowledge acquisition components appear to be central in intellectual functioning: (a) selective encoding, (b) selective combination, and (c) selective comparison.

Selective encoding involved sifting out relevant from irrelevant information. When new information is presented in natural contexts, relevant information for one's given purpose is embedded in the midst of large amounts of purpose irrelevant information. A critical task for the learner is that of sifting out the "wheat from the chaff"; recognising just what information among all the pieces of information is relevant for one's purposes (see Schank, 1980).

Selective combination involves combining selectively encoded information in such a way as to form an integrated, plausible whole. Simply sifting out relevant information is not enough to generate a new knowledge structure. One must know how to combine the pieces of information into an internally connected whole (see Mayer & Greenco, 1972).

My emphasis on components of knowledge acquisition is somewhat different from the focus of some contemporary theorists in cognitive psychology, who emphasize what is already known, and the structure of this knowledge (e.g., Chase & Simon, 1973; Chi, 1978; Keil, 1984). I should point out, again, therefore, that these various emphases are complementary. If one is interested in understanding, for example, differences in performance between experts and novices, clearly one would wish to look at the amount and structure of their respective knowledge bases. But if one wishes to understand how these differences came to be, merely looking at developed knowledge would not be enough. Rather, one would have to look as well at differences in the ways that the knowledge bases were acquired. It is here that understanding of knowledge acquisition components will prove to be most relevant.

We have studied knowledge acquisition components in the domain of vocabulary acquisition (e.g., Sternberg, 1987; Sternberg & Powell, 1983). Difficulty in learning new words can be traced, at least in part, to the application of components of knowledge acquisition to context cues stored in long-term memory. Individuals with higher vocabularies tend to be those who are better able to apply the knowledge acquisition components to vocabulary learning situations. Given the importance of vocabulary for overall intelligence, almost without respect to the theory or test one uses, utilization of knowledge acquisition components in vocabulary learning situations would appear to be critically important for the development of intelligence. Effective use of knowledge acquisition components is trainable. I have found, for example, that just 45 minutes of training in the use of these components in vocabulary learning can significantly and fairly substantially improve the ability of adults to learn vocabulary from natural language contexts (Sternberg, 1987).

To summarize, the components of intelligence are an important part of the intelligence of the individual. The various kinds of components work together. Metacomponents activate the performance and knowledge acquisition components. These latter kinds of components in turn provide feedback to the meta-components. Although one can isolate various kinds of information processing components from task performance using experimental means, in practice, the components function together in highly interactive, and not easily isolated ways. Thus, diagnoses as well as instructional interventions need to consider all three types of components in interaction, rather than any one kind of component in isolation.

Testing the Componential Aspect of Intelligence. There are three componential subtests in the Sternberg Triarchic Abilities Test:

1. *Componential: Verbal.* Verbal comprehension abilities are traditionally measured by vocabulary tests, taking forms such as synonyms or antonyms questions. Such items have been shown to correlate highly with overall IQ (see Sternberg & Powell, 1983). The problem with such test items is that they seem more to measure achievement than ability, or stated another way, they emphasize the products of learning over the processes of learning.

In the triarchic test, verbal comprehension abilities are measured by items assessing an examinee's ability to learn from context. The underlying notion is that vocabulary is a proxy for a fundamental ability—the ability to pick up information from relevant context. It is through context that most vocabulary is learned. The theory of verbal comprehension can be found in Sternberg (1987). An example of a learning from context item (Years 10–12) is:

The depression did not happen suddenly with the 1929 stock market crash, although the *laz* that preceded it seemed carefree and spendthrift. The twenties saw homeless workers beginning to wend their way across the country, and small business going bankrupt.

Laz most likely means:

a. economy
b. years
c. history
d. lifestyles

2. *Componential: Quantitative.* Quantitative componential abilities are measured by number series items. These items measure inductive reasoning ability in the numerical domain. The theory of inductive reasoning underlying them is

given in Sternberg and Gardner (1983). The items require the examinee to extrapolate a sequence of numbers. An example (Years 10–12) would be:

1,3,6,8,16,_____ .

a. 18
b. 24
c. 32
d. 48

3. *Componential: Figural.* Figural componential abilities are measured by figure classifications in the primary grades (K–3) and by figure analogies at all remaining levels. Classifications are used for the youngest children because they can be made easier than analogies can be. These items, like number series, measure inductive reasoning ability. The theory underlying them is in Sternberg and Gardner (1983). In the figure classification the examinee must indicate which figure does not belong with the others.

Intelligence and Experience.   Components of information processing are always applied to tasks with which one has some level of prior experience (including the null level) and in situations with which one has some level of prior experience (including the null level). Hence, these internal mechanisms are closely tied to one's experience. According to the experiential subtheory, the components are not equally good measures of intelligence at all levels of experience. Assessing intelligence requires one to consider not only components, but the level of experience to which they are applied.

During recent years, there has been a tendency in cognitive science to study script based behavior (e.g., Schank & Abelson, 1977), whether under the name of "script" or under some other name, such as "scheme" or "frame." There is no longer any question that much of our behaviour is scripted, in some sense. However, from the standpoint of the present subtheory, such behavior is nonoptimal for understanding intelligence. Typically, one's actions when one goes to a restaurant, a doctor's office, or a movie theatre do not provide good measures of intelligence, even though they do provide good measures of scripted behavior. What, then, is the relation between intelligence and experience?

According to the experiential subtheory, intelligence is best measured at those regions of the experiential continuum that involve tasks or situations that are either relatively novel, on the one hand, or in the process of becoming automatized, on the other. As Raaheim (1974) pointed out, totally novel tasks and situations provide poor measures of intelligence: One would not want to administer, say, trigonometry problems to a first grader of roughly 6 years of age. But one might wish to administer problems that are just at the limits of the child's understanding, in order to test how far this understanding extends. For further work see Raaheim's chapter in this volume.

Related is Vygotsky's (1978) concept of the zone of proximal development, in which one examines a child's ability to profit from instruction to facilitate his or her solution of novel problems. In order to measure automatization skill, one might wish to present a series of problems—mathematical or otherwise—and to see how long it takes for solution of them to become automatic, and to see how automatized performance becomes. Thus, both slope and asymptote (if any) of automatization are of interest.

Ability to Cope with Novelty.   Several sources of evidence converge on the notion that the ability to cope with relative novelty is a good basis for measuring intelligence. Consider three such sources of evidence.

First, we have conducted several studies on the nature of insight, both in children and in adults (Davidson & Sternberg, 1984; Sternberg & Davidson, 1982). In the studies with children (Davidson & Sternberg, 1984), we separated three kinds of insights: insights of selective encoding, insights of selective combination, and insights of selective comparison. Use of these knowledge acquisition components is referred to as insightful when they are applied in the absence of existing scripts, plans, frames, or whatever. In other words, one must decide what information is relevant, decide how to put the information together, or decide how new information relates to old in the absence of any obvious cues on the basis of which to make these judgments. A problem is insightfully solved at the individual level when a given individual lacks such cues. A problem is insightfully solved at the societal level when no one else has these cues either.

In our studies, our hypothesis was the children who are intellectually gifted are gifted in part by virtue of their insight abilities, which represent an important part of the ability to deal with novelty. Children were administered quantitative insight problems, of the kinds found in puzzle books, that measured primarily either selective encoding skills, selective combination skill, or selective comparison skill. Either the problems were uncued, or else cuing was given that essentially gave away the insights. We found that nongifted, but not gifted children benefited from the cuing. In other words, gifted children spontaneously had the insights, whereas nongifted ones did not. No children scored close to the ceiling of any test, and noninsight cuing did not benefit either group.

In another paradigm, adult subjects were given what I call conceptual projection problems (Sternberg, 1982). In these problems, one has to make predictions about future states of objects based on incomplete and sometimes partially faulty information about the current states of the objects. These problems generally employed a science fiction type of scenario. For example, one might be introduced to four kinds of people on the planet, Kyron: One kind of person is born young and dies young, a second kind of person is born young and dies old, a third kind is born old and dies old, and a fourth kind is born old and dies young. Given incomplete information about the person in the present, one has to figure out what kind of person the individual is (names such as "kwef," "pros," "balt" and "plin" were used) and determine what his or her appearance would be twenty years later. Performance on the conceptual projection task was experimentally decomposed, and the mathematical model of task performance accounted for most of the stimulus variance (generally more than 90%) in task performance.

Each of these component scores was then correlated with performance on a variety of psychometric tests, including tests of inductive reasoning ability, which are primary measures of general intelligence. The critical finding was that the correlation of overall response time with psychometric test scores assessing fluid abilities was due to correlations stemming from those performance components tapping the ability to cope with novelty, for example, changing conceptual systems from a familiar one (born young and dies old) to an unfamiliar one (e.g., born old and dies young). These correlations held up without regard to the particular surface structure of the problem, of which the scenario about birth and death states was only one of four. Thus, it was the ability to cope with novelty, rather than other abilities involved in solving the problems, that proved to be critical to general intelligence.

In a third paradigm, Sternberg and Gastel (1989b) presented subjects with presuppositions that were either actual or counterfactual, and then required subjects to use the presuppositions in their reasoning.

In the Sternberg and Gastel (1989b) experiment, subjects might see either a presupposition such as "kites fly in the air" or "kites run on gasoline." They would then receive a set of statements, and have to respond to each statement as quickly as possible. The response was "true" if the statement followed from the presupposition, and "false" if the statement did not follow. For novel presuppositions, a statement might be either true for the factual and counterfactual presuppositions, false for both presuppositions, true for the factual presupposition but false for the counterfactual presupposition, or true for the counterfactual presupposition and true for the factual one. Consider statements for the presuppositions about kites:

a. Kites emit exhaust.
b. Kites need fuel.
c. Kites have tails.
d. Kites need wind.
e. Kites have four wheels.
f. Kites are faster than airplanes.
g. Kites can explode when they crash.
h. Kites are sold in stores.

With the familiar presupposition, statements c, d, and h are true. With the counterfactual presupposition, statements a, b, c, g, and h are true.

The main datum of interest was whether the difference score between response times to factual and counterfactual premise items would correlate significantly with psychometric tests involving fluid reasoning. The idea was to see whether a fairly purified measure of the ability to cope with novelty in reasoning was, as the triarchic theory predicts, a good measure of intelligence. The results supported the hypothesis.

Sternberg and Gastel (1989a) also used factual and counterfactual presuppositions, where the presuppositions might be either relevant or irrelevant to the solution of an analogy, classification, or series completion problem. They, too, found that the ability to cope with novelty was an important component of intelligence.

Testing the Coping with Novelty Aspect of Intelligence.   Three different item types are used to measure coping with novelty ability in the triarchic tests: verbal, quantitative, and figural.

1. *Coping with novelty: Verbal.*   These items measure, within the verbal domain, the ability to think in relatively novel ways. Two kinds of items, based on the theory described in Sternberg and Gastel (1989b), are used. The first item type asks the examinee to imagine a counterfactual situation, and then to draw an inference based on it. An example (Year 8–9 level) is:

If a dog laid eggs, which of these would be most likely to be true?
a. Dogs would fly.
b. Puppies would have feathers.
c. Eggs would have tails.
d. Puppies would hatch.
e. Chickens would bark.

A second kind of item is the novel verbal analogy, which requires counterfactual reasoning also. An example (Year 6–7 level) is:

Assume: Snowflakes are made of sand.
Which solution is now correct, given this assumption?
WATER : DROP :: SNOW:
a. storm
b. beach
c. grain
d. ice

2. *Coping with novelty: Quantitative.* These items measure coping with novelty skills in the context of the quantitative domain. Examinees received number matrix items, but with an element of novelty beyond the numerical matrix format: A symbol is used in place of certain numbers in the item, and the examinee

must make a substitution. The theory behind these items is based on Sternberg and Lubart (in press). An example of a numerical matrix item (Years 6–7) is:

* + 4	* – 2	3	
36		* + 1	

* = 8

a. 15
b. *
c. 18
d. 9

3. *Coping with novelty: Figural.* These items are like figure completion items, except that they are novel in requiring examinees to complete the series in a new domain unlike the one in that they have inferred the rule. They are thus series completion items with the added element of mapping (see Sternberg & Gardner, 1983, for theoretical basis).

Ability to Automatize Information Processing.   Although we are only now testing the second aspect of the experiential subtheory, i.e., the ability to automatize information processing, there are several converging lines of evidence to support the claim that this ability is a key aspect of intelligence.

Sternberg (1977) found that the correlation between People–Piece (schematic–picture) analogy performance and measures of general intelligence increased with practice, as performance on these items became increasingly automatized. Skilled reading is heavily dependent on automatization of bottom-up functions, and the ability to read well is an essential part of crystallized ability, whether as viewed from the standpoint of theories such as Cattell's (1971) and Vernon's (1971), or from the standpoint of tests of crystallized ability, such as the verbal portion of the Scholastic Aptitude Test. Poor comprehenders often are those who have not automatized the elementary, bottom-up processes of reading, and hence who do not have sufficient attentional resources to allocate to top-down comprehension processes (Spear & Sternberg, 1987; Sternberg & Wagner, 1982).

Theorists such as Jensen (1982) and Hunt (1978) have attributed the correlation between tasks such as choice reaction time and letter matching to the relation between speed of information processing and intelligence. Indeed, there is almost certainly some relationship, although I believe it is more complex than these theorists suggest. A plausible alternative hypothesis to theirs is that at least some of the correlation is due to the effects of automatization of processing: Because of the simplicity of these tasks, they probably become at least partially automatized rapidly, and hence can measure both rate and asymptote of automatization of performance. In sum, then, although the evidence is far from complete, there is at least some support for the notion that rate and level of automatization are related to intellectual skill.

The ability to cope with novelty and the ability to automatize information processing are interrelated (Sternberg, 1985). If one is well able to automatize, one has more resources left over for dealing with novelty. Similarly, if one is well able to deal with novelty, one has more resources left over for automatization. Thus, performance at the various levels of the experiential continuum are related to one another.

These abilities should not be viewed in a vacuum with respect to the componential subtheory. The components of intelligence are applied to tasks and situations at various levels of experience: the ability to cope with novelty can be understood in part in terms of components applied to tasks and situations that differ in kind from those one is used to. Automatization is one of the components in the componential subtheory as well. Consider now how automatization is measured on the triarchic test.

Testing the Automatization Aspect of Intelligence. The automatization subtests, like all others, are divided into verbal, quantitative, and figural. These are the only subtests that are highly speeded.

In the *verbal automatization* test subjects are presented with an initial row of from 1 to 5 target letters. At lower grade levels, numbers of letters are smaller. Subjects then see a number of test rows, each of which contains one of the target letters. The examinee must mark the target letter as quickly as possible. For example, a subject might see the following at the Kindergarten level:

K
L M C K
K U T L
H C K Z
. . . .

The *quantitative automatization and figural automatization* tests are identical to the verbal ones, except for the use of digits rather than letters in the quantitative test and the use of figures rather than letters or digits in the figural test.

Intelligence and the External World of the Individual. According to the contextual subtheory, intelligent thought is directed toward one or more of three behavioral goals: (a) adaptation to an existing environment, (b) shaping of an existing environment, or (c) selection of a new environment.

These three goals may be viewed as the functions toward which intelligence is directed: Intelligence is not aimless or random mental activity that happens to involve certain components of information processing at certain levels of experience. Rather, it is purposefully directed toward the pursuit of these three global goals, all of which have more specific and concrete instances in people's lives. Although all three goals are important to the triarchic theory, only the first is assessed in the triarchic intelligence test, mainly because we do not yet know how to assess the other two. Because only adaptation is assessed, only it will be discussed here. Discussion of shaping and selection can be found in Sternberg (1985, 1988).

Most intelligent thought is directed toward the attempt to adapt to one's environment. The requirements for adaptation can differ radically from one environment to another—whether environments are defined in terms of families, jobs, subcultures, cultures, or whatever. Hence, although the components of intelligence required in these various contexts may be the same or quite similar, and although all of them may involve, at one time or another, coping with novelty and automatization of information processing, the concrete occurrences of these processes and levels of experience may differ substantially across contexts. This fact has an important implication for our understanding of the nature of intelligence. According to the triarchic theory, in general, and the contextual subtheory, in particular, the processes and experiential facets and functions of intelligence remain essentially the same across contexts; but the particular manifestation of these processes, facets, and functions can differ, and differ radically. Thus, the content of intelligent thought and its manifestations in behavior will bear no necessary resemblance across contexts. As a result, although the mental elements that an intelligence test should measure do not differ across contexts, the vehicle for measurement may have to differ. A test that measures a set of processes, experiential facets, or intelligent functions in one context may not provide equally adequate measurement in another context. To the contrary, what is intelligent in one culture may be viewed as unintelligent in another.

A nice example of this fact can be found in the work of Cole, Gay, Glick, and Sharp (1971). These investigators found that Kpelle tribesmen sorted objects into groups functionally, for example, sorting a knife with an orange because a knife can be used to cut an orange. In the West, this means of sorting would be considered developmentally immature, and would be a sign of low adult intelligence. This inference does not generalize to Kpelle society, however, because the Kpelle are not used to Western norms for taking tests. Indeed, they can easily sort in a taxonomic, hierarchic way—if asked to sort the way a "stupid" person would! They lack not our abilities, but our conception of what the intelligent way is to sort the objects. Or conversely, we lack theirs.

One of the most interesting differences among cultures and subcultures in the development of patterns of adaptation is in the matter of time allocation, a metacomponential function. In Western cultures, in general, budgeting of time and careful allocation of one's time to various activities is a prized commodity. Our lives are largely governed by careful scheduling at home, in school, at work, and so on. There are fixed hours for certain activities, and fixed lengths of time within which these activities are expected to be completed. Indeed, the intelligence tests we use show our prizing of time allocation to the fullest. Almost all of them are timed in such a way as to make completion of the tests a nontrivial challenge. A slow or very cautious worker is at a distinct disadvantage.

Not all cultures and subcultures view time in the same way that we do. For example, among the Kipsigi, schedules are much more flexible, and hence these individuals have difficulty understanding and dealing with Western notions of the time pressure that people are expected to live under (Super & Harkness, 1980). In Hispanic cultures, such as Venezuela, my own personal experience indicates that the press of time is taken with much less seriousness than it is in typical North American cultural settings. Even within the continental United States, though, there can be major differences in the importance of time allocation. Heath (1983) describes young children brought up in the rural community of "Trackton," in which there is very little time pressure and in which things essentially get done when they get done. These children can have great difficulty adjusting to the demands of the school, in which time pressures may be placed on the children for the first time in their lives.

The point of these examples has been to illustrate how differences in environmental press and people's conceptions of what constitutes an intelligent response to it can influence just what counts as adaptive behavior. To understand intelligence, one must understand it not only in relation to its internal manifestations in terms of mental processes, and its experiential manifestations in terms of facets of the experiential continuum, but also in terms of how thought is intelligently translated into action in a variety of different contextual settings. The differences in what is considered adaptive and intelligent can extend even to different occupations within a given cultural milieu.

Wagner and Sternberg (1985, 1986) sought to measure one aspect of adaptive intelligence; they referred to it as the use of "tacit knowledge." Tacit knowledge is knowledge that is needed for adaptive functioning in a real world environment, but that is not explicitly taught, and that is usually not even verbalized. They interviewed business executives and psychology professors who had been nominated as being highly practically intelligent in order to identify the skills needed for successful coping. On the basis of these interviews and other information, they constructed tests of tacit knowledge to administer to people in each of these two occupations. They found that the tests distinguished well between people with different levels of expertise in these occupations. Moreover, the tests were not correlated with conventional psychometric intelligence tests.

Testing the Practical Aspect of Intelligence. The practical subtests, like the rest, are divided into verbal, quantitative, and figural contents.

1. *Practical: verbal.* Practical verbal items require examinees to answer everyday inferential reasoning problems. In other words, the test taker must reason informally rather than formally, as would usually be the case for such items.

An example of a practical verbal item would be (Year 8-9 level):

Johnson's Service station adheres to its claim that it will not be undersold. Which of these is most likely to be true?
1. Garcia's Service Station charges more than Johnson's.
2. No other garage charges less than Johnson's.
3. Johnson's garage is the busiest garage in town.

2. *Practical: quantitative.* These items require the examinee to reason quantitatively with practical everyday problems of the kind he or she might face in everyday life. An example of part of a problem is (Year 10-12 level):

You plan to make some cookies for your club's bake sale. The recipe calls for the following ingredients:
1 stick butter, 1 cup sugar, 1 egg, 1 cup flour, 1 cup pecans.
Yield: 24 cookies
You have the following ingredients: 4 sticks of butter, 5 cups of sugar, 1 dozen eggs, 7 cups of flour, 2 8-oz. bags of chocolate chips and 3 cups of pecans.
If you decide to make pecan cookies, what is the largest number of cookies you can make, using the ingredients you already have?
a. 3 dozen
b. 4 dozen
c. 6 dozen
d. 8 dozen

3. *Practical: figural.* Items in this subtest require the ability to plan a route efficiently, given the information in a map or diagram. The examinee might be shown a map of a town, for example, and be asked which of several routes is the most efficient from one location to another.

USES OF THE STERNBERG
TRIARCHIC ABILITIES TEST

The Sternberg Triarchic Abilities Test measures each of the aspects of the triarchic theory, except for the environmental shaping and selection functions of the contextual subtheory. The test is not immune to effects of prior learning, nor is it culture free. It is impossible, I believe, to create a test that is genuinely immune to effects of prior experience or that is wholly culture free, because intelligence cannot be tested outside the boundaries of a culture. Intelligence is always used in some context, and must be measured in some context. The proposed test, however, seems broader and more comprehensive than other existing tests, and hence allows for more diversity in backgrounds than would be true of traditional tests.

The triarchic test has certain implications both for the assessment and the training of abilities. With regard to assessment, a full assessment battery would necessarily tap all of the abilities specified by the triarchic theory, something no existing test even comes close to. Although I believe my test is more nearly complete than current ones, even a test explicitly designed to measure intelligence according to the triarchic theory will be only an approximation to an ideal test, if only because the relativity of the contextual subtheory renders any one test adequate only for a limited population. Similarly, I have developed a training program for improving intellectual skills, based on the theory (Sternberg, 1986). But the training program could not possibly develop all of the skills posited by the theory, especially because contextual skills are so variable across environments.

I believe that the test will have use as a diagnostic and selection device in schools. It will give students and teachers alike a more nearly complete assessment of abilities than has been true of past tests. Moreover, it will pinpoint areas of strength and weakness, rather than merely giving one or two global scores. For admission to programs for the retarded or gifted, the test will be more valid than a test sampling just a limited range of abilities. And the test will have organizational uses for jobs in which more than just IQ-like abilities are needed, which includes almost all jobs!

In conclusion, the triarchic theory of human intelligence offers a relatively complete account of intelligent thought that draws on and partially subsumes many existing theories. This new theory, like all other theories, is only an approximation, one that will serve a constructive purpose if it, too, is eventually subsumed by a more complete and accurate theory of intelligence. For now, it forms a good approximation, something we have needed for a long time. We have been dependent on very old theories of intelligence to serve functions they were never intended to serve. The triarchic theory is broader, and can serve predictive and diagnostic functions that would not have been possible for earlier and narrower theories of intelligence.

REFERENCES

Binet, A., & Simon, T. (1916a). *The development of intelligence in children* (E. S. Kite, Trans). Baltimore, MD: Williams & Wilkins.

Binet, A., & Simon, T. (1916b). *The intelligence of the feeble-minded* (E. S. Kite, Trans). Baltimore, MD: Williams & Wilkins.

Butterfield, E. C., Wambold, C., & Belmont, J. M. (1973). On the theory and practice of improving short-term memory. *American Journal of Mental Deficiency, 77,* 654–669.

Campione, J. C., & Brown, A. L. (1979). Toward a theory of intelligence: Contributions from research with retarded children. In R. J. Sternberg & D. K. Detterman (Eds.), *Human intelligence: Perspectives on its theory and measurement.* Norwood, NJ: Ablex.

Carroll, J. B. (1982). The measurement of intelligence. In R. J. Sternberg (Ed.), *Handbook of human intelligence*. New York: Cambridge University Press.

Cattell, R. B. (1971). *Abilities: Their structure, growth, and action*. Boston, MA: Houghton Mifflin.

Chase, W. G., & Simon, H. A. (1973). The mind's eye in chess. In W. G. Chase (Ed.), *Visual information processing*. New York: Academic Press.

Chi, M. T. H. (1978). Knowledge structures and memory development. In R. S. Siegler (Ed.), *Children's thinking: What develops?* Hillsdale, NJ: Lawrence Erlbaum Associates.

Cole, M., Gay, J., Glick, J., & Sharp, D. W. (1971). *The cultural context of learning and thinking*. New York: Basic Books.

Cooper, L. A. (1982). Strategies for visual comparison and representation: Individual differences. In R. J. Sternberg (Ed.), *Advances in the psychology of human intelligence* (Vol. 1). Hillsdale, NJ: Lawrence Erlbaum Associates.

Davidson, J. E., & Sternberg, R. J. (1984). The role of insight in intellectual giftedness. *Gifted Child Quarterly, 28,* 58–64.

Flavell, J. H. (1977). *Cognitive development*. Englewood Cliffs, NJ: Prentice Hall.

Guilford, J. P. (1967). *The nature of human intelligence*. New York: McGraw Hill.

Heath, S. B. (1983). *Ways with words*. New York: Cambridge University Press.

Horn, J. L., & Cattell, R. B. (1966). Refinement and test of the theory of fluid and crystallized ability intelligences. *Journal of Educational Psychology, 57,* 253–270.

Hunt, E. B. (1978). Mechanics of verbal ability. *Psychological Review, 85,* 109–130.

Jensen, A. R. (1980). *Bias in mental testing*. New York: Free Press.

Jensen, A. R. (1982). The chronometry of intelligence. In R. J. Sternberg (Ed.), *Advances in psychology of human intelligence* (Vol. 1). Hillsdale, NJ: Lawrence Erlbaum Associates.

Keil, F. C. (1984). Transition mechanisms in cognitive development and the structure of knowledge. In R. J. Sternberg (Ed.), *Mechanisms of cognitive development*. San Francisco, CA: Freeman.

MacLeod, C. M., Hunt, E. B., & Mathews, N. N. (1978). Individual differences in the verification of sentence-picture relationships. *Journal of Verbal Learning and Verbal Behaviour, 17,* 493–507.

Mayer, R., & Greeno, J. G. (1972). Structural differences between learning outcomes produced by different instructional methods. *Journal of Educational Psychology, 63,* 165–173.

Raaheim, K. (1974). *Problem solving and intelligence*. Oslo: Universitetsforlaget.

Resnick, L. B., & Glaser, R. (1976). Problem solving and intelligence. In L. B. Resnick (Ed.), *The nature of intelligence*. Hillsdale, NJ: Lawrence Erlbaum Associates.

Schank, R. (1980). How much intelligence is there in artificial intelligence? *Intelligence, 4,* 1–14.

Schank, R., & Abelson, R. (1977). *Scripts, plan, goals, and understanding*. Hillsdale, NJ: Lawrence Erlbaum Associates.

Siegler, R. S. (1986). Unities across domains in children's strategy choices. In M. Perlmutter (Ed.), *Perspectives on intellectual development: The Minnesota Symposia on child psychology* (Vol. 19). Hillsdale, NJ: Lawrence Erlbaum Associates.

Snow, R. E., & Lohman, D. F. (1984). Toward a theory of cognitive aptitude for learning from instruction. *Journal of Educational Psychology, 76,* 347–376.

Spear, L. C., & Sternberg, R. J. (1987). An information-processing framework for understanding reading disabilities. In S. Ceci (Ed.), *Handbook of cognitive, social, and neuropsychological aspects of learning disabilities* (Vol. 2). Hillsdale, NJ: Lawrence Erlbaum Associates.

Spearman, C. (1904). General intelligence, objectively determined and measured. *American Journal of Psychology, 15,* 201–293.

Spearman, C. (1923). *The nature of "intelligence" and the principles of cognition*. London: Macmillan.

Spearman, C. (1927). *The abilities of man*. New York: Macmillan.

Sternberg, R. J. (1977). *Intelligence, information processing, and analogical reasoning: The componential analysis of human abilities*. Hillsdale, NJ: Lawrence Erlbaum Associates.

Sternberg, R. J. (1979). The nature of mental abilities. *American Psychologist, 34,* 214–230.

Sternberg, R. J. (1982). Natural, unnatural, and supernatural concepts. *Cognitive Psychology, 14,* 451–488.

Sternberg, R. J. (1983). Components of human intelligence. *Cognition, 15,* 1–48.

Sternberg, R. J. (1985). *Beyond IQ: A triarchic theory of human intelligence.* New York: Cambridge University Press.

Sternberg, R. J. (1986). *Intelligence applied: Understanding and increasing your intellectual skills.* San Diego, CA: Harcourt, Brace, Jovanovich.

Sternberg, R. J. (1987). Most vocabulary is learned from context. In M. McKeown (Ed.), *The nature of vocabulary acquisition.* Hillsdale, NJ: Lawrence Erlbaum Associates.

Sternberg, R. J. (1988). *The triarchic mind.* New York: Viking.

Sternberg, R. J. (1990). *Metaphors of mind.* New York: Cambridge University Press.

Sternberg, R. J. & Davidson, J. E. (1982). The mind of the puzzler. *Psychology Today, 16,* June, 37–44.

Sternberg, R. J., & Gardner, M. K. (1982). A componential interpretation of the general factor in human intelligence. In H. J. Eysenck (Ed.), *A model for intelligence.* Berlin: Springer Verlag.

Sternberg, R. J., & Gardner, M. K. (1983). Unities in inductive reasoning. *Journal of Experimental Psychology: General, 112,* 80–116.

Sternberg, R. J., & Gastel, J. (1989a). If dancers ate their shoes: Inductive reasoning with factual and counterfactual premise. *Memory and Cognition, 17,* 1–10.

Sternberg, R. J., & Gastel, J. (1989b). Coping with novelty in human intelligence: An empirical investigation. *Intelligence, 13,* 187–197.

Sternberg, R. J., & Ketron, J. L. (1982). Selection and implementation of strategies in reasoning by analogy. *Journal of Educational Psychology, 74,* 399–413.

Sternberg, R. J., & Lubart, T. I. (in press). An investment theory of creativity and its development. *Human Development.*

Sternberg, R. J., & Powell, J. S. (1983). Comprehending verbal comprehension. *American Psychologist, 38,* 878–893.

Sternberg, R. J., & Rifkin, B. (1979). The development of analogical reasoning processes. *Journal of Experimental Child Psychology, 27,* 195–232.

Sternberg, R. J., & Wagner, R. K. (1982). Automatization failure in learning disabilities. *Topics in learning and learning disabilities, 2,* July, 1–11.

Sternberg, R. J., & Weil, E. M. (1980). An aptitude-strategy interaction in linear syllogistic reasoning. *Journal of Educational Psychology, 72,* 226–234.

Super, C. M., & Harkness, S. (1980). The infants' niche in rural Kenya and metropolitan America. In L. L. Adler (Ed.), *Issues in cross-cultural research.* New York: Academic Press.

Thorndike, R. L., Hagen, E. P., & Sattler, J. M. (1986). *Stanford-Binet Intelligence Scale: Fourth Edition.* Chicago Il: Riverside Publishing Company.

Thurstone, L. L. (1938). *Primary mental abilities.* Chicago, Il: University of Chicago Press.

Vernon, P. E. (1971). *The structure of human abilities.* London: Methuen.

Vygotsky, L. S. (1978). *Mind in society: The development of higher psychological processes.* Cambridge, MA: Harvard University Press.

Wagner, R. K., & Sternberg, R. J. (1985). Practical intelligence in real-world pursuits: The role of tacit knowledge. *Journal of Personality and Social Psychology, 49,* 436–458.

Wagner, R. K., & Sternberg, R. J. (1986). Tacit knowledge and intelligence in the everyday world. In R. J. Sternberg & R. K. Wagner (Eds.), *Practical intelligence: Nature and origins of competence in the everyday world.* New York: Cambridge University Press.

12 Cognitive Models for Understanding and Assessing Spatial Abilities

James W. Pellegrino
Vanderbilt University

Earl B. Hunt
University of Washington

Over the last 15 years research and theory in cognitive psychology has significantly influenced contemporary views of intelligence (e.g., Carroll, 1976; Embretson, 1985; Hunt, 1980; Pellegrino, 1984; Resnick, 1976; Sternberg, 1982; Wolman, 1985). Many individuals have played a role in attempting to unite the large body of psychometric research with contemporary research and theory in cognition. This research has encompassed several different approaches. One example involves the search for relationships between information processing tasks and psychometric measures of intelligence (e.g., Hunt, 1978, 1980; Lansman, Donaldson, Hunt & Yantis, 1982; Jensen, 1982; Keating & Bobbit, 1978). A second example involves detailed modeling of the information processing components underpinning psychometric test item performance (e.g., Alderton, Goldman & Pellegrino, 1985; Pellegrino & Glaser, 1980; Sternberg, 1977; Sternberg & Gardner, 1983). A third example involves the complex integration of item response theory and componential analysis (e.g., Embretson, 1984; Whitely, 1980). Despite differences in the research approach, the goals have been identical, i.e., to develop an information processing explanation of intelligence as it manifests itself on traditional psychometric tests.

Some of the impetus for the attempts at unifying cognitive and differential psychology was the growing dissatisfaction with the limited predictive and prescriptive validity of tests of intelligence and specific aptitudes (e.g., Cronbach, 1970; Ghiselli, 1973; Glaser, 1972). The question is whether we are currently better off with regard to these issues of validity. Elsewhere, it has been argued that there are strong parallels and important ties between what is done in cognitive science research and what is done in typical test validation research (Pellegrino, 1988). Equally important, however, are the differences. The most critical difference is that emphasis has been given to detailed analyses of the

203

knowledge representations and processes underlying performance on the simple and complex cognitive tasks that define major intellectual ability constructs. As such, this collective body of work has theoretical and practical implications with regard to various validation issues associated with the construct, measurement, and improvement of intellectual abilities.

It is reasonable to ask whether we have concrete proof that the stage has been set for new concepts and measurement techniques. Have we reached a point where the knowledge from research and development activities is sufficient to significantly impact contemporary approaches to measurement? We believe that such is the case for various specific domains of cognition and aptitude. Our goal is to prove that this is the case by illustrating it for the domain for visual spatial ability.

There are several points that must be made about the accumulated knowledge in this area. The first is that current tests of visual spatial ability and typical data on individual differences in spatial ability can be understood when set in the context of underlying knowledge representations and processing activities. These representations and processes are not arbitrary but can be embedded in a general theory of spatial cognition (e.g., Just & Carpenter, 1985; Pellegrino & Kail, 1982; Lohman, Pellegrino, Alderton & Regian, 1987). Furthermore, such an orientation provides a necessary framework for understanding results from studies showing substantial ability changes following practice in various components of spatial processing (see Lohman et al., 1987). These issues are addressed in the next section of this chapter.

The second major point is that theory based assessment research can lead not only to a better understanding of individual differences on conventional tests but to the design of better testing procedures in which the construct representation of the tests is improved without changing substantially the nomothetic span of the instruments (Hunt, Pellegrino, Abate, Alderton, Farr, Frick & McDonald, 1987; Pellegrino, Hunt, Abate & Farr, 1987). Research related to the development and validation of theory based tasks is presented in the third section of this chapter.

The third major point is that the application of both contemporary theory and technology can lead to the discovery of heretofore unspecified cognitive abilities. An example is the evidence that reasoning about dynamically changing visual spatial displays defines a dimension of ability different from conventional tests of spatial ability (Hunt, Pellegrino, Frick, Farr & Alderton, 1988). This dimension of ability may be of great practical significance for predicting various real world visual spatial reasoning activities such as piloting and air traffic control. Work related to this issue is presented in the fourth major section of this chapter.

PSYCHOMETRICS AND INFORMATION PROCESSING

Spatial ability is the ability to reason about visual scenes. An example would be the reasoning a pedestrian does when deciding to cross a busy street. The positions of moving vehicles must be moved forward in time. Another, less serious, example is the reasoning one does in deciding to move a piece into an open position in a jigsaw puzzle. Spatial ability is a basic dimension of human intelligence, clearly separate from verbal intelligence or general reasoning ability. Virtually every comprehensive theory of intelligence makes reference to the domain of spatial ability (Carroll, 1982).

Spatial ability is better thought of as a domain of abilities than as a single ability or skill. Multivariate studies of the domain have identified three major factors (Lohman, 1979; McGee, 1979). The most clearly defined factor is *spatial relations* ability, which refers to the capacity to move objects *in the mind's eye* as required when one mentally rotates an object about its center (Shepard & Cooper, 1982). Conventional psychometric tests of spatial relations ability include the *Primary Mental Abilities* Space test (Thurstone & Thurstone, 1949). A second factor is *spatial visualization,* which is best thought of as the ability to deal with complex visual problems that require imagining the relative movements of internal parts of a visual image. The jigsaw puzzle example given earlier is a good illustration. Psychometric tests that tap spatial visualization include the paper folding (surface development) task in the *Differential Aptitude Battery (DAT)* (Bennett, Seashore & Wesman, 1974) and the *Minnesota Paper Form Board Test* (Likert & Quasha, 1970). The third primary spatial factor is *spatial orientation,* which is the ability to imagine how a stimulus or a stimulus array would appear from a different perspective. Distinguishing this factor from spatial relations is often difficult, however (Lohman, 1979).

Although three dimensions of spatial ability can be identified, they are typically correlated across individuals. Therefore, in terms of the technical aspects of multidimensional analysis, the scores from a variety of spatial ability tests may often be placed in a two rather than a three dimensional space. More precisely, depending upon the exact composition of the test battery, it may be the case that three dimensions are required for an excellent fit, but two dimensions will often be sufficient.

Correlational studies of spatial ability are perhaps more interesting for what they tell us spatial ability is not, than for what they tell us it is. For example, there is no clear separation of two dimensional from three dimensional stimuli and tasks, nor do the various transformations (rotation, folding, synthesis, etc) seem to depend on radically different skills. Further, complex spatial tests are highly correlated with figural reasoning tests, such as *Raven's Progressive Matrices* (Raven, 1962) and geometric analogy tests.

On logical grounds alone, one might expect tests of spatial ability to predict performance in certain nonacademic fields. Consider the examples given earlier, crossing a street and constructing a jigsaw puzzle. The first problem involves estimating the time and point of arrival of objects in the visual field, a task that appears to be a primary component of many machinery operation tasks. This component also appears to draw on spatial relations ability, as defined by typical psychometric tests. Consistent with this observation, spatial orientation tests have been used to screen candidates for flight training, where one would expect spatial orientation skills to be in high demand. Spatial relations and spatial visualization tests have also been related to performance in technical courses such as architecture and engineering courses, where they are reliable predictors of achievement (Alderton, 1988a; McGee, 1979). More detailed studies have shown that spatial ability test scores can be related directly to performance on problems involving analysis of engineering drawings (Pellegrino, Mumaw & Shute, 1985).

Outside of aviation, spatial ability tests have a rather mixed record as predictors of performance in military occupations. In spite of there being a strong logical case that the tests should predict performance in occupations involving either machinery operation or the analysis of drawings, only low to moderate correlations have been found. For that and other reasons, spatial tests are not included in the current version of the Armed Services Vocational Aptitude Battery (ASVAB).

It has been noted that the generally disappointing performance of spatial ability tests as predictors may be due to a technological restriction on the range of spatial abilities that can be tested (Hunt & Pellegrino, 1985). Current spatial tests virtually all depend on the conventional paper and pencil test format. This restricts the form of the test items severely because the visual scenes that the examinee must reason about cannot contain moving elements. Also, although it is possible to determine how many items an examinee can pass in a fixed time, it is not possible to examine the time that a person spends on an individual item, or the time spent on various identifiable subparts of the spatial problem posed by the given test item. This is an issue because speed and accuracy in solving parts of a problem may reflect different psychological skills (Pellegrino & Kail, 1982). More generally, different people may trade off between speed and accuracy of performance in different ways and measures of both speed and accuracy may be needed to adequately assess skill (Pachella, 1974).

Although the number of potentially identifiable spatial factors is quite large, the number of distinct psychological processes required by spatial tasks appears to be much smaller. Over the last decade, there has been a concerted effort to link psychological theories of spatial processing (e.g., Kosslyn, 1980) to psychometric measures of spatial ability (see e.g., Just & Carpenter, 1985; Lohman et al., 1987; Pellegrino & Kail, 1982; Poltrock & Brown, 1984). Detailed cognitive models have been developed and validated for a variety of spatial processing tasks that closely resemble or directly emulate the tasks associated with the spatial relations and visualization factors. Examples include mental rotation tasks, form board tasks, synthesis tasks, cube comparison tasks, and surface development tasks (see Just & Carpenter, 1985; Lohman et al., 1987). Such models have also been used as the basis for conducting detailed process, knowledge and strategy analyses of the sources of individual differences in measured spatial abilities.

A variety of general and specific conclusions can be reached from this body of research on the cognitive process basis of individual differences in spatial ability. By looking across tasks and studies one might initially conclude that spatial ability is not one thing but that it is a function of several capacities such as those included in Kosslyn's (1980) theory of mental imagery. One example is the ability to establish precise and stable representations of unfamiliar visual stimuli. Such representations can then be operated on or transformed with minimal information loss or degradation. It appears that individuals high in spatial ability are faster in representing unfamiliar visual stimuli and in constructing representations that are more precise. Differences in the quality of representation, and strategy of processing, may give rise to other speed of processing differences such as the superior mental rotation, search, and "folding" rates observed in different tasks. Problems of representation are most apparent in the more complex visualization tasks that require the representation and manipulation of stimuli having several interrelated elements. Differences between spatial relations and visualization tasks and factors may partially reflect a difference in the relative importance of coding versus transformation processes in a visual short term memory or buffer. Another difference between the two factors and their associated tasks appears to involve single versus multiple transformations and the coordination and monitoring of the latter.

A number of issues necessary for a complete understanding of spatial ability still need to be fully explored and resolved. One such issue is the use of different strategies in solving complex spatial problems. Both between and within individual differences can involve the use of different strategies and processes in item solution. Copper and Mumaw (1985) and Lohman (1988, see also Lohman & Kyllonen, 1983) have explored this possibility. It appears that individuals change strategies as a function of the complexity and difficulty of problems. An interesting issue is whether the selection and use of strategies is optimally matched to problem characteristics and whether ability differences result from the strategy repertoire available and/or the optimality of the decision rules for strategy application.

Given that there are differences in the speed and accuracy of executing spatial processes and in the selection and use of strategies for problem solution, another important issue is whether these differences are fixed or modifiable. Can individuals of low ability acquire skill in spatial processing as a function of experience, practice, and/or training? Some answers to these questions are considered in the next section.

PRACTICE AND SPATIAL APTITUDE

There is some old evidence that spatial ability can be increased following practice and/or training. For example, Brinkmann (1966) found substantial improvement on a complex spatial test (Differential Aptitude Test: Space Relations subtest, Bennett, Seashore & Wesman, 1974) following training in geometry that was directed to emphasize visual/imaginal aspects of geometry. However, simply learning geometry under usual conditions (emphasizing logical proofs) had no impact on spatial ability according to Brown (1954) and Ranucci (1952) (cited in Brinkmann, 1966). Blade and Watson (1955) found that students demonstrated gains in spatial ability following study in engineering. Stringer (1975) found similar results following directed training in drawing as did Dailey and Neyman (1967) (cited from Levine, Schulman, Brahlek & Fleishman, 1980). Even still, Levine et al., (1980) found virtually no increases in spatial ability following indirect training on tasks thought to require spatial ability, although practice did improve performance on the spatial training tasks.

More recent work on the effects of practice and/or training on spatial tasks comes from Embretson and Ackerman. Using *dynamic testing* principles, Embretson and Farha (1985; Embretson, 1987) conducted a study exploring the effects of practice and training on psychometric test performance. The authors used a pretest-train-posttest design to determine the effects of brief training on the psychometric properties of a complex spatial test (DAT: Space subtest, Bennett et al., 1974) including the predictive validity of the test. Following standardized administration procedures, the pretest was administered and followed by a brief training session that employed physical analogs of the test items to demonstrate how problems were to be solved. The posttest was then administered and performance data on a text editing task were collected. The results were completely consistent with predictions from the *dynamic testing* perspective. First, training significantly increased posttest performance. Second, the measurement properties of the posttest were greatly superior to those of the pretest (Cronbach's alpha increased as well as the fit of the one parameter logistic item response model). Finally, the posttest was clearly a better predictor of the text editing criteria (response time and time per accurate text correction). Whereas these data provide strong support for the *dynamic testing* hypotheses, they do not illuminate what changes occurred following practice/training.

Ackerman (1986) provides a partial answer to this question using substantially more practice than in the Embretson and Farha (1985) study. Ackerman used a practice-test-practice design where subjects received spatial task practice, then solved standardized spatial ability tests that were followed by more spatial task practice. All tallied, subjects solved 800 simple spatial problems over a four day period. Two results are important. First, the correlations between spatial task performance and spatial ability test scores increased initially and then dropped slightly; however, it is not clear if any of the changes in the correlations were significant. Second, using average solution time as the dependent measure, subjects became dramatically faster on the spatial task following practice; the decrement in mean response times followed the expected power function.

Combining the results from these studies, provides an interesting picture of the relationship between practice and spatial ability. Most importantly, the evidence for practice effects in spatial ability is generally positive, which is difficult to explain theoretically when spatial ability is viewed as a stable trait. There is clear evidence that practice and/or training produces increases in tested spatial ability and better performance on spatial problem solving tasks. Furthermore, the Embretson and Farha (1985) data plainly show that following practice/training, spatial ability tests can have better measurement properties and are more valid ability measures. Unfortunately, from an information processing perspective, these studies provide little insight into the nature or locus of change. For example, although average response times dramatically drop with practice, does this mean that there is a uniform increase in the speed of executing each of the component processes? Or, do some processes become faster and others remain stable? Or, are some processes omitted after time, implying a strategy change? Answers to these questions can only be obtained by monitoring process changes throughout practice.

Alderton and Pellegrino (1988) conducted a detailed investigation of the effects of practice on the information processing characteristics of two spatial tasks, a speeded mental rotation task and a complex visualization task. There were three general questions under consideration. The first was, what general and specific effects does practice have on the information processing components of the individual tasks? The second question was what impact does practice have on individual differences in the information processing components of these tasks? The third question was what effect does practice on spatial processing tasks have on tested spatial aptitude? The general design of their study involved a pretest battery of spatial tests representing perceptual speed, spatial relations and visualization tests. Subjects then received multiple sessions of practice on each spatial task. Practice was followed by readministration of the pretest battery. Subjects returned after 2-3 months and were again administered the spatial test battery and then were again presented with the two spatial processing tasks.

In general, the practice data showed that there were dramatic speed gains in the information processing components of both tasks during practice, and these gains were maintained over a very long delay period. As expected, based on the skill acquisition literature, mean latency dropped dramatically with additional practice. However, this general improvement masked several interesting differential changes occurring in separate component process measures. Some processes evidenced changes proportionally greater than mean response times, others less so, and some process measures showed no change whatsoever. With no corrective feedback, accuracy showed very little improvement with practice. The data provide substantial support for increased strategic consistency following practice. For example, subjects tended to better conform to the *ideal* solution strategy, with more practice (i.e., better estimates of model fit). Also, the parameter representing constants in item solution (orientation, process selection and response emission) showed particularly large improvements and these mapped onto task and stimulus complexity dimensions.

Average response times showed a lessening of high versus low ability group differences with low ability subjects gaining relatively more than their higher ability counterparts. Importantly, there were a number of ability effects that were masked in the global latency measures. Most notably, in the visualization task there was no same-trial ability effect for mean latency. In contrast, of the four visualization parameters derived from the latency measure, three showed large ability differences, and, two of these measures actually revealed that high ability subjects allocated *more* time for component execution. Furthermore, across both tasks, the data clearly indicate that many low ability individuals are capable of substantial and very durable improvements in various components of spatial information processing.

The retest performance gains for the spatial relations and visualization reference tests were substantial for the low ability group and near ceiling for the high ability individuals; these effects far exceeded normal retest effects and could not be attributed to regression toward the mean. The gains in reference test performance following spatial task practice were not exclusive to the tests being modeled, because there were also large gains in the two perceptual speed tests and a test of spatial relations using quite different stimuli than those employed in the practice tasks. Additionally, the practice tasks were different in format and content from the ability tests they were designed to emulate. Finally, the impact of practice was as evident following the long delay, and on all tests, as it was immediately following practice.

These data strongly argue for the utility and necessity of integrating psychometric, information processing and learning approaches to the study of individual differences in intellectual ability. The data on practice effects make it clear that test scores or process estimates based on short testing sessions are not the best (or at least not the only) representation of an individual's spatial ability. As with most tasks or skills, performance is subject to substantial improvement with practice. The large performance changes for low ability subjects in the Alderton and Pellegrino (1988) study make this particularly apparent. However, group changes mask the extraordinary variability among subjects with respect to the impact practice had on the experimental tasks and test scores. Some individuals, especially low ability subjects, showed tremendous changes in spatial processing whereas others did not. The important point is that typical testing procedures, whether they are intended to produce test scores or process estimates, are incapable of assessing such differences and therefore provide little information about the level of performance an individual could achieve. It is this handicap, among others that potentially limits the validity of tests for the prediction of practiced or trained performance.

THEORY BASED ASSESSMENT OF SPATIAL ABILITY

Given the material reviewed thus far, a strong argument can be made that there is now sufficient information available to conduct large scale, theory driven research focusing on how practice impacts spatial ability, components of spatial processing and, the predictive validity of various global and specific performance measures. To conduct such validation research, however, requires the existence of well designed tasks and testing procedures with reliable measures that can be exported to testing environments outside the laboratory. The most obvious way to emulate the testing procedures used for information processing analyses of spatial ability is to implement the tasks, item types and measurement procedures on computer. However, there is a necessary intermediate step. Data must be available that support the conclusion that computer based testing adds important information that could not otherwise be obtained and that subsumes the variance attributable to conventional testing procedures.

A large scale research and development project was conducted to address these issues of implementation and validation (Hunt, Pellegrino, Abate, Alderton, Farr, Frick & McDonald, 1987; Hunt, Pellegrino, Frick, Farr & Alderton, 1988; Pellegrino, Hunt, Abate & Farr, 1987). In this project we developed a computer administered test battery containing 11 spatial reasoning tasks. Five of the tasks involved static visual displays similar in content and format to typical paper and pencil tests of spatial ability. The remaining six tasks involved dynamic visual displays and these will be considered subsequently. The 11 computer based tasks were administered to a large sample of young adults (n=170) who also took a battery of conventional paper and pencil tests. A primary goal of this project was to determine whether the computer administered static display tasks evaluated the same abilities as standard paper and pencil tests of spatial ability. A secondary goal was examination of the reliability and utility of theory based measures of within problem process execution speed, measures that can be obtained in computerized testing but that cannot be obtained in paper and pencil tests.

The five static spatial reasoning tasks that were selected for computer implementation and administration had to fit within a set of criteria. First, the tasks had to have well defined information processing characteristics, i.e., the tasks had to have been previously analysed and internally validated with respect to underlying component processes. Second, whenever possible, the task and its derived performance/processing measures needed to have some history of use in the study of individual differences in spatial ability or imagery ability. Third, the full set of static tasks needed to represent major visual spatial factors such as perceptual speed, spatial relations and spatial visualization. The next sections briefly describe the five static display tasks and the justification for including each one in the task battery developed and implemented by Hunt et al., (1987).

Perceptual Comparison. This task was selected to provide measures of perceptual speed, i.e., the ability to rapidly encode figures and make visual comparisons. The computer task is based on visual comparison research conducted by Cooper (1976). On each trial a pair of random shapes is presented. The examinee is to indicate whether or not the shapes are exactly identical. The shapes are generated by connecting 6-14 randomly chosen points on a plane. Mismatching comparison figures are generated from a standard figure by slightly moving one or more of the original points. Two aspects of this task are of interest. First, on trials where there is a mismatch, the degree of mismatch is varied and decision time should be a monotonically decreasing function of this variable. The slope of the difference detection function provides an index of the speed (efficiency) of detecting feature differences. Second, stimulus complexity is manipulated by varying the number of points (6-14) used to generate the original shape. The slope of the stimulus complexity reaction time function provides an index of encoding and comparison efficiency. Measures derived from this task included average response time and accuracy, measures similar to those obtained from standard perceptual speed tests, as well as slope and intercept measures reflecting efficiency of different detection and efficiency of encoding and comparison process.

Mental Rotation.   This task was selected to provide a measure of spatial relations ability. The computer controlled mental rotation task was designed to closely resemble tasks used previously to assess individual differences in spatial relations ability (e.g., Mumaw, Pellegrino, Kail, & Carter 1984; Regian & Pellegrino, 1984). On each trial, a pair of polygons was presented on the computer display. The task was to judge their identity and respond by pressing one of two keys. The individual trials represented the combination of two variables: angular disparity of the stimuli (ranging from 0-180 degrees) and match type (same or different). Non-matching pairs were created by a mirror image reversal of the comparison stimulus. Measures of separate processes were estimated from the slopes and intercepts of the linear functions relating response time to angular disparity. General and specific latency and accuracy parameters were estimated separately for positive and negative match conditions because other research has shown that performance in the positive and negative conditions often differs (see Pellegrino & Kail, 1982).

Surface Development.   This task was selected to provide one example of a spatial visualization task. Spatial visualization ability is often assessed by surface development tasks that contain representations of flat, unfolded objects and completed three dimensional shapes. The task that was used in the computer battery is based on previous work on individual differences in spatial visualization ability (Alderton & Pellegrino, 1984; Pellegrino, 1984). On each trial, the individual is presented with two figures. The left hand figure shows a cube "unfolded" along its edges so that it lies flat. The base of the cube is labeled, and two of the three sides marked by dots. The right hand figure presents a two dimensional projection of a cube "refolded" and slightly rotated so that the top, front, and right lateral surfaces are visible. The task is to determine whether the flat figure on the left can be refolded and rotated (if appropriate) to form the cube shown on the right of the screen. Different folding patters are used, systematically varying the number of mental folds that have to be made and the number of surfaces that have to be mentally "carried along" during such folds (e.g., Shepard & Feng, 1972). Performance measures include mean latency and mean accuracy as well as slopes and intercepts of the linear functions relating response time to problem complexity as determined by the number of mental folding operations.

Integration of Detail in an Image.   This task was selected to represent a second prototypical spatial visualization task. Spatial visualization ability is often assessed by form board tasks that require the integration of elements to form a composite image. Examples include cases where a set of shapes must be concatenated in a certain way to form a completed shape or puzzle. Mumaw and Pellegrino (1984) and Poltrock and Brown (1984) have developed variants of this type of task that permit assessment of various image integration processes as well as the capacity of the visual buffer. The task that was used is similar to that developed by Poltrock and Brown (1984). On each trial, the individual is presented an array of regular shapes with various edges marked by specific letters. The number of pieces in the array varies from three to six. The individual inspects the pieces and tries to determine the composite image that would be created by appropriately aligning the pieces with corresponding edge markings. The time to perform the integration should vary with the number of shapes to be integrated. Following the integration phase, the individual is shown a completed shape and decides if it represents the correct integrated image. The slope of the latency function for image integration provides an index of the efficiency of several imagery processes whereas the accuracy score provides an index of buffer capacity.

Adding Detail to an Image.   One of the components of Kosslyn's (1980) imagery theory is the addition or deletion of detail in a mental representation (image). To do this, several subprocesses are required. Examples are the "Put" operation, in which a component part is placed at a point in an image, and the "Find" operation, in which an image is examined to determine whether or not it contains a feature. Poltrock and Brown (1984) developed a task that provides indices of the efficiency of these and other processes. Individuals are asked to image a base form and then add details (dots) to it at specified locations. A variant of this task was implemented for computer presentation. The base form is a six pointed star. Trials vary in terms of the total number of dots (four to seven) to be sequentially added to the base form prior to presentation of a single composite image containing the appropriate number of dots. The subject's task is to decide if the composite image is a correct or incorrect final product. From this task several latency measures are derived including a slope and intercept of the latency function for adding successive details. Changes in accuracy as a function of problem complexity provide an estimate of a person's visual memory buffer capacity.

The computer administered tasks produce a wide variety and range of individual performance scores. Of primary concern was whether the data support the conclusion that computer administered, "theory" based tasks of static spatial reasoning can be used to replace and augment current forms of spatial ability assessment. To address this issue a series of subsidiary issues had to be addressed. The first such issue is whether the computer based tasks and measures behave in a principled manner and have substantial reliability. Each of the five computer based tasks of static spatial reasoning had a systematically designed problem set permitting internal validation of a theory of task processing with simultaneous derivation of overall latency and accuracy measures as well as more refined component process measures.

The group and individual subject data revealed that performance in all five tasks was highly consistent with general expectations about within task processing. For example, in the perceptual comparison task, accuracy was generally high and response latency was a systematic function of stimulus complexity and degree of similarity between stimuli. In the mental rotation task accuracy was also generally high and response latency was a systematic function of angular disparity between stimuli. In the surface development task, latency and accuracy were systematic functions of the number of mental folding operations. In the integration of detail task, integration latency was a systematic function of the number of elements to be integrated to form a composite image. In the adding detail task, decision latency and accuracy were a systematic function of the number of details in the final image. The overall latency and accuracy measures had substantial reliabilities, with the majority of reliability coefficients above .90. Within each task various component process latency measures were also derived. Examples include the slope and intercept of the mental rotation function and the slope of the function relating integration latency to the number of elements to be integrated. These component process latency measures also had substantial reliability and the average reliabilities of such within task measures ranged from .67 to .91.

Given that the various overall performance and component process measures have substantial reliability, then the second issue is whether these measures encompass the variance produced by performance measures obtained form the paper and pencil tests. The analytic strategy for addressing this issue involved several stages. The first stage was to reduce the variables to be analysed to a manageable number. To do so, separate factor analyses were conducted for all variables within each computer administered task, using an orthogonal factor analysis followed by varimax rotation. At most, three factors were extracted from each set of within task measures and these typically represented separate latency and accuracy factors. Only the best marker for each of these factors was retained for further analyses.

The second stage of analysis was to conduct separate factor analyses of the paper and pencil task measures and the computer administered task measures to determine the dimensionality within each domain of performance. An orthogonal factor analysis of the paper and pencil tests followed by a varimax rotation identified two factors with eigenvalues greater than one. The two dimensional space accounted for 54% of the variance between measures. The first factor was closely related to two rotation tests in the paper and pencil test battery, but was also associated with all the other primary measures of spatial ability. The Raven Progressive Matrices test that was also in the test battery had only a small loading on this factor, and a vocabulary test was virtually orthogonal to this factor. The second factor was identified by relatively high loadings on the more complex, power oriented spatial visualization tests, and by a very high loading on the Raven test. The latter test depends both on spatial and abstract reasoning (Hunt, 1974). The factor analysis results indicated that the paper and pencil test scores were distributed much as one would expect them to be, given our discussion of previous factor analytic research on spatial ability.

A similar factor analysis was conducted for the selected measures from the computer administered static tasks. The first factor was identified by the highest loadings for measures of processing accuracy. The second factor generally had positive loadings for the latency measures. The third factor was associated with the latency measures from the adding detail task. The fourth factor appeared to be primarily associated with the measures from the perceptual comparison task and reflected a speed-accuracy tradeoff in performance within this task.

To examine these findings further, an oblique factor analysis was conducted. This method was chosen because the psychological processes would predict non-independence between measures of speed and accuracy, both within and across tests. Factor I had high loadings for latency measures, and only small loadings for accuracy measures. Factor II, conversely, was characterized by high loadings for accuracy measures. These two factors were essentially uncorrelated. Superimposed on this pattern, however, were factors III and IV. Factor III was a bipolar factor for the perceptual comparison task, again suggesting a strong speed-accuracy tradeoff across individuals for this task. (This is consistent with experimental results examining the task in detail and the within task factor analysis of performance measures.) Factor IV was a similar, somewhat less strongly defined speed-accuracy tradeoff for the adding detail and integrating details task.

The conclusion that could be drawn from these separate factor analyses within the domain of paper and pencil tests and the domain of computer based static display tasks was that the computer controlled static spatial reasoning tasks appear to encompass the same spatial relations and visualization factors as the paper and pencil tests while at the same time offering the potential for distinguishing between speed and accuracy of processing as well as speed-accuracy tradeoffs within tasks.

The third stage of analysis was to determine more precisely whether or not the two domains of tests tap the same psychological abilities. To determine whether the individual variation captured by the paper and pencil tests is embedded in the static task measures, Cohen's (1982) set correlation approach was used. A set correlation can be interpreted as the percent of generalized variance in a set of measures (e.g., paper and pencil spatial tests) that can be predicted by the variables in another set of measures (e.g., the computer based static spatial tests). This is analogous to the conventional correlation coefficient where only single variables are involved. The relevant set correlation between the paper and pencil tests and the computer based static tasks had an $R^2 = .82$. Therefore, it could be concluded that a substantial portion of the common variance in the paper and pencil domain is embedded within the (three or four dimensional) common variance of the computer controlled static tasks (see also Hunt, Pellegrino, Frick, Farr & Alderton, 1988).

The full set of results support the general conclusion that theory based, computer administered static spatial reasoning tasks can be used to replace and augment current paper and pencil procedures for the assessment of spatial ability. The computer based tasks and measures behave in theoretically predictable ways, have high reliability, encompass the variance contained in traditional paper and pencil tests, and provide measures of unique variance associated with speed versus accuracy of processing.

DYNAMIC SPATIAL REASONING ABILITY

Earlier we noted that another factor potentially limiting the predictive validity of spatial ability tests is the fact that all conventional tests are restricted to judgments about static spatial displays. In contrast, many real world activities that presumably tap visual spatial reasoning involve objects moving through space. Tasks that assess such reasoning skills can only be implemented within the context of computer technology. Thus, as part of our overall project on computer based assessment of spatial ability, we designed not only the static spatial ability tests described earlier but also a set of six dynamic spatial reasoning tasks that tested individual differences in motion extrapolation.

Unlike the tasks that require reasoning about static spatial information, there is little in the way of experimental literature on individual differences in motion extrapolation. Therefore the tests we used have less history of development than the ones discussed in the section dealing with static displays. We attempted to design tasks that coincided with a rational analysis of what appears to be required in this domain of performance. The basic dynamic visual spatial problem a person has to solve is to predict *where* a moving object is going and *when* it will arrive at its predicted destination. This skill can be divided into three components. First, an observer might need to remember the path the object has just travelled in order to extrapolate its future path. Second, given the path the object has travelled thus far, the observer must be able to predict or extrapolate the future path. Third, to predict when an object will arrive at a destination, the observer must extrapolate its speed. Thus, we developed three tasks that assessed these three separate components of dynamic spatial reasoning.

In addition to making judgments about the path and speed of a single moving object it would appear that many dynamic spatial problems required judgments of relative rather than absolute speed. For instance, if two objects are moving towards destinations, an observer may wish to know if they will arrive at the same time, or if not, which will arrive first. We developed two tasks that assessed the ability to make such comparative speed judgments.

Although it is reasonable to break up judgment about absolute and relative visual motion into component tasks, it is possible that judgments about motion are made in a holistic fashion. Therefore, at least one dynamic spatial reasoning task should require coordination of time, direction, and motor movement judgments. The act of making a coordinated judgement might itself be a significant source of individual differences and we designed a task that required such judgements. The next sections briefly describe each of the tasks.

Path Memory.   This task was designed to assess a person's memory for the path of moving objects. On each trial, a small square moved across the computer screen three times. The square followed a parabolic path, starting at the lower left of the computer screen. Either the first and second paths were the same and the third path was different, or the second and third paths were the same and the first path was different. The observer indicated which path differed from the second. The computer then reported whether or not the response was correct.

Three parameters determined the paths: the starting height of the parabola, the height of the apex of the parabola, and the horizontal distance from the start of the parabola to the apex. Within each of these dimensions, eight levels of difficulty were established. The easier the level of difficulty, the larger the difference between the unique path and the two identical paths. The dependent measure was the average difficulty level of the last ⅔ of the trials.

Extrapolation.   This task was intended as a measure of the ability to extrapolate from an observed to an expected path. Three types of curves were presented: a straight line, a sine wave, and a parabola. A portion of the curve was shown on each trial, starting from the left side of the computer screen and ending 41%, 52%, or 63% of the distance across the computer screen. The observer used a joystick to move an arrow up or down along a vertical line on the right side of the computer screen to indicate where the curve would intersect the line. The computer displayed the remaining portion of the curve as soon as the response was made. The dependent measure was the difference between the correct answer and the subject's answer.

Arrival Time for One Object.   In this task, the observer had to make an absolute judgment of velocity. On each trial a square moved horizontally from the left side of the computer screen towards a vertical line on the right. One quarter to one half of the way across the computer screen, the object disappeared. The observer pressed a key when he or she thought the object would have crossed the line, assuming that it would have continued moving on the same course at the same speed. The dependent measure was the difference in time between the correct answer and the subject's answer.

Arrival Time Comparison for Two Objects.   This task required judgements of relative speed of motion. On each trial, two different objects were presented, each moving towards its destination at a constant speed. The destinations were displayed as horizontal or vertical lines. A fifth of the way to the destination, the objects disappeared. The subject then reported which object would have arrived at its destination first. The computer informed the subject whether or not the response was correct.

There were five variations of this task. In the first variation, the objects moved in perpendicular paths towards different destinations. In the second variation, the objects moved in perpendicular paths towards the same destination. In the remaining three variations, the objects moved in parallel horizontal paths. Eight levels of difficulty were established by varying the size of the difference in arrival time for the two objects. The dependent measure was the average level of difficulty for the last ⅔ of the trials.

Arrival Time Comparison for Four Objects.   This task measured the ability to deal with relative motion in a somewhat different way. The task was something like guessing the winner of a horse race before the race is completed. The digits 1, 2, 3, and 4 moved horizontally from right to left at individually determined constant speeds. Their destination was a vertical line on the far left of the computer screen. The digits started at varying distances from the line. Half way to the vertical line, the digits disappeared. If they had continued travelling at the same speed three of them would have arrived at the line at the same time and one would have arrived earlier. The observer indicated which object would have arrived at the line first. There were again eight levels of difficulty, corresponding to the size of the time difference between the arrival time of the first object and the remaining objects. The subject's score was the level of difficulty for the last ⅔ of the trials.

Intercept.   This task was designed to measure the ability to combine the extrapolation of both speed and path. The task was like a video game, in which a player attempts to "shoot down" a moving object. A small rectangular target moved from left to right at a constant horizontal speed. The target moved along either a horizontal, sine wave, or parabolic trajectory. When the subject pressed a key on the keyboard, a triangularly shaped object began moving straight upwards at a constant velocity. The subject attempted to time the missile's "launch" so that the missile would collide with the target. The dependent measure was the vertical distance between the missile and the target when the target crossed the missile's path.

The issue of whether the computer based tests of dynamic spatial reasoning assess an ability separate from the abilities assessed by static spatial tasks required that a series of subsidiary issues be addressed. The first such issue was whether performance in the computer administered dynamic tasks was reliable. In three of the tasks (i.e., path memory, arrival time comparison for two objects and arrival time comparison for four objects) a staircasing method was used to adjust problem difficulty and the measure of performance was the average difficulty level for the last ⅔ of the problems presented. The reliability of the average difficulty level was moderate (.50 - .65) for two of these tasks, path memory and arrival time comparison for two objects, and low for the four object arrival time tasks (.30). The measures derived for the other three dynamic tasks, extrapolation, intercept, and arrival time for one object, had adequate to very high reliability levels (.79 - .99). Given the fact that none of these six tasks had large numbers of problems we considered the reliabilities to be satisfactory for all but one case.

The next issue to be considered was the dimensionality of the space defined by the measures from the dynamic spatial processing tasks. An orthogonal factor analysis was computed using the measures derived from the six tasks. The factor analysis before rotation indicated that a two factor solution was required, with 44% of the common variance between tests located in a two dimensional space. This solution was made simpler by a varimax rotation, which identified two factors. The first factor, which accounted for 71% of the common (two-space) variance, was marked by high loadings of the arrival time comparison for 2 and 4 object tasks and the intercept task. The second factor was associated primarily with the extrapolation task. Note that the extrapolation task can be solved without considering its dynamic aspects, because at the time the examinee must respond a static picture is present, and the information in the picture is sufficient to define the correct answer. (In actuality, other combined factor analyses support the conclusion that the extrapolation task is a static spatial reasoning task). The communalities of the path memory task and the measures in the time of arrival one object task were very low (less than .1 in all cases), suggesting that these measures do not tap processes associated with the other tasks.

Cohen's set correlation analysis procedure was again used to explore the connection between the dynamic tasks and the other two task domains. The R2 for the relationship between the computer-based static and dynamic spatial reasoning tasks was .65. The R^2 for the relationship between the dynamic spatial tasks and the paper and pencil tests was .52. The latter is substantially below the value obtained for the relationship between the paper and pencil static tests. In fact, the pattern of set correlations is exactly what would be expected if the dynamic tasks tapped some abilities that were different from the abilities tapped by the other two classes of spatial tasks. The fact that the R^2 values are substantial indicates that there is a correlation between static and dynamic spatial abilities.

The final stage of analysis was designed to test the hypothesis that the dynamic spatial reasoning tasks define an ability that is separate from those assessed by the static spatial reasoning tasks, either paper and pencil or computer based. In this analysis attention was restricted to measures from the intercept and two object arrival time task because these were the clearest markers from the separate factor analysis of the dynamic spatial tasks. Based on previous factor analytic research, we selected two of the paper and pencil tests as markers for the spatial visualization factor and two other tests as markers for the spatial relations factor. A confirmatory factor analysis was conducted to test the hypothesis that there were three factors, two static and one dynamic, with correlations among the factors. This model provided an excellent fit to the data and subsidiary analyses showed that none of the factors could be removed from the model without significantly decrementing the fit. Within this model, the spatial relations and visualization factors had a correlation of approximately .8, and both had a correlation of about .6 with the dynamic visual spatial factor.

A similar analysis was conducted with latency and accuracy measures derived from the battery of computer based static spatial reasoning tasks. As noted earlier, latency and accuracy measures represent the primary factors within the space of measures of the static tasks. A maximum likelihood confirmatory factor analysis was again computed to test the hypothesis that there were three factors, two static and one dynamic, with correlations among the factors. This model also provided an excellent fit to the data and subsidiary analyses again showed that none of the factors could be removed from the model without significantly decrementing the fit. There was a correlation of .4 between the dynamic and latency factors and .6 between the dynamic and accuracy factors. The latency and accuracy factors had only a low correlation of .12. We conclude from these two confirmatory factor analyses that there is strong initial evidence for a dynamic spatial reasoning factor that is separate from the static spatial reasoning factors previously identified.

The present results regarding existence of a dynamic spatial reasoning factor hold both theoretical and practical promise. From a theoretical perspective, there are numerous issues to be addressed about the nature of representation and processing of dynamically changing spatial information. This includes how such representations and processes relate to extant theories of imagery and static spatial processing. We have only begun to scratch the surface with respect to these (see Fischer, Pellegrino, McDonald, Mitchell, Abate & Hunt, 1990).

From a practical perspective, there is the distinct possibility that the ability to represent and reason about dynamically changing spatial relations may better predict real world performances that intuitively seem to require these abilities. Examples include machinery operation and piloting. Of further significance is the fact that this ability seems separate from those assessed by conventional spatial ability tests. Our results do not yet address the question of the utility of the computer controlled tests of either static or dynamic spatial reasoning as predictors of performance in situations outside the laboratory.

CONCLUSIONS

At the beginning of this chapter it was noted that part of the impetus for attempts at unifying cognitive and differential psychology was dissatisfaction with the limited predictive and prescriptive validity of tests of intelligence and specific aptitudes. Furthermore, it has been argued that contemporary research has theoretical and practical implications related to various validation issues associated with the construct, measurement, and improvement of intellectual abilities. A primary goal of this chapter has been to show that we are currently better off with regard to these issues of validity for the domain of visual spatial cognition and aptitude.

First, we have tried to show that current tests of visual spatial ability and typical data on individual differences in spatial ability can only be understood when set in the context of underlying knowledge representations and processing activities. This is not an arbitrary exercise but is driven by general theories of spatial cognition. A process and knowledge orientation also provides the necessary framework for understanding results from studies focusing on practice and training. The issues are: *What changes with practice? How does it change?* and *Will it transfer?* These questions can not be adequately addressed at a global test score level. It now appears from this entire body of research that individual differences in spatial ability are a function of very specific information processing capacities, many that are subject to modification. Obviously, the limits on training and performance have yet to be determined. These results raise interesting new questions about aptitude assessment and predictive validity.

Second, we have tried to show that theory based assessment research can lead not only to a better understanding of individual differences on conventional tests but to the design of better testing procedures. In these new testing procedures the classic construct validity problem is addressed because the construct representation of the tests is known and can be asserted with reference to existing cognitive theory. What is equally interesting is that improving construct representation does not necessarily change the nomothetic span of the instruments. Do any of our computer administered, theory based tests produce increased predictive validity? The answer is that the jury is still out, but the initial forays into this area have produced promising results (Alderton, 1988b).

Our third major point was that the application of contemporary theory and technology can lead to the discovery of heretofore unspecified cognitive abilities. As an example we reviewed initial evidence that reasoning about dynamically changing visual spatial displays defines a dimension of ability different from conventional tests of spatial ability. This dimension of ability may turn out to be of great practical significance for predicting various real world visual spatial reasoning activities such as piloting and air traffic control.

Obviously, there are many theoretical as well as applied issues that constitute future research agenda regarding visual spatial cognition and ability. However, many of these issues arise from the interesting and informative work to date uniting cognitive with differential theory and research. The union has been fruitful and it is clear that theory based assessment is possible, practical, and above all, necessary.

ACKNOWLEDGMENTS

The research reported in this paper and preparation of this manuscript was supported by Contract N660001-85-C-0017 from the Naval Personnel Research and Development Center and Contract N00014-86-C-0865 from the Office of Naval Research to Earl Hunt and James W. Pellegrino.

REFERENCES

Ackerman, P. L. (1986). Individual differences in information processing: An investigation of intellectual abilities and task performance during practice. *Intelligence, 10,* 101–136.

Alderton, D. L. (1988a, April). *Spatial tests in prediction and classification.* Paper presented at the Annual Meeting of the American Educational Research Association, New Orleans, LA.

Alderton, D. L. (1988b). *Development and evaluation of integrating details: A complex spatial problem solving test* (Technical Report, Navy Personnel Research and Development Center). San Diego, CA, July, 1988.

Alderton, D. L., & Pellegrino, J. W. (1984). *Analysis of mental paper folding.* Unpublished manuscript, University of California, Santa Barbara, CA.

Alderton, D. L., & Pellegrino, J. W. (1988). *Effects of practice on components of spatial processing.* Unpublished manuscript, University of California, Santa Barbara, CA, 1988.

Alderton, D. L., Goldman, S. R., & Pellegrino, J. W. (1985). Individual differences in process outcomes for verbal analogy and classification solution. *Intelligence, 9,* 69–85.

Bennett, F. K., Seashore, H. G., & Wesman, A. G. (1974). *Manual for the Differential Aptitude Test* (5th ed.). New York: Psychological Corporation.

Blade, M. F., & Watson, W. S. (1955). Increase in spatial visualization test scores during engineering study. *Psychological Monographs, 69,* (1, Whole issue No. 397).

Brinkmann, E. H. (1966). Program and instructions as a technique for improving spatial visualization. *Journal of Applied Psychology, 50,* 179–184.

Brown, F. R. (1954). *The effect of an experimental course in geometry on ability to visualize in three dimensions.* Unpublished doctoral dissertation, University of Illinois.

Carroll, J. B. (1976). Psychometric tests as cognitive tasks: A new "structure of intellect." In L. B.

Resnick (Ed.), *The nature of intelligence* (pp. 27–56). Hillsdale, NJ: Lawrence Erlbaum Associates.

Carroll, J. B. (1982). The measurement of intelligence. In R. J. Sternberg (Ed.), *Handbook of human intelligence* (pp. 29–120). Cambridge: Cambridge University Press.

Cohen, J. (1982). Set correlation as a general multivariate data analytic method. *Multivariate Behavioral Research, 17*, 301–342.

Cooper, L. A. (1976). Individual differences in visual comparison. *Perception & Psychophysics, 19*, 433–444.

Cooper, L. A., & Mumaw, R. J. (1985). Spatial aptitude. In R. F. Dillon (Ed.), *Individual differences in cognition, Vol. 2*. New York: Academic Press.

Cronbach, L. J. (1970). *Essentials of psychological testing* (3rd ed.). New York: Harper and Row.

Dailey, J. T., & Neyman, C. A. (1967). *Development of a curriculum and material for teaching basic vocational talents*. (Final report for Office of Education, Contract No. OE-5-85-023.) Washington, DC: George Washington University, Education Research Project.

Embretson, S. (1984). A general latent trait model for response processes. *Psychometrika, 49*, 175–186.

Embretson, S. E. (1985). *Test design: Developments in psychology and psychometrics*. New York: Academic Press.

Embretson, S. E. (1987). Improving the measurement of spatial aptitude by dynamic testing. *Intelligence, 11*, 333–358.

Embretson, S., & Farha, M. (1985, August). *Improving test validity by training spatial visualization skills*. Paper presented at the annual meeting of the American Psychological Association, Los Angeles, CA.

Fischer, S. C., Pellegrino, J. W., McDonald, T. P., Mitchell, S. R., Abate, R. J., & Hunt, E. B. (1990). *Perceptual and cognitive factors governing performance in a non-approach interception task*. Unpublished manuscript, Vanderbilt University, Nashville, TN.

Ghiselli, E. E. (1973). The validity of aptitude tests in personnel selection. *Personnel Psychology, 26*, 461–477.

Glaser, R. (1972). Individuals and learning: The new aptitudes. *Educational Researcher, 1*, 5–13.

Hunt, E. (1974). Quote the Raven? Nevermore! In L. Gregg (Ed.), *Knowledge and cognition* (pp. 129–157). Hillsdale, NJ: Lawrence Erlbaum Associates.

Hunt, E. (1978). Mechanics of verbal ability. *Psychological Review, 85*, 109–130.

Hunt, E. (1980). Intelligence as an information-processing concept. *British Journal of Psychology, 71*, 449–474.

Hunt, E., & Pellegrino, J. W. (1985). Using interactive computing to expand intelligence testing. *Intelligence, 9*, 207–236.

Hunt, E., Pellegrino, J. W., Abate, R., Alderton, D. L., Farr, S., Frick, R., & McDonald, T. (1987). *Computer-controlled testing of visual-spatial ability* (Technical Report 87-31, Navy Personnel Research and Development Center). San Diego, CA, August, 1987.

Hunt, E., Pellegrino, J. W., Frick, R. W., Farr, S., & Alderton, D. L. (1988). The ability to reason about movement in the visual field. *Intelligence, 12*, 77–100.

Jensen, A. R. (1982). The chronometry of intelligence. In R. J. Sternberg (Ed.), *Advances in the psychology of human intelligence* (Vol. 1, pp. 225–310). Hillsdale, NJ: Lawrence Erlbaum Associates.

Just, M. A., & Carpenter, P. A. (1985). Cognitive coordinate systems: Accounts of mental rotation and individual differences in spatial ability. *Psychological Review, 92*, 137–172.

Keating, D. P., & Bobbitt, B. L. (1978). Individual and developmental differences in cognitive-processing components of mental ability. *Child Development, 49*, 155–167.

Kosslyn, S. M. (1980). *Image and mind*. Cambridge, MA: Harvard University Press.

Lansman, M., Donaldson, G., Hunt, E., & Yantis, S. (1982). Ability factors and cognitive processes. *Intelligence, 6*, 347–388.

Levine, J. M., Schulman, D., Brahlek, R. E., & Fleishman, E. A. (1980). *Trainability of abilities: Training and transfer of spatial visualization* (Tech. Rep. No. TR-R80-3). Washington, DC: Advanced Research Resources Organization. (and *Selected Documents in Psychology, 10,* 82).

Likert, R., & Quasha, W. H. (1970). *Manual for the revised Minnesota Paper Form Board Test.* New York: Psychological Corporation.

Lohman, D. F. (1979). *Spatial ability: A review and reanalysis of the correlational literature* (Tech. Rep. No. 8). Palo Alto, CA: Stanford University, Aptitude Research Project, School of Education.

Lohman, D. F. (1988). Spatial abilities as traits, processes and knowledge. In R. J. Sternberg (Ed.), *Advances in the psychology of human intelligence* (Vol. 4). Hillsdale, NJ: Lawrence Erlbaum Associates.

Lohman, D. F., & Kyllonen, P. C. (1983). Individual differences in solution strategy on spatial tasks. In R. F. Dillon & R. S. Schmeck (Eds.), *Individual differences in cognition* (Vol. 1, pp. 105–135). New York: Academic Press.

Lohman, D. F., Pellegrino, J. W., Alderton, D. L., & Regian, J. W. (1987). Dimensions and components of individual differences in spatial abilities. In S. H. Irvine & S. E. Newstead (Eds.), *Intelligence and cognition: Contemporary frames of reference* (pp. 253–312). Boston, MA: Martinus Nijhoff.

McGee, M. G. (1979). *Human spatial abilities: Sources of sex differences.* New York: Praeger.

Mumaw, R. J., Pellegrino, J. W., Kail, R. V., & Carter, P. (1984). Different slopes for different folks: Process analysis of spatial aptitude. *Memory and Cognition, 12,* 515–521.

Pachella, R. G. (1974). The interpretation of reaction time in information-processing research. In B. H. Kantowitz (Ed.), *Human information-processing: Tutorials in performance and cognition* (pp. 41–82). Hillsdale, NJ: Lawrence Erlbaum Associates.

Pellegrino, J. W. (1984, April). *Information processing and intellectual ability.* Paper presented at the annual meeting of the American Educational Research Association, New Orleans, LA.

Pellegrino, J. W. (1988). Mental models and mental tests. In H. Wainer & H. Braun (Eds.), *Test validity.* Hillsdale, NJ: Lawrence Erlbaum Associates.

Pellegrino, J. W., & Glaser, R. (1980). Components of inductive reasoning. In R. E. Snow, P. A. Federico & W. E. Montague (Eds.), *Aptitude, learning, and instruction: Cognitive process analyses of aptitude* (Vol. 1, pp. 177–218). Hillsdale, NJ: Lawrence Erlbaum Associates.

Pellegrino, J. W., & Glaser, R. (1982). Analyzing aptitudes for learning: Inductive reasoning. In R. Glaser (Ed.), *Advances in instructional psychology* (Vol. 2, pp. 269–345). Hillsdale, NJ: Lawrence Erlbaum Associates.

Pellegrino, J. W., Hunt, E. B., Abate, R., & Farr, S. (1987). A computer-based test battery for the assessment of static and dynamic spatial reasoning abilities. *Behavior Research Methods, Instruments, & Computers, 19,* 231–236.

Pellegrino, J. W., & Kail, R. (1982). Process analyses of spatial aptitude. In R. J. Sternberg (Ed.), *Advances in the psychology of human intelligence* (Vol. 1, pp. 311–365). Hillsdale, NJ: Lawrence Erlbaum Associates.

Pellegrino, J. W., Mumaw, R. J., & Shute, V. J. (1985). Analysis of spatial aptitude and expertise. In S. E. Embretson (Ed.), *Test design: Development in psychology and psychometrics* (pp. 45–76). New York: Academic Press.

Poltrock, S. E., & Brown, P. (1984). Individual differences in visual imagery and spatial ability. *Intelligence, 8,* 93–138.

Ranucci, E. R. (1952). *The effect of the study of solid geometry on certain aspects of space perception abilities.* Unpublished doctoral dissertation, Teachers College, Columbia University.

Raven, J. C. (1962). *Advanced progressive matrices Set II.* London: H. K. Lewis.

Regian, J. W., & Pellegrino, J. W. (1984). *Practice and transfer effects in two-dimensional mental rotation.* Unpublished manuscript. University of California, Santa Barbara.

Resnick, L. B. (1976). *The nature of intelligence.* Hillsdale, NJ: Lawrence Erlbaum Associates.

Shepard, R. N., & Cooper, L. A. (1982). *Mental images and their transformations*. Cambridge, MA: MIT Press.

Shepard, R. N., & Feng, C. (1972). A chronometric study of mental paper folding. *Cognitive Psychology, 3,* 228–243.

Sternberg, R. J. (1977). *Intelligence, information processing and analogical reasoning: The componential analysis of human abilities*. Hillsdale, NJ: Lawrence Erlbaum Associates.

Sternberg, R. J. (1982). *Advances in the psychology of human intelligence*. (Vol. 1). Hillsdale, NJ: Lawrence Erlbaum Associates.

Sternberg, R. J., & Gardner, M. K. (1983). Unities in inductive reasoning. *Journal of Experimental Psychology: General, 112,* 80–116.

Stringer, P. (1975). Drawing training and spatial ability. *Ergonomics, 18,* 101–108.

Thurstone, L. L., & Thurstone, T. G. (1949). *SRA primary abilities*. Chicago: Science Research Associates.

Whitely, S. E. (1980). Modeling aptitude test validity from cognitive components. *Journal of Educational Psychology, 72,* 750–769.

Wolman, B. B. (1985). *Handbook of intelligence: Theories, measurements & applications*. New York: Wiley.

13

The Control of Complex Systems and Performance in Intelligence Tests

Rainer H. Kluwe
Carlo Misiak
Hilde Haider
Universitaet der Bundeswehr, Hamburg

During the last 10 years cognitive psychology in West Germany developed a special interest in research into the problem solving behaviours of individuals whose task is to operate a complex, dynamic system. The basic research strategy in this domain of cognitive psychological research is the use of computer driven *microworld* systems as an experimental instrument. Such systems are described with respect to attributes like complexity, dynamics and connectivity. Implemented on a computer, the systems are conceived of as instruments that allow the systematic study in the laboratory of processes of human decision making and problem solving in dynamic task environments. The subjects' tasks in these experiments can be categorized either as *ill-defined* or *well-defined* problems. Ill-defined tasks refers to experimental settings where the subjects are instructed to operate the system, but they are not provided with any details about the goal states they have to reach. As well-defined one can describe those tasks where subjects receive instructions about specific system states that have to be reached or to be kept during a certain time interval or during a number of trials, when operating a specific system.

Central research issues that have been addressed so far in this domain of cognitive science include: the process of acquisition and use of knowledge when operating a system (Funke, 1985; Kluwe et al., 1985; 1986; 1990; Opwis & Spada, 1985), conflict resolution, metacognitive regulation of the control process, characteristics of successful and of unsuccessful performance (Doerner, 1978; Doerner et al., 1983), and learning by doing when operating a system (Kluwe, Misiak, Ringelband & Haider, 1986; Kluwe, Haider & Misiak, 1990). Especially in the work of Doerner, the question has been raised as to which factors might affect individual control performance. In this chapter we examine whether general intelligence, as assessed by means of tests, is a predictor of how individuals perform in system control tasks.

INTELLIGENCE TESTS VERSUS SYSTEM CONTROL TASKS

If the cognitive demands of operating a complex microworld simulated on a computer are comparable to the cognitive requirements that individuals meet in everyday problem situations, then intelligence tests - because they claim to assess general problem solving abilities - should predict control performance. The conclusion, that intelligence tests are useful predictors for problem solving ability and decision making in complex environments in reality would hold only, if empirical examinations of this implication revealed no contradictory results.

One could expect that performance in intelligence tests is based on cognitive operations that are also required for operating a complex system. If one accepts, for example, the coding scheme for cognitive tasks appearing in psychometric tests provided by Carroll (1976; see also Sternberg & Powell, 1982) then there are numerous cognitive operations and memory processes that may be shared by both types of tasks, i.e., intelligence tests and system control.

The results of 11 studies, published in West Germany that report coefficients for the correlation between scores obtained on intelligence tests and performance data derived from system control tasks are provided in Table 13.1. The work of Putz-Osterloh is of special importance here (1981; Putz-Osterloh & Luer, 1981; Putz-Osterloh, 1985). She initiated the empirical investigation of this problem and her results gave rise to subsequent studies.

As can be seen in Table 13.1, the overall results fail to fulfill the expectation of a close positive relationship of intelligence test scores and performance scores derived from system control. The reported correlation coefficients are remarkably low; in most cases they are close to zero. Few coefficients reach values of .4 to .5. Only in four studies (Putz-Osterloh & Luer, 1981, second study; Hesse, 1982; Putz-Osterloh, 1985; Hoermann & Thomas, 1988) can correlation coefficients of this size be found. Thus the reported results from these studies do not support the general assumption that intelligence tests are good predictors of an individual's performance when operating a complex system.

Table 13.1 provides additional information about the systems used as research instruments as well as about characteristics of the experimental settings. One has to take into account the fact that the studies differ considerably in research design: systems with different characteristics are used as instruments (e.g., the number of system variables); the control tasks for the subjects vary (see Vemouri, 1978, for a taxonomy of control tasks; for example, specification of goals for control versus no specification); the experimental conditions are different (instruction to think aloud while operating the system versus quiet control; direct

TABLE 13.1

Studies of the Relationship Between Performance on Intelligence Tests and Control of Complex Systems

Author	System	Characteristics	Criterion	Test	Correlation
Putz-Osterloh (1981)	Tailorship (business) thinking aloud; interaction with experimenter necessary; no goals specified	no formal description available; 24 variables; 11 for inputs; system has a trend towards catastrophy	number of months with capital assets increasing	APM Raven	low transparency τ=.22(N = 35) High transparency τ =-.013(N = 13)
Putz-Osterloh & Luer (1981)	Tailorship (business) thinking aloud; interaction with experimenter necessary no goals specified	no formal description available; 24 variables; 11 for inputs; system has a trend toward catastrophy	number of months with capital assets increasing	APM Raven	no diagrams of relations τ =.00(N = 35) diagram of relation τ =.31(N = 33)
	Ocean (biology) specific goals provided	no formal description available 6 variables	number of goals accomplished in time interval	APM Raven	no diagram of relations r =.40(N = 34) diagram of relations r =.46(N = 35)
Hesse (1982)	Dori (ecology) interaction with experimenter necessary; no thinking aloud; no goals specified	no formal description available 12 variables; 6 for inputs	combined criterion	APM Raven	no cover story, diagram of relations*: r =.38. no cover story, no diagram of relations: r =.46. cover story, diagram of relations: r =.06. cover story, no diagram of relations: r =.17. (N = 35 each condition)

(Continued)

229

TABLE 13.1 (Continued)

Dörner et al (1983)	Lohhausen (act as mayor); thinking aloud; interaction with experimentrer necessary; no goals specified	ca. 2000 variables no formal description available	combined criterion correlated with expert judgment	APM Raven Kit of Ref. CFT 3	$r = .12(N = 48)$ $r = .02(N = 48)$ $r = .03(N = 48)$
Funke (1983)	Tailorship (business) no thinking aloud; direct interaction at the computer; feedback about system state; no goals specified	optimization of linear equations of system not possible 24 variables; 11 for inputs	(a)number of months with capital assets increasing (b)combined criterion	APM Raven	(a) $\eta = .14(N = 35)$ (b) $\eta = .28(N = 53)$
Gediga et al. (1984)	Hamurabi (ecology) no thinking aloud; no goal specified	no formal description available; 11 variables	combined criterion	IST 70	$\tau = .19(N = 14)$
	Serum (Company) no thinking aloud; no goals specified	no formal description available; 11 variables	number of years existence of company	IST 70	$\tau = .03(N = 12)$
Putz-Osterloh (1985)	Moro (ecology) thinking aloud; no goal specified	no formal description available; system is less dynamic 49 variables; 22 for inputs	5 performance variables 1 combined criterion	BIS 6 subsets total score	Control group (N = 25) no substantial correlation coefficients Experimental group (N = 25; received self-reflection training); Correlation total score X combined criterion $r = .36$; 21 out of 42 coefficients significant (-.52 to .46)

Study	System	Task/Input	Performance measure	Test	Results
Funke (1985)	Ecology system no thinking aloud; no interaction with experimenter; goal specified	mathematically defined optimal input; 6 variables; 3 for inputs	distance to goal state	BIS	N=43 5 out of 12 coefficients $\geq .10(-.17$ to $.15)$ no correlation between BIS subtests and different forms of acquired system knowledge (11 out of 36 coefficients $\geq .10$; -.20 to 37)
Misiak and Kluwe (1986)	SIM 005 (fictitious business); no thinking aloud; direct interaction with the computer; goal specified	mathematically defined; optimal input; 16 variables 14 for inputs	distance to goal state	IST 70	N=65 Correlations for IST total score, subtests and criterion (a) for 3 control intervals (b) for 2 different groups of variables 25 out of 520 coefficients $\geq .30$ (max. -.42)
Hormann and Thomas (1988)	Tailorshop see Funke (1983)	see Funke (1983)	number of months with capital assets increasing	BIS 4 subscales total score	no diagram of relations: r = .03 (N = 22) diagram of relations*: r = .46(N = 19; subscales .43 to 54)
Reichert and Dorner (1988)	Cooling house direct interaction goal specified thinking aloud	mathematically defined 2 variables 1 for input	mean deviation from set point (temperature)	BIS	correlations for 7 subtests between r = .2-.32; N = 54.

interaction with the system at the computer keyboard versus interaction via an experimenter). These different experimental conditions limit the comparability of the studies listed in Table 13.1. The differences between the studies also prevent a statistically based meta-analysis.

Although there is considerable heterogeneity in the research designs, all studies have in common the use of tasks with the same crucial components: The subjects are provided with a set of system variables that are connected and dynamical. Thus, the effects of inputs on one system variable spread out, and changes of system states occur also without inputs of the individual.

In addition, most studies agree with respect to the interpretation of the results in two important ways:

1. It is argued that the tasks (i.e., simulated systems) have higher ecological validity and are closer to reality than problem situations, such as intelligence test items or the Tower of Hanoi (see also Kreuzig, 1983) which have traditionally been studied by cognitive psychologists.

2. The low correlation coefficients allow us to infer that intelligence test scores can not be regarded as valid predictors for problem solving and decision making in complex real-life environments.

The far reaching evidence of the value of complex systems as experimental tasks on the one hand and the low correlations between performance on such tasks and intelligence test scores on the other hand, makes it necessary to examine the obtained data more carefully. The following discussion refers to some of the essential factors that appear to influence the correlation between intelligence test scores and performance data obtained from system control. In this context consideration is being given also to the question of whether the psychometric approach, as it is being applied to system control is appropriate.

FORMAL ASPECTS

As early as 1973, Newell pointed out that the task selection procedures of information processing psychology are questionable. Investigators ran the danger of separating tasks from psychological theory. In response to this criticism Sternberg (1982) proposed four criteria for the selection of tasks: quantifiability, reliability, construct validity and empirical validity. These criteria will provide the framework for the following discussion of complex systems as tasks compared to intelligence tests.

Quantifiability.   The first criterion, quantifiability refers to the possibility of assigning numbers to the subjects according to rules (Sternberg, 1982, p. 229). Although this is not usually a problem in research on reasoning and problem solving, it raises serious problems where complex systems are used as tasks. Clearly, there are several possibilities for assigning numbers to the performances of individuals operating complex systems. The problem, however, relates to the selection of the appropriate performance variables. So far there are no criteria available to base decisions about which variables determine a subject's control performance.

In order to evaluate the state of a system, it is possible to consider various parameters. It is, however, not evident which of these parameter oriented criteria are appropriate for the evaluation of an individual's control performance. For example, different criteria may well lead to different reliability estimates, and as a consequence to different correlations with intelligence (Funke, 1983). The difficulty here is due to the fact that the complex and complicated process of system control that lasts for hours or even days can not be summarized easily into a zero dimensional score. In situations where such scores are computed as indicators of control performance it is essential that reasons are provided for the selection of specific variables and for the rejection of others. The arguments should then refer to the formal characteristics of the system that can reveal essential control variables.

The use of single performance scores also raises the question of when to assess control performance. The system's state as indicated by the value of one or more variables at a certain point in time totally ignores the system's developmental history. The same score obtained by two individuals may indicate completely different system developments: it can be reached either after a monotonously decreasing system state or in the course of a monotonously increasing system state (and, of course, by an oscillating one; see also Strohschneider, 1986, on this point).

It should be clear by now that it is necessary to take into account information about the course of system control that presumably covaries with transitions between stages of knowledge acquisition. The goal has to be a structural description of the process in the time domain, because it is not possible to obtain an adequate estimation of performance at only one point in the time domain. This position is strongly supported by the results of single case studies that reveal highly different courses of system development for different individuals (Kluwe et al., 1986, 1990).

With respect to criteria, like objectivity, stability and reliability, which are applied in test theory and construction, there are hardly any data available for the performance in system control. However, these criteria are well documented for intelligence tests scores, and in most cases satisfactory values are reported.

Standardization. One of the preconditions for valid and reliable measurement is providing for standardized conditions. The experimental settings reported for some studies in Table 13.1 make it difficult to achieve this. Standardization in terms of equal treatment of all subjects is not warranted. The conditions of system control should be clearly specified with regard to instruction, time and method of scoring. However, it is difficult to establish conditions in such a way that each subject controlling a particular system is treated exactly the same. This is especially the case where the subject's control actions are translated to the computer by means of verbal interaction with the experimenter. A standardization of the experimental conditions is much easier to attain when the subject is allowed to interact with the system directly at the computer keyboard. With respect to methods for the generation of data, objectivity is difficult to achieve where raters' judgments are applied to evaluate a subject's performance.

Reliability.   Reliability refers to the imprecision or precision of measurements. There are several methods to estimate reliability: test-retest, parallel forms and the internal analysis methods (Lord & Novick, 1968, p. 134). The correlation between measurements obtained by administering the same instrument at different times may also be conceived of as a coefficient of *stability*. Such coefficients are expected to be low when determined for control performance data. In the course of controlling the system, subjects learn about the system's characteristics, they acquire useful as well as misleading heuristics and strategies that govern their control behaviour, and they collect facts and develop beliefs about the system's structure and behaviour. Due to this diversity of ongoing processes in a subject's cognitive system, stability cannot be expected to be high with respect to a performance criterion.

Strohschneider (1986) addressed this question. The system *Moro,* used in this study, is considered to be a system with rather low dynamics, i.e., the system does not run easily into catastrophies when there are no inputs from the subject (contrary to the often used *Tailorshop* system, see Table 13.1). The test-retest correlation coefficients for a variety of behavioural measures were found to be between $r = .33$ and $r = .85$ (N = 25; repeated measurements were obtained after 11 to 55 days). Performance was assessed by applying a combined criterion based on seven variables. The test-retest correlations for this score at different points of measurement during system control varied between $r = .26$ and $r = .44$. Estimation of lower-bound reliability lead to coefficients around .50.

It is interesting to note in this context that Strohschneider (1986) himself rejects the zero-dimensional performance criterion used in his study as an appropriate measure for a subject's quality of system control. The selected criterion is assessed after a fixed, but arbitrarily determined, number of trials (inputs); this does not take into account the previous development of the system state nor its future state.

In another study (Funke, 1983) test-retest correlation coefficients are reported for two different performance criteria applied to the same system (Tailorshop). The first criterion that is usually derived for the Tailorship system is the number of months in that capital assets increase. The reported correlation coefficient is r

= .199 (N = 14). For the second criterion, determined on the basis of the states of several system variables, a coefficient of r = .798 (N = 14) is reported. However, the author points out, that the retest data have been obtained from a sample that cannot be considered to be a random sample of the original group of N = 53 subjects.

The second method to estimate reliability of performance scores is the application of parallel forms, i.e., structurally equivalent systems. This possibility has to be excluded for dynamic task environments. Minor changes of a system's structure, of its dynamic behaviour, or with respect to its cover story will engender different viewpoints and approaches on the part of the subjects. Estimating reliability by means of the internal analysis methods, i.e., dividing the control task into two parts (split half) proves to be difficult, also. There is no appropriate method to distinguish between items or to form two essentially equivalent halves of a control task.

Validity. The third criterion for the selection of tasks proposed by Sternberg (1982) is that of validity, in this case construct validity and empirical validity. By construct validity, Sternberg (1982) refers to tasks that have been chosen on the basis of some psychological theory. "A task that is construct-valid is useful for gaining psychological insights through the lens provided by some theory of cognition" (p. 229). However, so far there is no appropriate theory that might guide the selection of dynamic task environments as tasks in cognitive psychological research, and that makes statements about what is involved in the performance of these tasks. Therefore, it is not possible to state that the selection of complex system environments is theory-based. However, the work of Doerner (Doerner, 1984; Doerner et al., 1983) provides a promising approach towards a comprehensive theory of acting in a complex environment that might well provide a basis for the construction and selection of such tasks.

Empirical Validity assures that the task serves the purpose in the theory that it is supposed to serve. Thus, whereas construct validity guarantees that the selection of a task is motivated by a theory, empirical validity tests the extent to which the theory is empirically supportable. Empirical validation is usually performed by correlating task performance with an external criterion (Sternberg, 1982, p. 229).

With respect to the criterion of empirical validity, there is a widespread assumption held for complex systems that can be characterized as a *complexity bias*. This bias might be explained as follows: In contrast to intelligence tests, the laboratory task of operating a complex dynamic system implemented on a computer has higher ecological validity. The bias has two components (a) the dynamic task environment, the "microworld" is assumed to be rather similar to complex environments in reality and (b) what is even more important, the cognitive requirements for operating a complex system are similar to those met in real problem situations. This latter assumption however, has yet to be proven. There are no data that justify the assumed higher ecological validity of systems implemented on a computer.

> An ecologically valid task, as opposed to a highly artificial one, may be defined as one whose performance is required in adaptation to real-world environments (Sternberg & Powell, 1982, p. 991).

But ecological validity is difficult to determine. Neisser (1985), for example, points out the ambiguity of this concept. In order to specify the meaning of this term he provides prototypes of research that are judged to be exemplars of ecologically valid tasks.

So far one gains the impression that ecological validity is assigned to complex task environments on the basis of plausible judgments. However, cover stories that sound interesting, that motivate the subjects and that seem to be related to everyday experience do not necessarily have external or ecological validity. Even worse, cover stories for systems elicit individual knowledge structures in subjects controlling the system in question that may vary remarkably. These knowledge structures have not been examined so far.

Furthermore, it must be emphasized that the operation of complex dynamic systems provide subjects with new and unfamiliar requirements in the laboratory. The control of an economical system, of a traffic system or operating a fictitious technical system are by no means every day experiences for most human subjects. Thus, one has to take into account that subjects in these studies, at least in the first trials, experience an unfamiliar environment and unfamiliar demands. Therefore, one should provide the opportunity for extended learning before assessing a subject's performance (see also Moray, 1986, on this point). This finding is well documented by the learning curves that have been obtained from single case studies (Kluwe et al., 1986, 1990).

The initial decrease of control performance in the first sessions shown in Figure 13.1 corresponds to the amount of experience allowed for in most studies reported in Table 13.1. Therefore, the results of those studies with respect to control performance refer to a period where the search for information about the unfamiliar environment dominates control activity and it occurs at the cost of system control.

There are only a few studies of the external validity of complex systems. The results yielded so far are not satisfactory (Norris & Snyder, 1982; for a 5-year longitudinal study with respect to a business game see Wolfe & Roberts, 1986). A major problem is, of course, the selection of appropriate performance criteria, as discussed earlier.

To summarize, with regard to formal aspects such as quantifiability, reliability and validity the use of performance scores obtained from complex system control reveals serious deficits. The present state of research considering psychometric

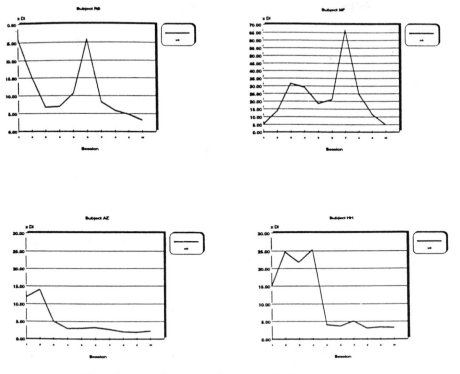

FIG. 13.1.   Learning curves from four single case studies.

criteria does not yet exclude intelligence, as assessed by traditional tests, as a potential predictor for performance in dynamic task environments of reality.

COGNITIVE ASPECTS

Task Complexity and Cognitive Activity.   One of the reasons for varying correlation coefficients in this domain may be that subjects accomplish two tasks at different levels of processing.

The correlation becomes stronger as the level of processing of the laboratory-type task gets closer to the level of processing required by the verbal ability test (Sternberg & Salter, 1982, p. 5).

It has to be assumed that both type and level of processing have an impact on the observed relationship between two kinds of activities. Discrepancies with respect to these factors may be the reason for low correlations. In the following discussion it will become obvious that specific assumptions are being made with respect to this issue.

The widespread complexity bias, mentioned earlier, implies a second potential explanation that relates to the cognitive requirements of complex system control and intelligence tests respectively. Operating a complex system imposes intellectual demands that are not present when the task is to solve intelligence test items. The solution of intelligence test items requires only a subset of those cognitive activities that are necessary for system control. Related to this assumption is the belief that system control requires more cognitive activity and higher levels of processing, because it is more complex (see, for example, Kreuzig, 1983). This is considered to be a major reason for the low correlation coefficients (Fig. 13.2).

There are serious problems with the complexity bias because its conceptualization is unclear and because it is not supported by data. First, the term complexity is by no means well defined. What makes a task or an environment complex? There are numerous approaches towards mathematically well founded descriptions of complexity for systems. When using the term complexity, researchers often refer only to the number of variables that constitute a system. However, attributes of the system, such as the strengths and the type of relationships between the system variables are also of importance. Time-lagged effects of inputs and inner-system relations also contribute to a system's complexity. Crawford's chapter, in this volume, provides excellent food for reflection on this issue.

Another point is that the complexity of a task does not have generality. It is always a question of the subject's representation of the dynamic task environment. It is argued here that it is by no means clear that a situation described as complex because of its formal structure, is also internally represented at a higher level of complexity than, say, an intelligence test item. As a consequence, it is not legitimate to infer in advance that the high complexity of an environment requires high level processing, i.e., the application of more and higher level cognitive operations. Instead, the type and number of operations applied depend on the individual's elaboration of the problem space and on the individual's goals while accomplishing the task.

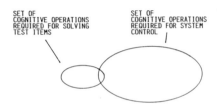

SET OF
COGNITIVE OPERATIONS
REQUIRED FOR SOLVING
TEST ITEMS

SET OF
COGNITIVE OPERATIONS
REQUIRED FOR SYSTEM
CONTROL

FIG.13.2.   The assumed sets of cognitive operations necessary for solving intelligence test items and for systems control respectively.

Kreuzig (1983) argues that compared to simulated complex systems, intelligence tests contain little, if any demands that might be related to rational, reasonable behaviour in reality (p. 316). Intelligence test items tend to only require a narrow range of cognitive operations, because they are static, less complex, and more transparent. However, this is just the impression of an external observer, not a view based on precise task analysis. Kreuzig (1983) among others provides a list of 20 global cognitive activities that he regards as necessary for the operation of a complex system. These include cognitive activities such as information search (the acquisition, reduction and storage of data about the system), predictions of trends, estimation of side effects, monitoring inputs, planning and conflict resolution. The activation and combination of these cognitive operations, however, strongly depends on a subject's view of the system, on the internal representation developed by the subject and the goals established by an individual when operating it.

In single case studies it was found that some subjects operate the system similarly to a control loop, i.e., the subject acts just like the control component in the loop (Kluwe, Haider & Misiak, 1990; Ringelband et al., 1990). These subjects do not search for information about relationships between system variables, they just adapt their inputs to the perceived deviations from a desired reference value. Instead of considering the connectivity of the system, the system variables are treated as independent "problems". It is highly questionable whether the distinctions made by Kreuzig (1983) with respect to intelligence tests and complex systems are appropriate for those subjects, though the applied task has all the characteristics of complex dynamic systems.

Intuitively assigned characteristics to complex systems need to be examined more thoroughly. And, even more importantly, the internal representation of a task, be it a complex system or an intelligence test item, depends on the individual's approach. Kreuzig (1983) and others explain low correlations between intelligence test scores and control performance on the basis of differences between the hypothetical set of cognitive operations necessary for solving test items and that necessary for operating a system. There may be a small intersection, but operating a complex system requires a larger set of additional operations.

One course of action might be to reduce the complexity of systems in order to reach higher correlations with intelligence test. The reduction of system complexity would imply a reduction of the set of operations necessary for system control, thus roughly equalizing the cognitive requirements for intelligence tests and system control.

Providing Information About the System.   One of the experimental manipulations of a system's complexity is referred to as variation of the system's *transparency*. This is accomplished by introducing two conditions: (a) A nontransparent condition that provides the subjects with no more than the description of the control task, i.e., there are no specific goals, also there is no further information about the structure or the behavior of the system. (b) A transparent condition that differs with respect to the information given as subjects are supplied with data about the structure of the system. In most studies this is done by providing the subjects with data about the relationships between the system variables in terms of a diagram of the connections between the system variables (see Table 13.1).

However, only for two out of four studies essential differences between the correlation coefficients are reported: Putz-Osterloh & Luer (1981; first study) as well as Hoermann & Thomas (1988). Obviously, transparency is a rather vague concept. Before deciding on the conditions for system control in terms of transparency, one would have to examine if the information about the system variables provided in a diagram is in fact relevant information for system control. It is by no means clear that this information is actually searched for and used by the subjects when operating the system (for an extended discussion of this problem see Misiak et al., 1988). Some empirical results fail to support the assumption that subjects search for information about relationships between system variables and that they would use such information (Broadbent, Fitzgerald & Broadbent, 1986; Ringelband et al., 1990). Thus, before a systematic variation of control conditions in terms of transparency is feasible one has to analyze more detailed formal characteristics of the system and the cognitive requirements it imposes on the subjects.

The Number of System Variables. It is assumed that the task requirements in operating a complex system become more similar to those of intelligence tests when the number of system variables is reduced, i.e., the correlation coefficients will be higher. Few system variables are considered to indicate low complexity of the system.

The correlation coefficients shown in Table 13.1 do not support the aforementioned assumption. There are coefficients of .46 and .40 for a system with only 6 variables (Putz-Osterloh & Luer, 1981), of .31 and of .46 for a system with 24 variables (Putz-Osterloh & Luer, 1981; Hormann & Thomas, 1988), and of .36 for a system with 49 variables (Putz-Osterloh, 1985). In a recent study Reichert and Doerner (1988) report no substantial correlation between intelligence as assessed with the *Berliner Intelligenz Struktur Test (BIS;* Jaeger, 1984) and a one-variable system (see Table 13.1). There may be one factor inherent in these and other conditions that in fact could raise correlation coefficients: Putz-Osterloh (1981; Putz-Osterloh & Luer, 1981) obtained higher correlations when subjects were provided with verbal information or with a diagram about the system to be controlled; This is also true for the study of Hoermann and Thomas (1988); furthermore, Putz-Osterloh (1985) obtained higher correlations for an experimental group that was instructed to reflect retrospectively the solution approach; this result did not match her expectations.

One possible explanation for these increases of the correlation coefficients is that the heterogeneity of the individual internal representations and strategies when operating the system is indeed reduced when the subjects are provided with additional information about the system and with the instruction to monitor and evaluate their own strategies. This is the position taken by Putz-Osterloh (1985).

Heterogeneity of Cognitive Activity.   Heterogeneity refers to the fact that subjects when operating complex systems elaborate highly different mental representations of the simulated complex environment, establish different goals for system control and apply different strategies. Thus, the same performance score obtained by two subjects does not indicate that they used of the same process of control. This is especially true for dynamic task environments, in which no goals are provided for operating the system. In group studies process differences do not emerge, but they can be observed in case studies. Due to the complex environment, subjects will elaborate mental models for the system on the basis of samples of the system behavior. However, different subjects will not consider the same samples. As a result of her earlier studies Putz-Osterloh (1985) concludes that the diversity and heterogeneity of the individual approaches may well be one of the main reasons for the low correlation coefficients obtained so far.

The fact that different subjects elaborate different mental representations with regard to the same system, that they also change idiosyncratically as a result of different control behaviour during the control process, poses a major problem for any trait model of cognition (Hunt, 1987). Different representations and changing representations may also imply different types of information processing.

This challenges a basic assumption of all psychometric methods: that the same linear combination of abilities can be used to predict the test score of every examinee (Hunt, 1987, 28).

Especially when tasks are performed in unfamiliar, complex and uncertain environments one has to consider the individual mental representations of the system as one of the major factors determining control performance.

CONCLUSION

In this chapter it has been shown that the results of correlational studies do not support the assumption that intelligence, as measured by traditional intelligence tests, is a predictor for performance in system control. There are serious shortcomings with the psychometric approach when applied to complex system control. In addition, there are no empirical data that would support a position described as complexity bias, according to which dynamic task environments as research instruments would possess higher ecological validity, and would require higher levels of cognitive processing.

Quite complex systems can be controlled on the basis of simple declarative knowledge and a limited number of rules. An individual may control a system without understanding the relationships between its variables. It is not necessary for the operator of a system to search for information in order to understand the system. Rather, he/she may search for inputs that produce acceptable system states. The subject does not have to ask *why* something works, instead the question is *whether* it works. This is similar to engineering psychology, where operators presumably control systems on the basis of incomplete knowledge about the system (see also Bainbridge, 1981).

It must be noted that intelligence test items that are considered to be of low complexity may nevertheless elicit considerable cognitive activity. For example, Hunt and Poltrock (1974) showed that 82 production rules were required to solve letter series tasks as used by Thurstone. These 82 rules were found to constitute six production systems that finally solved 11 out of the 15 Thurstone letter series tasks. This finding would suggest that the complexity bias described earlier is unlikely to provide an explanation of the low correlations between intelligence test scores and control performance.

Another issue that has been neglected in the analyses discussed in this paper is *domain specificity,* understood in this context as the availability and applicability of mental abilities that generalize or transfer to many problem situations, e.g., different systems.

It is highly questionable whether the cognitive requirements of intelligence tests and system control should continue to be investigated on the basis of intercorrelations. When subjects work on system control tasks, changes in systems' activities and in the cognitive processes occur in the time domain. This is not the case when the task is to solve a test item. What is required are detailed task analyses that might reveal the cognitive demands of system control. One of the prerequisites for this is a system that can be described formally, i.e., a system with known characteristics. In psychometrics the processes that engender performance are usually not considered. They are, however, at the core of cognitive science. We must examine the *knowledge structures* and the *processes* that underlie cognitive performance.

There is considerable support in the literature for single case studies of the control of complex systems. Individual differences in goals, the development of internal representations, information search and processing, and other cognitive and metacognitive strategies and their interaction with the demand characteristics of tasks in microworlds appear to provide a promising framework for further research in cognitive science.

REFERENCES

Bainbridge, L. (1981). Mathematical equations or processing routines. In J. Rasmussen & W. B. Rouse (Eds.), *Human detection and diagnosis of system failures.* New York: Plenum.

Broadbent, D., Fitzgerald, P., & Broadbent, M. (1986). Implicit and explicit knowledge in the control of complex systems. *British Journal of Psychology, 77,* 33–50.

Carroll, J. B. (1976). Psychometric tests as cognitive tasks. A new "Structure of intellect". In L. Resnick (Ed.), *The nature of intelligence*. Hillsdale, NJ: Lawrence Erlbaum Associates.

Doerner, D. C. (1978). Merkmale der kognitiven Struktur 'guter' und 'schlechter' Versuchspersonen beim Umgang mit sehr komplexen Systemen. In H. Ueckert & D. Rhenius (Eds.), *Komplexe menschliche Informationsverarbeitung*. Bern: Huber.

Doerner, D. (1984). Denken, Problemloesen, und Intelligenz. *Psychologische Rundschau, 35,* 10–20.

Doerner, D., Kreuzig, H. W., Reither, F., & Staudel, Th. (1983). *Lohhausen: Vom Umgang mit Unbestimmtheit*. Bern: Huber.

Funke, J. (1983). Einige Bemerkungen zu Problemen der Problemloeseforschung: Ist Testintelligenz doch ein Praediktor? *Diagnostica. 29,* 283–302.

Funke, J. (1985). Steuerung dynamischer Systeme durch Aufbau und Anwendung subjektiver Kausalmodelle. *Zeitschrift fuer Psychologie, 19,* 443–465.

Gediga, G., Schottke, H., & Tucke-Bressler, M. (1984). *Problemloesen und Intelligenz*. Psychologische Forschungsberichte, Fachbereich Psychologie, Universitaet Osnabruck, Nr. 34.

Hesse, F. W. (1982). Effekte des semantischen Kontexts auf die Bearbeitung komplexer Probleme. *Zeitschrift fuer experimentelle und angewandte Psychologie, 29,* 62–91.

Hoermann, J. J., Thomas, M. (1988). *Fuer wen sind transparente Probleme transparent? Ein Beitrag zum Zusammenhang zwischen Intelligenz und komplexem Problemloesen*. Vortrag gehalten auf der 30. Tagung experimentell arbeitender Psychologen, Marburg 1988.

Hunt, E. B., & Poltrock, S. E. (1974). The mechanics of thought. In B. H. Kantowitz (Ed.), *Human information processing: Tutorials in performance and cognition*. Hillsdale, NJ: Lawrence Erlbaum Associates.

Hunt, E. B. (1987). Science, technology and intelligence. In R. Ronning, J. Glover, J. Conoley & J. Witt (Eds.), *The influence of cognitive psychology on testing*. Hillsdale, NJ: Lawrence Erlbaum Associates.

Jaeger, A. O. (1984). Intelligenzstrukturforschung: Konkurrierende Modelle, Neue Entwicklungen, Perspektiven. *Psychologische Rundschau, 35,* 21–35.

Kluwe, R. H., Haider, H., & Misiak, C. (1990). Learning by doing in the control of a complex system. In H. Mandl, E. de Corte, N. Bennett, & H. F. Friedrich (Eds.), *Learning and Instruction*. Oxford: Pergamon Press.

Kluwe, R. H., Misiak, C. & Haider, H. (in press). Modelling the process of system control. In P. Milling & E. Zahn (Eds.), *Proceedings of the 1989 International Conference of the System Dynamics Society*. Berlin: Springer Verlag.

Kluwe, R. H., Misiak, C., & Ringelband, O. (1985). *Learning to control a complex system*. Paper presented at the 1st European Conference on Learning and Instruction. University of Leuven. Belgium.

Kluwe, R. H., Misiak, C., Ringelband, O., & Haider, H. (1986). *Learning by doing in the control of complex systems: The benefits from experience and the effects of system characteristics on the learning process*. Paper presented at the 35th Congress of the German Society for Psychology, Heidelberg.

Kreuzig, H. W. (1983). Intelligenz als Praediktor fuer Problemloesen. In D. Doerner, H. W. Kreuzig, F. Reither, & Th. Staudel, *Lohhausen: Vom Umgang mit Unbestimmtheit*. Bern: Huber.

Lord, M. F., & Novick, M. R. (1968). *Statistical theories of mental test scores*. Reading, MA: Addison-Wesley.

Misiak, C. & Kluwe, R. H. (1986). *Complex system control*. Research Report No. 13. Institut fuer Kognitionsforschung, Universitaet der Bundeswehr Hamburg.

Misiak, C., Haider, H., & Kluwe, R. H. (1988). *Formale Strukturen von Systemen zur Erfassung kognitiver Leistungsmerkmale*. Paper presented at the 36th Congress for Psychology of the German Society for Psychology, Berlin: October 1988.

Moray, N. (1986). Modelling cognitive activities: human limitations in relation to computer aids. In E. Hollnagel, G. Mancini & D. D. Woods (Eds.), *Intelligent decision support in process environments*. Berlin: Springer Verlag.

Neisser, U. (1985). Toward an ecologically oriented cognitive science. In Th. M. Shlechter, & M. P. Toglia (Eds.), *New directions in cognitive science*. Norwood, NJ: Ablex.

Newell, A. (1973). You can't play 20 questions with nature and win. In W. G. Chase (Ed.), *Visual information processing*. New York: Academic Press.

Norris, D. R., & Snyder, Ch. A. (1982). External validation of simulation games. *Simulation & Games, 13*, 73–85.

Opwis, K., & Spada, H. (1985). Erwerb und Anwendung von Wissen ueber oekologische Systeme. In D. Albert (Hrsg.) *Bericht ueber den 34. Kongress der Deutschen Gesellschaft fuer Psychologie*, Wien 1984. Goettingen: Hogrefe.

Putz-Osterloh, W. (1981). Ueber die Beziehung zwischen Testintelligenz und Problemloeseerfolg. *Zeitschrift fuer Psychologie, 189*, 79–100.

Putz-Osterloh, W. (1985). Selbstreflexion, Testintelligenz und interindividuelle Unterschiede bei der Bewaeltigung komplexer Probleme. *Sprache & Kognition, 4*, 203–216.

Putz-Osterloh, W., & Luer, G. (1981). Ueber die Vorhersagbarkeit komplexer Problemloeseleistungen durch Ergebnisse in einem Intelligenztest. *Zeitschrift fuer experimentelle und angewandte Psychologie, 28*, 309–334.

Reichert, U., & Doerner, D. (1988). Heurismen beim Umgang mit einem "einfachen" dynamischen System. *Sprache & Kognition, 7*, 13–24.

Ringelband, O., Misiak, C., & Kluwe, R. H. (1990). Mental models and strategies in the control of a complex system. In D. Ackermann & J. Tauber (Eds.), Mental models and human-computer-interaction. *Proceedings of the 6th Workshop on Informatics and Psychology*. Amsterdam: North Holland.

Sternberg, R. (1982). REasoning, problem solving, and intelligence. In R. J. Sternberg (Ed.), *Handbook of human intelligence*. Cambridge, MA: Cambridge University Press.

Sternberg, R. J., & Powell, J. S. (1982). Theories of intelligence. In R. J. Sternberg (Ed.), *Handbook of human intelligence*. Cambridge, MA.: Cambridge University Press.

Sternberg, R., & Salter, W. (1982). Conceptions of intelligence. In R. J. Sternberg, (Ed.), *Handbook of human intelligence*. Cambridge, MA.: Cambridge University Press.

Strohschneider, St. (1986). Zur Stabilitaet und Validitaet von Handeln in komplexen Realitaetsbereichen. *Sprache & Kognition, 1*, 42–48.

Vemouri, V. (1978). *Modelling of complex systems*. New York: Academic Press.

Wolfe, J., & Roberts, C. R. (1986). The external validity of a business management game: A five-year longitudinal study. *Simulation & Games, 17*, 45–59.

14 New Intelligence with Information Technologies

Andrea A. diSessa
University of California, Berkeley

In his *Meditations,* Descartes claimed that the source of fallibility in human knowledge is the will. Man's need or desire to act frequently outpaces and outstrips his capability to know for certain. Thus people guess rather than check, presume rather than reason, all for the sake of acting. If we had the time to think slowly and carefully before acting, our rational souls could come to Truth in the clarity and distinctness it exhibits to us.

As a constructivist, I am not generally overwhelmed by rationalist pronouncements. But this one strikes me as a deep insight, at least for the subculture of researchers in education. In fact, the need or desire to act, strongly thrust on us by the dire problems of education in the practical world, constantly drive "application" far beyond the meager state of the art.

But, we can't just sit by the fire with Descartes until we have things straight in order to escape mistakes. The temptation to act and prescribe beyond our confident knowledge base is an unavoidable "original sin" for us. A significant part of the social value of our craft is in what we can or will be able to do to help people learn. And what's more, I think that, if we are careful, the combination of reflective research and more impulsive action can be a much more powerful technique for building a strong scientific basis for education than each alone. So we should act while thinking.

In this chapter I want to consider aspects of my current work that, in my opinion, lie outside ground that provides a really firm theoretical or empirical footing. I do not wish to insult those who have tried for such a footing, but my own judgments are that our scientific understanding clearly falls short here. Nor is this to say that all aspects of my current work are unscientific. Instead, I want to reflect about some important aspects that just are not scientific—yet.

THE CONCEPT OF A COMPUTATIONAL MEDIUM

In the Boxer Project at the University of California, Berkeley we are designing and building a prototype of a "computational medium." We are just now beginning to try it out in educational contexts. The idea of a computational medium is rather simple and can be understood by analogy with a very familiar representational medium. Written text is a technology that has entered the very fabric of our culture and provides us with intellectual capabilities far beyond those we could have without it. This may be most evident in education, where much of our knowledge and skills are developed and exercised through this medium.

Imagine, then, that we can extend the capabilities of text as an intellectual medium with some radically different ones. Imagine we free text from its linear and flat structure so that it can be easily hierarchically organized and cross connected in any way we choose. So overviews and organization can graphically become part of the documents we create. Perusing can be a much more efficient act, because we can scan at a high level and only zoom into details when we want to see them. We can also zip quickly, via provided links, from one corner of the document to another in order that the document approximate much more closely our personal needs for reminders of things past, previews of what is to come and access to important central ideas or data from any place we need it. This medium is strictly more useful than text because it can be used simply as a text (in the form of a text processor), if one chooses to do so. This is not a trivial point, because many attempts at hypertext are dramatically more clumsy than simple text.

But hypertext is only the beginning. Next we add dynamic graphical capabilities. You can have pictures in this medium, and they move if you so chose. Yet more. The pictures are interactive, and can be poked and manipulated to reveal even more structure in our interactions with them and their responses.

Finally, we add one essential ingredient to an interactive medium: the ability of *all* users to build and modify any kinds of structure the medium affords. It is not a one-way medium in which productions are created by experts and given to consumers, like books or movies. But everyone learns and becomes competent to build in this medium, even if only in small and perhaps often seemingly unimpressive pieces. This is much like textual literacy. It is well worth everyone learning to write as well as read, even if they may never write a book.

Because it entails dynamic structure, it seems we must call this last constructive and reconstructive capability "programming," although it may look very little like what we think of as programming now both in its form and in its breadth of uses by just plain folks.

I find it almost inconceivable that such a medium, if it came to exist in practical forms, would not have profound effects on our culture and especially on education. Given a few assumptions e.g., that the skills it took to operate were not excessive, that the hardware in which it is implemented became cheap, easily portable and widely available, the medium could not logically fail to be more than what it would replace, writing. That follows from the fact that it contains written text in essentially familiar form as a start. This is unlike ordinary programming languages, or even typical hypertext systems that are aimed dominantly at presentation rather than a more evenhanded treatment of production and consumption. But I expect a substantial lot more from such a medium than "at least as good as writing." We turn to these expectations soon.

Some parts of the development of such a medium are, I would argue, scientific. For one, the study of comprehensibility of programming systems is coming to the point that substantial and demonstrable improvements in design and instruction of programming are possible. For another, the design of learning environments can benefit from whatever we do know about learning in general and the learning of particular subject areas. This is happening already as, for example, the present psychological and cognitive community frequently works with computers as a fine new tool to apply and test what they think they know about learning.

But again, the points I wish to make do not relate centrally to these instrumental levels. Instead, I wish to presume them and look at some of the larger scaled effects of such a medium, some of the reasons and modes in which more than just barely noticeable effects on education might come about. Thus, I am examining the reasons why our work, or some successor, may have dramatic effects on education that are beyond our current scientific capabilities to really predict or control. These are at the core of why I have the commitment to act in the way I have, and have chosen to do the related instrumental scientific and engineering work. It is not just scientific curiosity or the expectation that the science to which I contribute will provide us with powerful leverage in education. Rather, I believe that this particular combination of science and invention may have important effects for entirely other reasons than I know how scientifically to explain or predict.

INTELLIGENCE AND LITERACY

To set the stage, let me approach computational media from this perspective: What can information technology, centrally computers, contribute to the development of human intelligence? Again, these brief comments are intended to be speculative and personal. I don't think the grounds for debating them deeply are in hand.

Modes of Human/Machine Intelligence. The first notion that comes to mind is that information technology may provide extraordinary means for training intelligence in individuals, where the kind of intelligence at issue is something like the traditional meaning of the term. Although I think there is a grain of truth in this possibility, it may be overrated. In the first instance, the concept of intelligence is assumed to be an invariant that does not change substantially from context to context, nor should it change much even from instruction and learning. The very presumptions around which the present concept of intelligence has been built oppose the directions in which I wish to move here.

Will simply learning more effectively count as improving intelligence? It may or may not, depending on your definition of intelligence. In any case, this is certainly what many hope for. But from the perspective advanced here and stated in this simple way, "improved learning" assumes that not much really changes in the intellectual lives of humans. The same things happen, just a bit more and faster. In net, I think we have, in principle, rather little to expect from computing making us "smarter" by the measure of traditional conceptions of intelligence. Rather, it is the presumption of a computational medium that context can make dramatic changes.

Starting close to "making us smarter" are two more promising directions. The first is that a new medium can unlock skills and intelligences that have been largely ignored or have been untappable with past media. I do not think it is a secret that schools are dominated by verbal activities. And I think it quite clear as well that children vary widely in those skills, and in particular, that many have their strongest suits elsewhere. What if this new medium relied on, and therefore developed, very different skills—say, dynamic spatial imagery, and the ability to act, design and build without the usual verbal accoutrements of school? I consider many people I have met gifted in these ways, though not many of those excel in usual academic settings. This may be because those skills are currently blocked from use; the intellectual medium of academic development simply does not fit them and therefore leaves them unengaged. What if this new medium did so much more? I believe this is the case, and provide an example and a pointer to "data" later.

Those who are more talented in the area of traditional literacy have little to fear from the introduction of this new medium. It will serve their purposes as well or better than standard text. (Not to mention that what are now nonstandard general skills in the classroom may be quite learnable if they came to be exercised, as some research suggests concerning learnability of spatial skills.) Indeed, I think many subjects will be much more approachable even if the style of approach relies on the usual set of academic skills. Some of these new subjects may have important leverage. For example, I believe the ability of such a new medium to organize large amounts of data effectively may be critical to students developing better metaconceptualizations of what knowledge in a field is about. One concept our group has been toying with is that of a "knowledge space" in which, say, a group of children over an extended period of time try to scope out what a domain is about: What are the most central ideas? What are the peripheral ones? What are the relations among all the elements? What is the evidence for believing the central ideas? and so on. Traditional media have been impoverished for such tasks (diSessa, 1990). The mode of "improved intelligence" here is that the medium happens to match not so much the skills of individuals, but new kinds of potentially very powerful subject matter, such as metaknowledge.

So far our images of improved intelligence, although different from what is measured by conventional intelligence tests, are still more or less compatible with capabilities that eventually (as learning progresses), reside more or less in individuals' heads. There are important other ways to think about intelligence. In particular, consider the possibility of *symbiotic intelligence,* that individuals in concert with computers (via our new medium) simply are able to accomplish much more in intellectual tasks than individuals alone, no matter how well trained, or what general intellectual skills they have.

Bits and pieces of this are common sense and already realized. Productivity tools are everywhere, and few of us (although there are some) doubt that they are contributing to the quality of our civilization. But, to take the high road, can we really think of these as improved intelligence? Mechanical power technology allows us to do much more than if we did not have it. But it does not qualify as improved intellectual resources.

Instrumental effectiveness lacks one fundamental characteristic that I would expect of anything that I wanted to call intelligence—flexibility. So, could our new medium foster a move from productivity tools defined by narrow niches, to a genuinely creative general instrumentality? A central image for me is that of a tool rich culture where individuals borrow and share and invent a broad range of tools to serve their purposes. All along the way, the medium serves to embody the inventive capabilities of individuals and of the culture into instruments that effectively accomplish more. The nature of that "more" that is accomplished is crucial, of course. Doing more assignments would not constitute a reasonable measure of improved learning in schools. But just as computers now serve scientists in research, learning more about the unknown, I believe the same might be true for some future tool-rich learning culture for young learners and their mentors.

Finally, consider the image of this medium serving us as the basis of a new and extended literacy. I note in passing that such a literacy is rather far from what passes as computer literacy in schools these days. For one, the school image is almost vocational, and focused on awareness or low level skills. The new literacy I look forward to, if it comes to exist, will be as foundational to learning and the development of intellectual skills as reading and writing are now. Essentially every school class will be affected, and some of them deeply in the most fundamental aspects of the style of instruction. We may hope for a change from, let us caricature, a style that is didactic and oriented toward fixed artifacts (texts and materials), toward one that is much more fundamentally interactive and presumes substantial invention on the part of both students and teachers. As well, learning will be affected even in basic focus, in what constitutes the content of worthwhile learning. New subjects will emerge. For example, just as calculus is a text-based technology for thinking about motion and change, and it is a course subject as well, so may computer modeling become both such a fundamental instrument and curricular topic. Similarly, old subjects will look dramatically different. Say, history may become historical and cultural research, and biology may not be so much a fact intensive, static discipline, but a place to solve biological problems with computer support.

This image of a new literacy is encompassing, for certainly it embraces the infrastructure of a tool-rich learning culture. It also embraces new expositional modes, new kinds of books that contain interactive graphical representations and even modifiable tools as part of them. It presumes people may well find very different kinds of things to say and ways to say them; new masters of this medium will emerge to create classics for future generations in the way Dickens and Shakespeare created classics in the mode of our present literacy.

The image of literacy contains, at the opposite extreme, the reminder of a critical barrier any proposed new medium must pass if it is to be the foundation of a literacy. That is menial utility. A very broad range of people in a very broad range of everyday tasks had better find the medium not only accessible, but just plain useful, if the society at large is to decide that the cost of changing the common infrastructure of its literacy is worth the price. For educators, I believe this means that being a good educational tool will simply not be enough, that the decision to have a new medium available will be beyond what any single community can decide for itself. Perhaps this is an overly expansive estimate of how the decision to adopt a new medium must come about. But it is certainly indicative of the scale of issue that might be involved, and for me, another indication of how little we know of the general principles of media development and appropriation into literacies.

In the remainder of this paper I wish to return to our efforts to create a computational medium, which we call Boxer. I do not presume Boxer will be the medium like that sketched here, although that is our hope. Instead, I wish to raise in more concrete form some issues drawn out earlier concerning computational media.

EXAMPLES

Engaging Untapped Intelligence.   My first example will be very sketchy as it is reported in more detail elsewhere (diSessa, 1989). As part of our modest program to show the effectiveness of Boxer in teaching traditional school subjects, we are aiming to build a year-long course for elementary school students to teach them some of the essentials of motion that are now usually taught in high school or university physics courses. These include concepts of speed and distance, acceleration, components, composition of motions, relative motion, and even versions of the fundamental theory of calculus in a computer- and child-appropriate form. One of the central aims is not just intellectual mastery, but to show that mastery can be accompanied by the children's appreciation of the power of those intellectual tools to enhance their own personal goals. A modest expectation along these latter lines is that children can easily program their own computer games using what they have learned about motion.

One of the first microworlds we built in this program was one we assumed would be an advanced one, concerning relative motion. Just to get a little base-line data, we started working with some children. To our surprise, two of the first three groups showed a substantial degree of learning, even though we intended only to look at initial competence with the microworld's ideas, not to test a fully developed pedagogical program. One pair of children, in particular, were strikingly competent after an hour of work with the microworld, much more so than our experience with students having a master's degree in physics by coming "cold" to the kind of problems presented in the microworld.

We have since extended that work with about a dozen more students. Preliminary analysis leads us to believe that the kind of expertise our exceptional pair developed is not all that exceptional.

It is important to know what is happening here. We have begun investigating in depth what exactly are the skills and knowledge these children come with that allow them to learn so quickly and perform so well. So far, it appears that a diversity of skills and knowledge are at issue. Perhaps most centrally, we have identified skills with dynamical imagery and the ability to reason on dynamical presentations, either provided by the computer or generated (e.g., with hand motions) by themselves. What's more, these do not appear to be the same skills that traditional trained experts bring to bear on these problems. There is actually some real overlap on the coverage or focus of the skills; but this is a complex story that cannot be told here.

What is most exciting to us about these developing possibilities is that we may be able to model a "child's expertise" that may be built with the help of the dynamic representational capabilities available in Boxer. This expertise may be very different than the expertise we might try to teach by looking at present day experts who were trained with a substantially different medium. We have good reason to expect that this child's expertise will be much more learnable even by those who have initial difficulties. In contrast to the literature that finds that typically 50% of students coming out of physics courses have fundamental problems with basic concepts in the course, we see that it may be true that there is an expertise with which very many students enter a course, an expertise that is currently not tapped.

Menial Utility.   The next example serves to show some details of Boxer, and at the same time explores the concept of menial utility that emerged in the earlier discussion. In this case, we consider a not quite menial, but still everyday utility that may serve to enhance teachers "creative instrumentality."

The example is a thought experiment that grew out of an encounter with an expert high school teacher, Jim Minstrell, who is developing computer tools to help teachers understand and employ his strategies of enhancing conceptual development based on analysis of the naive conceptions with which students come to physics classes. The set of tools should be helpful not only in managing everyday interactions with children, but also in changing the teacher's view of him/herself as "just a teacher" toward more of a "teacher-researcher" who *thinks* about his/her students' learning as well as trying to enhance it.

Minstrell does not yet have access to Boxer and is developing his tools with more traditional computer facilities. But I thought it would be well worthwhile exploring how Boxer could contribute to his goals.

In the course of a few hours, Minstrell and I developed pretty much the entirety of what will be displayed here. The essence of the environment is a transparent database capability that Boxer has, and an ability to add simple tools at essentially no programming cost.

Figure 14.1 shows the top level of this teacher's toolbox. Basic Boxer is evident here. Text may be typed and edited at any place in Boxer. There is never any distinction between the developer and users of a piece of software. The

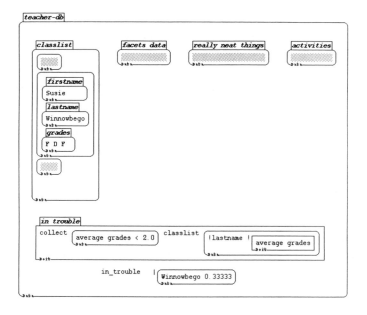

FIG. 14.1. A teachers toolbox, containing four databases.

major structuring device in Boxer, the box, has organized this world. You can make a box with a keystroke, and delete or move it around as if it were a large character in a text editor. Boxes automatically expand to enclose as much as you put in them. If you want to hide the insides of a box, you can just shrink it with a mouse click, leaving a small grey box. Clicking on a shrunken box, opens it up again. If a box is large and complex, you can enter it by expanding it from its normally open size to full screen. Thus very complex entities can be kept in context, but inspected in great detail, if necessary. This control of visible presentation via trivial operations is central to Boxer's capability to make complexity of many kinds manageable. Any box can be named by poking the box to cause a nametab to appear at its top, then typing in the tab.

The four boxes at the top of Figure 14.1 are databases. The first, which is open, is just the class listing. Notice the simple structure of the records, just named boxes inside boxes. By following the model you can see in the database, you can make more entries just by typing more boxes and data in a similar form. Perusing the database can be done with no more than basic point and expand or shrink capabilities.

One of the nice features of Boxer is that computational capabilities are totally integrated into the basic form of the medium. So, for example, although you may just type in your database, it is computationally accessible at the same time. I programmed a utility program called *collect* that looks through a database for boxes in which you are interested and culls out whatever information you want from each. The program *in trouble,* whose entire code is shown in the figure, collects all entries of students whose average marks are below 2.0 (C) from the database named *classlist,* and prints out the last name and the average mark from each such entry. (The exclamation point in the last input to *collect,* which specifies what information to print out, means to use the data from the database entries, rather than to print literally the words "last name" or "average grades.")

The bottom line of the figure shows what happens when *in trouble* is executed. A box appears with the list of students who are in trouble, in the format specified in the third input to *collect.* In this case, just one student, Winnowbego, appears. Looking back at the classlist, we could have seen that Susie is having problems.

That much is quite menial, but also quite useful. You can easily imagine utilities to print school reports that include specific data for each student. This "print merge" capability is available in Boxer simply because there is no distinction between anything you type and computational data.

Figure 14.2 shows a simple tool that we built to assist in inspecting databases, which might get quite big, complex, and hard to peruse intelligently in concrete form. The program *inspect* takes the name of a database as input and returns a complete working tool that you may use to inspect that database. The inspector tool contains a "port" (picture-frame box labelled *entry*) to one entry at a time.

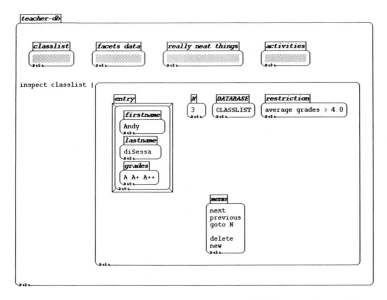

FIG. 14.2. The program *inspect* generates a fully interactive tool for inspecting the entries of a database.

Ports are views of boxes that actually "live" someplace else. They constitute the basic hypertext capability built into Boxer. Ports are active views, so that any change you make in the *entry* will actually be reflected in the database itself.

The menu at the bottom of the inspector tool can be poked to bring up any item in the named database, or even make a new entry or delete an old entry. Changes to entries, as mentioned, can be made directly in the port. Any restriction typed into the *restriction* box means *next* and *previous* commands will be restricted to items that have the specified property. In this case, we have found a student who has better than a straight A average.

Figure 14.3 shows a more interesting database than a class list. It contains entries made by a teacher that describe instances of use of various intuitive ideas, here called *facets.* An entry contains the student's name, the type of activity in which an observation was made, the date, the facet observed (or not observed, which is displayed in the *status* field) and some commentary, *result,* on what happened.

Perusing a database like this can be useful for the teacher. But a tool like *collect* can make it much more useful in discovering really important things about student learning. The database *really neat things* is meant to hold such discoveries. Figure 14.4 shows an entry in that database. Here a *collect* has been executed on the *facets data* database, which collects information on uses of a particular intuition called "overcoming". The returned data shows an intriguing

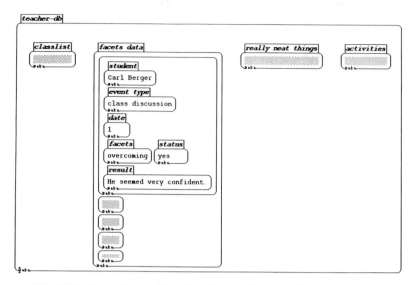

FIG. 14.3.   A database of intuitive facets of students' understanding.

pattern of use and unexpected lack of use. Fields that describe the category of "neat thing" and other commentary are useful for lookup and interpreting the entries in this database.

Figure 14.5 shows an entry in the final database, which is a collection of activities for students, keyed by what problems they are intended to help with. A

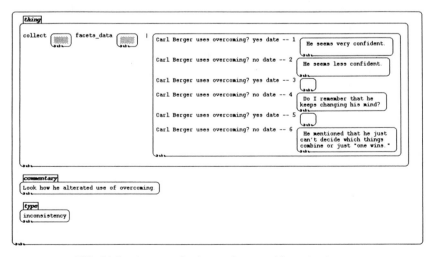

FIG. 14.4.   An entry in the *really neat things* database.

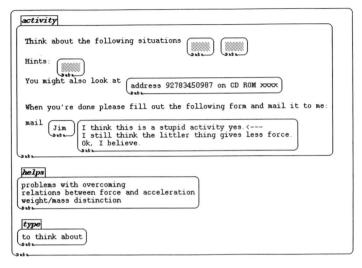

FIG. 14.5. An entry in the *activities* database, that contains suggestions for things for students to do.

beginning teacher can get a lot of hints from such a database, and an experienced teacher can be helped managing the complexities of making individual assignments to students. Note that because Boxer is totally integrated, the activities can be complete and working microworlds to be given directly to students. They can contain other active capabilities, such as the return (electronic) *mail* line shown, for the student to execute having completed the activity. Such a database containing good things to do keyed to areas that are aided by the activities may even be used by enterprising students.

Finally, Figure 14.6 shows the complete "program" for implementing a notebook for a teacher to use from anywhere inside the Boxer universe. To fetch the

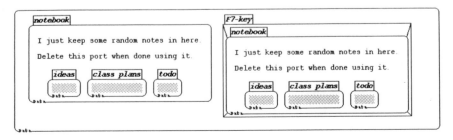

FIG. 14.6 The "program" for a notebook that appears and disappears at will.

notebook, you just press the F7 function key, and a port to your notebook appears. After perusing your notes and making any additions or modifications you want, you can just delete the port with a "delete" keystroke, but the changes will remain in your actual notebook box. Two small pieces of quite general magic implement this notebook. First, the suffix "-key" in the name of any box makes that box be executed when the named key is pressed. Secondly, the meaning of executing a port is defined in Boxer to be creating a copy of the port. Executing the port named F7 by pressing it gives you a port to your notebook wherever you are located. So, in net, central system capabilities combine trivially to make importantly useful extensions to a user's world.

Reconstructibility or Capturing Process. The second microworld I wish to display here was also constructed in a few hours. It is a heat and temperature microworld that allows students to play with the flow of heat.

In Figure 14.7 the central box, *temperatures,* contains an array of numbers that represent the temperature of various parts of an object, or the temperatures of an array of objects in contact with one another. You can think of the temperatures box as showing an object with a collection of digital thermometers attached to it.

The box *conductivities* allows one to specify how conductive the material is between the places where temperature is indicated. The asterisks in the *conductivities* box represent the places where temperature is measured, and a number representing conductivity appears between each pair of asterisks. Because this box would not normally be needed, it can be shrunk most of the time. Similarly, the box *sources* lets one declare which temperature locations are held at a fixed

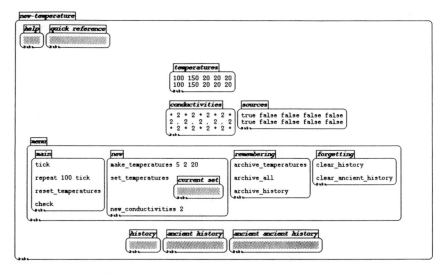

FIG. 14.7.   A heat and temperature microworld.

temperature (the default being that the left hand edge of the array is held fixed), and it can be kept shrunken in most instances.

Any of the data, temperature, and so forth, can be changed with usual Boxer editing functions. One of the reasons it is so easy to implement such a micro-world in Boxer is that you need no input or output programming at all. The boxes shown *are* the data the program works with, and changing them changes what the program will see and act on. Similarly, readout is trivial, for any changes the program makes in causing heat to flow are automatically made visible to the user by having those boxes open for display.

In the menu box are commands to be poked by a mouse to activate the microworld. In particular, the main submenu contains the command *tick,* which causes a unit of time to pass, and hence heat to flow and temperatures to change. The menu, like everything in Boxer, is instantly editable, and the second line was just typed in to make available long intervals of time for checking heat equilibration.

The boxes at the bottom of the microworld are simple extensions of the basic capabilities of the system. These are meant to help users keep track of what they are doing. So, for example, you might open the history box and begin typing your intentions in doing an experiment. Whenever you want data from the rest of the microworld in your history, you can just cut and paste. Alternatively, some rapid-fire capabilities are provided under the *remembering* menu. Execution of the *archive temperatures* item puts a copy of the current temperature array at the end of the history box. Similarly, *archive all* puts a copy of all the settings of the temperature simulation in *history,* so that complete experimental setups and results can instantly be saved. The *archive all* facility also generates a menu item *retrieve,* which we will see shortly, in the entry added to *history. Retrieve* will put the state of the simulator instantly back to what it was when the *archive all* command was executed. Thus you can replay your own experiment, or the teacher can rerun the lab report that you construct in the history box.

Archive history means all the work you have done in the history box is moved into a box in the *ancient history* box. Thus, it is easy to keep a series of related experiments. *Ancient ancient history* is useful to keep a student's long term work, or to keep some experimental setups or demonstrations provided by the teacher.

In general, archiving in this way is part of Boxer's general capability to help support users by concretizing their activities for purposes such as replay or reflection. At the everyday end of the spectrum, externalizing one's plans, goals, reflections and current work state in complex tasks like experimentation, can provide important support for students in valuable intellectual tasks. We believe similar uses could support everyday work of all sorts of people, from scientists to secretaries. More deeply, the opportunity to react concretely to what one has done, and experiment easily with improving long time-scale work patterns can provide opportunities to learn at entirely different levels. And these capabilities are not exotic ones programmed on top of Boxer, but intrinsically available because there is no distinction between the user's seen world and the computational substrate. So, one can easily type personal commentary into *history*. But as well, a one line program can take part of the system's computational state, for example, the variable *temperatures,* and add it to the history for purposes of documentation or replay.

Figure 14.8 shows a simple experiment/demonstration that I built in about 5 minutes, pretending to be a teacher preparing a lesson. First, I set up an array of temperatures with an unusual distribution in a "bar." The temperatures are generally cold (20 degrees F), but with a hot surface (150 degrees) right next to the heat reservoir (100 degree source). Recall that the heat source is the leftmost column in the temperature array. Then I just ran *tick* a few times, and after each

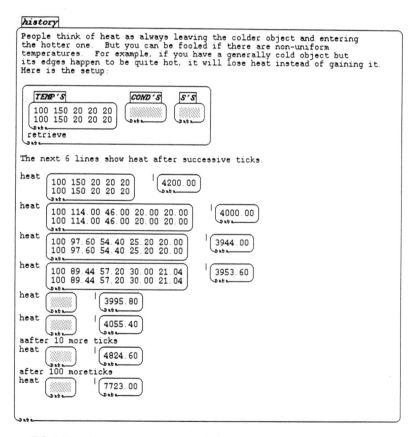

FIG. 14.8. An experiment to see a "cold" bar initially decrease in heat content because its surface is hot and radiates heat.

run, clicked on *archive temperature*. Finally, I just ran a simple program *heat* on each of the temperature distributions. *Heat* finds the total amount of heat in the object with the temperature distribution specified. The sequence of heats demonstrates that the "cold" object cools off more before it begins to heat up to equilibrium. The transition from unexpected cooling to heating occurs when the surface temperature (originally 150 degrees) falls below the source temperature.

Figure 14.9 shows a similar experiment I left in the *ancient ancient history*

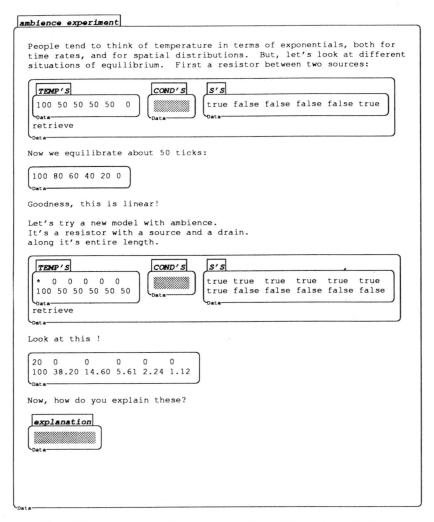

FIG. 14.9. A demonstration of exponential and linear heat distributions in a bar.

box. The point of the experiment is that people spontaneously expect heat distributions to have a characteristic exponential falloff. But, in fact, temperatures will equilibrate to a linear function between two different fixed temperature sources. The latter part of the experiment shows how the characteristic exponential distribution can be brought about by adding a fixed temperature ambience, a source along the length of our simulated bar.

Note how the box demonstrating exponential and linear temperature distributions contains entire setups with temperatures, conductivities, and sources, so that students can retrieve these by clicking on the *retrieve* command, and rerun or modify the experiment as they wish. This little experiment contains an extended explanation of what it represents and how these phenomena work inside the shrunk *explanation* box at the bottom of the experiment.

WHERE WE STAND

It is too early to make strong empirical statements about how the program to create a computational medium is progressing. But that does not mean there is nothing to say. In this section, I briefly report on our experiences to date. Some of these can and will be documented as scientific results. Others are more interpretative, but are suggestive as to how the prospects for the grander goals of establishing a new kind of literacy may be assessed. We start with the more instrumental side of these issues.

> Children can induce quite reasonable models of important parts of Boxer structure just from observing its action in examples.

In general we have been working with children in the age range of 11 to 14. Graduate student Chuen-Tsai Sun has created a microworld that teaches and assesses student comprehension of one of the important technical aspects of Boxer, scoping of variables. *Scoping* refers to the mechanisms that establish the connection between names and objects, especially if there exists more than one object with the same name. Sun found that a carefully rationalized sequence of critical examples in which students are asked to predict and explain the way Boxer works can allow most students to induce for themselves the general mechanisms Boxer uses for scoping.

> Some of the most complex parts of Boxer can be acquired through combinations of example demonstrations and visual model presentations.

The most advanced aspects of scoping are complex enough that substantial state of the computer needs to be visualized intermediate to start and end state. However, we have carefully designed Boxer not only to have relatively easily visualizable models, but also so that Boxer can easily represent these models in the same terms as it shows in its surface structure. Thus, Sun was able to produce materials that explicated underlying operations of Boxer well enough that children could, within a few minutes, not only produce appropriate explanations on their own, but extend them to predict behaviour in different circumstances.

Similarly, graduate student Michael Leonard has been developing materials to teach Boxer's general function-calling mechanisms and recursive programming, which is generally considered one of the most advanced and difficult of programming concepts. He has documented children developing a series of partial models that are more and more adequate to the task (Leonard, in press). We believe this is working in large measure because, as with scoping, Boxer's surface presentational capabilities are up to the task of representing its (usually) hidden computational state.

> Some parts of Boxer are much easier to use than, for example, Logo; saving up to two thirds in time and effort.

One of the earliest controlled experiments on the ease of use of Boxer was conducted outside of our group, by Schweiker and Muthig (1986) at an IBM research laboratory in Germany. Although the experiment investigated only a small part of Boxer's programming capabilities (specifically, compound object construction out of precomputed pieces), and although the experiment was limited by being done with naive adults and on the basis of pencil and paper tasks, the results were still impressive. After a period of learning the constructs available in Boxer and Logo, the experimental subjects very reliably performed the same tasks of constructing and debugging compound objects taking approximately one third the time in Boxer that they took on Logo.

> Expert programmers can produce workable and interesting microworlds in a day or two.

As has been exemplified with the teachers tools and the temperature microworld, quite usable systems can be created in Boxer in significantly less than a day of programming. In fact, one day seems to be about the norm. Much of this capability can be credited to the fact that Boxer shows its own structure so well and allows changes to be made so easily that, frequently, essentially no programming needs to be done on input/output behaviour or on user interface. Thus, time reverts to the really essential jobs, inventing, empirically testing and revising the microworlds. Additional credit is due to Boxer's extended graphical capabilities and object orientated programming facilities. These make interactive graphics relatively easy to program and also make building computational models conceptually and practically much easier.

> Teachers and "non-programming" graduate students with less than a year's work in Boxer can produce serviceable materials in less than a week.

Graduate students with essentially no programming background have created materials in less than a week that were successful in use with children. Similarly, the (admittedly very few) teachers that have worked with Boxer have all ended up making their own materials, some of these entirely for their own purposes and without our instigation. Indeed, we have incorporated some of the tutorial materials generated by students, who had a year or less experience with Boxer, into our motion course. These indications are extraordinarily important for our goals of spreading the responsibility for the creation of the content of Boxer literacy from researchers and curriculum developers, to teachers and even to children.

Some children become expert enough in Boxer to truly appropriate the medium for their own purposes.

Two or three admittedly exceptional students among the first to have Boxer accessible for roughly a year have shown extraordinary competence and inventive capabilities in taking over the system for their own goals. Although we can not describe and catalog these accomplishments here, it has been important to our judgment that these are likely indicators of future forms of literacy. These students did these things on their own initiative, clearly serving their own personal goals, and they were substantially innovative in taking novel Boxer structures (compared to prior computer environments) and extending them in clever and unanticipated ways.

Children and teachers share code dramatically more in Boxer than with Logo.

In the first course in which Boxer was used as a resource (Picciotto, 1989) we saw very good signs indicating that hopes for the development of tool-rich learning cultures are warranted. In the course children learned both subject matter (statistics) and programming. Though some of the students entered the six week course having essentially no prior programming experience, all managed to produce finished, working and conceptually interesting programming projects by the end of the course. What is especially intriguing was that several of the projects relied in substantial ways on children spontaneously appropriating tools or code written by other students or by the teacher into their own projects.

Far from cheating, we view this kind of social support as essential for developing an effective cultural matrix for computational literacy. Although it is very difficult to quantify, or even briefly to characterize the extent and nature of this computer–mediated distanced collaboration (the students and teacher did not intend to write part of someone else's project), my impression is that this worked dramatically better than in our prior experience with Logo. We believe credit goes largely to Boxer's ease of inspection and interactive trying out of other's codes. As well, it seems likely credit must go to the "trivial" capability to deal with programs as visible, transportable units.

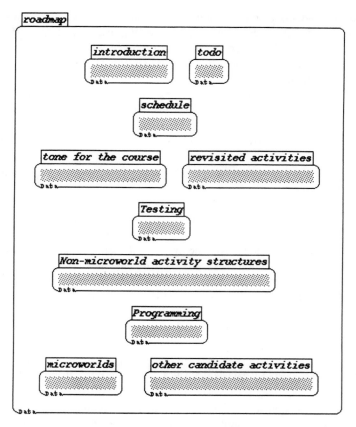

FIG. 14.10   The top level of a database containing discussions of issues, plans and completed materials with commentary for a course on
motion for elementary school students.

Boxer is useful enough that we use it ourselves in our everyday research tasks.

We have used Boxer for the infrastructure of planning and managing our own
motion course project. For example, Figure 14.10 shows the top level of a
database that contains our community plans, issues to debate and even completed
materials (working, microworlds, etc.) and commentary on them. Similarly, we
have constructed databases containing schematized transcripts of students working with our materials that are annotated by a hierarchically organized companion
database of theoretical issues and categories of analysis. The connection between
analysis and data is maintained by including in the analysis part of the database
ports to sections of transcript that illustrate theoretical points.

CONCLUSION

The possibility of a computational medium and a new, extended literacy involving it are exciting prospects. It has been the contention of this chapter that along with the more tractable issues, such as comprehensibility of programming systems, this idea raises a host of larger scaled and much less tractable issues. Centrally, we would like to understand how information technology can extend the intelligence of humans and how tools of this sort may be appropriated by society at large or by significant segments of it. In a more specifically educational framework, we want to understand how such a medium can support new expectations for learning, different conceptions of knowledge and knowing, new ways of tackling old and new problems, and how the critical infrastructure of literacy, capability with the new medium, can develop.

If Boxer succeeds even in a small degree, we will have an opportunity to test our conjectures and, we hope, calibrate and refine our efforts toward realizing the motivating prospects.

ACKNOWLEDGMENTS

This is an extended version of a paper presented at the Third Annual Conference of the European Association for Research on Learning and Instruction.

This work was supported, in part, by the National Science Foundation under grant number MDR-88-50363. Opinions expressed are those of the author and not necessarily those of the Foundation.

REFERENCES

diSessa, A. A. (1990). Social Niches for Future Software. In M. Gardner, J. Greeno, F. Reif, A. Schoenfeld, A. diSessa & E. Stage (Eds.) *Toward a Scientific Practice of Science Education.* Hillsdale, NJ: Lawrence Erlbaum Associates.

diSessa, A. A. (1989). A child's science of motion (Boxer Technical Report G4). *The Boxer Project,* School of Education, University of California, Berkeley, California.

Leonard, M. (in press) Learning the Structure of Recursive Programs in Boxer, *Journal of Mathematical Behavior.*

Picciotto, H. (1989). Teacher-created educational software: BASIC, Logo, Boxer (Boxer Technical Report E4). *The Boxer Project,* School of Education, University of California, Berkeley, California.

Schweiker, H. & Muthig, K. (1986). Solving Interpolation Problems with Logo and Boxer. In P. Gorny & M. J. Tauber (Eds.), *Visualization aids in programming.* Heidelberg: Springer.

15

Improving Intelligence by Fostering Creativity in Everyday Settings

Arthur J. Cropley
University of Hamburg

The problem. In an oral examination a few months ago I asked a candidate what he understood by the term "age." He replied that age is defined by the amount of time that has passed between an individual's birth and the present moment. Because the examination in question was in psychology, I asked him if he could make some suggestions about the elements of a psychological definition of age. He replied that the concept "age" already exists with a set meaning (he had just given it) and that speculating in the way I had invited would be a very dangerous matter, because it would lead to a situation where we could never be sure what an expression meant. Several years ago I asked a 14-year-old school girl if she could offer a few suggestions about the consequences that would follow if the clouds suddenly had strings hanging down from them. She replied that it was impossible for her to imagine such a situation, because she knew that clouds are only water vapor, and water vapor could not support the weight of strings long enough to reach down to the earth. When I asked her to use her imagination and pretend that such strings really existed, she replied that she could not imagine something that she *knew* to be impossible.

Although it is quite clear that the answers given by both the students were strictly correct and even in a certain sense admirable, I myself (and I believe many readers of this chapter) have the feeling that something is lacking in the students' reactions to the invitation to speculate, imagine or phantasize. Despite the fact that both were highly intelligent young people (the girl achieved an IQ of 140), their application of intelligence to the questions just outlined left something to be desired. Employers, teachers, parents, as well as the people in question themselves, frequently emphasize the importance and the practical value both to society and to individuals of getting ideas, trying the new, seeing issues from an unexpected angle and the like - some of the advantages of these modes of thinking will be outlined shortly. My aim here is to define what was missing in the examples of thinking outlined earlier, and to show how to encourage the appearance of the missing factor, in other words to "improve" intelligence.

Raising IQ Versus Altering Ways of Thinking.   The idea of improving intelligence is by no means new. In the 1920s and 1930s a number of famous studies demonstrated the beneficial effects on IQ scores of transfer to a more stimulating environment (e.g., Skeels & Dye, 1939; Dennis, 1960). More recently, hopes were raised of being able to increase IQ scores through the administration of glumatic acid, whereas I myself investigated a possible relationship between intelligence and uric acid (see Raina, 1986, for a recent summary of this kind of research). In North America the most famous program for improving intelligence was *Head Start* which focused on early educational intervention in the family environment. However, disappointing results of evaluation studies and, in particular, the scandal surrounding the *Milwaukee Project* have damaged the reputation of such measures.

In any case, "improvement" as conceptualized in the strategies just mentioned does not address itself to the issue raised at the beginning of this chapter. One more promising approach that has aroused repeated interest during the last 30 years involves an emphasis on such strategies as combining ideas, breaking existing cognitive sets and seeing unexpected relationships as a means of improving the way intelligence is applied rather than trying to develop more of it. A number of German speaking psychologists have concentrated on the nature of intelligent processes. Meili (e.g., 1964, although he had already published papers on this topic in the 1930s) theorized that intelligence has four main properties: complexity, plasticity, totality and fluency. *Complexity* involves bringing the elements of a set of information into relationship with each other. *Plasticity* refers to the changing of existing cognitive structures. *Totality* is seen in the relating of new material to existing mental structures, while *fluency* consists in moving from one idea to another. Other theorists from German speaking countries (Meili worked in Switzerland) emphasized the importance in intelligent thinking of making combinations and imagining (Amthauer, 1973) or of recognizing general laws underlying apparently unrelated stimuli (Horn, 1962). These writers saw the changing of mental structures or the use of imagination as integral elements of intelligent thinking, whereas the pragmatic North American approach to defining intelligence has been dominated by its emphasis on rapidly finding the "best" or "correct" answer.

Creativity as a Mental Style.   Since the famous Guilford Presidential Address to the American Psychological Association (Guilford, 1950) this extension of the definition of what was understood as "intelligence" has usually been discussed in the English speaking world in terms of "creativity," a usage that was popularized by Getzels and Jackson (1962) in another seminal work. This use of the term creativity is now also well established in German-language psychology.

Initially, creativity and intelligence were treated as separate dimensions of intellect, creativity being seen, for instance, as capable of compensating for lack of intelligence in the mastery of school learning tasks. Over the years, however, creativity and intelligence have increasingly come to be seen as elements of a more general phenomenon of "mental power." Recently, Wallace (1985, p. 362) referred to a general dimension of mental "extraordinariness," of which intelligence is one aspect and creativity another. Extraordinary individuals may manifest intelligence without creativity (or presumably creativity without intelligence, although this situation is seldom discussed), or display some combination of both.

Of particular interest is the attempt by a number of authors to conceptualize creativity as a qualitative improvement in mental functioning: About 20 years ago I argued for a concept of creativity as a "style" of applying intelligence, rather than as a separate ability; in a similar vein, Gardner (1983) described creativity as the highest form of application of intelligence, whereas Horowitz & O'Brien (1986) regarded it as a qualitative reorganization of a specific domain of knowledge or skill. Horn (1988) distinguished between two basic styles of reacting to novelty, the one involving avoidance, the other attraction.

For the present purposes, the style approach argues that, at all levels of ability, people may deal with situations requiring intelligence either by trying to reapply the already learned, concentrating on proven tactics, relating the new situation to the familiar and so on, or by searching for the novel, backing intuitions, taking a chance, and so forth. For brevity's sake, I call the first tactic *convergent,* the second *divergent.* In real life these are probably stereotypes, as few people would be expected to function permanently at the one or other extreme, most tending towards a combination, the nature of the mix varying according to the particular situation in question and the psychological properties of the individual person.

The Need for Creativity.　Obviously, there are many situations where strictly convergent application of intelligence is highly desirable. One obvious example would be the behavior of airline pilots. On the other hand, McLeod and Cropley (1989) argue that convergence is overrepresented and overvalued, both in schools (including universities) and in society in general. Thus, the improving of intelligence is seen as involving, among other things, encouraging people to be more creative. McLeod and Cropley offer a number of arguments supporting the importance of divergent application of intelligence. Reasons for its importance include the following:

1. It makes school learning more effective. Cognitive processes and personal and motivational characteristics such as those that will be outlined shortly greatly enhance, among other things, *learning to learn.*

2. It increases the ability of people to cope with the social and scientific changes that the next 50 years will bring; flexibility, originality, readiness to try something new, and so forth are becoming, and will become even more, important.

3. It promotes the spiritual wellbeing of people; the ability and readiness to deal in an open and flexible way with life situations is vital to mental health.

4. It protects our human dignity; in the age of the computer it is not routine, programmable thinking that will confirm our unique position as human beings, but creative processes and products.

5. It offers new perspectives for making equality of opportunity a reality. An expanded concept of excellence that takes account of hitherto neglected areas, and also emphasizes the importance of noncognitive aspects, opens up new possibilities.

As can be seen, these arguments do not conceptualize divergent application of intelligence or creativity as something for a small group of highly creative individuals, but as offering ways of improving intelligence for all. Nicholls (1972) was one of the first to make this point explicit, in a paper entitled *Creativity in the person who will never produce anything original and useful: The concept of creativity as a normally distributed trait.* This idea is at the heart of the present deliberations.

Defining Creativity. Because of the obvious connection with novelty, the term creativity is often misused, and has come to mean, for some, little more than "doing your own thing" or mere unconventionality. Simply being different is regarded as synonymous with being creative. In fact, approaches emphasizing unconventionality and the like are not absurd: Brown (1977) argued that creative breakthroughs in science frequently involve an apparently irrational jump. However, reduction of creativity merely to unconventionality or irrationality is dangerous: In the school setting, not only may teachers be seduced into tolerating or even encouraging disruptive behavior, but an erroneous notion of creativity may also be harmful for children falsely labelled as creative, by leading them to think that they are being creative when they are doing nothing more than indulging in trivial activities.

Fox (1981) suggested that much of the uncertainty stems from confusion over whether creativity is a personality trait, a specific cognitive ability or a type of problem solving strategy that might be learned. Fox's evaluation is similar to that in a review by Barron and Harrington (1981), who observed that creativity is usually defined in terms of achievement (creativity as product), as a personal disposition (creativity defined in terms of the person involved) or as a special kind of ability. A further problem centers on the question of whether it is really possible to speak of creativity as a unitary phenomenon.

Necka (1986) distinguished between "aesthetic," "artistic," "professional" and "scientific" creativity. Barron (1969) even suggested that creativity need not require being creative oneself, but is also seen in the ability to foster it in others. Wallach (1985) argued that creativity is difficult to define except in terms of a specific domain, whereas Renzulli (1984) pointed out that a child may show creativity in different areas at different times. Nonetheless, Altshuller (1984) concluded that it is possible to develop a general theory of creativity, which would encompass artistic, technical, scientific and practical domains.

Taylor (1975) referred to "levels" of creativity. At the lowest level is what he called "expressive spontaneity," to be found for instance in the uninhibited production of ideas often seen in children. Originality is unimportant at this level, as is the quality of the product (i.e., its usefulness or degree of adaptation to the demands of the real world is irrelevant). Higher levels of creativity include "technical" creativity, characterized by unusual skill or proficiency; "inventive" creativity in which the already known is utilized in novel ways; "innovative" creativity, which requires that existing principles be taken a step further; and finally "emergent" creativity, where new abstract principles are recognized and stated. Sternberg (1988) identified six "facets" of creativity in everyday life: *insight,* leading to selection in information processing; *knowledge* (although as will be discussed later in more detail, knowledge can block flexibility); *personal factors,* e.g., flexibility, tenacity, and the willingness to take risks; *courage of one's convictions; intrinsic motivation;* and *relevance.*

An important point in the present discussion is that creative thinking should lead to worthwhile results if it is to involve an improvement in intelligence. This distinguishes it from blind unconventionality or simple expressive spontaneity. The products of processes labelled creative should, to use the words of Sappington and Farrar (1982), conform to reality constraints. Furthermore, they should involve some genuine transformations (Besemer & Treffinger, 1981) and not simply a slick use of the well known. Not infrequently, these products have a compelling quality about them that causes a perceptible shock of recognition in the observer, perhaps the thought: "Now why didn't I think of that?". This is the property that Bruner (1967) referred to as *effective surprise,* whereas Sternberg labelled it *relevance.*

The call for effectiveness deals squarely with an interesting issue: The possibility of a fundamental incompatibility between creativity and exact knowledge of a field (expertise). Some practitioners assume that trying the novel, breaking with the conventional, and so forth can only occur at the expense of precision, accuracy and similar properties. Others assume that creative products cannot, of necessity, meet conventional criteria of relevance, effectiveness, and so on - otherwise they would not be creative. However, this view involves a trivialization of creativity in the form of "pseudocreativity" or "quasicreativity" (see McLeod and Cropley, 1989, p. 61). Fantasy is needed, but it should be what Goethe called "exact fantasy." At the school level, creativity oriented learning is not an excuse for abandoning standards or giving up the effort to reach high levels of achievement. On the contrary, improving intelligence in the sense of this chapter incorporates such goals, but goes beyond them.

Finally, the issue of morality, ethics and the like raises itself. Most writers agree that the products of creative intelligence should be socially desirable before they can be labelled creative; otherwise, as Cropley (1982) has pointed out, it would be necessary to speak of the creativity of a burglar or a terrorist - something that most people would be unwilling to accept. In a similar vein, a number of writers call for emphasis on responsibility and concern for others in the orientation of measures aimed at fostering creativity. Otherwise, improved intelligence could foster the emergence of manipulators, white collar criminals, even dictators.

Diagnosing Creativity.   As might be expected, increasing interest in creativity saw the emergence of a new kind of test, the test of creativity. Strictly speaking, such tests had already existed for many years. Binet himself had suggested that interpretations of inkblots could be used to assess creativity and, as Barron and Harrington (1981) pointed out, there was a proliferation of studies by creativity investigators prior to 1915, adopting Binet's open ended multiple solution format. Later authors also proposed various ways of testing creativity. However, such tests had largely fallen into disuse, and were exerting little influence at the time of Guilford's address. Some psychologists (including Guilford himself) thus began to construct tests of divergent thinking - usually called creativity tests. Many of these were incorporated into the battery of tests published by Torrance (1966), nowadays referred to as the *Torrance Tests of Creative Thinking (TTCT)*. An often cited creativity test of the same period was the *Remote Associations Test* (Mednick, 1962) although this has since been criticized on the grounds that it is really a test of convergent thinking. The other influential set of creativity tests to appear during this period was that of Wallach and Kogan (1965), whose major contribution was perhaps their emphasis on a gamelike atmosphere, and the absence of time limits in the testing procedure.

The crucial difference between creativity tests and conventional intelligence tests is the way that they are scored. There is no single best or correct answer, and subjects are asked to invent answers to open ended items. In general, responses are assessed either by counting the sheer number of answers to an item (fluency), or else by assessing the degree of unusualness of answers (flexibility, originality).

A very recent creativity test is that of Urban and Jellen (1986). This test, the *Test for Creative Thinking - Drawing Production (TCP-DP)*, differs from the tests of Torrance, Guilford and Wallach and Kogan in that its scores are derived not from the statistical uncommonness of verbal or figural associations, but from what the authors call "image production." Although respondents are asked to complete incomplete figures, as in several other tests, scoring of responses is based not on statistical uncommonness of the figures created, but on nine dimensions derived from Gestalt psychology: these include, for instance, "boundary breaking", "production of new elements" and "humor . " A major difference between this approach and those discussed earlier in this section is thus that the *TCT-DP* is based on a theory of the nature of creative thinking, and that scoring procedures derive from this theory rather than simply from the quantitative and statistical characteristics of answers.

A final approach to creativity testing that can be mentioned here is that of Facaoaru (e.g., Facaoaru & Bittner, 1987). Her basic argument is that the successful carrying out of real life activities requiring creativity depends on a combination of divergent and convergent processes. For this reason, a "two track" testing procedure is needed, which assesses the "area of overlap" between the two kinds of thinking. The *Divergent-Convergent Problem Solving Processes Scale* assesses among others, "goal directed divergent thinking," "flexibility" and "task commitment."

Training Creativity.   Defining improved intelligence as encompassing not only intelligence as it is defined conventionally, but also creativity, raises the question of whether it is possible to train children to be more creative. The provision of such training would be an indispensable part of any program aimed at improving intelligence. Because creativity, as the term is used in the present paper, involves branching out from the conventional, seeing unusual implications, recognizing relationships that most people would not notice, and so forth, training designed to foster creativity would not be limited to transmission of information, but would consist on the one hand of nurturing skills, and on the other of encouraging attitudes, values, motives and self-image. Furthermore, such training need not be confined to children who have in some way demonstrated high levels of creative potential; all children are in principle capable of becoming more willing and able to be innovative and original.

A number of procedures for training creativity have been developed in the last 20 years, including both short term and long term programs. The variety of procedures that exist is illustrated by the fact that 20 years ago Treffinger and Gowan (1971) were able to describe nearly 50 different approaches. Despite reported success in the raising of test scores via such procedures, there is only limited evidence that they actually increase creativity. Rather, they seem to improve performance only on activities that closely resemble the training procedures. In a detailed review of the evidence, Rump (1979) came to the conclusion that the effects of training are at their strongest when the criterion closely resembles the training procedure, and at their weakest when this similarity is low. In the case of personality, interests and preferences, only limited effects are obtained. Consequently, it is possible to conclude that short term training procedures have little effect on general creative skills, attitudes, values, self-image and motivation. There is even a danger that creativity training procedures have the opposite effect from the desired one. For example, children can become aware in the course of training that certain kinds of behavior are preferred by the teacher, and can alter their behavior accordingly. Although children may be encouraged by the training to work hard on the various tasks presented, they can learn that it is easy to give original answers by engaging in hair splitting, giving rambling answers without regard to accuracy or relevance, or offering banalities in the name of creativity. In this way, creativity can quickly degenerate to a special form of conformity.

Torrance (1972) acknowledged that many researchers would be likely to discredit his evaluation of some 142 studies of attempts to enhance creativity. However, he still maintained that many procedures really do have a positive effect, especially those that emphasize not only cognition (getting ideas, combining information, etc.) but also affect (having the courage to try something different, wanting to reach a novel solution, etc.). As Wallach (1985) put it, the basic idea of promoting creativity by means of appropriate training procedures is by no means foolish. Unfortunately, however, simply training divergent thinking does not seem to achieve the desired results. To adapt an analogy suggested by Wallach: teaching sprinters preparing for a race how to hammer down the starting blocks is not irrelevant to their chances of running a fast time, but it can hardly be regarded as training them how to run faster. To take an actual example he mentions: students in a creative writing program practiced with divergent thinking tests for two years - at the end they were noticeably better on such tests, but their writing had hardly become more creative at all!

Improving Intelligence in Practice.   Despite the relatively short life of intensive modern interest in creativity, a considerable literature has emerged in recent years. Three main thrusts can be discerned that are of special relevance to the present discussion: the search for a definition of creativity, the attempt to design valid diagnostic instruments (mostly in the form of tests) and the design of training procedures thought likely to foster creativity. However, much of this work has led only into a blind alley. The search for a satisfactory definition of creativity has yielded a great deal of interesting material, but has still not led to a brief statement that captures the quintessence of the phenomenon in question. (In all fairness, it must be pointed out that this is a common state of affairs, not only in psychology but in all science; the subject of this whole volume, *intelligence,* has never been satisfactorily reduced to a brief, simple, universally accepted definition.)

From my point of view, the mistake lies in attempting to define a global concept of creativity in the first place. In a similar way, creativity diagnosis has not yielded a unitary line of attack that has been demonstrated to be valid - see Wallach (1985) for a recent review of the situation. Finally, as I have just shown, it has not been possible to establish that creativity training makes people creative (whatever that means).

The approaches generally adopted have yielded a great deal of important material, whose value I do not wish to denigrate here. However, they have been dominated by what Hofer (1987) called the *context* approach: tried and trusted general and basic methods and concepts in psychology have simply been applied in a new context; leading in this case to the search for a definition, the attempt to develop tests, and the trying out of training procedures. A more fruitful line of attack, however, is what he calls the *epistemological* approach: in the present context this involves recreating the phenomena that occur "in the heads" of people when they think creatively. The task of encouraging them to display intelligence improved by the appearance of the creative, or as I called it earlier, the divergent approach, then becomes that of promoting the states or activities identified by this reconstruction. A second shortcoming of conventional approaches has been that they have frequently regarded creativity as an ability.

The problem relating to the fostering of creativity can be seen, according to Richelle (1988), as that of maintaining a "system of generative viability" in the face of influences to the contrary. Without laying any claim to completeness, McLeod and Cropley (1989) have sketched out how this task could be attacked. They argue that three psychological *prerequisites* are essential for creative use of intelligence: knowledge of a field (expertise), possession of divergent abilities and skills (ability to see unexpected implications, to make connections between apparently unrelated pieces of information, etc.) and appropriate personal characteristics (willingness to take risks, confidence in oneself, task commitment, etc.). Table 15.1 contains a schematic overview.

The relevant practical question for improving intelligence in the sense described here then becomes that of the degree to which it is possible to foster the

TABLE 15.1
The Three Component Model of Practical Creativity

Component	Examples of Contents	Possibility of Faciliation
1. 'Expertise'	special talents or inborn abilities	low
	thorough knowledge of a content area, special skills	
2. Creativity related abilities and skills	general thinking skills (recognizing problems, evaluating possible alternative, etc.)	Intermediate
	special thinking skills (e.g., divergent thinking)	theoretically high
3. Personal characteristics	task commitment and courage	
	intrinsic motivation	all theoretically high
	'expectation of mastery'	

growth of these components, and how this can be done. The empirical part of the present chapter describes a number of projects carried out by my students at the University of Hamburg, which cast some light on this issue. All of the projects described focus on everyday life. They are all modest in scope and scientific rigor, but close to reality.

SOME RELEVANT STUDIES

Cognitive Games. Endriss (1982) developed a number of simple games (e.g., bridge building, idea production, transformations, creative connections), and conducted a 12 week training program with a total of 56 adults aged between 20 and 30. The purpose of these activities was to promote the development of fluency, flexibility and originality by training participants in associating, elaborating, producing, and so on. In addition, she sought to promote appropriate metacognitive skills: recognizing the problem, finding related ideas, seeing possible solution tactics, evaluating alternative approaches, and the like. Test-retest data showed that there were significant changes over time, which were not present in an untrained control group.

Craft Projects. Schwarzkopf (1981) carried out a longitudinal study with nine adult women who met once a week and worked creatively on sewing, knitting, weaving, crocheting and similar projects. Factors such as making unexpected combinations, trying out new ideas, or seeing the familiar in a new way were emphasized. At the beginning of the year each woman was rated on a number of personality traits by several relatives and close friends, who had no knowledge of the project or its intentions. At the end of the year the women were again rated and the more recent scores compared with those from a year earlier. There were significant differences in the ratings for a number of personality dimensions: in day to day life the women showed less anxiety in unfamiliar situations, were more playful, more self-critical and less cautious. They were judged to be positively motivated by the need to make difficult decisions, more independent and lively, to show more phantasy, be more goal oriented and to show more task persistence.

Coaching in Sports. Herrmann (1987) compared two soccer teams in a league for 10–12 year old boys. The one team was coached in an authoritarian way, the other democratically. Emphasis in the latter situation was on taking personal responsibility, spontaneously doing the unexpected, even having fun. The democratically trained boys produced significantly more novel elements in a creativity test as well as making a significantly larger number of cross relationships. Correlating these with data on a personality test, Herrmann concluded that the democratic training style in the sporting domain had fostered self-confidence and reduced anxiety, and these had generalized to the test domain. He also showed that the democratically trained boys made significantly more humorous responses, and concluded that the democratic soccer training style encouraged the expression of aggression in the form of humor rather than of on the field violence.

Dyslexic Students.   Stranger (1987) worked with a group of 48, 10–13 year-old boys and girls and showed that children diagnosed as dyslexic produced the same number of responses on a divergent thinking test as "normal" readers, and also showed the same degree of originality. However, there was a large and significant difference between the two groups in the area of elaboration: Dyslexic children were as capable as the members of the control group of producing novel ideas, but they were inhibited in extending and carrying through these ideas. Stranger interpreted this as reflecting the effects of lack of self-confidence and negative self-evaluation, and recommended emphasis in instruction with dyslexic children on elaborating ideas and developing personal (internal) criteria for their evaluation.

Jazz Musicians.   Scheliga (1988) tested a group of dedicated amateur jazz musicians, mainly playing in jazz cellars along the famous (or infamous) Hamburg Reeperbahn, with a paper and pencil test. They scored significantly higher than a control group of laboratory technicians on dimensions such as spontaneity, wealth of ideas, power of association, willingness to take risks, flexibility, and so on. An important conclusion by Scheliga was that latent creativity had been released by participation in music making, which offers (especially in the form of jazz improvisation) special psychological opportunities: stress on individuality, elimination of inhibitions, encouragement of phantasy, confrontation with one's own emotions, use of nonverbal forms of expression, and the like. Nonetheless, the musician must remain within a particular framework; the product must be relevant to the main musical theme; so that blind nonconventionality is not called for.

Transfer.   Of considerable importance in all these studies is the fact that a degree of *transfer* seemed to have occurred in the personal domain. However, this took the form of a mirror image of the usual creativity training procedures: a divergent way of going about a real life activity was judged to have promoted personal properties (self-confidence, phantasy, openness to new situations, etc.), whereas the conventional procedure involves attempting to train personal properties in a formal laboratory or classroom setting. This suggests that intelligence may be improved by encouraging people to attack everyday situations in a creative way, rather than by means of relatively abstract creativity training programs. From the point of view of the practical question of how to improve intelligence by promoting creativity, the argument developed here would mean that real life activities should be suffused with creativity enhancing elements: In terms of Table 15.1, fostering the development of the various prerequisites listed should be a conscious goal in, for example, school lessons, training, coaching, reviewing, and the like.

PROMOTING CREATIVITY IN SCHOOLS

To turn to the school setting, the right hand column of Table 15.1 indicates the extent that these prerequisites are amenable to promotion by teachers. Innate talents can scarcely be implanted where they are absent (although teachers may be very important for their emergence - see Bloom, 1985). Schools are well equipped for and strongly interested in passing on knowledge and specific skills, so that the prospects of fostering these are high. I have labelled the possibility of promoting divergent thinking, courage, intrinsic motivation, and so forth as only theoretically high because they are characteristics that run counter to existing school practice to such a degree that their practical facilitation is probably more difficult than theory suggests.

Although the specific studies outlined here offer some ideas about how the facilitation of these characteristics could be carried out, what is needed are general guidelines and rules for practitioners. To focus on a common practical setting, the school, Facaoaru (1985) has developed detailed guidelines on promoting creativity in the classroom through appropriate teaching materials, teaching tactics, learning methods, forms of evaluation and so forth that can be applied at all levels and in all subject areas. McLeod and Cropley (1989) have also developed general guidelines for classroom practice, which to some extent go beyond Facaoaru's suggestions, for instance by examining issues such as the position of social outgroups, physically handicapped youngsters, or ethnic minorities. Although a detailed presentation here would exceed the limits of this chapter, both these publications attack the question of how to carry out everyday teaching in a way likely to foster divergent application of intelligence. Although the final step in the case of everyday educational practice involves the design of specific, concrete contents, methods and materials, this goal is definitely within reach of appropriately informed and motivated curriculum developers.

REFERENCES

Altshuller, G. S. (1984). *Creativity as an exact science.* New York: Gordon and Breach.
Amthauer, R. (1973). *Intelligenz-Struktur Test (IST).* Goettingen: Hogrefe.
Barron, F. X. (1969). *Creative person and creative process.* New York: Holt, Rinehart and Winston.
Barron, F., & Harrington, D. M. (1981). Creativity, intelligence and personality. *Annual Review of Psychology, 32,* 439–476.

Besemer, S. B., & Treffinger, D. J. (1981). Analysis of creative products: Review and synthesis. *Journal of Creative Behaviour, 16,* 68–73.

Bloom, B. S. (1985). *Developing talent in young people.* New York: Ballantine.

Brown, R. A. (1977). Creativity, discovery and science. *Journal of Chemical Education, 5,* 720–724.

Bruner, J. S. (1967). *On knowing: Essays for the left hand.* New York: Athaneum.

Cropley, A. J. (1982). *Kreativitaet and Erziehung.* Muenchen: Reinhardt.

Dennis, W. (1960). Causes of retardation among institutional children: Iran. *Journal of Genetic Psychology, 90,* 47–59.

Endriss, L. (1982). *Entwicklung und Auswirkung eines Kreativitaetstrainings—Foerderung des spielerischen Denkens bei jungen Erwachsenen.* Unpublished master's thesis, University of Hamburg.

Facaoaru, C. (1985). Kreativitaet und schulische Leistung. *Engagement, 1,* 20–35.

Facaoaru, C., & Bittner, R. (1987). Kognitionspsychologische Ansaetze der Hochbegabungsdiagnostik. *Zeitschrift fuer differentielle und diagnostische Psychologie, 8,* 193–205.

Fox, L. H. (1981). Identification of the academically gifted. *American Psychologist, 36,* 1103–1111.

Gardner, H. (1983). *Frames of mind: The theory of multiple intelligences.* New York: Basic Books.

Getzels, J. W., & Jackson, P. W. (1962). *Creativity and intelligence.* New York: Wiley.

Guilford, J. P. (1950). Creativity. *American Psychologist, 5,* 444–454.

Herrmann, W. (1987). *Auswirkungen verschiedener Fussball-Trainingsstile auf Leistungsmotivation.* Unpublished master's thesis, University of Hamburg.

Hofer, M. (1987). Paedagogische Psychologie: Fuenf Ueberlegungen zum Selbstverstaendnis eines Faches. *Psychologische Rundschau, 38,* 82–95.

Horn, W. (1962). *Das Leistungspruefsystem.* Goettingen: Hogrefe.

Horn, J. L. (1988, August). Major issues before us now and for the next few decades. Paper presented at Seminar on Intelligence, Melbourne.

Horowitz, F. D., & O'Brien, M. (1986). Gifted and talented children: State of knowledge and direction for research. *American Psychologist, 41,* 1147–1152.

McLeod, J., & Cropley, A. J. (1989). *Fostering academic excellence.* Oxford: Pergamon.

Mednick, S. A. (1962). The associative basis of creativity. *Psychological Review, 69,* 220–232.

Meili, R. (1964). Die faktorenanalytische Interpretation der Intelligenz. *Schweizerische Zeitschrift fuer Psychologie, 23,* 135–155.

Necka, E. (1986). On the nature of creative talent. In A. J. Cropley, K. K. Urban, H. Wagner & W. H. Wieczerkowski (Eds.), *Giftedness: A continuing worldwide challenge.* New York: Trillium.

Nicholls, I. G. (1972). Creativity in the person who will never produce anything original and useful: The concept of creativity as a normally distributed trait. *American Psychologist, 27,* 717–727.

Raina, M. K. (1986). *Biochemicals and behaviour.* Delhi: Natural Council of Educational Research and Training.

Renzulli, J. S. (1984). The triad/revolving door system: A research-based approach to identification and programming for the gifted and talented. *Gifted Child Quarterly, 28,* 163–171.

Richelle, M. N. (1988, August). Variations on learning, problem solving and creativity. Paper presented at Symposium on Intelligence, Melbourne.

Rump, E. E. (1979). *Divergent thinking, aesthetic preferences and orientation towards Arts and Sciences.* Unpublished doctoral dissertation, University of Adelaide.

Sappington, A. A., & Farrar, W. E. (1982). Brainstorming v. critical judgement in the generation of solutions which conform to certain reality constraints. *Journal of Creative Behaviour, 16,* 68–73.

Schwarzkopf, D. (1981). *Selbstentfaltung durch kreatives Gestalten.* Unpublished master's thesis, University of Hamburg.

Scheliga, J. (1988). *Musik machen und die Foerderung der Kreativitat.* Unpublished master's thesis, University of Hamburg.

Skeels, H. M., & Dye, H. B. (1939). A study of the effects of differential stimulation on mentally retarded children. *Proceedings of the American Association of Mental Deficiency, 44,* 114–136.

Sternberg, R. J. (1988, August). Beyond IQ. Paper presented at Seminar on Intelligence, Melbourne.

Stranger, A. (1987). *Lese-Rechtschreibschwaeche und divergentes Denken.* Unpublished master's thesis, University of Hamburg.

Taylor, I. A. (1975). An emerging view of creative actions. In I. A. Taylor & J. W. Getzels (Eds.), *Perspectives in creativity.* Chicago: Aldine.

Torrance, E. P. (1966). *Torrance Test of Creative Thinking.* Columbus, OH: Personnel Press/Testing.

Torrance, E. P. (1972). Predictive validity of the Torrance Test of Creative Thinking. *Journal of Creative Behavior, 32,* 401–405.

Treffinger, D. J., & Gowan, I. C. (1971). An update representative list of methods and educational materials for stimulating creativity. *Journal of Creative Behavior, 6,* 236–252.

Urban, K. K., & Jellen, H. (1986). Assessing creative potential via drawing production: The Test for Creative Thinking—Drawing Production (TCT-DP). In A. J. Cropley, K. K. Urban, H. Wagner, & W. H. Wieczerkowski (Eds.), *Giftedness: A continuing worldwide challenge.* New York: Trillium.

Wallace, D. B. (1985). Giftedness and the construction of a meaningful life. In F. D. Horowitz & M. O'Brien, (Eds.), *The gifted and talented: Developmental perspectives.* Washington, D. C.: American Psychological Association.

Wallach, M. A., & Kogan, N. (1965). *Modes of thinking in young children.* New York: Holt, Rinehart and Winston.

Wallach, M. A. (1985). Creativity testing and giftedness. In F. D. Horowitz & M. O'Brien (Eds.), *The gifted and talented: Developmental perspectives.* Washington, D. C.: American Psychological Association.

16 Intelligence, Economics, and Schooling

Kevin Harris
Macquarie University

Every social formation has its own historical-cultural construction of which human capacities are desirable, and thus to be fostered and developed; as well as micro and macro economic constraints on the number and types of resources that can be directed towards formal provisions for such development.

IDEALISM AND MATERIALISM

At the very broadest level there are two distinctly identifiable approaches to educational issues and schooling practices—idealism and materialism. Idealism, with its stress on essentialism and formalism, and its concern for timeless social, moral and personal ideals, provides the background or basic presuppositions for most past and contemporary educational practice and theory. Materialism, on the other hand, is nonfoundationalist and antiformalist; and sees educational values, theories and practices as deriving from nonessential material contexts. In materialist terms things such as "education," "knowledge," "the worthwhile" and "intelligence" have no essential or formal universal timeless nature; rather they are issues to be understood and determined by analyzing particular material contexts, and the interests and needs involved therein.[1]

---

[1] Some details of the specific material context under analysis here may not be familiar to readers outside of Australia. At the time of writing this paper (March 1988 to February 1989) a number of highly significant developments were taking place with regard to the structure and financing of schooling and higher education in Australia. Of most importance was the Federal Government's proposal or "Green Paper," which in modified form is now official policy (Dawkins, 1988) for the

In practical terms this means that production of educational theory, along with establishing related practices such as the implementation of curricula, seeking certain ends, and fostering specific cognitive skills and so forth, is determined by existential conditions, social issues and problems, and the existence of interest groups, along with the level of control and influence such groups have over circumstances at any particular time. In a more extreme form of materialism - one that I adopt in this paper—economic determinants are regarded as the central and basic conditions influencing practice.

An extended example here can indicate certain differences between idealist and materialist approaches to educational issues, and also lay some useful ground for later argument. Consider, then, curriculum theory: And the relationship between school curricula and the fostering and development of intelligence.

Curriculum and the Development of Intelligence.   All knowledge might, at least prima facie, be regarded as potential curriculum content. But given that the period of formal schooling is temporarily finite, and that curricula have to select from an infinite body of knowledge, those concerned with such selection im-

---

virtual total restructuring of higher education. The four key issues are: Developing a unified system of tertiary education, producing more graduates yet maintaining or improving academic standards while resources for the higher education sector are held static, improving graduation rates, and lowering standards of entry and increasing retention rates within tertiary education. The underlying concern is unquestionably a matter of cost-efficiency, and the Minister charged with the restructuring declared quite openly that a central aim of the proposal was 'to bring higher education into line with the economic needs of the country.' A lot, of course, hangs on how those economic needs are defined and theorized.

A second major development was the canvassing of plans for, and the eventual implementation of, a "user pays" policy for higher education, thus ending a 15 year period in which the recipients of higher education had, for all intents and purposes, made no direct and immediate contribution to the cost of such education. There are now to be up-front fees, and a tax on graduates' salaries, as parts of the new Higher Education Contribution Scheme. The third major development was the series of restrictions and modifications imposed onto schooling in the State of New South Wales by the newly elected Greiner Government in its first months of office. The Premier, with some hindsight, still stands by the policies, but has admitted that they were conceived and executed too hastily and with too little consultation with affected interest groups.

All three developments were concerned, in their specific ways, with altering and rerationalizing the material context of schooling within Australian social relations, and much of the detail involved can be found in proposals and practices formulated and implemented in Britain in the last two decades. It would not be unfamiliar to American experience as well. The issues also focussed public attention on education in a way untypical in Australia. Had those behind the proposals been aware of, or felt free to espouse, the materialist account of the economy and the labour market developed in this paper, they would have otherwise, and more simply and elegantly, realized and articulated that, given the structural constraints of our present economic base and system of social relations, we can no longer provide our existing form of tertiary offerings, or a continuing emphasis on liberal studies in secondary schools.

As an illustration of how materialist analyses must focus on, and change in accordance with specific contexts, this present account might usefully be compared and contrasted with my previous application of similar methodology and central concepts to the material situation of a mere few years ago (Harris, 1984).

plicitly ask Herbert Spencer's question: "What knowledge is of most worth?" (Spencer, 1963: pp. 1–44). They might disagree strongly about the substantive content they seek to include, but they all surely believe that the particular knowledge they champion is the most important that can be included in a finite and severely limited curriculum. Spencer himself wanted education based on and around science; Matthew Arnold plumped for the humanities; M. V. C. Jeffreys envisaged a religious centre for education; F. R. Leavis saw literary criticism as the central discipline; Herbert Read sought education based on art; the Harvard Report (General Education in a Free Society - 1945) saw education as developing the logical, relational and imaginative modes of thinking; A. D. C. Peterson went for the logical, moral, empirical and aesthetic modes of experience; Cassirer and Phenix put forward other particular modes; L. A. Reid championed his "ways of knowledge and experience"; Oakeshott wanted education to tune into the voices of practical activity, science, poetry and history; and most prominently of all in recent debate P. H. Hirst saw liberal education as the development of mind, which in turn was allegedly initiation into forms of knowledge that have become differentiated out over human history (Hirst, 1974).

In all but one of the aforementioned cases the Spencerian question has been addressed from an idealist perspective, and contextualized within epistemology and metaphysics. However, as Aristotle indicated long ago in his *Politics and Ethics,* conclusions regarding what is to be studied, by whom, and to what extent, must derive from premises other than epistemological ones. Epistemological theories are simply neither necessary nor sufficient to establish conclusions about the content of education; i.e., about the curriculum, or what knowledge shall be transmitted; nor even to establish conclusions about education, or what knowledge is worthwhile, in general. Epistemology may raise issues relevant to formulating answers to such questions; but even the merest materialist consideration reveals that education, along with its curriculum, is politically determined. Formal education may be charged with transmitting knowledge, but it does this neither in a metaphysical vacuum nor in a mystical epistemological realm. Such transmission occurs nowhere else but within the material conditions of existing social relations: and education, almost in contrast to what idealist epistemologists proclaim, is a major factor in the production and legitimation of certain kinds of knowledge that serve particular ruling interests in particular societies. It is thus first and foremost a political act, and never a pure application of essentialist epistemological theory (Harris, 1979: 137–64).

Let us now connect this to the matter of "intelligence." As Hamlet well knew, human beings are infinite in faculty. They can do any number of things; and they can do each of these things along a continuum of skill level from the pathetically poor to the utterly brilliant. And, just as all knowledge might, at least prima facie, be regarded as potential curriculum content, so too might the performance of each of these things be regarded as an instance of the use of intelligence.

Western academic and philosophical traditions, however, bear a strong tendency to distinguish between physical and mental skills, and to recognize only the latter (or even only some of the latter) as displays of intelligence. These distinctions are commonly made in terms of a "mind/body" dualism; or are otherwise justified on the grounds that labelling all conscious goal-directed human behaviour intelligent, or even regarding all human activity as the exercise of intelligence, would be to render the term "intelligence" vacuous. Such distinctions, however, are idealist abstractions; and can be nothing more than arbitrary stipulations made on essentialist metaphysical grounds, or else mere tautologies relating mental skills with skills requiring or displaying intellectual activity.

A materialist approach to the issue of intelligence would avoid dualisms and essentialism, and could allow that all conscious goal-directed human behavior might be regarded as intelligent behavior (just as all knowledge is potential curriculum content). But this does not entail that all such behavior should be regarded as important or valuable, let alone equally important or valuable, or important or valuable in every social instance. What, from a materialist context, makes behavior valued, and thus to be fostered and rewarded, are (again) not metaphysical and/or essentialist criteria, but rather specific considerations of social and political utility, and the service of particular interests and needs of particular social formations. The identification, then, of valued behavior, and even the identification of intelligence itself, need be no more an application of essentialism, nor of metaphysical and/or epistemological criteria, than is the determination of curriculum content.

But there was another major reason for raising the matters of curriculum and intelligence together here. They are matters that tend to be otherwise frequently linked; in the common view that mastering particular curriculum content not only requires, but can also actually quantify the operation of intelligence. Such a claim can now be usefully identified as one of contingency, and anything but essentialist. Or, to put it slightly differently and tie some important strings together: to identify certain forms of knowledge acquisition and curriculum mastery fostered and rewarded by schools and universities as instances of the operation of intelligence, is to state a contingency established by definition, rather than to recognize an essentialist association.

Failure to realize this has had much to do with the unprofitable preservation of aspects of idealism within an historical conjuncture in which reassessment of the role of schooling in general, along with the type of human potential that might be sought and developed, is a vital requirement, and one that would be better served by other approaches.

THE CONTEMPORARY CONTEXT: IDEALIST EDUCATIONAL THEORY

As indicated earlier, most of the educational theory currently legitimated, employed, generated and taught, is idealist. Its roots are planted firmly in Platonic idealism, formalism and liberalism; and its central premises can be found in the very scheme set out in Plato's *Republic*.

There are three themes central to Plato's proposal, and the idealist liberal tradition stemming from it. One, there is the notion that real education, as distinct from things like socialization and vocational training, is a matter of cognitive struggle with particular forms of intellectually demanding content. Two, we have the idea that not everybody is equipped for or suited to this form of cognitive struggle. Real (idealist liberal) education, although on offer to everybody, is really for a naturally predisposed intellectual elite, who can be identified by testing.[2] And three, the educated are to rule the State through the just application of their acquired wisdom. Thus it was part of Plato's overall theory that there be a form of rule by intellectual merit, with schooling playing a part in determining class location. Those who succeeded best at school (the most intellectually able, as the theory would have it) were to gain social status (albeit, for Plato, without financial reward) by becoming rulers, or members of the ruling class.

Interestingly, an aspect of this last point encountered significant resistance at a time when certain conditions might have seemed to have been favoring it. In the nineteenth century Plato's unashamedly elitist social and educational theory, and his theory of human ability and intelligence (leaning heavily as it did in the direction of heredity) was under challenge by those who had attended to Voltaire, Rousseau, von Humbolt, and Mill, and were learning to speak in terms of equality, mobility, egalitarianism, and the rights and worth of all mankind. At the same time universal schooling was in the process of becoming a reality. And yet it was here that the idea of making liberal education (and consequently positions of power) available to all, was paradoxically taken as problematic.

Egalitarian programs were confronted with prevailing idealist notions of human nature, and beliefs and values concerning differing human abilities; not to mention the problem of finding and deploying the financial resources necessary for such undertakings. Fears were expressed that an attempt to universalize liberal education, however nobly conceived, might not raise the intellectual and cultural standard for all, but instead interfere with the prospects of those who were capable of benefiting in the first place, and consequently for society as a whole. And eventually the issue of providing universal liberating education, along with equal social opportunity, became reduced in to the wider issue of the growing need for schooling to incorporate multiple functions: on the one hand an educative function of providing high level intellectual fare for those who could benefit from it; whereas on the other hand an instrumental function of socializa-

---

[2]Under the scheme set out for the education of Plato's future guardians, instruction was initially offered to every citizen, both male and female. This was limited to physical and instrumental skills: But as tests proceeded to eliminate more and more of the population the content became increasingly abstract, or what might be now called "intellectual." Towards the top, intense cognitive engagement in areas considered by Plato to be most beneficial to the production and development of the wise person was being offered to the few whom it was judged could both handle and benefit from the exercise.

tion (including a minimal level of instruction in literacy, numeracy and morals) for the majority.

Liberal education discourse thus retreated from hopes of providing *universal* liberating education, to a concern to introduce intellectual pursuits to as many as possible of those who could benefit from them; and to do this in a context of compulsory schooling accommodating the entire youth population, and performing multiple social functions. Many then comfortably declared the real job of the school to be that of performing an essential intellectual-educative function as far as possible and for as many as possible; whereas at the same time providing the best of instrumentality (arguably social control) for those who could not benefit fully from the educative (intellectual, cognitive) aspect (Peters, 1966, pp. 74; 167; 252). Such a position is commonly voiced today.

The retreat was clearly in the direction of Plato. Educative activities still tend to be identified as those requiring cognitive struggle with particular intellectually demanding content; and have some special status in schools. The educated still tend to be identified as the most intellectually able who best assimilate and master the specifically intellectual content schooling offers. And finally the educated, as defined, possessing their particular cognitive skills and specific esoteric and demanding content, are proclaimed as best equipped to undertake prestigious, supposedly intellectually demanding jobs, to form opinions and have them respected, and to occupy certain privileged social positions. Conversely, those judged not intellectually gifted or suited to benefiting from the school's essential values and content, are to receive instrumental training, socialization and basic instruction, and become the modern artisans of the contemporary Republic, namely the working class in industrial capitalist society.

SCHOOLING, EDUCATION, AND INTELLIGENCE: A MATERIALIST INTERPRETATION

The above might all sound well and good, with its emphases on individual ability and effort in mastering essential valuable content, and the distribution of just deserts according to intellectual merit. But there are numerous problems involved. To begin with, it makes continued and untenable reliance on human nature to justify its observations and conclusions. Further, it conflates concrete social institutions with abstracted ideals (e.g., it conflates schooling with education, then education with intelligence, and thus presents the contingent link between "success at school" and "displaying intelligence" as a conceptual and essentialist one). But the most important problem is that it simply overlooks actual manifestations of material existence. For instance, a central factor like the increasing need for, and the actual role of schooling in, the production of a progressively deskilled and proletarianized work force (Braverman, 1974) has been ignored, or rendered unproblematic.

Basically, and central to this present analysis, idealist theory is oblivious to the matter of *production relations,* and their effects on and relationships with all aspects of material reality, including the practice and provision of schooling and education, and the exercise and valuing of human abilities. The materialist interpretation that follows here, in deliberate contrast, concentrates on these very real, if less commonly recognized, relationships. It might best begin at the point of the introduction of universal compulsory schooling itself.

Schools as an Intermediary Institution Between Family and the Labour Market. In the early nineteenth century the western world was experiencing the establishment of radically altered socialized and collectivized production processes; and along with this massive migration concentrating populations in industrial and commercial cites. As this occurred, the family unit became increasingly expelled from the production process; and consequently its informal educational function became delegitimized. A three-fold need thus arose. Reproduction of labour power had to be rationalized, in the sense of inculcating attitudes and values in future workers which, rather than being specific to performing particular jobs, were conducive to accepting and promoting certain general social and production relations. An institutionalized transition from family relations to collectivized work relations was also needed. And an alternative arena became necessary for passing on the actual skills and knowledge required by the newly collectivized workers, which the family alone could no longer provide. A single answer to all these needs was the institution of free, compulsory, universal elementary (and later secondary) schooling.

Given that the social conditions that brought about universal compulsory schooling still prevail, this form of schooling thus continues to function broadly very much as it did in the beginning - as the intermediary institution between the family and the labor market. As such it does three basic things.

First, schooling provides certain skills and knowledge required by most, if not all, future workers (e.g., literacy, numeracy), as well as socially specific highly valued esoteric skills and knowledge to a small proportion of pupils headed for specialized regions in the labor market. Second, it transmits to all future adults (with varying degrees of proficiency and success) the behaviors, values, norms and attitudes required by people occupying different positions within the existing relations of production. And third, it diverts part of the cost of producing trained and "pre-sorted" workers for the labor market from the employers to the State, or more specifically to the taxpayers.[3]

The Economic Context. The importance of the first two of those points cannot be underestimated, but it is actually the third that is of most significance

---

[3]To the extent that employers are also taxpayers, they thus also make some contribution in this regard.

here, in that it highlights schooling's place with an economic context. From the viewpoint afforded by such a context we can profitably examine the role of schools in general, as well as in fostering particular abilities and rewarding success within social formations.

Idealist liberal theory is committed to the principles that all should be educated, in the sense of achieving "the highest degree of individual development of which they are capable" (Nunn, 1921, p. 12), or having their intellectual powers extended and developed to the full, and that the central function of schooling is to get on with that educating.[4] It does not, as indicated earlier, see contemporary schooling as being exclusively concerned with such educating, nor does it expect all pupils to emerge from the schooling experience as equally educated people.

Constraints on schooling and on individual pupils (which include supposed natural constraints) are commonly recognized. But what this theoretic context fails to recognize is the economic impossibility of, in its own terms, educating everybody under existing social conditions, and the related economic absurdity (and impossibility) of having the liberal education and intellectual development it speaks of as the main business of the school. This, however, is only marginally a matter of how much money the treasury has, or how much it might desire to lay out on schooling. It can be better understood in terms of production relations, which I now examine in the context of Marx's classical identification of "productive labor" and "unproductive labor ," and the interrelation of these in political economy (Marx, 1961, 1969).

In Marx's categorization productive and unproductive labor are differentiated according to exchange relations.   Productive labor is that labor exchanged with capital to produce surplus value or profit. It is thus the very source of capital accumulation, which in turn is the basic requirement for maintaining the capitalist mode of production, and its attendant social relations. Unproductive labour, on the other hand, is exchanged with something other than capital, and does not produce surplus value. It is usually exchanged with revenue, which is largely (but not only) made up from part of the surplus produced by productive labourers, and is most commonly (but not only) manifested in taxes.

A key issue can now be recognized. Virtually the entire expenditure on State provided schooling (including higher education) comes from taxes, or, largely from a part of the surplus generated by productive labor.[5] Thus schooling is, to

---

[4]The rhetoric is commonplace and enduring. Compare the 1921 statement with this of March 1988, by the University of New South Wales in its response to the "Green Paper" (see Note 1): "Any country which is dependent for its economic (and therefore social) success on modern technological development must ensure that its citizens have the right to proceed in their education to the highest standard of which they are capable and to which they aspire."

[5]Unproductive laborers pay taxes too, but that tax revenue by definition is not part of surplus value. Tax revenue to be spent on schooling is not, of course, earmarked according to the status of its contributor, and so even though some must come from the levies on unproductive laborers it is still true to say that the expenditure on schooling comes largely (but not totally) from generated surplus value.

begin with, purely and simply a drain on surplus, and so a potential threat and impediment to capital accumulation. But the matter has been further compounded by a historical development within western capitalism, resulting in a dramatic increase in the proportion of unproductive laborers in the workforce. The tiny figure of little more than a century ago, when universal compulsory schooling began, has grown to a present day level of 40–50%. What this means is that about half the population now passing through schools will, if present production relations are maintained, engage in unproductive labor, and thus, along with the unemployed, they will not directly generate surplus value. We see, then, that since the beginnings of universal compulsory schooling an ever growing proportion of expenditure on schooling has been consumed unproductively, and has not been directed back into surplus. Thus contemporary schooling has become more than an inefficient contributor or potential threat to capital accumulation. It has in fact become an extremely serious real drain on surplus value, serious enough to generate possibly unprecedented political concern regarding its financing and restructuring in advanced capitalist societies.

Restructuring?   This drain cannot be ignored. In the interests of capital accumulation it must be offset or plugged up, either through modifications internal to the provision of schooling, or else external modifications to production relations and the financing of schooling. The most obvious internal solution would be to modify what is taken to be universal and/or compulsory schooling.

State schooling might be made non-universal by offering it to fewer people, or less universal by encouraging a drift or defection to private schools. It could be made less compulsory through measures like lowering the minimum leaving age, or making advanced attendance subject to examination success. But none of these things, all of which have actually been mooted, could be achieved comfortably in the present conjuncture (apart from the very obvious failure in Britain and Australia to discourage a drift to private schools), basically for two reasons. On the one hand, existing ideological commitment to universal compulsory schooling is extremely strong, which is testimony to the pervasiveness of idealist liberal theory. And on the other hand there are political, as well as conflicting economic needs to actually extend rather than merely maintain the present form of schooling, needs that have contributed to current proposals for restructuring the provision of tertiary education in Australia, and that have been voiced more universally regarding raising the school leaving age. (Keeping more at school and university longer, while draining capital further in this area, actually decreases other government outlays, and so acts as a minor, immediate, and highly visible short term diversion. It could have long term effects only if the eventual outcome is, as proposals seem to suggest it will be, increased productive labor.)

There is another internal possibility. Schooling expenditure could directly counteract the drain, simply by being used to enhance the basic training of future productive workers at school. If this were done, workers would require less training elsewhere, and their future productivity would offset not just the drain but also the increased cost of their reproduction (schooling is getting dearer to provide). But once again so simple and obvious a solution turns out to be less simple and less easy to effect than it might at first seem.

Two things stand in its way. First, what would suffer most would be the liberal and educative function of schooling, namely that aspect of schooling related to education, and to fostering and developing what are taken to be cognitive skills and intelligence. The result would be a very marked and serious divorce between a historically established continuing rationale for the role of schools in fostering intelligence and promoting "the highest degree of individual development" of each child, and actual practice that would elevate and promote the instrumental function of schooling as the norm. Second, because the specific problem is not that of merely reducing a drain, but of reducing a drain brought about largely through schooling so many future unproductive workers, such a restructuring could only succeed if a large majority of pupils were heading for productive labour: and whereas that may have been the situation when universal compulsory schooling was first instituted, at the present moment, as we have seen, this is no longer the case.

The growth in the numbers of these future potential unproductive laborers raises a closely related complication. In the way in which labor relations have become historically constructed, it is the unproductive labourers who have tended to stay on longest at school, engage with the cognitive intellectual pursuits, and whose production is regarded and displayed as the paradigm instance of the school performing an educative function for society. To fail to concentrate on this area, and/or to crudely redirect school resources to increase productivity by decreasing the number of unproductive laborers, would again focus unwelcome emphasis on the instrumental function of schooling.

It would appear, then, that the answer might not lie simply in an internal modification of schooling directed towards producing fewer unproductive workers. But much the same economic effect can be achieved externally. Trivial (if tangible) results can be achieved by any of the increasingly proliferating schemes presently under consideration or use, which offer variations on the "user pays" principle. Having pupils pay for their own schooling, either through voucher systems, loans, fees, or a tax on their future salaries, clearly requires less input from, and thus less drain on, capital. But there are dangers and counter-productive tendencies in such schemes. A much more significant and global effect can be achieved by modifying production relations themselves in order to redirect present unproductive labor back into the realm of productivity.

Such modification has been taking place gradually within advanced capitalism over the last two decades. It has, however, suddenly gained pace dramatically in places like Britain and Australia through a practice once considered unthinkable by many, namely privatization. Under privatization the State sells off certain institutions and functions, such as the railways, the telephone and postal systems, and so forth to private enterprise, and whatever else it might achieve by this move, it also changes the status of the labor involved.   Labor provided and paid for by the State, necessarily out of revenue, is by definition unproductive, and privatization immediately ensures that most of the same labor will now be paid for out of surplus, and thus become productive. The State, however, cannot privatize its own civil or public service (although this too is actually being mooted, and there have even been calls in Australia for the privatization of schools). The most the State can do in this regard is minimize its services and administration, but it cannot totally relieve itself of unproductive labor.   The question that must now be considered, given that materialist accounts have to take note of, and be continually modified in terms of changing historical conditions, is how the once gradual and now rapidly accelerating redirection of labor from the unproductive to the productive realm will impinge on the role of schools, and particularly their educative function.

From Unproductive to Productive Labor.   Basically, if capital accumulation is to continue with minimal political and theoretical disruption and disjunction concerning both education and the role of the State as provider in general, we could expect to see an interactive application of all the possible solutions noted earlier. Our schools' growing expenditure on both productive and unproductive labour is most likely to be offset by increasing the return from expenditure on present productive labor, as well as by making present unproductive labour more productive in the future (O'Connor, 1973; Harris, 1982).

The effects of these moves are already evident in schools (and in Australia and Britain particularly, in government proposals and newly implemented policies). Discipline, or socialization and behavior control, has reemerged as a major issue that schools are becoming increasingly required to be concerned with. In addition to this, concentration in schools has again been directed, and almost daily becomes increasingly directed, to transmission of the "basics," i.e., those skills required by all future workers, and that tend to be viewed instrumentally rather than as manifestations of intellectual excellence, let alone "the highest degree of development" that people are capable of. And the open emphasis on the role of schooling in job orientation and preparation is also growing daily, commonly rationalized by the absurd claim that having pupils learn marketable skills in school will make a significant contribution to overcoming unemployment. Schools (and universities) are coming under increasingly centralized control (from governments paradoxically bent on privatization, and which claim to promote decentralization and free market monetarism). They are being asked, and forced, to "cut out the frills," which tends to mean reducing both the breadth of options offered, and the number of liberal options offered, and instead to direct effort towards making pupils employable, more so now at the productive level. And finally, State funding has been massively redirected away from the public sector, (and in the process withdrawn from schools, thus resulting in larger classes, fewer resources, less options etc.); while within the public sector itself funding has been directed away from liberal arts programs towards centrally selected vocational and technical programs.

Thus at one and the same time valued abilities are being redefined, and the entire schooling system is being asked to produce greater numbers of modified ideal end-products, all with less direct input from capital. The eventual graduates, irrespective of whether the numbers at the higher end will increase or not, will have neither the form nor the level of general intellectual development that we have traditionally expected, or which idealist theory advocates. And so, although idealist theory still dominates in academia, and other marginal places, and still infiltrates educational policy statements in a rationalized way, economic reality, which is now more at odds with such theory than it ever has been, determines, as it always has, the ongoing practices of schooling. Idealist theory has, of course, always been at odds with material reality, and what has changed historically have been the terms (such as the recent issue of privatization), the playing out, and the rationalization of the conflict, rather than the conflict itself. So, to tie up this particular argument it would be well to direct further attention to the contemporary situation regarding schooling and productive and unproductive labor.

Schooling and Productive Labor.   If we relate productive and unproductive labor to years and type of schooling, productive laborers (like Plato's artisans) generally, but by no means universally, are the first to drop out, most commonly at or very near the point where legal compulsion ceases. They are also the ones who swim in lower streams and/or do the more vocationally oriented courses in schools. They have traditionally been regarded as less intelligent, and more suited to doing practical courses rather than cognitive studies. On the other hand, unproductive laborers generally, although again not universally, do more schooling in higher streams, undertake more "intellectual" studies, attend beyond the point of legal compulsion, and need higher certificates (which ostensibly require higher intelligence to obtain, and are regarded as indicators of possession of such intelligence) in order to get their particular jobs. This is, and will continue to be the case, for civil servants and most future government officials and administrators, who will remain unproductive laborers, whereas it is less often the case for those laborers who will be made productive by privatization.

Now the type and content of schooling encountered by future unproductive laborers does, at least in the later years, begin to cohere with idealist liberal educational theory and contingent definitions of intellectual achievement, just as it is the case that this theory has always been more in harmony with the particular production, as in the past, of a small highly schooled, supposedly intellectually superior social elite. Thus, with more and more staying on longer at school, and in a situation that from one aspect suggests (if we ignore the economic relations imbedded in privatization) that increasing numbers are heading for unproductive labor, it could appear on the surface that idealist theory regarding education and intellectual development is becoming more and more compatible with schooling practice. It is, however, the reverse of this common illusion that is actually the case. There is a general point to be considered here as well as a historically specific one.

The general point is one of basic economics and has been touched on before, namely that globally, production of unproductive laborers must at least be counterbalanced by the production, at minimal cost, of productive laborers equipped for increased productivity. The brutal fact to emerge from this is that the success schooling will actually have in turning children into unproductive laborers (which, regardless of privatization in some areas, it must continue to do), in fostering intellectual development according to classical idealist notions, or in actually putting the principles of idealist liberal theory into practice, must be at least balanced by the production of more productive workers. The production of the former impels the production of the latter. Children elevated or directed into unproductive levels, or educated in the cognitive/intellectual sense, (and they are not necessarily the most able, even within the definitional set that links success at school with intelligence) are so elevated, developed, directed, or educated at the expense of others who must, at the very basic level of economics, see the ideals of liberation and liberalism evaporate before them. The end result can be nothing less than massive increasing global wastage of human resources and potential.

The historically specific point is concerned with changing production relations. When universal compulsory schooling began, only a small proportion of unproductive laborers was required, and schooling came to be seen as doing its job if it fulfilled liberal educative ideals for a minority while offering literacy, numeracy, and sound moral values to the rest. "Education for all" (with its specific contingently defined intellectual development) was rationalized as a hope for the future. Changing production relations, allied with economic expansion, however, resulted in an acceleration in practice. The ranks of the unproductive laborers swelled, people stayed on at school longer to better themselves, education did become a significant means towards social advancement, and more of this education was offered to more and more people (the zenith of this process produced the current generation of senior academics, researchers and educational administrators).

But economic expansion not merely stumbled, as it occasionally does. Rather the western world moved into its present contractive phase, in which less unproductive laborers are required, and where, in the interests of capital accumulation the work of more of those still remaining has to be rechanneled into the productive sector. The present situation, then, is that although idealist notions still linger, and are championed by those recently well served by them, and although schools and teachers will continue to assist in the education of unproductive labourers, the number and proportion of these laborers is highly likely to decrease, and their required skill level and intellectual development (as classically defined) will certainly decrease. As privatization gathers pace it is most likely that entrepreneurs will continue the existing trend of taking on, directly or indirectly, the narrow, specialized intellectual instruction of their most skilled functionaries, and leave schools with the task of socialization and basic training of the largest body of newly defined productive labor. And even if there is to be an increased number of university graduates, as so many governments' proposals for restructuring higher education want to insist there will be, then, as indicated earlier, these people are unlikely to possess either the type or level of intellectual development and excellence traditionally promoted by idealist theory.

The overall situation, expressed in more familiar if unpalatable terms, is that State schooling (at all levels) will be required to exercize more social control, engage in further instrumental functions, and educate fewer people less well. Its role in promoting traditionally valued liberal cognitive pursuits, and fostering what are commonly regarded as intellectual virtues and excellences, will seriously and markedly decline.

CONCLUSION

Advanced corporate capitalism in a late contractive phase cannot coexist easily with universal liberal education because the latter is not well suited to provide the very workforce and system of social and production relations necessary to maintain the former. There is no doubt that our schools and institutions of higher education will continue to produce higher and higher skilled functionaries displaying perhaps inconceivably high levels of intellectual development—but increasingly there will be proportionately fewer of them.[6] On the other hand, the need for more and continually deskilled productive labor will result in undeveloped and unrealized human potential, and increasingly greater proportional wastage of human resources.

This trend, and the wastage accompanying it, is hardly likely to be stemmed or reversed, even by the most well meaning of educators, while idealist liberal educational theory continues to prevail within the context of advanced corporate capitalism. Such a conjunction is a recipe for making schooling a living contradiction, stumbling from crisis to crisis while the wastage of human potential

---

[6]There may also be proportionately less employment opportunities for them. Australian Bureau of Statistics (1987) figures show that although more people are gaining higher educational qualifications, an increasing proportion of them are either out of work and/or on the dole. Of Australians aged 15 years and over, 36.6% had post-school qualifications (psq). Of those with psq 75.6% participate in the workforce (i.e., only 3 in 4 seek work); and the unemployment rate within those seeking work is 5.3%, against the national figure of 9.1%. That, taken alone, seems very promising. However, 25.8% of the total unemployed have psq (and 5 out of 8 of those have a degree, certificate or diploma). This is an increase of almost 2% over the last 5 years. In rough terms 1 out of 3 Australians over age 15 has psq. whereas 1 out of 4 Australians over 15 on the dole has psq.

grows daily. If the trend is to be properly understood, and then possibly reversed, it will not be through trying harder to implement idealist theory regarding intellectual development in schools. What would be required, at the least, would be continued refinement of constructions relating to desirable human development, along with fundamental reconstruction of socioeconomic contents in which human potential actually could be fully valued and fostered.

One cannot prophesy what those constructions and contexts will look like, as their forms will be contingent on and shaped by historical development. But whatever the specific form, the task of achieving universal human liberation, remains—and the development and progress towards that end, like all social development, will be the result basically of human labor, whether or not that labor be practical or theoretical. It is thus unarguably in the interest of the whole of humanity that the full potentialities of human labor be continually fostered and extended. This in turn requires a commitment to developing, fostering and extending our human capacity to labor: that is, our potential to learn, to acquire skills and abilities, and to act creatively and constructively. If "intelligence" were reconceptualized in materialist terms relating to the human capacity for labor, and if schools sought to promote the development of this "intelligence" for the purpose of liberation, debate on details of substance, along with the achievement of tangible results, might proceed more profitably than it has in the past.

REFERENCES

Australian Bureau of Statistics (1987). *Labour force status and educational attainment*. Cat. No. 6235.0.

Braverman, H. (1974). *Labour and monopoly capital*. London: Monthly Review Press.

Dawkins, J. S. (1988). *Higher education: A policy statement*. Canberra: Australian Government Printing Service. Cat. No. 88 1089 6.

Harris, K. (1979). *Education and knowledge*. London: Routledge & Kegan Paul.

Harris, K. (1982). *Teachers and classes*. London: Routledge & Kegan Paul.

Harris, K. (1984). Teachers: Grist for the Laurentian millstones. *Education Research and Perspectives, 11*, 34–51.

Hirst, P. H. (1974). *Knowledge and the curriculum*. London: Routledge & Kegan Paul.

Harvard University. Committee on the Objectives of a General Education in a Free Society. (1945). *General education in a free society: report of the Harvard Committee*. Cambridge, MA: Harvard University Press.

Marx, K. (1961). *Capital*. Vol. 1, Moscow: Progress Press.

Marx, K. (1969). *Theories of surplus value*. Part 1, Moscow: Progress Press.

Nunn, T. P. (1921). *Education: Its data and first principles*. London: Edward Arnold.

O'Connor, J. (1973). *The fiscal crisis of the state*. New York: St Martins Press.

Peters, R. S. (1966). *Ethics and education*. London: George Allen & Unwin.

Spencer, H. (1963). *Essays on education*. London: J. M. Dent & Sons.

Author Index

A

Abate, R. J., 204, 211, 220, 223, 224
Abelson, R., 191, 201
Ackerman, P. L., 99, 111, 116, 125, 126, 141, 208, 222
Alderton, D. L., 203, 204, 206, 209, 210, 211, 212, 216, 221, 222, 223, 224
Allport, D. A., 126, 131, 132, 135, 138, 139, 141
Altshuller, G. S., 271, 278
Amthauer, R., 268, 278
Anderson, J. A., 134, 135, 141, 142
Anderson, J. E., 111, 112, 116
Anderson, J. R., 59, 74, 81, 93
Ashcraft, M. H., 81, 93
Ashlock, R. B., 81, 93
Atkinson, J. R., 127, 129, 142

B

Bainbridge, L., 242
Baisden, R. H., 174, 181
Baltes, P. B., 98, 117
Barron, F. X., 270, 271, 272, 278
Bartlett, F., 47, 55
Beaumont, J. G., 174, 179
Belmont, J. M., 187, 200
Bennett, F. K., 205, 207, 208, 222
Berg, C. A., 77, 95
Berman, M., 3, 17
Bernstein, R. J., 3, 9, 17
Besemer, S. B., 271, 279
Beveridge, E., 71, 74

Biggs, J. B., 60, 61, 64, 65, 68, 69, 74, 75
Bigler, E. D., 178, 179
Binet, A., 57, 74, 184, 200
Bittner, R., 273, 279
Blade, M. F., 208, 222
Bliezner, R., 98, 117
Bloom, B. S., 278, 279
Bloom, F. E., 174, 179
Bobbit, B. L., 203, 223
Bobrow, D. G., 124, 131, 144
Bolter, J. E., 175, 179
Boring, E. G., 77, 93
Borke, H., 60, 75
Borkowski, J. G., 127, 142
Boud, D., 71, 75
Bracken, B. A., 178, 179
Braden, W., 145, 147, 161
Brahlek, R. E., 208, 244
Bramble, W. J., 123, 142
Bransford, J. D., 79, 95
Braverman, H., 286, 295
Brinkmann, E. H., 207, 208, 222
Broadbent, D., 240, 243
Broadbent, M., 240, 243
Broadhurst, P. L., 145, 160
Brown, A. L., 79, 92, 93, 127, 129, 142, 187, 200
Brown, F. R., 208, 222
Brown, P., 206, 213, 224
Brown, R. A., 270, 279
Bruner, J. S., 62, 71, 72, 75, 80, 93, 271, 279
Bryant, N. R., 127, 129, 142
Bullock, D., 60, 67, 68, 95

297

Burke, R. J., 36, 45
Burns, M. S., 79, 95
Burt, C., 150, 151, 152, 155, 160
Butterfield, E. C., 5, 17, 187, 200

C

Caharack, G., 126, 142
Caley, M. T., 2, 18
Campione, J. C., 79, 93, 127, 129, 142, 187, 200
Capra, F., 2, 3, 8, 17
Carpenter, P. A., 204, 206, 223
Carroll, J. B., 104, 116, 123, 128, 142, 183, 200, 203, 205, 222, 223, 228, 243
Carter, P., 212, 224
Carter-Saltzman, L., 20, 33
Case, R., 60, 61, 62, 67, 75
Cattell, R. B., 13, 17, 98, 115, 116, 120, 123, 133, 136, 138, 142, 157, 160, 185, 195, 201
Ceci, S. J., 72, 75
Chase, W. G., 189, 201
Chelune, G. J., 178, 179
Chen, K., 99, 100, 101, 103, 117
Chi, M. T. H., 50, 55, 59, 75, 189, 201
Chipman, S., 59, 75
Christensen, A. L., 175, 179
Church, M., 125, 142
Cicerone, K. D., 175, 176, 179
Clark, C. M., 177, 179
Cohen, J., 216. 223
Cohen, R. L., 129, 142
Cole, M., 6, 17, 78, 93, 197, 201
Collis, K. G., 60, 61, 64, 65, 68, 74, 75
Commons, M. C., 64, 75
Cooper, L. A., 187, 201, 205, 207, 211, 223, 225
Corballis, M. C., 112, 116
Cosden, M. A., 80, 88, 94
Crawford, J. D., 122, 127, 130, 142
Cronbach, L. J., 111, 116, 203, 223
Cropley, A. J., 269, 271, 272, 275, 278, 279

D

Dailey, J. T., 208, 223
Damasio, A. R., 175, 178, 179
Darrow, C., 64, 76
Das, J. P., 163, 166, 169, 171, 172, 175, 176, 177, 178, 179, 180
Davidson, J. E., 36, 39, 40, 46, 192, 201, 202
Davis, E. J., 81, 94
de Lemos, S., 125, 142
Dean, R. S., 174, 177, 180
Delclos, V. R., 79, 95
Demetriou, A., 58, 60, 64, 75
Dennis, W., 268, 279
diSessa, A. A., 250, 265
Dessart, D. J., 81, 95
Detterman, D. K., 13, 17, 77, 95, 163, 181
Dickinson, D. K., 88, 94
Dodds, A., 64, 76
Dodson, J. D., 145, 161
Doerner, D. C., 227, 235, 240, 243, 244
Donaldson, G., 203, 223
Donaldson, M., 60, 75
Driver, R., 71, 75
Dye, H. B., 268, 280

E

Easley, J., 71, 75
Edelman, G. M., 24, 32
Edwards, W., 45
Efklides, A., 58, 60, 64, 75
Egan, K., 63, 75
Ellis, N. R., 129, 142
Embretson, S. E., 203, 208, 209, 223
Endriss, L., 176, 179
Erickson, E., 64, 75
Erickson, F., 6, 7, 17
Eysenck, H. J., 123, 140, 142, 157, 160
Eysenck, M. W., 136, 142
Eysenck, S. B. G., 157, 160

F

Facaoaru, C., 273, 278, 279
Farha, M., 208, 209, 220
Farr, M., 50, 55
Farr, S., 204, 211, 216, 223, 224
Farrar, W. E., 271, 279
Feng, C., 213, 225
Fensham, P., 71, 75
Ferguson, G. A., 98, 105, 116
Ferguson, W., 178, 179
Ferrara, R. A., 79, 92, 93, 94
Feuerstein, R, 79, 94
Fischer, K., 60, 61, 62, 67, 68, 75, 220
Fischer, S. C., 220, 223
Fitzgerald, P., 240, 243
Flavell, J. H., 187, 201
Fleishman, E. A., 110, 116, 208, 224
Fogarty, G., 125, 142
Fox, L. H., 270, 279
Fraisse, P., 30, 32
Frick, R. W., 204, 211, 216, 223
Funke, J., 227, 233, 234, 243

G

Gallistel, C. R., 49, 56
Gardner, H., 58, 62, 63, 64, 75, 125,
    126, 132, 139, 142, 269, 299
Gardner, M. K., 188, 191, 195, 202,
    203, 225
Gastel, J., 192, 194, 202
Gault, A., 151, 161
Gay, J., 197, 201
Gazzaniga, M. S., 174, 180
Gelman, R., 49, 56
Gergen, K., 5, 17
Getzels, J. W., 269, 279
Ghiselli, E. E., 203, 223
Gilbert, J., 71, 95
Glaser, R., 47, 50, 53, 55, 56, 59, 75,
    128, 187, 201, 203, 223, 224
Glick, J., 197, 201
Goldman, S. R., 77, 79, 80, 81, 82, 83,
    84, 87, 88, 94, 203, 222

Gopher, D., 126, 132, 138, 144
Gowan, I. C., 273, 280
Greeno, J. G., 189, 201
Guba, E. G., 2, 9, 11, 17
Guilford, J. P., 120, 142, 185, 201, 268,
    279
Gunstone, R., 69, 75
Guttman, L., 121, 142

H

Hadamard, J., 63, 76
Hagen, E. P., 184, 202
Hagtvet, K. A., 43, 45
Haider, H., 227, 239, 240, 243
Haier, R. J., 145, 147, 161
Halford, G. S., 60, 61, 67, 76
Hannay, H. J., 174, 180
Harkness, S., 198, 202
Harrington, D. M., 270, 272, 278
Harris, K., 283, 291, 295
Hawkins, H. L., 125, 142
Heath, S. B., 198, 201
Hebb, D. O., 135, 142, 146, 161
Heemsbergen, D. B., 172, 180
Hempel, E. E., Jr., 110, 116
Hendrickson, D. E., 147, 161
Hermann, W., 276, 279
Heron, J., 10, 17
Hess, W. R., 167, 180
Hesse, F. W., 228, 243
Hesse, M., 3, 17
Hicks, R., 134, 143
Hine, M. A., 88
Hine, M. S., 80, 94
Hinton, G. E., 134, 142
Hirst, P. H., 283, 295
Hirst, W., 126, 142, 144
Hoemann, J. J., 228, 240, 243
Hofer, M., 275, 279
Hofstadter, L., 174, 179
Horn, J. L., 104, 116, 117, 120, 123,
    125, 126, 139, 142, 201,268, 269,
    279
Horn, W., 268, 279

Horowitz, F. D., 269, 279
Hughes, O. L., 130, 143
Humphreys, L. G., 97, 117, 143
Hunt, E. B., 123, 124, 125, 127, 128, 137, 138, 143, 187, 195, 201, 203, 204, 206, 211, 215, 216, 220, 223, 224, 241, 242, 243
Hunt, J. McV., 68, 76

J

Jackson, P. W., 269, 279
Jacob, E., 2, 6, 11, 17
Jaeger, A. O., 240, 243
Jantsch, E., 3, 17
Jarman, R. F., 166, 169, 175, 176, 177, 180
Jellen, H., 272, 280
Jenkinson, J. C., 122, 143
Jensen, A. R., 97, 117, 122, 123, 129, 139, 140, 143, 188, 195, 201, 203, 223
Jensen, M. R., 79, 94
Johnsen, T. B., 43, 45
Johnson, M., 2, 17
Jones, M. B., 111, 117
Joreskog, K. G., 172, 180
Jung, C. G., 64, 76
Just, M. A., 204, 206, 223

K

Kahneman, D., 124, 131, 134, 135, 143
Kail, R. V., 204, 206, 212, 224
Kaniel, S., 79, 94
Kantowitz, B. H., 131, 144
Keating, D. P., 203, 223
Keele, J., 128, 143
Keil, F. C., 49, 56, 189, 201
Kerr, B., 131, 143
Ketron, J. L., 188, 202
Kinsbourne, M., 133, 134, 143
Kirby, J. R., 166, 169, 171, 175, 176, 180

Kirby, N. H., 128, 144
Klein, E., 64, 76
Kluwe, R. H., 227, 233, 236, 239, 240, 243, 244
Knight, J. L., 131, 144
Knox, A. B., 64, 76
Kogan, N., 272, 280
Kosslyn, S. M., 206, 207, 213, 223
Krause, A., 127, 142
Krengel, M., 145, 147, 161
Kreuzig, H. W., 227, 232, 238, 239, 243
Kuhn, D., 64, 75
Kuhn, T. S., 2, 5, 17
Kyllonen, P. C., 207, 224

L

Lachman, J., 5, 17
Lachman, R., 5, 17
Lajoie, S., 53, 56
Lakoff, G., 2, 17
Lansman, M., 124, 125, 137, 138, 143, 203, 223
Lashley, K. S., 167, 180
Lather, P., 10, 11, 17
Laughery, K. R., 130, 143
Lautrey, J., 30, 32
Lave, J., 6, 18
Lawrence, J., 64, 76
Lazerson, A., 174, 179
Ledbetter, M. F., 172, 180
Lesgold, A. M., 53, 56
Leshan, L., 3, 9, 17
Levine, J. M., 208, 224
Levinson, D., 64, 76
Levinson, H., 64, 76
Lewandowski, L. J., 175, 180
Lezak, M. D., 133, 143
Lidz, C. S., 79, 86, 94
Liker, J., 72, 75
Likert, R., 205, 224
Lincoln, Y. S., 2, 9, 11, 17
Lindman, H., 45

Lohman, D. F., 121, 143, 188, 201, 204, 205, 206, 207, 224
Long, C. J., 175, 179
Lord, M. F., 234, 243
Lubart, T. I., 195, 202
Luchins, A. S., 36, 41, 45
Luer, G., 228, 240, 244
Luria, A. R., 164, 165, 166, 168, 174, 175, 178, 180
Lynn, R., 151, 161

M

MacLeod, C. M., 187, 201
Magoun, H. W., 146, 161
Maier, N. R. F., 36, 45
Manis, J., 6, 17
Margenau, H., 3, 9, 17
Marshalek, B., 121, 143
Marton, F., 69, 76
Marx, K., 288, 295
Matarazzo, J. D., 128, 143
Mathews, N. N., 187, 201
Mayer, R., 189, 201
McArdle, J. J., 102, 117
McClelland, J. L., 134, 144
McDonald, R. P., 100, 112, 117
McDonald, T. P., 204, 211, 220, 223
McGee, M. G., 205, 206, 224
McKee, B., 64, 76
McLoed, J., 269, 271, 275, 278, 279
Meadows, S., 60, 76
Mednick, S. A., 272, 279
Mehler, J., 20, 32
Meili, R., 268, 279
Meltzer, B. N., 6, 17, 18
Mertz, D. L., 81, 84, 94
Messick, S., 10, 18
Misiak, C., 227, 239, 240, 243, 244
Mitchell, S. R., 220, 223
Moehle, K., 178, 179
Monty, R. A., 130, 143
Moray, N., 130, 143, 236, 244
Morgan, G. M., 11, 12, 18
Moruzzi, G., 146, 161

Mounoud, P., 60, 61, 62, 67, 76
Mumaw, R. J., 206, 207, 212, 213, 223, 224
Muthig, K., 262, 265

N

Naglieri, J. A., 163, 172, 177, 179, 180
Navon, D., 132, 138, 144
Necka, E., 271, 279
Neisser, U., 126, 142, 144, 236, 244
Nettlebeck, T., 128, 144
Newell, A., 232, 244
Neyman, C. A., 208, 223
Nicholls, I. G., 270, 279
Norman, D. A., 124, 129, 144
Norris, D. R., 236, 244
Novick, M. R., 234, 243
Nunn, T. P., 288, 295

O

O'Brien, M., 269, 279
O'Connor, J., 291, 295
Ogilvy, J., 2, 18
Oleron, P., 20, 32
Opwis, K., 227, 244
Osborne, R., 71, 75

P

Pachella, R. G., 206, 224
Paivio, A., 70, 76
Pavlov, L. P., 164, 180
Pellegrino, J. W., 77, 79, 81, 84, 94, 128, 144, 203, 204, 206, 209, 210, 211, 212, 213, 216, 220, 222, 223, 224
Peters, R. S., 286, 295
Petras, J. W., 6, 18
Phillips, L. D., 45
Piaget, J., 30, 32, 59, 62, 76, 80, 94
Picciotto, H., 263, 265
Pieron, H., 30, 32
Pipp, S., 61, 75

Polkinghorne, D., 11, 18
Poltrock, S. E., 206, 213, 224, 242, 243
Popkewitz, T. S., 2, 18
Popper, K. R., 31, 32
Post, T., 52, 56
Powell, J. S., 24, 33, 189, 190, 202,
  228, 236, 244
Pressley, M., 81, 94
Pribram, K. H., 134, 144, 166, 180
Prigogine, I., 2, 3, 9, 18, 28, 32
Putz-Osterloh, W., 228, 240, 241, 244

Q

Quasha, W. H., 205, 224

R

Raaheim, A., 44, 46
Raaheim, K., 36, 39, 40, 42, 43, 44, 45,
  46, 191, 201
Raina, M. K., 268, 279
Ramsden, P., 69, 76
Rand, Y., 79, 94
Ranucci, E. R., 208, 224
Raven, J. C., 205, 224
Reaves, C. C., 126, 142
Rees, E., 59, 75
Regian, J. W., 204, 206, 212, 224
Reichert, U., 240, 244
Renzulli, J. S., 271, 279
Resnick, L. B., 58, 76, 187, 201, 203,
  224
Reynolds, L. T., 6, 18
Richards, F. A., 64, 75
Richelle, M. N., 25, 26, 30, 32, 59, 275,
  279
Rifkin, B., 187, 202
Ringelband, O., 227, 239, 240, 243,
  244
Roberts, C. R., 236, 244
Roberts, J. K. A., 178, 181
Robinson, D. L., 145, 147, 148, 149,
  153, 154, 155, 156, 161
Roediger, H. L., 131, 144

Rogoff, B., 6, 18
Rueda, R., 87, 94
Rumelhart, D. E., 134, 144
Rump, E. E., 273, 279
Russell, E. W., 175, 181

S

Sadawa, D., 2, 18
Saljo, R., 69, 76
Salter, W., 237, 244
Samuels, I., 146, 151, 161
Sandberg, T., 129, 142
Sappington, A. A., 271, 279
Sattler, J. M., 184, 202
Scarr, S., 20, 33
Schaie, K. W., 64, 76
Schank, R., 189, 191, 201
Scheliga, J., 277, 279
Schenk, S. M., 69, 76
Schneider, W., 105, 117, 125, 126, 141,
  144
Schulman D., 208, 224
Schwarzkopf, D., 276, 279
Schweiker, H., 262, 265
Scribner, S., 6, 17, 58, 72, 76
Seashore, H. G., 205, 207, 222
Segal, J., 59, 75
Sharp, D. W., 197, 201
Shepard, R. N., 205, 213, 225
Shiffrin, R. M., 105, 117, 126, 127,
  129, 142, 144
Shrager, J., 81, 94
Shute, V. J., 206, 224
Siegler, R. S., 81, 94, 187, 201
Silvern, L., 60, 61, 75
Simmelhag, V. L., 29, 33
Simon, H. A., 52, 56, 189, 201
Simon, T., 57, 74, 184, 200
Skeels, H. M., 268, 280
Skinner, B. F., 29, 33
Snow, R. E., 111, 116, 121, 143, 144,
  188, 201
Snyder, C. A., 236, 244
Sorbom, D., 172, 180

Spada, H., 227, 244
Spear, L. C., 195, 201
Spearman, C., 119, 124, 137, 144, 150, 155, 161, 184, 185, 201
Spelke, E. S., 126, 142, 144
Spencer, H., 283, 295
Sperry, R. W., 174, 181
Staddon, J. E., 29, 33
Stankov, L., 98, 99, 100, 101, 103, 104, 114, 117, 122, 125, 126, 142, 144
Stengers, I., 2, 3, 9, 18, 28, 32
Sternberg, R. J., 20, 24, 33, 35, 36, 37, 39, 40, 46, 57, 58, 59, 76, 77, 95, 97, 117, 127, 128, 144, 163, 181, 183, 187, 188, 189, 190, 191, 192, 194, 195, 197, 198, 201, 202, 203, 225, 228, 232, 235, 236, 237, 244, 271, 280
Stevens, J. J., 172, 180
Stranger, A., 277, 280
Stringer, P., 208, 225
Strohschneider, S. 233, 234, 244
Super, C. M., 198, 202
Suydam, M. N., 81, 95
Sverko, B., 125, 144

T

Taub, H. A., 130, 143
Taylor, I. A., 271, 280
Thomas, M., 228, 240, 243
Thorndike, R. L., 184, 202
Thurstone, L. L., 120, 144, 185, 202, 205, 225
Thurstone, T. G., 205, 225
Torgesen, J. K., 2, 18
Torrance, E. P., 274, 280
Treffinger, D. J., 271, 279, 280
Tupper, D. E., 175, 176, 179
Tyler, L. E., 59, 76
Tzuriel, D., 79, 94

U

Urban, K. K., 272, 280

V

Valle, R. S., 4, 9, 18
Van Rossum, E. J., 69, 76
van Parreren, C., 81, 95
Varnhagen, C. K., 163, 180
Vemouri, V., 228, 244
Vernon, P. A., 144, 178, 181
Vernon, P. E., 120, 195, 202
Volet, S., 64, 76
Voss, J., 52, 56
Vye, N. J., 79, 95
Vygotsky, L. S., 6, 18, 68, 76, 78, 80, 87, 95, 192, 202

W

Wagner, R. K., 57, 58, 59, 76, 195, 198, 202
Wallace, D. B., 269, 280
Wallach, M. A., 271, 274, 280
Walsh, K. W., 133, 144, 176, 178, 179, 181
Wambold, C., 187, 200
Washbon, C. A., 81, 93
Watkins, D. A., 69, 76
Watson, W. S., 208, 222
Waugh, N. C., 129, 144
Weil, E. M., 188, 202
Wesman, A. G., 205, 207, 222
White, P. O., 123, 144
White, R. T., 69, 75
White, R. W., 68, 76
Whitely, S. E., 203, 225
Wickens, C. D., 107, 117, 125, 131, 132, 134, 136, 141, 144
Williams, D., 145, 147, 161
Willis, S. L., 98, 117
Wilson, G., 151, 161
Wittenborn, T. R., 126, 130, 140, 144
Wolf, F. A., 3, 18
Wolfe, J., 236, 244
Wolman, B. B., 203, 225
Woo-Sam, J. M., 128, 144

Wood, R. E., 122, 123, 144
Woodruff, M. L., 174, 181

Y

Yantis, S., 203, 223
Yerkes, R. M., 145, 161

Z

Zimmerman, I. L., 128, 144

Subject Index

A

ability, 7, 10
accretion, 111
action, 9, 10, 25, 26, 196
ad hominem, 22
adaptation, 196, 197
adults, 24, 49, 62, 63, 68, 72, 147, 149,
    192, 211
aesthetics, 63, 283
analogical reasoning, 187
analogies, 128, 185, 188, 191
analogy, 194, 195
anatomy, 71
animal, 21, 25, 28, 32, 69
Aristotle, 28, 69, 283
arithmetic, 187
Arithmetic, 157, 158
Armed Services Vocational Aptitude
    Battery, 206
arousal, 15, 145-155, 164-168
artificial intelligence, 21, 31
assessment, 10, 78-80, 163, 169-174,
    176-179, 185-200, 203- 221, 262
assumptions, 7, 10, 53, 57, 99, 236,
    247, 282
attention, 53, 81, 124, 127, 130-133,
    135-137, 146, 151-153, 157, 164-
    170
automation, 51, 55, 77, 78, 104, 105,
    131, 133-135, 186, 192, 195, 196

B

Bain, 150
Bartlett, 99
behavioral objectives, 4
behaviorism, 22
beliefs, 2
Berliner Intelligenz Struktur Test, 240
Bertalanffy, 9
Binet, 20, 183, 184, 272
black white difference, 114
Block Design, 158
Boltzman, 28
Boxer, 16, 246, 247, 252, 265
Buehler, 23

C

capacity, 129
case studies, 233
Cattell, 99, 124
cause-and-effect, 4, 9, 27, 86
central processing, 138, 167
chance, 28
change, 30,67, 68, 72, 102, 110-114,
    210, 213, 221
chess, 59
Chomsky, 20
classifications, 185, 191, 194
coding, 165, 167
cognitive

components, 128
correlates, 128
skills, 4
cognitivism, 26
collaborative writing, 80, 87-92
comparison, 214
competing task, 105-110
complementarity, 23
complexity, 22, 35, 64-68, 119-130,
    136-139, 155, 227, 235, 237-240,
    253, 268
components, 190, 191, 196, 203, 204,
    209, 232
computational medium, 16, 246, 247
computer, 2, 16, 21, 26, 27, 43, 45, 83,
    88, 211, 212, 214, 216, 219, 227,
    236, 237, 250, 270
computerized testing, 211, 214, 219
concentration, 120
concurrent tasks, 134, 138
conflict resolution, 227, 239
constructivist, 23, 245
context, 3, 6, 7, 9, 50, 58, 71, 190, 275,
    281, 283
control, 4, 105, 228-232
convergence, 269
correlation, 35, 36, 39-41, 99, 110-114,
    119, 120, 122, 123, 126, 128, 129,
    137, 140, 146-149, 156, 157, 185,
    195, 205, 208, 216, 228, 234, 240
cortical localization, 132, 133
creativity, 16, 35, 38-40, 42, 99-101,
    267-268
criteria, 233
crystallized intelligence, 14, 98-110,
    120, 122, 138-140, 157-159, 195
culture, 20

D

decision making, 175, 227
declarative knowledge, 50, 59, 72
Descartes, 3, 245
detail, 213

development, 6, 10, 13, 23, 24-27, 30,
    49, 51, 67, 71, 79-81, 92, 98, 175
    187, 204, 212, 288, 293
Dienes Blocks, 71
Differential Aptitude Test, 207
Differential Aptitude Battery, 205
differential psychology, 30
diffuse neural pathways, 138
Digit Span, 122, 123, 157, 171
distraction, 152
divergence, 269-270, 275, 278
Divergent-Convergent Problem Solving
    Processes Scale, 273
domain, 14, 19, 47, 49-51, 57, 86, 185,
    186, 204, 277
dual task performance, 131
dynamic assessment, 25, 92, 93, 179,
    208
dynamic variability, 13, 26, 27

E

economics, 281-294
eduction, 120, 155, 159, 185
EEG, 15, 145-149, 166
efficiency, 134, 137, 141
egalitarian programs, 285
Einstein, 8
Einstellungseffekt, 41
empowerment, 10
encoding, 185, 189
engagement, 11
environment, 5, 6, 9, 29, 43, 51, 61, 77,
    78, 87, 186, 196-198, 227, 235, 241
    everyday, 14
epistemology, 2, 14, 27, 31, 275, 283
equality, 30
errors, 10, 70, 154
ethics, 283
ethnography, 10, 88
ethology, 23
etiology, 21
everyday life, 14, 16, 35, 49, 57, 72,
    186, 250, 267-278
evolution, 27, 29-31

expectations, 37, 41-43, 240, 265
experience, 43, 47, 49, 58, 163, 168,
   186, 191, 196, 236, 283
expert, 49, 51, 52, 59, 67, 72, 73
expertise, 48, 64, 79, 251, 275
extraverts-introverts, 155
Eysenck, 124
Eysenck Personality Questionnaire, 157

F

facets, 271
factor, 57, 68, 101, 104, 112, 113, 119,
   122, 125, 130, 138, 150, 152, 157,
   184, 188, 215, 275
factor analysis, 19, 53, 126, 157, 163,
   177, 184, 185, 215
factors, 30, 35, 67, 98, 136, 158, 169,
   171, 185, 220
feedback, 10, 51, 88, 190
flexibility, 273
fluency, 268
fluid intelligence, 14, 98-110, 120, 122,
   136, 138-140, 157-159, 194
Fodor, 31
forms of knowledge, 59
frames, 191, 192
freedom from distractibility, 157
Freud, 23

G

Galton, 163
Gantt, 25
Gazzaniga, 174
general heuristics, 52, 53
Gestaltists, 99
goals, 6, 196, 203, 228, 238, 284
Guilford, 99, 104

H

habits, 168
Halstead Reitan Neuropsychological
   Test Battery, 178

Hatrack Problem, 36
Head Start, 268
Hebb, 149
Heisenberg, 8
helplessness, 43
hemispheres, 164
heritability, 98
Hidden Figures test, 106
higher order processes, 20, 27, 67, 71,
   77, 78, 128, 131, 169, 184
Horn, 98, 114
Hull, 25
Humbolt, von, 285
Humphreys, 98
hypertext, 246

I

idealism, 281-284
ill-defined problem, 227
ill-structured problem, 52
ill-structured tasks, 14
imagery, 207, 213, 220
imagination, 283
indivudual differences, 6, 14, 48, 99,
   122, 126, 127, 129, 137, 183, 204,
   207, 241
inductive reasoning, 19, 188, 190
information processing, 24, 79, 120
input-output, 10
insight, 192
instruction, 187, 192, 234, 241
integration, 15, 23, 65, 159, 163-169,
   186, 213, 214
intelligence
   and creativity, 269-276
   and knowledge, 49-50
   and literacy, 247-250
   and school curricula, 282-284
   and the Newtonian paradigm, 3-7
   assessment, 127
   at work, 45
   complexity, 124-130

crystallized, 14, 98-110, 120, 122, 138-140, 157-159, 195
differential theories, 183-189
everyday, 57
fluid, 14, 98-110, 120, 122, 136, 138-140, 157-159, 194
machine, 248
properties, 50, 51, 67-73
scources of discontent in current research, 21-23
symbiotic, 249
system control, 228-240
untapped, 250-252
inter-task interference, 130
interaction, 5-7, 25, 87, 91, 190
interference, 134, 136, 138
interpersonal, 80
interpretation, 19, 42
intervention, 4, 79, 92, 97, 99, 190
intra-individual, 30, 101
intrapersonal, 80
introversion-extraversion, 145, 150, 151, 153-155
IQ-tests, 4, 7, 16, 35, 57
item response theory, 203

J

Jensen, 104, 124
Johnson-Laird, 31

K

Kahneman, 124, 125
Kaufman Assessment Battery for Children, 178
knowledge, 3, 5, 7, 9-15, 22, 32, 47-55, 58, 59, 63, 68, 69, 72, 78, 80, 81, 163, 168, 175, 187, 189, 198, 204, 227, 236, 249, 251, 265, 271, 281, 282, 284, 287
declarative, 50, 59, 72
forms of, 59
mathematical, 49
proceduralized, 50

school, 69
spatial, 49
stages of, 233
Kuhn, 22
Kvashchev, 99-103, 114

L

Lamarck, 31
language, 6, 25, 49, 58, 69, 100, 158, 159, 170, 185, 187, 194, 234
Language Acquisition Device, 20
language contexts, 190
learning
cycle, 64-67
difficulties, 26
disabilities, 80, 88, 277
everyday, 72
higher order, 71
laws of, 27
paired associate, 122
problems, 4
process, 29
letter lists, 122
letter matching, 195
letter reordering, 109
liberal education, 286
Liddell, 25
limited capacity, 104
LISREL, 172
literacy, 287
literary criticism, 283
Logo, 263
longitudinal studies, 25
Lorenz, 23, 29
Luria, 163-166, 174-179
Luria-Nebraska Neuropsychological Battery, 178

M

materialism, 281-284
materialist approach, 284, 286-294
mathematical
abilities, 6

knowledge, 49
mathematicians, 63
meaning, 3, 9
measurement, 53-55
memory, 50, 51, 67, 69, 84, 104, 106,
    114, 115, 122, 127, 151-153, 157,
    164, 167-169, 184, 187, 214, 217,
    258
mental
    energy, 15, 120, 124, 126, 137, 185
    puzzles, 36, 39
    rehearsal, 70
    rotation, 187
    tests, 13, 20, 28, 45, 77, 79, 120,
        126, 140, 145, 183, 203, 228-232,
        239, 267
metacognition, 51, 77, 78, 175, 227
metacomponents, 187-190
metaphor, 5, 9, 26, 32
methodology, 99
microworld, 16, 227-241, 251, 254, 262
Mill, 285
Milwaukee Project, 268
Minnesota Paper Form Board Test, 205
mnestic processes, 166
monitoring, 239
Moro, 234
motivation, 10, 58, 60, 68, 269, 271
multidisciplinary, 21
multiprocessor, 126, 138
musical talent, 49

N

natural selection, 31
nature and nurture, 48
Neural Darwinism, 32
neural processes, 15, 119, 132, 141,
    155-159
    constricted, 134
    diffuse, 138
neurobiology, 24, 27, 31, 32
neurological functioning, 119
neurophysiology, 4, 15
neuropsychology, 145-159, 163, 177

Newton, 2, 3, 8
novelty, 27, 36, 37, 39, 42, 48, 52, 59,
    100, 127, 186, 191-196, 268, 270
novice, 59, 67, 72, 73
number series, 109, 110, 191

O

ontogenesis, 19, 20, 23

P

paired associate learning, 122
paradigm, 1-12, 22, 26
pattern recognition, 45, 50
Pavlov, 149
Peabody Individual Achievement Test,
    82, 83
peers, 80, 87-92
perceptions, 2
performance components, 187-189
phenotype, 98
phylogeny, 31
physics, 27, 59, 72, 251
    quantum, 8
Piaget, 6, 14, 19, 23-26, 29, 60-62, 78,
    99, 174, 175, 179
Picture Arrangement, 158
Planck, 8
planning, 166, 169, 170, 175, 192, 239
plasticity, 14, 175, 268
Plato, 285, 286
Poincare, 28
practice, 2, 14, 16, 47, 51, 79, 81-86,
    92, 97, 103-114, 126, 207-210, 274,
    275
prediction, 4
prerequisities, 275
Primal Mental Abilities Test, 205
primary mental abilities, 120
principles, 49, 54
problem
    definition, 7
    ill-defined, 227

ill-structured, 52
learning, 4
water-jar, 36
water lilies, 40
well-defined, 227
series, 42
solving, 30, 36, 39, 58, 79, 120, 129, 152, 187, 227, 232-233
space, 238
proceduralized knowledge, 50
procedure, 42
processes, 170
automatic, 104, 105, 131, 133, 134
controlled, 105
higher order, 20, 27, 67, 71, 77, 78, 128, 131, 169, 184
learning, 29
neural, 15, 119, 132, 134, 138, 141, 155-159
spatial, 174
processing
central, 138, 167
information, 24, 79, 120
simultaneous, 165, 167, 169, 170
successive, 165, 167, 169, 170
productive labor 288
proficiency, 49, 50
programming, 246, 252-254, 263
protocol, 11
psychoanalysis, 23
psycholinguistics, 26
psychometrics, 15
purpose, 9
puzzle, 40, 43, 192, 205

Q

quantum physics, 8

R

rationality, 9
Raven's Progressive Matrices, 122, 123, 130, 171, 205, 215
real life, 78, 99, 232, 236

reality, 2, 10
reasoning, 6, 49, 120, 185, 205, 211, 216, 232
analogical, 187
higher order, 184
inductive, 19, 188, 190
syllogistic, 188
reconstructibility, 257-261
reductionist, 9, 10
reinforcement, 25, 29, 42
relationships, 239, 240, 268
relevance, 271
reliability, 13, 28, 128, 211, 214, 216, 219, 233, 234
Remote Associations Test, 272
repertoire, 25, 207
representation, 49, 50, 52, 54, 61-64, 79, 204, 207, 239, 241, 251
research
designs, 232
method, 11
methodology, 2, 3, 252
questions, 7
Reticular Analysis Model, 102
rotation, 205-207, 212, 214
rote learning, 154
Rousseau, 285
rules, 54, 232

S

scheme, 191
Scholastic Aptitude Test, 195
scientists, 63, 71
Scrambled Words, 107
script, 191, 192
search, 51
selective stabilization, 32
self-regulatory skills, 14, 53, 55
sequence, 40, 42, 167
series completion, 128, 185, 194
Similarities, 158
simplicity, 3, 111
simultaneous processing, 165, 167, 169, 170

Skinner, 25, 29, 30
SOLO Taxonomy, 14, 64-71
solution
    principle, 40
    process, 43
spatial
    abilities, 16, 49, 58, 203-221
    knowledge, 49
    processes, 174
    skills, 248
    tests, 205, 206
Spearman, 15, 58, 99, 104, 120, 125, 126, 184
species, 20, 27, 29
speed, 115, 209, 216, 217
stages, 60-62, 67, 71, 122, 233
Stanford Binet Intelligence Scale, 184
Sternberg, 24
strategies, 4, 30, 45, 52, 59, 69, 80-92, 127, 140, 141, 187, 188, 207, 241, 268
Stroop cards, 171
structure, 52
style, 16, 48, 88, 268, 269
successive processing, 165, 167, 169, 170
Sully, 150
surface approach, 69
surface-structure, 50
Swaminathan, 112
syllogistic reasoning, 188
syndrome analysis, 176-177

T

Tailorshop, 234
task, 39, 41, 45, 60, 64, 65, 70, 80, 87, 97, 104, 121, 122, 126, 127, 131, 132, 134, 135, 168, 169, 188, 195, 203, 204, 207, 214, 227, 232, 276-277
    complexity, 15
    concurrent, 134, 138
    control, 228-232

difficulty, 122, 131-133, 219, 237-239
elementary, 128
everyday, 250
ill-structured, 14
stories, 88
teacher-researcher, 252
technology, 16, 245-265
test anxiety, 43
Test for Creative Thinking-Drawing Production, 272
testing
    computerized, 211, 214, 219
theoretical and ideological debate, 23
theory, 4, 5, 13, 19, 20, 24, 53, 65-73, 86, 99, 119, 203, 210-221, 278, 282, 285
think aloud, 228
threshold, 36, 37, 43, 147, 151
Thurstone, 29, 99, 104, 184
time, 198, 218, 19, 234
Tolman, 29
Torrence, 99
Torrance Tests of Creative Thinking, 272
Tower of Hanoi, 232
training, 14, 16, 97-103, 111-114, 273, 274
transfer, 14, 16, 48, 51, 98, 99, 101, 129, 221, 277
transformation, 9, 10, 31, 72, 205
transition, 67
transmission, 283
transparency, 239, 240
Triarchic Abilities Test, 186, 190-200
Triarchic theory, 15, 24, 127, 183, 186-199
truth, 5, 11

U

uncertainty, 4, 8
understanding, 6, 30, 99, 191, 246, 267
unifying concepts, 22, 26-30

V

validity, 203, 210, 214, 221, 232, 235, 236
values, 2
variation, 31, 51
verbalization, 70, 80
vocabulary, 107, 123, 158, 189, 190, 215
Voltaire, 285
Vygotsky, 6, 23, 25, 99

W

WAIS, 15, 128, 147, 149, 151, 155, 157-159
WAIS-R, 110, 111, 178
Walton, 23
water lilies problem, 40
water-jar problems, 36
well-defined problem, 227
Wide Range Achievement Test, 178
WISC-R, 82, 88, 178
Wundt, 152

Y, Z

Yerkes-Dodson law, 145
zone of proximal development, 25, 68, 80, 192